D0253243

WEST'S LAW SCHOOL
ADVISORY BOARD

JESSE H. CHOPER
Professor of Law,
University of California, Berkeley

DAVID P. CURRIE
Professor of Law, University of Chicago

YALE KAMISAR
Professor of Law, University of Michigan
Professor of Law, University of San Diego

MARY KAY KANE
Chancellor, Dean and Distinguished Professor of Law,
University of California,
Hastings College of the Law

WAYNE R. LaFAVE
Professor of Law, University of Illinois

ARTHUR R. MILLER
Professor of Law, Harvard University

GRANT S. NELSON
Professor of Law, University of California, Los Angeles

JAMES J. WHITE
Professor of Law, University of Michigan

AMERICAN INDIAN LAW

IN A NUTSHELL

Fourth Edition

By

WILLIAM C. CANBY, JR.
Senior Judge, United States Court of Appeals
For the Ninth Circuit
formerly
Professor of Law,
Arizona State University

Property of:
California Indian Legal Services
510 16th Street, Fourth Floor
Oakland, CA 94612

THOMSON

WEST

Mat #40148922

TEXT IS PRINTED ON 10% POST
CONSUMER RECYCLED PAPER

PREFACE

The purpose of this book remains as it was in the first three editions. It is to set forth in succinct form the essentials of the very complex body of federal Indian Law, with attention when necessary to the governmental policies underlying it.

The scope of this edition is substantially the same as that of the third edition. In the interest of economy, I have omitted treatment of some subjects that fall within the field of Indian Law or are related to it. For example, I have not dealt individually with the special problems peculiar to Oklahoma or New York, although I have discussed decisions from both states when generally relevant. I have not treated the subject of the Native Hawaiians, who seek to apply some of the principles of Indian Law to their situation.

Revisions for this edition have been quite extensive. This treatment is necessary largely because of the significant changes wrought by the Supreme Court in the area of civil jurisdiction over non-Indians, and because of the Court's ever-narrowing approach to questions of tribal sovereignty generally. I have also had to take account of many of the increasing number of Indian law cases in the lower courts, which probably reflect the added economic activity flowing from Indian gaming.

My citation form generally follows the Uniform System of Citation (Blue Book). In accordance with that manual, I have not indicated denials of certiorari or other discretionary review unless the case cited is less than two years old.

The views expressed in this book are attributable to me individually as a student and former teacher of Indian Law. They do not represent the views of the United States Court of Appeals for the Ninth Circuit, Arizona State University, or even of myself in any official capacity.

WILLIAM C. CANBY, JR.

Phoenix, Arizona
December, 2003

OUTLINE

*

TABLE OF CASES

References are to Pages

A

B

C

D

G

H

I

L

M

N

O

P

Q

R

S

T

U

TABLE OF CASES

V

W

TABLE OF CASES

Y

Z

*

AMERICAN INDIAN LAW

IN A NUTSHELL

Fourth Edition

*

CHAPTER I

INTRODUCTION

A. THE NATURE AND SCOPE OF INDIAN LAW

The term "Indian Law" is a catchall with various meanings, but it refers primarily to that body of law dealing with the status of the Indian tribes and their special relationship to the federal government, with all the attendant consequences for the tribes and their members, the states and their citizens, and the federal government. In this application, "Indian Law" might better be termed "Federal Law About Indians."

The unique legal posture of the tribes in relation to the federal government is deeply rooted in American history, and a knowledge of historical context is perhaps more important to the understanding of Indian Law than of any other legal subject. Indian Law has always been heavily intertwined with federal Indian policy, and over the years the law has shifted back and forth with the flow of popular and governmental attitudes toward Indians. Yet a few themes have persisted and form the doctrinal bases of present law. At the risk of oversimplification, they may be reduced to four. *First*, the tribes are independent entities with inherent powers of self-

1

government. *Second*, the independence of the tribes is subject to exceptionally great powers of Congress to regulate and modify the status of the tribes. *Third*, the power to deal with and regulate the tribes is wholly federal; the states are excluded unless Congress delegates power to them. *Fourth*, the federal government has a responsibility for the protection of the tribes and their properties, including protection from encroachments by the states and their citizens. These principles, while enduring, are not static. The boundaries of tribal self-government referred to in the first proposition, for example, have been considerably narrowed in recent years by the Supreme Court, particularly with regard to tribal authority over non-Indians. Recent assertions of state power also have subjected the third proposition to great stress.

As all of these themes suggest, Indian Law is greatly concerned with actual or potential conflicts of governmental power. When such conflicts arise in a legal setting, they appear as issues of jurisdiction. It is not surprising, therefore, that controversies in Indian Law usually have at their core a jurisdictional dispute.

Indian Law includes within its scope those situations in which a legal outcome is affected by the Indian status of the participants or the subject matter. Obviously, there are many legal disputes involving Indians that do not turn upon points of Indian Law. If an Indian commits a traffic offense in Chicago, his case will be governed by the same law and decided by the same court that would govern and decide a case against a non-Indian; the defendant's Indian status is irrelevant and Indian Law does not enter at all. But if that same Indian commits a similar offense upon the Navajo Reservation in Arizona, his Indian status and the location will combine to confer jurisdiction upon a different court and will result in the application of different law from that which would decide and govern the case if the defendant were a non-Indian. (See Chapter VII, Section D.) The latter situation is very much controlled by Indian Law—that is, by the federal law that allocates jurisdiction over Indian affairs.

Although the subject of "Indian Law" legitimately might be thought to include the internal law that each tribe applies to its own affairs and members, that is not the common definition nor the one used here. Instead, that body of law is separately referred to as "tribal law," and it may range from oral tradition to entire codes borrowed nearly intact from non-Indian sources. No attempt will be made in this volume to set forth the content of the various bodies of tribal law. Instead, the concern will be to determine *when* tribal law (rather than state or federal law) governs a particular situation.

B.   WHAT IS AN INDIAN TRIBE?

The Indian tribe is the fundamental unit of Indian Law; in its absence there is no occasion for the law to operate. Yet there is no all-purpose definition of an Indian tribe. See Duke v. Absentee Shawnee

Tribe of Oklahoma Housing Authority, 199 F.3d
1123, 1125 (10th Cir.1999). A group of Indians may
qualify as a tribe for the purpose of one statute or
federal program, but fail to qualify for others. See
Golden Hill Paugussett Tribe of Indians v. Weicker,
39 F.3d 51, 57–58 (2d Cir.1994). Definitions must
accordingly be used with extreme caution.

At the most general level, a tribe is simply a
group of Indians that is recognized as constituting a
distinct and historically continuous political entity
for at least some governmental purposes. See Paugussett Tribe, 39 F.3d at 59. The key problem with
this definition lies in the word "recognized." Recognized by whom? The answer is that recognition may
come from many directions, and the sufficiency of
any given recognition is likely to depend upon the
purpose for which tribal status is asserted. See
Joint Tribal Council of Passamaquoddy Tribe v.
Morton, 528 F.2d 370 (1st Cir.1975).

By far the most important and valuable recognition is that of the federal government. Such recognition binds the state courts. John v. Baker, 982
P.2d 738 (Alaska 1999). Indeed, unequivocal federal
recognition may serve to establish tribal status for
every purpose, and the Department of the Interior
insists upon federal recognition as a prerequisite for
entitlement to the many federal Indian services
administered by the Department. Federal recognition may arise from treaty, statute, executive or
administrative order, or from a course of dealing
with the tribe as a political entity. Any of these
events, or a combination of them, then signifies the

existence of a special relationship between the federal government and the concerned tribe that may confer such important benefits as immunity of the Indians' lands from state taxation. The Kansas Indians, 72 U.S. (5 Wall.) 737 (1866). In recognizing a tribe, the federal government has not always been governed by ethnological realities; there are numerous instances where ethnologically distinct tribes or bands were gathered into one common reservation and thereafter treated as a single tribe.

The failure of the federal government to recognize a particular group of Indians as a tribe cannot deprive that group of vested treaty rights. Greene v. Babbitt, 64 F.3d 1266, 1270–71 (9th Cir.1995); Timpanogos Tribe v. Conway, 286 F.3d 1195, 1203–04 (10th Cir.2002). The group must have maintained itself as a distinct community, however, with some defining characteristic that permits it to be identified as the group named in the treaty. United States v. Washington, 641 F.2d 1368 (9th Cir.1981). Similarly, a federally unrecognized tribe that met common-law requirements of ethnicity, continuity, leadership and territoriality has been held to enjoy the same immunity from state-law tort suit as that enjoyed by federally recognized tribes. Koke v. Little Shell Tribe of Chippewa Indians of Montana, Inc., 315 Mont. 510, 68 P.3d 814 (2003).

The action of the federal government in recognizing or failing to recognize a tribe has traditionally been held to be a political one not subject to judicial review. United States v. Holliday, 70 U.S. (3 Wall.) 407, 419 (1866). Although it is still true that Con-

gress or the Executive can establish standards of
recognition without court direction, federal courts
today will review grants or denials of recognition
under the Administrative Procedure Act to determine whether the Department of the Interior followed its own regulations and other controlling law,
and adhered to the requirements of due process. See
Miami Nation of Indians v. United States Dept. of
Interior, 255 F.3d 342, 347–49 (7th Cir.2001);
Greene v. Babbitt, 64 F.3d 1266, 1274–75 (9th Cir.
1995). Once granted, however, the recognition will
bind the courts until it is removed by the Executive
or Congress. Oneida Indian Nation of New York v.
City of Sherrill, 337 F.3d 139, 166–67 (2d Cir.2003).
A court may order the executive branch of the
federal government to honor tribal status for a
particular purpose when that is deemed to have
been the intent of Congress. Joint Tribal Council of
Passamaquoddy Tribe v. Morton, 528 F.2d 370 (1st
Cir.1975). There may be other substantive limits to
the executive power to recognize in extreme instances; the government would not be permitted to
confer tribal status arbitrarily on some group that
had never displayed the characteristics of a distinct-
ly Indian community. See United States v. Sandoval, 231 U.S. 28, 46 (1913).

In 1978, the Department of the Interior published
criteria for the "acknowledgment" of the status of
tribes that were not otherwise federally recognized.
The Department revised those criteria in 1994. See
25 C.F.R. Part 83 (2003). The criteria are designed
to achieve eligibility for federal services and other

benefits of tribal status for Indian groups that have maintained a "substantially continuous tribal existence and which have functioned as autonomous entities throughout history until the present." 25 C.F.R. § 83.3. Acknowledgment thus amounts to recognition. A group seeking acknowledgment must, among other things, have been identified as an American Indian entity on a substantially continuous basis since 1900. It may establish the requisite tribal identity by various types of evidence, including dealings as a tribe with federal, state or local governments or other tribes, and recognition by historical records or scholarly opinion. The group must show that it is a distinct community and exercises political influence or authority over its members, and that it has maintained these characteristics from historical times until the present. 25 C.F.R. § 83.7. The Department's decision to acknowledge or deny acknowledgment is subject to administrative review before the Interior Board of Indian Appeals. 25 C.F.R. § 83.11. A group seeking acknowledgment as a tribe must exhaust administrative remedies before seeking relief in federal court. United Tribe of Shawnee Indians v. United States, 253 F.3d 543 (10th Cir.2001). The current acknowledgment process is a slow one, with several petitions waiting in line for years. The District of Columbia Circuit held, however, that it was error for a district court to require the Department to rule on a particular delayed petition without first considering the BIA's limited resources and the effect of such an order on others in the waiting line.

Mashpee Wampanoag Tribal Council, Inc. v. Norton, 336 F.3d 1094 (D.C.Cir.2003).

Even when a tribe clearly has been recognized, as by a treaty, Congress has the power effectively to end the recognized status by legislating a "termination" of the tribe's special relationship to the federal government. (See Chapter III, Section E). In addition, a tribe may totally lose its tribal status by voluntarily ceasing to function as a distinct and identifiable entity. Mashpee Tribe v. New Seabury Corp., 592 F.2d 575 (1st Cir.1979). If a tribe once recognized simply ceases to exist, voluntarily or involuntarily, it is not presently entitled to acknowledgment. Miami Nation of Indians v. United States Dept. of Interior, 255 F.3d 342, 350–51 (7th Cir.2001).

Congress in 1994 required the Secretary of the Interior to publish annually in the Federal Register a list of all tribes recognized to be eligible for federal services because of their Indian status. 25 U.S.C.A. § 479a–1. Publication in fact has been somewhat less than annual. The 2002 list included 562 recognized tribes, of which some 225 were Alaska Native entities. 67 Fed. Reg. 46328 (July 12, 2002).

C. WHO IS AN INDIAN?

"Indian" is another term the meaning of which varies according to the purpose for which the definition is sought. In the most general terms, a person must meet two requirements to be an Indian: he or she must (1) have some Indian blood, and (2) be regarded as an Indian by his or her community. See F. Cohen, Handbook of Federal Indian Law 2 (1942).

To have Indian blood is to have had ancestors living in America before the Europeans arrived, but this fact is obviously never provable as such. It is enough that a parent, grandparent, or great-grandparent was clearly identified as an Indian. Because the general requirement is only of "some" blood, a person may be classified as an Indian despite a very low quantum of Indian blood, such as one-sixteenth. Particular statutes, however, may set higher blood requirements.

For many federal jurisdictional and statutory purposes it is not enough that the individual be regarded as an Indian by his or her community; the person must be considered a member of a *federally recognized* tribe. LaPier v. McCormick, 986 F.2d 303, 305 (9th Cir.1993); State v. Sebastian, 243 Conn. 115, 701 A.2d 13 (1997); United States v. Antoine, 318 F.3d 919 (9th Cir.2003). In the jurisdictional context, individual status follows tribal status, and there can be no Indian without a tribe. See Epps v. Andrus, 611 F.2d 915 (1st Cir.1979). Thus, where Congress has terminated a tribe's special relationship with the federal government, the individual members of that tribe are no longer Indians for purposes of federal criminal jurisdiction. United States v. Heath, 509 F.2d 16 (9th Cir.1974). Even in the case of tribes that continue to be federally recognized, individual members have been held in the past to have lost their Indian status by leaving the tribe and adopting non-Indian ways. E.g., Nagle v. United States, 191 Fed. 141 (9th Cir.1911). It is unlikely, however, that such behavior today would be considered an unequivocal abandonment of the tribe by the individual.

It is not always necessary for an individual to be formally enrolled in a recognized tribe to be regarded as a member for jurisdictional purposes. United States v. Broncheau, 597 F.2d 1260 (9th Cir.1979); United States v. Keys, 103 F.3d 758, 761 (9th Cir.1996); but see United States v. Lawrence, 51 F.3d 150 (8th Cir.1995). Nevertheless, enrollment is commonly a prerequisite for acceptance as a member of the tribal community, and it provides by far the best evidence of Indian status. Individual tribes have varying blood requirements for enrollment, with the result that the general definitional requirement of "some" blood may be substantially increased for persons seeking to establish status as members of certain tribes. Many tribes require one-fourth tribal blood, and at least one requires five-eighths.

CHAPTER II

HISTORICAL OVERVIEW OF FEDERAL INDIAN LAW AND POLICY

A. INTRODUCTION

Indian Law is a reflection of national Indian policy, which has undergone numerous shifts in direction in the course of American history. At some times, the prevailing view has regarded the tribes as enduring bodies for which a geographical base would have to be established and more or less protected. At other times, the dominant position has been that the tribes are or should be in the process of decline and disappearance, and that their members should be absorbed into the mass of non-Indian society. The dominance of one position at any given time does not, of course, mean that the other disappears entirely; its influence is diminished but usually observable. That is as true today as it has been in the past, and the continuing tension between the two views makes it unsafe to assume that national Indian policy has found its final direction.

B. ESTABLISHMENT OF THE FEDERAL ROLE: COLONIAL TIMES TO 1820

During the colonization of America, the British Crown dealt with the Indian tribes formally as foreign sovereign nations. Britain and several of its colonies entered treaties with various tribes. As the colonies grew in strength and population, it became apparent that individual colonists were encroaching upon Indian lands and were otherwise treating the Indians unfairly or worse. In order to avoid prolonged and expensive Indian wars, and perhaps also to enforce a measure of justice, the Crown increasingly assumed the position of protector of the tribes from the excesses of the colonists. It is accordingly not surprising that when the colonies revolted from Britain, nearly all of the tribes allied themselves with the Crown.

Upon independence, the new nation found itself with the same problems of aggression by state citizens and threatened Indian retaliation that had faced the Crown. If wars were to be avoided and stability achieved, Indian affairs had to be placed in the hands of the central government. After a period of uncertainty under the Articles of Confederation, the Constitution did just that. Congress was granted the power to "regulate Commerce * * * with the Indian Tribes" while the President was empowered to make treaties, necessarily including Indian treaties, with the consent of the Senate. U.S.Const. Art. I, § 8, cl. 3; Art. II, § 2, cl. 2.

Congress set the basic pattern of federal Indian Law in a series of Trade and Intercourse Acts passed between 1790 and 1834. E.g., 1 Stat. 137 (1790); 2 Stat. 139 (1802); 4 Stat. 729 (1834). The central policy embodied in the Acts was one of separating Indians and non-Indians and subjecting nearly all interaction between the two groups to federal control. For this reason, some courts refer to the Acts as Non–Intercourse Acts. The Acts established the boundaries of Indian country and protected against incursion by non-Indians in several ways. Non–Indians were prohibited from acquiring Indian lands by purchase or treaty (other than a treaty entered pursuant to the Constitution), or from settling on those lands or entering them for hunting or grazing. Trading with the Indians was made subject to federal regulation. Depredations by non-Indians against Indians were made a federal crime, and federal compensation was provided to victims of depredation by either group, so long as the victims took no private revenge. The Trade and Intercourse Acts made no attempt to regulate the conduct of Indians among themselves in Indian country; that subject was left entirely to the tribes.

During these years when federal control over Indian affairs was being consolidated, the federal government continued to deal with Indian tribes by treaty. Indian agents were appointed as the federal government's liaison with the tribes. These agents were generally under the jurisdiction of the War Department.

C. THE CHEROKEE CASES AND INDIAN REMOVAL: 1820 TO 1850

Despite the Trade and Intercourse Acts, friction grew between the burgeoning non-Indian population and the tribes, particularly as non-Indian demands for additional land became more acute. The solution of "removal" of the tribes to Indian country beyond the Mississippi gained currency and was espoused by Presidents Monroe, John Quincy Adams and, most vigorously, Jackson. At the same time that this executive policy was hardening, however, the Supreme Court under John Marshall's leadership was independently fashioning legal doctrines that would influence Indian Law for the next century and a half.

The first decision in which the Supreme Court attempted to formulate its views of Indian tribes and their legal and historical relation to the land was Johnson v. McIntosh, 21 U.S. (8 Wheat.) 543 (1823). The case concerned the validity of a grant of land made by tribal chiefs to private individuals in 1773 and 1775 (before passage of the Trade and Intercourse Acts, which would have prohibited such transactions). The Court held the conveyance invalid. Discovery of lands in the new world, said the Court, gave the discovering European sovereign a title good against all other Europeans, and along with it "the sole right of acquiring the soil from the natives * * *." 21 U.S. at 573. The Indians retained a right of occupancy, which only the discovering sovereign could extinguish, either "by purchase or by conquest." The sovereign (now the United States) was free to grant land occupied by Indians, but the grantee received title subject to that right of occupancy. The result of this decision was to recognize a legal right of Indians in their lands, good against all third parties but existing at the mere sufferance of the federal government. This right of occupancy is frequently referred to as "aboriginal title," or simply "Indian title."

A few years later, the attempts of Georgia to extinguish Indian title within the state gave rise to the Cherokee Cases—perhaps the two most influential decisions in all of Indian Law. The state of Georgia had given up western land claims in return for a federal promise to extinguish Indian title to lands within Georgia, but the state tired of waiting for federal action. Between 1828 and 1830, Georgia enacted a series of laws that divided up the Cherokee territory among several Georgia counties, extended state law to the divided territory, invalidated all Cherokee laws, and made criminal any attempts of the Cherokees to act as a government. To combat these actions of Georgia, the Cherokees brought an original action in the Supreme Court, Cherokee Nation v. Georgia, 30 U.S. (5 Pet.) 1 (1831). The ability of the tribe to bring such a suit depended on its being a "foreign state" within the meaning of Art. III, § 2 of the Constitution, which defines the federal judicial power. Chief Justice Marshall, writing for the Court, first determined that the Cherokee tribe had succeeded in demonstrating that it was a "state," "a distinct political society separated from others, capable of managing its own affairs and governing itself," and that treaties between the tribe and the United States had so recognized it. 30 U.S. (5 Pet.) at 16. But Marshall determined that tribes could not be considered "foreign" states:

They may, more correctly, perhaps, be denominated domestic dependent nations. They occupy a territory to which we assert a title independent of their will, which must take effect in point of possession, when their right of possession ceases. Meanwhile, they are in a state of pupilage; their relation to the United States resembles that of a ward to his guardian.

30 U.S. (5 Pet.) at 17. Thus, while the language of the opinion was obviously sympathetic to the Cherokee cause, the tribe was out of court. Marshall's characterization of the tribes as "domestic dependent nations" turns out to have been a mixed blessing for them. Its emphasis on nationhood laid the groundwork for future protection of tribal sovereignty by Marshall and his immediate successors, but the characterization also created an opportunity for much later courts to discover limits to tribal sovereignty inherent in domestic dependent status. Marshall's reference to tribes as "wards" was to have an equally mixed history; it provided a doctrinal basis for protection of the tribes by the federal government, but it also furnished support for those who disagreed with Marshall's view that the tribes were states capable of self-government.

The Cherokee question returned to the Supreme Court the very next term. Several missionaries were arrested by Georgia authorities for violating a state law requiring non-Indians residing in Cherokee territory to obtain a license from the state governor. Two of them appealed their convictions to the Supreme Court in Worcester v. Georgia, 31 U.S. (6 Pet.) 515 (1832). In a strongly-worded opinion, Marshall reviewed the history of relations with the Indians, the treaties with the Cherokees, and the Trade and Intercourse Acts which "manifestly consider the several Indian nations as distinct political communities, having territorial boundaries, within which their authority is exclusive * * *." 31 U.S. (6 Pet.) at 557. Marshall then concluded:

> The Cherokee nation, then, is a distinct community, occupying its own territory, with boundaries accurately described, in which the laws of Georgia can have no force * * *.

31 U.S. (6 Pet.) at 561. The conviction of the missionaries was thereupon reversed.

Marshall's ruling in *Worcester* was even more pivotal than his language in *Cherokee Nation*. His opinion is the foundation of jurisdictional law excluding the states from power over Indian affairs, and it has much vitality today even though it is not applied to the full extent of its logic. Certainly in its own day, it was an exceptionally forthright declaration against the view that the tribes should be dispossessed at all costs. President Jackson probably did not make the statement about the decision that is popularly attributed to him: "John Marshall has made his decision; now let him enforce it," but there is little question that the decision was not popular with the Jacksonians who were anxious to hasten the exodus of the tribes from lands east of the Mississippi.

In the end, however, all but a few remnants of tribes east of the Mississippi were moved to the West under a program that was voluntary in name and coerced in fact. The journeys were often attended with extreme hardship and some became symbols of imposed suffering, such as the Trail of Tears traveled by the Five Civilized Tribes (Cherokee, Choctaw, Creek, Chickasaw and Seminole) from the Southeast to what is now Oklahoma. In 1849, with the East nearly free of tribal Indians, the Bureau of Indian Affairs was moved from the War Department, where it had existed since 1824, to the Department of the Interior.

D. MOVEMENT TO THE RESERVATIONS: 1850 TO 1887

As non-Indians continued to move westward, further pressures were exerted upon the Indian land base. The federal government consequently evolved a policy of restricting the tribes to specified reservations. This goal was typically accomplished by treaty, exacted with varying degrees of persuasion, reward, and coercion, in which the tribe ceded much of the land it occupied to the United States and reserved a smaller portion to itself (hence the term "reservation"). On other occasions, the tribe was moved entirely away from the lands it was occupying to a distant reservation.

In 1871, Congress passed a statute providing that no tribe thereafter was to be recognized as an independent nation with which the United States could make treaties. Existing treaties were not affected. 25 U.S.C.A. § 71. While it is questionable that Congress could limit the constitutional treaty-making power of the President, the statute did effectively end the making of Indian treaties by serving as notice that none would thereafter be ratified. Reservations established after 1871 were accordingly created either by statute or, until Congress ended the practice in 1919, by executive order. 43 U.S.C.A. § 150.

Reservations were originally intended to keep distance and peace between Indians and non-Indians, but they came to be viewed also as instruments for "civilizing" the Indians. Each reservation was placed in charge of an Indian agent whose mission was to supervise the Indian's adaptation to non-Indian ways. The appointment of Indian agents came to be heavily influenced by organized religions, and when reservation schools were first set up in 1865, they too were directed by religious organizations with a goal of "Christianizing" the Indians. In 1878, off-reservation boarding schools were established to permit education of Indian children away from their tribal environments.

In 1883, Courts of Indian Offenses were authorized, with judges to be appointed by the Indian agents. Neither these courts nor the codes they administered were fashioned after indigenous Indian institutions; they were imposed as federal educational and disciplinary instrumentalities in furtherance of the civilizing mission of the reservations. See United States v. Clapox, 35 Fed. 575, 577 (D.Or. 1888). Accordingly, certain religious dances and customary practices, as well as plural marriages, were outlawed.

Also in 1883, the Supreme Court decided the case of Ex parte Crow Dog, 109 U.S. 556 (1883), which held that murder of one Indian by another in Indian country was within the sole jurisdiction of the tribe; federal territorial courts had no power over the case. Congress reacted by passing the Major Crimes Act, 23 Stat. 385 (1885), declaring murder and other serious crimes committed by an Indian in Indian country to be federal offenses triable in federal court. The result was a further erosion of the tribes' traditional role in dispute resolution.

E.   ALLOTMENTS AND ATTEMPTED ASSIMILATION: 1887 TO 1934

In the 1870's and 1880's, there was increasing dissatisfaction in governmental circles with the reservation policy. Those friendly to the Indians recognized that the tribal economies were frequently a shambles, that individual Indians were living in hopeless poverty, and that no progress was being made toward overcoming either of these conditions. Others not so friendly resented large tracts of land being excluded from white settlement. The combination of these two sentiments produced the most important and, to the tribes, the most disastrous piece of Indian legislation in United States history: the General Allotment Act of 1887, also known as the Dawes Act, 24 Stat. 388.

There is little question that the leadership for passage of the Dawes Act came from those sympathetic to the Indians. They believed that, if individual Indians were given plots of land to cultivate, they would prosper and become assimilated into the mainstream of American culture as middle-class farmers. The tribes, which were viewed as obstacles to the cultural and economic development of the Indians, would quickly wither away. Such a prospect was not, of course, offensive in the least to those non-Indians anxious to break up the tribal land mass.

The Allotment Act authorized the President to allot portions of reservation land to individual Indians. There was no provision for consent of the tribes or individual Indians. Allotments of 160 acres were to be made to each head of a family and 80 acres to others, with double those amounts to be allotted if the land was suitable only for grazing. (These quantities were subsequently cut in half. 25 U.S.C.A. § 331.) Title to the allotted land was to remain in the United States in trust for 25 years (or longer if extended by the President), after which it was to be conveyed to the Indian allottee in fee free

of all encumbrances. The trust period was intended
to protect the allottee from immediate state taxation and to permit him to learn the arts of husbandry and to acquire the capacity to manage his land
and affairs. The Act provided that upon receiving
allotments (or, after amendments in 1906, fee title),
the allottees became United States citizens (as did
other Indians residing apart from their tribes and
adopting "the habits of civilized life"), and were
subject to state criminal and civil law. Finally, and
perhaps most notably, the Act authorized the Secretary of Interior to negotiate with the tribes for
disposition of all "excess" lands remaining after
allotments, for the purpose of non-Indian settlement.

The primary effect of the Allotment Act was a
precipitous decline in the total amount of Indian-
held land, from 138 million acres in 1887 to 48
million in 1934. Of the 48 million acres that remained, some 20 million were desert or semidesert.
Much of the land was lost by sale as tribal surplus;
the remainder passed out of the hands of allottees.
Allottees who received patents after 25 years found
themselves subject to state property taxation, and
many forced sales resulted from non-payment. In
addition, the Indians' new power to sell land provided many opportunities for non-Indians to negotiate
purchases of allotted land on terms quite disadvantageous to the Indians. The allottees were frequently left with neither their land nor with any benefits
that might have resulted from its disposition.

Other circumstances combined to render the allotment system a failure even where the land remained in trust. Leasing of allotted trust land to non-Indians became common, defeating the intention of the Act to turn the Indians into small farmers. The Allotment Act had subjected allotted land, whether or not in trust, to state intestacy laws that resulted in highly fractionated ownership which effectively rendered the land unusable. Passage of many of the fee allotments out of Indian hands left large "checkerboard" areas of alternate non-Indian and Indian ownership, making sizable farming or grazing projects impractical.

Some reservations, particularly those in the West that were established late in the allotment period, largely escaped allotment and its baneful effects. But in much of the country the long-range effect of the Act was to separate Indians from their lands without accomplishing any of the benign purposes intended by the Act's sponsors.

In 1924, as the Allotment period was drawing to a close, Congress passed a statute conferring citizenship upon all Indians born within the United States. 8 U.S.C.A. § 1401(b). This action completed a process by which many Indians had already become citizens under the Allotment Act or other special statutes. By reason of the 14th Amendment, the grant of federal citizenship had the additional effect of making the Indians citizens of the states where they resided.

F. INDIAN REORGANIZATION AND PRESERVATION OF THE TRIBES: 1934 TO 1953

In 1928, the now-famous Meriam Report documented the failure of federal Indian policy during the Allotment period. Institute for Gov't Research, The Problem of Indian Administration (1928). The Report provided part of the impetus for a sweeping change in federal policy marked by passage of the Indian Reorganization Act of 1934, also known as the Wheeler–Howard Act. 25 U.S.C.A. § 461 et seq.

The Indian Reorganization Act was based on the assumption, quite contrary to that of the Allotment Act, that the tribes not only would be in existence for an indefinite period, but that they *should* be. The Act consequently sought to protect the land base of the tribes, and to permit the tribes to set up legal structures for self-government.

Perhaps the most important and effective provision of the Indian Reorganization Act was that which ended the practice of allotment, and extended indefinitely the trust period for existing allotments still in trust. The Act also authorized the Secretary of the Interior to restore to tribal ownership any "surplus" lands acquired from the tribes under the Allotment Act, so long as third parties had not acquired rights in that land. The Act authorized the Secretary to acquire lands and water rights for the tribes, and to create new reservations.

To aid in tribal self-government, the Act authorized tribes to organize and adopt constitutions and by-laws subject to ratification by vote of tribal members. This recognition of the tribal right of self-government was not complete, however; the constitutions and by-laws were subject to approval of the Secretary of the Interior. Tribes were authorized to employ their own counsel, but again subject to the approval of the Secretary. The Secretary was also authorized to issue charters of incorporation to petitioning tribes, subject to ratification by a majority of tribal members. Finally, the Act provided that its provisions would not apply to any tribe that voted against its application at a special election to be called by the Secretary within one year of the passage of the Act.

The Act was overwhelmingly successful in preventing further rapid erosion of the tribal land base. Its encouragement of tribal self-government enjoyed a more limited success; the tribal constitutions adopted under the Act were suggested by federal authorities and followed the non-Indian pattern of divided executive, legislative and judicial authority. They were consequently often unsuited to tribal needs and conditions. Some of the tribes rejected coverage of the Act, fearing additional federal direction. But on the whole the Act must be considered a success in providing a framework, however flawed, for growing self-government by the tribes in the decades following its passage.

G. TERMINATION AND RELOCATION: 1953 TO 1968

By 1950, fashions in federal Indian policy were beginning once again to change radically. In 1953, Congress formally adopted a policy of "termination," its express aim being "as rapidly as possible, to make the Indians within the territorial limits of the United States subject to the same laws and entitled to the same privileges and responsibilities as are applicable to other citizens of the United States, [and] to end their status as wards of the United States * * *." H.Con.Res. 108, 83rd Cong., 1st Sess., 67 Stat. B132 (1953). Pursuant to this policy, several tribes were "terminated" by statute. Their special relationship with the federal government was ended, they were subjected to state laws, and their lands were converted into private ownership and in most instances sold. See Chapter III, Section E, infra. While the intentions of many of the congressional supporters of termination had once again been benevolent (one purpose had been to "free" the Indians from domination by the Bureau of Indian Affairs), the results were generally tragic. The two largest terminations, those of the Klamaths of Oregon and the Menominees of Wisconsin, were typical. The Klamath lands were sold and the proceeds quickly dissipated. The Menominees were plunged into even deeper economic troubles than they had previously endured; in 1973 they were successful in securing legislation to restore their special relationship with the federal government and to place their lands back in federal trust.

While the number of tribes terminated was a very small percentage of the total, the policy cast a pall over the futures of most of the tribes during the years when it was officially endorsed by Congress.

At the same time that Congress was stressing the goal of termination, the Bureau of Indian Affairs was attempting to encourage Indians to leave the reservation under its "relocation" program. As a response to unquestionably high unemployment rates on the reservations, the B.I.A. offered grants to Indians who would leave the reservation to seek work in various metropolitan centers. Some were successful in securing lasting employment. All too often, however, the effect of the program was to create in the target cities a population of unemployed Indians who suffered all the usual problems of the urban poor along with the added trauma of dislocation.

The final major piece of legislation of the 1950's that further attenuated the relationship between the federal government and the tribes was Public Law 280. 67 Stat. 588 (1953), as amended, 18 U.S.C.A. §§ 1161–62, 25 U.S.C.A. §§ 1321–22, 28 U.S.C.A. § 1360 (1953). That statute extended state civil and criminal jurisdiction to Indian country in five specified states: California, Nebraska, Minnesota (except Red Lake reservation), Oregon (except Warm Springs reservation), and Wisconsin. Alaska was added to the list in 1958. In addition, Public Law 280 provided that any other state could assume such jurisdiction by statute or state constitutional amendment. Several states assumed partial or total jurisdiction pursuant to this authority. See Chapter VIII, infra. Consent of the concerned tribes was not required and in several cases was not sought.

The effect of Public Law 280 was drastically to change the traditional division of jurisdiction among the federal government, the states and the tribes in those states where the law was applied. Assumption of jurisdiction by the state displaced otherwise applicable federal law and left tribal authorities with a greatly diminished role. It ran directly counter to John Marshall's original characterization of Indian country as territory in which the laws of the state "can have no force." Worcester v. Georgia, 31 U.S. (6 Pet.) 515, 561 (1832). Indeed, it went much further, for it not only gave state laws and courts force in Indian country, it gave them power over the Indians themselves. Yet an assumption of Public Law 280 jurisdiction by the state did not amount to a termination of the federal trust relationship. The Act disclaimed any grant to the states of power to encumber or tax Indian properties held in federal trust or to interfere with treaty hunting and fishing rights. The Act was subsequently held not to have conferred upon the states general regulatory power within Indian country. Bryan v. Itasca County, 426 U.S. 373 (1976); see Chapter VIII, infra. In these respects, Public Law 280 represented a compromise between termination and continuation of the relative immunity of the tribes from state jurisdiction. It was a compromise that satisfied almost no one. The tribes, fearing that the extension of state jurisdiction was but a first step toward termination, objected to the lack of any requirement of tribal consent. The states, finding that new enforcement responsibilities involved substantial expense, resented their inability to tax tribal properties to help pay the cost. This latter consideration frequently led to neglect of law enforcement in Indian country by Public Law 280 states, and probably explains the reluctance, despite the assimilationist tenor of the times, of many states to assume general jurisdiction.

H.   TRIBAL SELF–DETERMINATION: 1968 TO PRESENT

By the late 1960's, the policy of termination was largely regarded as a failure, and the assimilationist ideal began to fade. Partly as a result of this movement, and partly for independent reasons, Congress passed the Indian Civil Rights Act of 1968. 82 Stat. 77, 25 U.S.C.A. § 1301 et seq.

The primary effect of the Act was to impose upon the tribes most of the requirements of the Bill of Rights. Traditionally, the tribes had not been subject to constitutional restraints in their governmental actions, because those restraints are imposed in terms either upon the federal government or, by the 14th Amendment, upon the states. Since the tribes were neither, the constitutional restrictions did not apply to them. Talton v. Mayes, 163 U.S. 376 (1896). The Civil Rights Act imposed upon the tribes by statute such basic requirements as the protection of free speech, free exercise of religion, due process and equal protection of the laws, among others. See Chapter XI, infra. In so doing, the Act represented a federal intrusion upon the independence of the tribes, and some tribal members have opposed it upon that ground. On the other hand, congressional action to require constitutional procedures by tribal governments seemed to contemplate the continued existence of those governments, rather than their withering away. In that sense, the Indian Civil Rights Act had a thrust quite inconsistent with the earlier termination policy.

One provision of the Civil Rights Act of 1968 was unequivocally welcomed by the tribes. The Act amended Public Law 280 so that states could no longer assume civil and criminal jurisdiction over Indian country unless the affected tribes consented at special elections called for the purpose. 25 U.S.C.A. §§ 1321–22, 1326. This amendment brought such extensions of jurisdiction to a virtual halt. In addition, the Act set forth a procedure by which states that had assumed Public Law 280 jurisdiction could retrocede such jurisdiction to the federal government. 25 U.S.C.A. § 1323. Numbers of these retrocessions have occurred.

In 1970, President Nixon issued a statement on Indian affairs that set the current direction of federal policy. 116 Cong.Rec. 23258. He declared termination to have been a failure, and called upon Congress to repudiate it as a policy. He stressed the continuing importance of the trust relationship between the federal government and the tribes. Finally, he urged a program of legislation to permit the tribes to manage their affairs with a maximum degree of autonomy.

In the ensuing years, Congress passed several measures along the lines indicated by President Nixon. The Indian Financing Act of 1974, 25 U.S.C.A. § 1451 et seq., established a revolving loan fund to aid in the development of Indian resources. In 1975, Congress passed the Indian Self–Determination and Education Assistance Act, 25 U.S.C.A. § 450 et seq., which authorized the Secretaries of the Interior and of Health, Education and Welfare to enter contracts under which the tribes themselves would assume responsibility for the administration of federal Indian programs.

Congress in 1975 also established the American Indian Policy Review Commission to undertake a comprehensive review of federal Indian policy and to consider, among other things, "alternative methods to strengthen tribal government * * *." 88 Stat. 1910. The Commission, which included Indian representation, issued its report in 1977 and called for a firm rejection of assimilationist policies, reaffirmation of the status of tribes as permanent, self-governing institutions, and increased financial aid to the tribes.

Subsequent congressional and executive policies have continued to favor tribal self-development. The Indian Tribal Government Tax Status Act of 1982, 96 Stat. 2607, accorded the tribes many of the federal tax advantages enjoyed by states, including that of issuing tax-exempt bonds to finance governmental projects. In 1983, President Reagan reaffirmed the policy of strengthening tribal governments, with the additional goal of reducing their dependence upon the federal government. He repeated President Nixon's repudiation of the termination policy. Statement on Indian Policy, 19 Weekly Comp.Pres.Doc. 98 (Jan. 24, 1983). In 1988, Congress declared the nation's commitment to "the development of strong and stable tribal governments," 25 U.S.C.A. § 450a(b), and it enacted the Tribally Controlled Schools Act of 1988, 25 U.S.C. § 2501 et seq., which provided grants for tribes to operate their own tribal schools. In 1994, President Clinton instructed each agency of the federal government to operate "within a government-to-government relationship with federally recognized tribal governments." 59 Fed.Reg. 22951 (1994). That principle was further endorsed by President Clinton in 2000, 65 Fed.Reg. 67249, and President George W. Bush in 2002, 67 Fed.Reg. 67773.

At present, then, congressional and executive federal Indian policy seems clearly to be based on a model of continuing pluralism; it recognizes that the tribes are here to stay for the indefinite future, and seeks to strengthen them. The assimilationist viewpoint, which has intermittently predominated in the past, is not now in favor. National policy is not monolithic, however. At the same time that Congress and the Executive have been acting to strengthen the tribes, the Supreme Court has been narrowing tribal power over nonmembers within tribal reservations. E.g., Nevada v. Hicks, 533 U.S.

353 (2001). (See Chapter V, Section A; Chapter VII, Section F(2)(a)). Nevertheless, it is fair to say that all branches accept the continuing vitality, for the indefinite future, of Indian tribes and their governments.

It is perhaps possible that the contending forces in Indian affairs have reached some sort of final balance, and that no further major changes of direction will occur. Nothing in the history of federal Indian policy, however, justifies confidence in such a conclusion.

CHAPTER III

THE SPECIAL RELATIONSHIP BETWEEN THE FEDERAL GOVERNMENT AND THE TRIBES

A. INTRODUCTION

Much of American Indian Law revolves around the special relationship between the federal government and the tribes. Yet it is very difficult to mark the boundaries of this relationship, and even more difficult to assess its legal consequences. At its broadest, the relationship includes the mixture of legal duties, moral obligations, understandings and expectancies that have arisen from the entire course of dealing between the federal government and the tribes. In its narrowest and most concrete sense, the relationship approximates that of trustee and beneficiary, with the trustee (the United States) subject in some degree to legally enforceable responsibilities. Unfortunately, the same terms of fiduciary obligation are often used by the courts whether they are referring to the broadest or the narrowest definition. Care must be exercised, therefore, to determine whether the type of fiduciary obligation in question in any given case is merely a moral command or is an enforceable legal duty.

34

The degree to which the courts are willing to enforce fiduciary responsibilities of the federal government depends upon both the branch of government involved and the subject matter of the dispute. Although it has been stated on several occasions that Congress owes a fiduciary duty to the tribes, no court has ever enforced such a duty. In the case of Congress, then, the duty is essentially a moral or political obligation. The executive branch, on the other hand, sometimes has been subjected to court enforcement of its trust responsibilities. The duty of the executive branch to the tribes is therefore increasingly a legal one. In general, it has been enforced in regard to the executive's management of Indian lands or other properties, such as water rights. See Section C, infra. It should not be assumed, however, that the broader areas of the special relationship between the federal government and the tribes are unimportant simply because they have not been held to be judicially enforceable on a theory of trust.

B. EVOLUTION OF THE RELATIONSHIP

Some form of special relationship between the federal government and the Indian tribes was probably implicit in the decision, made immediately after the Revolution, to keep Indian affairs in the hands of the federal government as a means of protecting the tribes from the states and their citizens (thereby avoiding Indian wars). See Chapter II,

Section B, supra. The evolution of that relationship into fiduciary form took place slowly. The Constitution itself certainly contains no explicit delineation of a relationship, fiduciary or otherwise, but it does grant powers to the federal government that have been held to authorize its role as a trustee. Most crucial are the congressional power to regulate commerce with the Indian tribes, Art. I, § 8, cl. 3, and the presidential power to make treaties, Art. II, § 2, cl. 2. Additional support for the role of trustee sometimes has been found in the congressional power to make regulations governing the territory belonging to the United States, Art. IV, § 3, cl. 2.

Primary support for the trust relationship came, however, from the judiciary, beginning with Chief Justice John Marshall's decision in Cherokee Nation v. Georgia, 30 U.S. (5 Pet.) 1 (1831). There he characterized the tribes as "domestic dependent nations" with a right of occupancy of the land until the federal government chose to extinguish their title. Marshall added:

Meanwhile, they are in a state of pupilage; their relation to the United States resembles that of a ward to his guardian.

30 U.S. (5 Pet.) at 17. While Marshall's reference was perhaps more literary than legal and did not attempt to spell out the incidents of the guardian-ward relationship, his statement served as a conceptual basis for further evolution of the doctrine. Thus, fifty years later the Supreme Court was able to uphold Congress's Major Crimes Act (defining

certain offenses committed by Indians as federal crimes), on the following theory:

> These Indian tribes *are* the wards of the nation. They are communities *dependent* on the United States,—dependent largely for their daily food; dependent for their political rights. They owe no allegiance to the states, and receive from them no protection. Because of the local ill feeling, the people of the states where they are found are often their deadliest enemies. From their very weakness and helplessness, so largely due to the course of dealing of the federal government with them, and the treaties in which it has been promised, there arises the duty of protection, and with it the power. This has always been recognized by the executive, and by congress, and by this court, whenever the question has arisen.

United States v. Kagama, 118 U.S. 375, 384–85 (1886); see also United States v. Sandoval, 231 U.S. 28 (1913).

This view of the trust relationship as a source of congressional power was buttressed in Lone Wolf v. Hitchcock, 187 U.S. 553 (1903). In that case, the Supreme Court upheld a statute distributing tribal lands despite a claim by some tribal members that an earlier treaty required consent of tribal members for any such distribution. The Court stated:

> The contention in effect ignores the status of the contracting Indians and the relation of dependency they bore and continue to bear towards the government of the United States. To uphold the

claim would be to adjudge that the indirect operation of the treaty was to materially limit and
qualify the controlling authority of Congress in
respect to the care and protection of the Indians,
and to deprive Congress, in a possible emergency,
when the necessity might be urgent for a partition and disposal of the tribal lands, of all power
to act, if the assent of the Indians could not be
obtained.

* * *

Plenary authority over the tribal relations of the
Indians has been exercised by Congress from the
beginning, and the power has always been
deemed a political one, not subject to be controlled by the judicial department of the government.

187 U.S. at 564–565. Thus where Congress was
concerned, the trust responsibility had become far
more of a sword for the government than a shield
for the tribes.

C. ENFORCEMENT OF THE TRUST RESPONSIBILITY

It was with regard to the executive branch that
the Supreme Court began to enforce the federal
trust responsibility toward the Indians. The guardian-ward relationship was held not to authorize the
Secretary of Interior to dispose of lands claimed by
an Indian Pueblo in the same manner that he could
dispose of other public lands. "That would not be

an exercise of guardianship, but an act of confiscation." Lane v. Pueblo of Santa Rosa, 249 U.S. 110, 113 (1919). In Cramer v. United States, 261 U.S. 219, 229 (1923), the Court construed a doubtful statute to protect Indian-occupied lands from being patented to third parties, because to fail to protect the Indians' right of occupancy "would be contrary to the whole spirit of the traditional American policy toward these dependent wards of the nation." It also held that the United States had standing to assert the Indians' interest, by reason of its position as guardian. Some years later, the Court observed that, at least in the case of lands owned by an Indian tribe in fee, the federal powers of management arising from the trust relationship were "subject to limitations inhering in such a guardianship * * * ". United States v. Creek Nation, 295 U.S. 103, 110 (1935). Then, in 1942 the Supreme Court held that where a treaty required the United States to pay funds to tribal members, it was liable when it paid the money instead to the tribal government that was known to be misappropriating it. In regard to the treaty, the Government was more than "a mere contracting party;" it was to "be judged by the most exacting fiduciary standards." Seminole Nation v. United States, 316 U.S. 286, 296–97 (1942); see also Loudner v. United States, 108 F.3d 896, 901–02 (8th Cir.1997).

The trust responsibility and its consequences were further defined in the 1980's by the Supreme Court in two decisions arising from the same lawsuit. Indian allottees of forested land in the Quinault Reservation sued the United States for damages for mismanagement of the forest resources. In the first decision, United States v. Mitchell, 445 U.S. 535 (1980) ("Mitchell I"), the Court held that the General Allotment Act itself "created only a limited trust relationship between the United States and the allottee that does not impose any duty upon the Government to manage timber resources." 445 U.S. at 542. In the second decision, United States v. Mitchell, 463 U.S. 206 (1983) ("Mitchell II"), the Court held that a trust duty *did* arise from several statutes and regulations that, unlike the General Allotment Act, expressly authorized or directed the Secretary of the Interior to manage forests on Indian lands. E.g., 25 U.S.C.A. §§ 406(a), 466. In addition, the Court stated that

a fiduciary relationship necessarily arises when the Government assumes such elaborate control over forests and property belonging to Indians. All of the necessary elements of a common-law trust are present: a trustee (the United States), a beneficiary (the Indian allottees), and a trust corpus (Indian timber, lands, and funds).

463 U.S. at 225. In these circumstances, a trust relationship exists " 'though nothing is said expressly in the authorizing or underlying statute * * * about a trust fund, or a trust or fiduciary connection.' " 463 U.S. at 225 (quoting Navajo Tribe of Indians v. United States, 224 Ct.Cl. 171, 183, 624 F.2d 981, 987 (1980)). The Court went on to hold that "it naturally follows that the Government should be liable in damages for the breach of

its fiduciary duties." 463 U.S. at 226. Finally, it held that the Tucker Act, 28 U.S.C.A. § 1491, and the Indian Tucker Act, 28 U.S.C.A. § 1505, waived the sovereign immunity of the United States for such claims.

Two recent decisions of the Supreme Court further delineated the boundaries between the "bare trust" of Mitchell I, which gave rise to no duties of management on the part of the United States, and the more active trusteeship of Mitchell II, which permitted a remedy against the United States for breach of trust. In United States v. Navajo Nation, 537 U.S. 488 (2003), the Court held that the Indian Mineral Leasing Act, which required secretarial approval of mineral leases negotiated by the tribe, gave rise to no fiduciary duty enforceable in damages when the Secretary allegedly caused the tribe to receive below-market royalties for its coal. The Court relied on the fact that the Act gave the Secretary no duties of management beyond approval (which was constrained only by a minimum royalty rate) and contained no express declaration of trust duty. The decision is a restrictive one; it is hard to imagine a purpose for the requirement of secretarial approval if it creates no duty to protect the interests of the tribes. In the wake of the decision, it remains to be seen whether the Navajo Nation can recover on the ground that a network of other statutes and regulations gave rise to an enforceable trust duty. See Navajo Nation v. United States, 347 F.3d 1327 (Fed.Cir.2003) (on remand).

On the same day that it handed down *Navajo Nation*, the Supreme Court decided United States v. White Mountain Apache Tribe, 537 U.S. 465 (2003), which held that the United States was subject to a fiduciary duty to maintain and preserve Fort Apache, which it held in trust for the benefit of the Tribe on whose reservation it was located. A 1960 statute had provided that the fort be so held, and permitted the Secretary to use the property for administrative and school purposes as long as needed. 74 Stat. 8 (1960). The Court concluded that the United States could be held liable for letting the fort fall into decay because the statute expressly provided that the facility was held in trust, and the government not only exercised daily supervision of the property, but occupied portions of it.

The Supreme Court has thus demonstrated willingness to hold the executive accountable for breaches of its fiduciary duties to Indians when the trust is an active one. It must be kept in mind, however, that in the cases where recovery has been permitted, the federal government was acting in its most narrow and specific role as trustee—that of manager of assets held by the United States for the benefit of the Indians. Although the Court relied on the more general, overall trust relationship to buttress its decision in *Mitchell II*, 363 U.S. at 225, it has never granted relief for breach of that general duty by itself. Nor is the Court always ready to apply the law of private trusts to the federal trustee, as it appears to have done in *Mitchell II*, 363 U.S. at 226, and *White Mountain Apache Tribe*, 537

U.S. at 475–76. When the United States litigates on behalf of the tribes, the Court has said that the government "cannot follow the fastidious standards of a private fiduciary" with regard to potential conflicts of interest. Nevada v. United States, 463 U.S. 110, 128 (1983). Similarly, when the United States administers an irrigation project for the benefit of tribes and non-Indian users, the trust responsibility to the tribes does not protect communications between the tribes and the United States from disclosure under the Freedom of Information Act. Department of the Interior v. Klamath Water Users Protective Ass'n, 532 U.S. 1 (2001).

In the lower courts as well, the trust responsibility of the United States is most readily invoked with regard to the active management of Indian assets. One huge lawsuit, still pending, involves a determination that the United States breached its fiduciary duties over a period of many years in managing Individual Indian Money trust accounts (representing revenues produced by trust assets held for the benefit of individual Indians). See Cobell v. Norton, 240 F.3d 1081 (D.C.Cir.2001). This litigation, which has resulted in numerous reported decisions, potentially involves hundreds of millions of dollars. The problem of mismanagement of these accounts had induced Congress in 1994 to enact the Indian Trust Management Reform Act, 25 U.S.C.A. § 4001 et seq., which called for the government to provide an accounting, and established (but failed to fund) an Office of Special Trustee for American Indians within the Department of the Interior. Id. at § 4041; see

Cobell, 240 F.3d at 1092. A major difficulty in the case, largely caused by faulty records, is in determining the amount of loss or damages. An accounting was ordered by the court, Cobell v. Norton, 283 F.Supp.2d 66 (D.D.C.2003), but Congress, in an action of dubious constitutionality, provided that no funds of the Department of Interior could be used for such an accounting until Congress amended the 1994 Act. Pub. L. 108–108 (Nov. 10, 2003). The accounting has been stayed until the circuit court determines the effect of this legislation. Cobell v. Norton, 2003 WL 22711642 (D.C.Cir.2003). This saga is far from over.

Several lower courts have invoked the trust responsibility to compel the government to undertake litigation to protect tribal lands or resources. One example is Joint Tribal Council of Passamaquoddy Tribe v. Morton, 528 F.2d 370 (1st Cir.1975). In that case the Tribe sued the federal government to require it to bring an action against the state of Maine to recover land ceded by the tribe in 1794 without the approval of the federal government, in violation of the Trade and Intercourse Act of 1790. From 1794 on, all the Tribe's dealings with government had been with the state of Maine (or its predecessor, Massachusetts); it had no dealings with the federal government and Congress passed no legislation specifically in regard to the Passamaquoddy. In its decision, the court of appeals held: (1) that the Trade and Intercourse Act included the Passamaquoddy within its terms as a "tribe," regardless of the fact that the federal government had not taken any action to "recognize" the tribe; (2) that at least insofar as the preservation of tribal lands was concerned, the Act created a trust relationship between the federal government and the tribe; and (3) that Congress had never acted to terminate this trust relationship. The Government accordingly was ordered to file suit as trustee for the tribe.

The trust responsibility also figured prominently in litigation concerning water rights of several of the western tribes. One such controversy involved the Pyramid Lake Paiute Tribe, which for years had been aggrieved by the declining water levels in its reservation lake, caused by certain reclamation projects along its feeder streams. After several years of prodding, the tribe succeeded in having the United States bring a water rights suit on its behalf. In the meantime, the tribe successfully attacked a regulation of the Secretary of Interior that allocated water among the various users in the watershed. The Secretary's allocation had been an accommodation to the demands of the competing users (including the tribe) and was defended as a "judgment call." The district court struck down the regulation on the ground that, in making a mere accommodation, the Secretary had failed to fulfill his fiduciary duty to protect the water rights of the tribe. Pyramid Lake Paiute Tribe of Indians v. Morton, 354 F.Supp. 252 (D.D.C. 1972). Once a tribe establishes priority water rights, the Bureau of Reclamation has a trust responsibility to honor those rights in allocating water in the operation of an irrigation project. Klamath Water Users Protective Ass'n v. Patterson, 204 F.3d 1206, 1213–14 (9th Cir.1999).

Courts continue to find new ways to apply trust principles to the management of tribal property. In the case of In re Blue Lake Forest Products, Inc., 30 F.3d 1138 (9th Cir.1994), the United States and the tribe had sold logs cut on the reservation to a non-Indian buyer off-reservation who received but did not pay for them. In an ensuing bankruptcy, "the heightened protection for property held in trust for Indian tribes" was held to override a state security interest in the logs that a financing bank held under the Uniform Commercial Code.

Courts in recent years have delineated additional characteristics or limitations of the federal trust responsibility. The federal government's responsibility runs to *all* Indian tribes; it therefore cannot be invoked to prevent the Indian Health Service from terminating a program favoring one Indian subgroup in order to use the resources in programs benefitting Indians generally. Lincoln v. Vigil, 508 U.S. 182, 194–95 (1993). A tribe seeking judicial redress for federal mismanagement of its resources ordinarily must first exhaust administrative remedies. White Mountain Apache Tribe v. Hodel, 840 F.2d 675, 677–78 (9th Cir.1988). The trust duty does not extend to the federal government in its disposition of an off-reservation Indian school; the school was not trust property, even though operated for the benefit of Indian tribes. Inter Tribal Council of Arizona, Inc. v. Babbitt, 51 F.3d 199 (9th Cir. 1995). Congress may authorize state governments to exercise the trust responsibility in specific instances. See Pelt v. Utah, 104 F.3d 1534 (10th Cir.1996); Peyote Way Church of God, Inc. v. Thornburgh, 922 F.2d 1210, 1219 (5th Cir.1991). A violation of federal trust responsibility toward an individual Indian has been held to create a right of action under state law, enforceable by incorporation in the Federal Tort Claims Act. Marlys Bear Medicine v. United States ex rel. Secretary of Interior, 241 F.3d 1208 (9th Cir.2001).

From time to time Indian litigants have urged the enforcement of a broader trust responsibility, going beyond protection of tribal lands and resources and encompassing a duty to preserve tribal autonomy or to contribute to the welfare of the tribes and their members. As yet these attempts have not met with success in the courts, which tend to insist upon a statute or regulation establishing trust responsibility, or upon the existence of federal supervision over tribal funds or other property. See United States v. Wilson, 881 F.2d 596, 600 (9th Cir.1989). Thus no general trust responsibility precluded the Secretary of Labor from enforcing provisions of the Safe Drinking Water Act against a tribe. Osage Tribal Council v. U.S. Dept. of Labor, 187 F.3d 1174, 1183–84 (10th Cir.1999). When a generalized trust responsibility has been recognized, as in the case of the Federal Energy Regulatory Commission, it has entitled the tribes to no greater rights than they would otherwise have under the Federal Power Act and agency regulations. Skokomish Indian Tribe v. FERC, 121 F.3d 1303 (9th Cir.1997). An agency's trust responsibility is discharged by compliance with regulations and statutes not aimed at protecting Indian tribes. Morongo Band of Mission Indians v. Federal Aviation Admin., 161 F.3d 569, 574 (9th Cir.1998); Okanogan Highlands Alliance v. Williams, 236 F.3d 468, 479 (9th Cir.2000). The broad view of the trust responsibility is not utterly without effect, however; it can influence the decision of cases brought on other grounds. In McNabb v. Bowen, 829 F.2d 787 (9th Cir.1987), the court required the Indian Health Service to pay for medical care of an Indian child when the state, which arguably had the primary responsibility, refused to do so. The court found the sources of the federal duty in the congressional intent underlying the Indian Health Care Improvement Act, 25 U.S.C.A. § 1601 et seq., "brought into sharper focus by the trust doctrine." 829 F.2d at 793. Similarly, the broad trust obligation permits an agency to assume that disputed land is Indian country for purposes of regulation, see HRI, Inc. v. EPA, 198 F.3d 1224, 1246–48 (10th Cir.2000), or to maintain an informal policy of not enforcing against members of recognized tribes the Migratory Bird Treaty Act's prohibition of possession of hawk parts, see United States v. Eagleboy, 200 F.3d 1137 (8th Cir.1999). The broad trust obligation of the United States thus casts its shadow beyond cases involving Indian lands, resources and proprietary treaty rights. See also Morton v. Ruiz, 415 U.S. 199, 236 (1974). Efforts to expand the enforcement of the doctrine may be expected to continue. See, generally, Chambers, *Judicial Enforcement of the Federal Trust Responsibility to Indians*, 27 Stan.L.Rev. 1213 (1975).

D. ROLE OF THE BUREAU OF INDI- AN AFFAIRS AND THE DEPART- MENT OF THE INTERIOR

The primary instrument for carrying out the federal trust responsibility has been the Bureau of Indian Affairs, located for the past one hundred fifty years within the Department of the Interior. From a system of Indian agents under the loose control of a small Washington office, the Bureau has evolved into a complex bureaucracy of many thousands of employees. The Washington office is headed by the Commissioner of Indian Affairs, who reports to the Assistant Secretary of the Interior for Indian Affairs (whose position was recently created to reflect an increased executive commitment to tribal development). While the Washington office is at the organizational top of the Bureau, an unusually great degree of decision-making authority has been delegated to the twelve Area Offices, located in various parts of the country and each headed by an Area Director. Below the Area Offices are the eighty-odd agencies, each usually responsible for one or more reservations. The Agencies are located on reservations and each is directed by a superintendent.

At one time the Bureau represented virtually the entire governing authority in Indian country. Today the activities of the Bureau are more narrowly directed toward the fulfillment of the federal trust responsibility to the tribes, although its overall influence on tribal affairs remains great. The most substantial activities of the Bureau are probably the provision of education and the management of tribal resources, particularly lands. The Bureau has for years run Indian boarding schools, which were originally designed as instruments of assimilation and which have been the focus of controversy and resentment partly because of that heritage. In recent years, the Bureau has been phasing out its boarding schools in favor of day schools located in reservation communities. The Bureau also has entered contracts permitting local tribal or community control of some of the schools, and this trend is likely to continue. (Much Indian education, of course, is provided by the states, with federal financial assistance. See 20 U.S.C.A. §§ 236–44, 631–47 ("impact aid"); 25 U.S.C.A. §§ 452–54 (Johnson O'Malley Act)).

Management of lands and other resources, including mineral and water rights, held in trust is a very significant portion of Bureau activity. Because the United States is legal titleholder of all trust resources, the federal government is of necessity a participant in all leases or other dispositions of these assets. Even a will by an individual allottee disposing of his or her beneficial interest is invalid without the approval of the Secretary of the Interior. 25 U.S.C.A. § 373. Indeed, the Secretary must approve any contract providing for payment or grants of privilege by a tribe in consideration of services for the Indians "relative to their lands." 25 U.S.C.A. § 81; see Penobscot Indian Nation v. Key Bank, 112 F.3d 538 (1st Cir.1997). The result of trusteeship is therefore a considerable degree of Bureau supervision, whether the assets are held in trust for the tribe or for individual Indians.

There are many other activities of the Bureau too numerous to mention here. Examples are the administration of Bureau housing programs, building and maintenance of roads, licensing of Indian traders, provision of emergency relief, and the administration of various grant programs.

Over the years the Bureau has been subjected to repeated and bitter criticism on a variety of counts. If has been contended that the complex and burdensome administrative structure of the Bureau eats up an undue share of the appropriations that Congress intends for the benefit of the Indians, and that it has "lost" large portions of those appropriations. The Bureau has also been charged with simply not doing its job, and with being more sensitive to non-Indian than to Indian interests. Examples that attracted judicial attention were the Bureau's failure to issue regulations governing Indian traders, see Rockbridge v. Lincoln, 449 F.2d 567 (9th Cir.1971), and its failure in one instance to provide irrigation for Indian farmers while providing it for non-Indians—behavior that the court of appeals said "borders on the shocking," Scholder v. United States, 428 F.2d 1123, 1130 (9th Cir.1970). Recently, the failure of the Bureau to maintain adequate records in its management of Individual Indian Money accounts, with the likely loss of huge amounts of funds, has come into focus. See Cobell v. Norton, 240 F.3d 1081 (D.C.Cir.2001), Section C, supra.

A more fundamental complaint against the administration of the trust responsibility goes beyond the Bureau to the Department of the Interior and even to the Department of Justice. The Bureau has the responsibility of defending the tribes' trust assets when they are threatened by other interests. Unfortunately, many of these threats come from other agencies within the Department of the Interior and their constituencies. Indian land and water interests frequently conflict with the activities or designs of the Bureau of Reclamation, the Bureau of Land Management, the National Park Service and, occasionally, the Bureau of Mines and the Office of Surface Mining Reclamation and Enforcement. Indian fishing interests have conflicted with those of the Fish and Wildlife Service. All of these agencies are within the Department of the Interior, and many of them have political support far in excess of that of the Bureau of Indian Affairs. As a result, Indian interests may suffer when compromises are made at the Secretary's level between competing bureaus. Although this type of political compromise goes on within every executive agency, it carries the danger that the tribes will be viewed merely as a weak political interest rather than as a group to whom a fiduciary duty is owed.

The trust relationship runs into even more severe problems when the battle for preservation of trust assets moves into court. The Bureau of Indian Affairs is represented initially by the Solicitor of the Department of Interior and, if the matter goes to court, by the Department of Justice. Both of these offices are charged with representing not only Indian interests, but also those of the agencies with which the tribes frequently come into conflict. In addition to the agencies within the Department of Interior listed above, the tribes find themselves competing on occasion with the Forest Service of the Department of Agriculture, which is also represented in court by the Justice Department. A private law firm could not ethically undertake the representation of such clearly competing clients, but the government attorneys regularly do. The Supreme Court has made it clear that, in those circumstances, the government may not disregard its obligations to its other beneficiaries in favor of its responsibility to the tribes. Nevada v. United States, 463 U.S. 110, 127 (1983).

[I]t may well appear that Congress was requiring the Secretary of the Interior to carry water on at least two shoulders when it delegated to him both the responsibility for the supervision of the Indian tribes and the commencement of reclamation projects in areas adjacent to reservation lands. But Congress chose to do this, and it is simply unrealistic to suggest that the Government may not perform its obligation to represent Indian tribes in litigation when Congress has obliged it

> to represent other interests as well. In this re-
> gard, the Government cannot follow the fastidi-
> ous standards of a private fiduciary * * *.

463 U.S. at 128. Accordingly, the tribes are not
relieved of the res judicata effect of a judgment
merely because the government represented both
the tribes and those who competed with them. 463
U.S. at 134–43; Arizona v. California, 460 U.S. 605,
626–28 (1983).

The tribes believe that the government's representation of conflicting interests results in less-
than-satisfactory advocacy of Indian trust interests.
One alternative, frequently employed, is for the
tribes to use their own attorneys. The tribes generally may intervene in litigation affecting their interests, even if they are already represented by the
United States as trustee. E.g., Arizona v. California,
460 U.S. 605, 613–15 (1983). This alternative may
be an expensive one, however; the tribe that used
its own attorney to sue to enforce the trust responsibility in the *Pyramid Lake* case was unable to
recover attorneys' fees from the government after it
prevailed on the merits. Pyramid Lake Paiute Tribe
v. Morton, 499 F.2d 1095 (D.C.Cir.1974).

To avoid these problems of conflict of interest,
President Nixon proposed the establishment of an
independent Indian Trust Counsel Authority that
would undertake legal representation of Indian
trust interests. 116 Cong.Rec. 23258, 23261 (1970).
The American Indian Policy Review Commission
went even further; it recommended a cabinet level

Department of Indian Affairs with its own Office of Trust Rights Protection to litigate trust cases. Neither proposal has been enacted by Congress.

The final, recurrent criticism of the federal administration of Indian affairs focuses on the Bureau of Indian Affairs itself. It is the charge of excessive paternalism. Initially, the reservations themselves and the schools established by the Bureau had the very purpose of changing and molding the Indians to the non-Indian way of life—a process that was paternalistic by definition. Today the emphasis of federal policy is upon tribal self-determination, and the Bureau has certainly receded from its monolithic control of tribal affairs. Many of the Bureau's management functions have been contracted to the tribes under the Indian Self–Determination and Education Assistance Act of 1975, 25 U.S.C.A. § 450 et seq. Moreover, the Bureau is no longer the only presence of the federal government within Indian country. The Departments of Health and Human Services, of Education, of Housing and Urban Development, as well as the Legal Services Corporation and other agencies now play a considerable part in tribal development. Nevertheless, the Bureau is still the most important agency for the tribes, and on some occasions may influence tribal affairs to a degree greater than is consistent with present notions of tribal autonomy. There are several reasons for this persistent condition.

The first reason may simply be that old habits die hard; neither a bureaucracy nor those accustomed to relying upon it are likely to change overnight.

Habit in this case is supported by the legal framework. Tribal elections are held and approved by the Secretary of the Interior. See Thomas v. United States, 189 F.3d 662 (7th Cir.1999); 25 U.S.C.A. § 476. Most tribes have constitutions adopted pursuant to the Indian Reorganization Act of 1934, and those constitutions can be changed only after an election supervised by the Secretary of the Interior, with the Secretary having the power to review determinations of voter eligibility and to disapprove the amendments if they do not comply with federal law. See Shakopee Mdewakanton Sioux (Dakota) Community v. Babbitt, 107 F.3d 667 (8th Cir.1997). Typically, those constitutions provide either that tribal ordinances must be approved by the Secretary of the Interior or that the Secretary has the power to rescind ordinances passed by the tribal council. The Secretary's approval or disapproval is based upon the recommendation of the agency superintendent. While the policy today is that tribal ordinances will be approved almost automatically, there are still exceptions. See Moapa Band of Paiute Indians v. United States Dept. of Interior, 747 F.2d 563 (9th Cir.1984), upholding the Secretary's rescission of a tribal ordinance licensing prostitution. It is consequently quite natural for a tribal council, when considering passage of a controversial measure, to be interested in knowing whether the superintendent approves of it. From this position it is a short step to fairly frequent guidance of the council by the superintendent, who is the federal authority consistently on the scene. The degree to which this tendency occurs will depend upon the character of the tribal officials and of the superintendent, the attitudes of both toward tribal independence, and the respect those parties have for each other.

Another reason why the Bureau may continue to guide many tribal affairs is found in the trust responsibility itself. The concept of trusteeship is, unfortunately, opposed in principle and to some degree in practice to that of tribal independence. If the tribal council wants to enter a particular lease upon terms that the bureau deems disadvantageous, the trust responsibility (and the possible trustee liability that follows from it) encourages the Bureau to frustrate the desires of the tribal authorities. While it may be argued that this example arises but rarely (as there are all too many instances of the Bureau's having entered disadvantageous leases), the fact remains that the trust responsibility exerts some pressure toward continued paternalism.

An outsider's reaction to the criticisms of the Bureau might simply be to call for its abolition, but this suggestion inevitably encounters opposition from the tribes. While joining in criticism of the Bureau, tribal leaders recognize that it is much less paternalistic than it once was. It has substantial Indian representation within its ranks, partly as a result of Indian preference. Most important, the Bureau is seen as the embodiment of the federal trust responsibility. An attempt to end the Bureau is perceived as an attempt to do away with the trust relationship itself—in other words, to "terminate."

The experience of the tribes whose relationship with the federal government was terminated in the 1950's was sufficiently dismal that any hint of the policy's revival triggers instant opposition.

E. TERMINATION OF THE FEDERAL–TRIBAL RELATIONSHIP

Termination of the special relationship between the federal government and the tribes became an official goal of Congress in 1953, and was pursued for the following fifteen years. See Chapter II, Section G, supra. During that period, the relationship with over 100 tribes or bands was terminated. Nearly all of these were small, consisting of a few hundred members at most. The two exceptions were the Menominee of Wisconsin, with 3,270 members, and the Klamath of Oregon, with 2,133. All of these terminations were accomplished, as they must be, by acts of Congress. Since the provisions of these acts differ, the particular legal effects of termination upon any given tribe can be determined only by examination of the governing statute. The termination of the Mixed Blood Utes of the Uintah and Ouray Reservation, for example, has spawned endless litigation concerning its effects. See Hackford v. Babbitt, 14 F.3d 1457, 1463–64 (10th Cir.1994). Nevertheless, terminations do have enough common consequences to permit a general description of the effects of the process.

One of the most important features of termination is that the tribal land base passes out of trust into some form of private ownership. This means that the land may be sold or mortgaged. Federal government supervision, for good or ill, is no longer available for land and resource management. The land may be taxed by state and local governments, which was not possible when the land was in federal trust, and non-payment of taxes may result in loss of the land. In the case of many of the terminated tribes, the tribal lands were sold as part of the termination process and the proceeds were distributed to tribal members per capita (often to be consumed by routine living expenses).

Another element of termination is the transfer of jurisdiction over the tribal territory from the federal government to the state. The state and local governments acquire complete legislative power; they can regulate all activity taking place on the former reservation. State laws may be applied to the tribe itself. South Carolina v. Catawba Indian Tribe, Inc., 476 U.S. 498, 506 (1986). The state also acquires judicial jurisdiction; civil and criminal matters that were formerly tried in federal or tribal court go to state court instead. Individual members of the tribe, should they be found in Indian country, will not even be considered "Indians" for purposes of jurisdictional questions arising there. United States v. Heath, 509 F.2d 16 (9th Cir.1974).

Termination also brings to an end a number of federal services arising from the trust responsibility. Virtually all services administered by the Bureau of Indian Affairs including education, housing and emergency welfare are discontinued. Tribal members are no longer eligible for health care provided by the Indian Health Service. The tribe itself loses the ability to participate in a number of federal grant programs available to federally recognized tribes. A few federal programs serving "Indians" remain available to individual members, however, because the governing statute or regulation does not make eligibility depend upon federal recognition of the tribe.

A common practical result of termination is the disappearance of the entire tribal governmental structure. While termination statutes do not decree such a result, it is hardly surprising that the structure of self-government collapses when there is no tribal land base and no area of legislation or adjudication reserved for the exercise of tribal authority. Without territory and without government, tribal identity itself is severely threatened. While it is technically inaccurate to refer to "terminated tribes" because it is the federal-tribal relationship and not the tribe that is terminated by statute, that common shorthand term sometimes reflects the true state of affairs.

If the tribe is able to maintain its existence, termination will not put an end to its treaty rights in the absence of a clear expression of legislative intent to accomplish that purpose. Thus the Menominee and Klamath tribes were held to have hunting and fishing rights that survived each tribe's "termination." Menominee Tribe v. United States, 391 U.S. 404 (1968); Kimball v. Callahan,

493 F.2d 564 (9th Cir.1974), and Kimball v. Callahan, 590 F.2d 768 (9th Cir.1979).

The social and economic effects of termination were almost uniformly disastrous. See Chapter II, Section G, supra. After several years of political effort, the Menominees in 1973 convinced Congress to restore the federal-tribal relationship and place their remaining lands back in federal trust. 25 U.S.C.A. §§ 903–903f (Supp.1980). Since that time, Congress has restored the federal relationship with several other tribes or bands. That includes the Klamath, although restoration could not return their lost lands to them. See 25 U.S.C.A. § 566. The American Indian Policy Review Commission recommended general legislation permitting restoration of any "terminated" tribe whose members vote for it, but no such legislation has been forthcoming. In the meantime, many tribes or bands continue a precarious existence without the benefits, flawed as they may be, of a special relationship with the federal government.

CHAPTER IV

INDIAN TRIBAL GOVERNMENTS

A. ORGANIZATION OF THE TRIBES; TRIBAL CONSTITUTIONS

At the time of their first contact with the Europeans, Indian tribes were characterized by a variety of traditional forms of government. As the tribes were pushed westward and ultimately confined to reservations, these ancient systems were totally disrupted. The social fabric of most of the tribes was severely damaged, and federal administration replaced traditional forms of communal decision-making and internal control. Only a few tribes, most notably the Pueblos, escaped this fate and retained most of their customary ways.

Tribal organization was further distorted by the tendency of the federal government to create a tribe where none existed. In cases where independent bands shared a common language, federal authorities sometimes found it convenient to lump them all together into a "tribe" that could enter a single treaty opening up Indian lands for settlement. On some occasions the federal government selected "chiefs" to sign these treaties even though the concept of a chief (or the choice of those particular chiefs) was wholly foreign to the existing traditional system. The federal government in several instances also gathered disparate or even hostile groups together on one reservation and dealt with them administratively as a single unit.

By the 1920's, when the allotment policy came to be acknowledged as a failure, very little was left of the once-healthy tribal structures. The Indian Reorganization Act of 1934, which marked the shift in federal policy toward preservation of the tribes, did little to revive them in their familiar form. Instead, the Act built upon the tribal situation as it found it, and created an entirely new framework for tribal self-government.

The Indian Reorganization (Wheeler–Howard) Act provided that any tribe or tribes "residing on the same reservation" had the right to organize and adopt a constitution and by-laws which became effective upon a majority vote of the adult members of the tribe and upon approval by the Secretary of the Interior. 25 U.S.C.A. § 476. The Act also permitted the tribe to incorporate under a charter issued by the Secretary and approved by a majority vote of the members. 25 U.S.C.A. § 477. Under these provisions, a large number of the tribes adopted constitutions within a few years of passage of the Act, and many also became incorporated as an aid to the transaction of tribal business. Because these measures were adopted for entire reservations, the new constitutional "tribes" often included more than one ethnic tribe.

In light of the degree of tribal disorganization prevailing at the time of passage of the Reorganization Act and the novelty of the governmental structures proposed by the Act, it is not surprising that the newly constituted tribes were in a poor position to take immediate charge of their destinies. Indeed, the Act itself was not designed to confer complete autonomy. An election to adopt or amend a constitution could be precipitated by a request from the tribe (its government, not its individual members). 25 U.S.C. § 476(c); Split Family Support Group v. Moran, 232 F.Supp.2d 1133 (D. Mont. 2002). The election itself, however, was called and conducted by the Secretary, and the constitution or its amendment was not effective until approved by the Secretary. 25 U.S.C. § 476(a); see Thomas v. United States, 189 F.3d 662 (7th Cir.1999). The conditions for continued federal guidance were therefore abundantly present. As a consequence, virtually all of the new constitutions were reproductions, with insignificant variations, of a model produced in Washington with little attention to the needs of individual tribes.

The standard constitution contained provisions describing the tribal territories, specifying eligibility for membership, and establishing the governing bodies and their powers. It also contained provisions for amendment (subject, of course, to the approval of the Secretary of the Interior), and many of the tribes have since revised their constitutions to reflect individual tribal concerns and a desire to exercise more complete tribal autonomy. Nevertheless, the original structure persists in most cases, so that it is still possible to generalize about the components of tribal government with the caveat that individual tribal constitutions should be consulted to resolve specific problems.

B. THE TRIBAL COUNCIL

Most of the tribes vest the legislative authority in a tribal council, although it is not always called by that name. The council members are normally elected for a specified number of years. In some tribes they are elected by district, in others at large. The council is given general governmental powers over internal affairs of the tribe, with one important qualification. Virtually all ordinances or resolutions of the tribal council that have an operative effect are subject to review by the Secretary of the Interior. Some constitutions provide that the ordinances and resolutions are not effective until the Secretary approves; others provide that the Secretary may rescind ordinances of which he disapproves. Either way, the requirement represents a very substantial limitation upon the self-government of the tribes.

The present policy of the Secretary (through the Bureau of Indian Affairs) is to approve nearly all ordinances, but the existence of the veto power has its effect nonetheless. When the council is unsure of itself, or when the agency superintendent or area director is particularly assertive, the council may seek guidance from those federal officials before taking important action.

C. THE TRIBAL CHAIRMAN

Most of the tribal constitutions provide for a tribal chairman, sometimes called president or governor. In some of the tribes, the chairman is elected by a vote of the council; in others, he or she is directly elected by the voting tribal members. The chairman is commonly perceived as the leader and spokesperson for the tribe, but the duties and powers of the position are often not set forth in the constitution. Tribal by-laws typically recite that it is the chairman's duty to preside over the tribal council, and then confer varying degrees of executive authority. The role of the chairman consequently differs substantially from tribe to tribe, depending upon both the governmental structure of the tribe and the individual characteristics of the particular chairman.

D. TRIBAL COURTS

The tribal courts have a history long antedating the Indian Reorganization Act. Their forerunners were Courts of Indian Offenses, first established in the eighteen-eighties by the Secretary of the Interior to help "civilize" the Indians. Those courts administered a code promulgated by the Secretary and incorporated in volume 25 of the Code of Federal Regulations (C.F.R.). Courts of Indian Offenses continued in existence even after the passage of the Indian Reorganization Act, because the tribes lacked the resources to establish new courts on their own authority. Some still function today. During the past thirty years, however, most tribes have organized their own tribal courts that administer tribal codes passed by the council and approved by the Secretary of the Interior. The jurisdiction of these courts is discussed in Chapter VII, Section D(2) and F(2) infra. Tribal court systems vary from the highly structured, multiple court system of the Navajo Nation, served by tribal prosecutors and defense advocates, to very informal single-judge courts operated on a part-time basis without supplementary services. Some of the Pueblos utilize their traditional governing councils to adjudicate cases under the guidance of customary law. In recent years there has been an emphasis on re-establishing traditional methods of dispute-resolution, either by creating alternative courts such as the Navajo Peacemaker Court, or by providing alternative litigation tracks in existing tribal courts.

In many tribes, the tribal judges are popularly elected; in some others, they are appointed by the tribal council. They are usually, but not always, tribal members. Until the last decade, tribal judges rarely were lawyers, but recently the numbers of law-trained tribal judges has been increasing. Even if not lawyers, nearly all tribal judges undergo some form of training while in office. They commonly serve for a fixed term, although in at least one case (the Navajo) they enjoy indefinite appointments. The degree to which the judges are independent of the tribal council and its political forces varies widely, depending upon the method of judicial selection, the traditions of the council, and the character of the individual judge. In the strongest systems there is a high degree of independence, and the trend is unquestionably in that direction. Tribal judges, like other judges, are protected by absolute immunity from liability for their judicial actions. Penn v. United States, 335 F.3d 786 (8th Cir.2003).

Appellate court structures have only recently been developed by most of the tribes. In many tribes, panels of tribal judges are assembled *ad hoc* for each appeal. In others, judges from other tribes are used. Some tribal appellate courts employ outside lawyers or law professors as judges. In the Navajo system, there is a regularly sitting supreme court that issues written opinions.

E. THE TRIBAL ATTORNEY

While not a part of the formal tribal government, the tribal attorney is often a major influence on tribal affairs, particularly the tribe's dealings with third parties. The hiring of attorneys by the tribal council is generally authorized by tribal constitutions, but is made subject to approval of the Secretary of the Interior, as required by statute. 25 U.S.C.A. §§ 81–82a. This requirement became an obvious source of conflict of interest on the part of the federal government when tribes began to engage in litigation against federal authorities for breach of their trust responsibilities. The Department of Interior could, by design or inadvertence, forestall hostile litigation simply by failing to approve the tribal attorney's contract. Inaction by the

Department became such a severe problem for the tribes that Congress included in the Indian Civil Rights Act of 1968 a provision that failure of the Secretary to approve or disapprove an attorney's contract within ninety days resulted in automatic approval. 25 U.S.C.A. § 1331.

The client of the tribal attorney is the entire tribe, not its individual members. Of necessity the attorney's relationship is with the tribal council or the tribal chairman, and that fact creates a potential for the tribe's interest to be confused with its leaders' individual interests. The problem is diminished somewhat by the fact that most tribal attorneys concentrate their efforts on the tribe's external affairs—particularly its dealings with the federal government and with third parties involved in the development of tribal resources or in conflict over them. The more complicated these matters are, the more the tribal council and its chairman find it necessary to rely on the guidance of the attorney. Because the tribal attorneys are often not tribal members or even Indians, they must to some degree be considered an outside influence affecting tribal self-government.

In recent years, some of the larger tribes have organized offices of in-house counsel, under the direction of a tribal attorney-general or general counsel. This tendency has been accelerated by the increase in tribal gaming operations, with their attendant increase in tribal economic activity of various kinds. The development of in-house counsel does not necessarily end a tribe's resort to the employment of outside law firms, however, particularly for litigation or complex negotiations with non-tribal parties.

F. TRIBAL CORPORATIONS

Those tribes that incorporated under the provisions of the Indian Reorganization Act did so under charters that were also formulated in Washington and standardized to a greater degree even than the tribal constitutions. These charters, designed to permit the tribes to engage in economic activity in corporate form, created perpetual membership corporations encompassing all tribal members. Usual corporate powers were conferred, but many actions such as the pledging of tribal income or the entering of leases were made subject to approval of the Secretary of the Interior. The charters also provided for termination of the Secretary's supervisory powers upon a vote of the tribe, but again with the requirement that the Secretary approve such termination. The corporate power to "sue and be sued" has caused conflict in the courts over whether the tribes by those terms have waived their sovereign immunity. See Chapter V, Section C, infra.

G. TRIBES NOT ORGANIZED UNDER THE INDIAN REORGANIZATION ACT

The Indian Reorganization Act (I.R.A.) provided that tribes could vote not to be governed by its organizational provisions, and several tribes rejected application of the Act. The Navajos and many of the Pueblos are examples. As a consequence, these tribes do not necessarily follow the constitutional pattern described above, and it is unsafe to generalize about their characteristics. For example, the Navajo Nation has no written constitution although provisions are made for one in the Navajo–Hopi Rehabilitation Act of 1950, 25 U.S.C.A. § 631 et seq. Yet the Navajos operate under a detailed tribal code, and have an elected tribal council and chairman in much the same manner as the I.R.A. tribes. On the other hand, many of the Pueblos operate entirely under unwritten customary law, with traditional leaders and a governmental structure wholly different from the I.R.A. constitutional model.

CHAPTER V

INDIAN TRIBAL SOVEREIGNTY

A. ORIGINS AND DEVELOPMENT OF TRIBAL SOVEREIGNTY

Sovereignty is a word of many meanings, and it is used frequently and loosely in Indian affairs. At its most basic, the term refers to the inherent right or power to govern. At the time of the European discovery of America, the tribes were sovereign by nature and necessity; they conducted their own affairs and depended upon no outside source of power to legitimize their acts of government. By treating with the tribes as foreign nations and by leaving them to regulate their own internal affairs, the colonial powers and later the federal government recognized the sovereign status of the tribes. On the other hand, the Europeans clearly claimed dominion over all the territories of the new world, and those claims seemed to limit in some degree the sovereignty of the tribes living there. The legal status of the tribes as nations was therefore clouded by uncertainties, and it was left to the Supreme Court to attempt to resolve them.

In Johnson v. McIntosh, 21 U.S. (8 Wheat.) 543 (1823), Chief Justice Marshall held that Indian tribes had no power to grant lands to anyone other than the federal government. In describing the effects of European discovery on the tribes, Marshall said:

[T]he rights of the original inhabitants were, in no instance, entirely disregarded; but were, necessarily, to a considerable extent, impaired. They were admitted to be the rightful occupants of the soil * * * but their rights to complete sovereignty, as independent nations, were necessarily diminished, and their power to dispose of the soil, at their own will, to whomsoever they pleased, was denied by the original fundamental principle, that discovery gave exclusive title to those who made it.

21 U.S. (8 Wheat.) at 574. The principles of discovery were, of course, European (and, by adoption, federal) law which the Indian tribes might have thought quite irrelevant, but in Marshall's view that was the only kind of law that the Supreme Court could apply.

Having thus established a serious limitation on tribal sovereignty, Marshall ten years later emphasized the affirmative governmental power of the tribes. In Cherokee Nation v. Georgia, 30 U.S. (5 Pet.) 1 (1831), the Court held that the Cherokees could not be regarded as a "foreign state" within the meaning of Article III of the Constitution, so as to bring them within the federal judicial power and permit them to maintain their action in the Supreme Court. But in ruling the tribe not "foreign,"

Marshall was careful to acknowledge that it qualified as a "state":

> So much of the argument as was intended to
> prove the character of the Cherokees as a state,
> as a distinct political society separated from oth-
> ers, capable of managing its own affairs and gov-
> erning itself, has, in the opinion of a majority of
> the judges, been completely successful.

30 U.S. (5 Pet.) at 16. He then went on to characterize the tribes, in a famous phrase, as "domestic
dependent nations."

In Worcester v. Georgia, 31 U.S. (6 Pet.) 515, 559
(1832), Marshall had a further opportunity to dis-
cuss the status of the tribes.

> The Indian nations had always been considered
> as distinct, independent, political communities,
> retaining their original natural rights, as the un-
> disputed possessors of the soil, from time imme-
> morial, with the single exception of that imposed
> by irresistible power, which excluded them from
> intercourse with any other European potentate
> than the first discoverer of the coast of the partic-
> ular region claimed * * *.

The opinion then held that the laws of Georgia
could have no force in Cherokee territory.

Marshall, then, left a view of the tribes as nations
whose independence had been limited in only two
essentials—the conveyance of land and the ability
to deal with foreign powers. For all internal purposes, the tribes were sovereign and free from state

intrusion on that sovereignty. Although Marshall's position has been subject to considerable erosion in recent decades, it still provides the foundation for determining the governmental role of the tribes.

Because a tribe is sovereign, it is in a very different position from a city or other subdivision of a state. When a question arises as to the power of a city to enact a particular regulation, there must be some showing that the state has conferred such power on the city; the state, not the city, is the sovereign body from which power must flow. A tribe, on the other hand, is its own source of power. Thus a tribe's right to establish a court or levy a tax is not subject to attack on the ground that Congress has not authorized the tribe to take these actions; the tribe is sovereign and needs no authority from the federal government. Iron Crow v. Oglala Sioux Tribe, 231 F.2d 89 (8th Cir.1956); Merrion v. Jicarilla Apache Tribe, 455 U.S. 130, 149 (1982). The relevant inquiry is whether any limitation exists to *prevent* the tribe from acting within the sphere of its sovereignty, not whether any authority exists to *permit* the tribe to act. See National Farmers Union Ins. Cos. v. Crow Tribe, 471 U.S. 845, 852–53 (1985). To determine whether sovereignty has been limited, it may be necessary to examine relevant statutes, treaties, executive policies, and administrative or judicial decisions. Id. at 855–56.

Two additional consequences have followed from the fact that tribal powers are inherent and not derived from the federal government. The provisions of the Bill of Rights that restrict the federal government do not to apply to the tribes. Talton v. Mayes, 163 U.S. 376 (1896); see Chapter XI, infra. Nor does it violate the Fifth Amendment provision against double jeopardy for the tribe and the federal government to prosecute a defendant for the same offense; both independent sovereigns are entitled to vindicate their identical public policies. United States v. Wheeler, 435 U.S. 313 (1978).

The self-governing character of the tribes also has enabled Congress to delegate power to them that could not properly be delegated to a non-governmental private association. In United States v. Mazurie, 419 U.S. 544 (1975), the Supreme Court upheld a federal statute prohibiting the introduction of liquor into Indian country unless the tribe involved permitted it. The delegation was valid because the tribes already possessed some independent regulatory authority over the subject matter.

B. TRIBAL SOVEREIGNTY TODAY; ITS MEANING AND LIMITS

1. DOMESTIC DEPENDENT STATUS

John Marshall described only two disabilities arising from the domestic dependent status of the tribal sovereigns–tribes could not freely alienate their land and they could not treat with foreign powers. For nearly 150 years following the Cherokee cases, no additional limitations on tribal sovereignty were found to inhere in domestic dependent status. Then, in Oliphant v. Suquamish Indian Tribe, 435 U.S. 191 (1978), the Supreme Court announced another.

The Supreme Court held that the exercise of criminal jurisdiction over non-Indians was inconsistent with the domestic dependent status of the tribes. The Court also referred to 200 years of federal legislation that seemed to assume an absence of tribal criminal jurisdiction over non-Indians, but those statutes were not held to have removed such jurisdiction by their own operative effect. The Court based its decision squarely on the status of the tribes.

By opening the door to discovery of new inherent limitations on tribal sovereignty, *Oliphant* represented a significant potential threat to tribal governmental power. The threat was not long in being realized. Tribes were held, rather surprisingly, to have lost any preemptive power to regulate liquor sales on their reservations, as a consequence of domestic dependent status. Rice v. Rehner, 463 U.S. 713, 726 (1983). Two years earlier, in Montana v. United States, 450 U.S. 544 (1981), the Court held that, at least where there was no showing that tribal interests were affected, a tribe lacked inherent power to regulate hunting and fishing by non-Indians on non-Indian-owned land within its reservation. Ownership of land within a reservation had not previously been held relevant to determinations of jurisdiction. The Court recited that tribes retained inherent power to protect self-government and to control "internal relations," which the Court described quite narrowly as including "the power to punish tribal offenders, ... to determine tribal membership, to regulate domestic relations among members, and to prescribe rules of inheritance for members." 450 U.S. at 564. The Court then stated:

> But exercise of tribal power beyond what is necessary to protect tribal self-government or to control internal relations is inconsistent with the dependent status of the tribes, and so cannot survive without express congressional delegation.

450 U.S. at 564. The Court then added two qualifications to its ruling. Tribes retained inherent sovereign power, even on fee lands: (1) to regulate by taxation, licensing or other means, activities of nonmembers who enter consensual relationships with the tribe or its members, as by commercial dealings; and (2) to regulate conduct of non-Indians that threatens or directly affects "the political integrity, the economic security, or the health or welfare of the tribe." 450 U.S. at 565–66.

Although *Montana* announced an exception to the general rule that a tribe has governmental power over its territory unless some statute or treaty takes it away, subsequent Supreme Court opinions have tended to refer to the *"Montana* rule," not the *"Montana* exception." As a "rule" limiting inherent tribal sovereignty, it continues to gain strength; indeed, it appears to have become the foundation case for contemporary Indian law in the Supreme Court. Thus the plurality opinion in Brendale v. Confederated Tribes and Bands of the Yakima Indian Nation, 492 U.S. 408 (1989), applied the "general principle" of *Montana* to preclude a tribe from zoning fee lands within the reservation that were owned by nonmembers. Because of split votes of other Justices, the judgment in *Brendale* permitted the tribe to zone non-member fee lands in the "closed" portion of the reservation (where the general public was not freely admitted) but not in the "open" portion—a territorial distinction that had never before been made. Justice Blackmun in dissent argued that *Montana* should be recognized as a relatively narrow exception to the presumption of tribal governmental power. 492 U.S. at 450–51. His view, shared by many Indian law scholars and practitioners at the time *Montana* was decided, has not prevailed.

In Duro v. Reina, 495 U.S. 676 (1990), the Supreme Court held that the retained sovereignty of an Indian tribe did not include criminal jurisdiction over nonmember Indians on its reservation, despite a pattern of federal legislation that based criminal jurisdiction on defendants' status as Indians, rather than as tribal members. See, e.g., 18 U.S.C.A. §§ 1152, 1153. Congress promptly overruled the Court, defining tribal powers of self-government to include "the inherent power of Indian tribes, hereby recognized and affirmed, to exercise criminal jurisdiction over all Indians." 25 U.S.C.A. § 1301(2). This legislation raised the question whether Congress, by so acting, had *conferred* power on the tribes to punish nonmember Indians, or whether Congress had merely recognized inherent tribal power to assert such jurisdiction. The issue is of importance for double jeopardy purposes; if the tribes are exercising delegated federal power in asserting criminal jurisdiction over nonmember Indians, then it would violate the double jeopardy clause of the Constitution for the federal government also to prosecute for the same offense. If, as Congress seems clearly to have intended, the tribal power is inherent and merely recognized by the legislation, then each sovereign acts on its own and both can prosecute. One circuit held that the legislation recognized inherent tribal power (permitting dual prosecution), and that Congress had the power thus to contradict the Supreme Court's decision in *Duro*. United States v. Enas, 255 F.3d 662 (9th Cir.2001) (en banc). Another circuit held that Congress had no power to overturn the *Duro* ruling, and that a prosecution after Congress's corrective legislation accordingly was an exercise of newly delegated federal power (precluding dual prosecution). United States v. Lara, 324 F.3d 635 (8th Cir.2003). The Supreme Court has granted certiorari in *Lara*, ___ U.S. ___, 124 S.Ct. 46 (2003), and thus will have an opportunity to elaborate on the nature of inherent sovereignty of the tribes, as well as the power of Congress to recognize inherent sovereignty that the Court had negated in *Duro*.

In a somewhat related vein, the Seventh Circuit decided that, after Congress restored the "terminated" Menominee Tribe, the tribe's criminal prosecution of a member was an exercise of reinstated inherent power, not delegated congressional power, so that dual tribal and federal prosecution was permissible. United States v. Long, 324 F.3d 475

(7th Cir.2003), cert. denied, ___ U.S. ___, 124 S.Ct. 151 (2003).

Congress's prompt reaction against the decision in *Duro* did not slow the Supreme Court in finding additional limitations on tribal power arising from dependent domestic status as formulated in *Montana*. In Strate v. A–1 Contractors, 520 U.S. 438 (1997), the Court held that a tribal court lacked jurisdiction over a civil case between nonmembers arising out of a vehicle accident on a state highway traversing the reservation. The Court held that the grant of right-of-way to the state, which precluded the tribe from exercising proprietary rights of exclusion, rendered the highway the equivalent of non-Indian fee land. 520 U.S. at 454. The Court stated that *"Montana* thus described a general rule that, absent a different congressional direction, Indian tribes lack civil authority over the conduct of nonmembers on non-Indian land within a reservation." The tribe's interest in safe driving within the reservation was not sufficient to qualify for the second *Montana* exception (matters affecting the tribe's political integrity, economic security, health, or welfare) because such a construction "would severely shrink the [*Montana*] rule." 520 U.S. at 458. Because the tribe could not regulate nonmember activity on the highway, the tribal court could not entertain the action. "As to nonmembers, we hold, a tribe's adjudicative jurisdiction does not exceed its legislative jurisdiction." 520 U.S. at 453. One court of appeals has interpreted *Strate* to preclude tribal court jurisdiction over a civil suit by a *tribal mem-*

ber against a nonmember arising from an accident on a right-of-way within a reservation. Burlington Northern R. Co. v. Red Wolf, 196 F.3d 1059 (1999); Wilson v. Marchington, 127 F.3d 805 (9th Cir.1997).

In Atkinson Trading Co. v. Shirley, 532 U.S. 645 (2001), the Supreme Court held that a tribe, under the rule of *Montana*, lacked the power to tax non-Indian activities on non-Indian land within the reservation. The tax was a hotel occupancy tax imposed on hotel guests but collected by the resident hotel owner. The Court rejected arguments that hotel guests, who enjoyed the protection of tribal police, fire and emergency services, were in a consensual relationship with the tribe, to bring them within the first *Montana* exception. It also rejected claims that the hotel and associated trading post, which employed nearly 100 tribal members, threatened or directly affected "political integrity, the economic security, or the health or welfare of the tribe" so as to qualify for the second *Montana* exception. 532 U.S. at 657 (quoting *Montana*). The Court distinguished Merrion v. Jicarilla Apache Tribe, 455 U.S. 130 (1982), which had upheld a tribal severance tax on non-Indian lessees with language broadly suggesting an inherent power of the tribe to tax economic activity within its reservation. The Court in *Atkinson*, while acknowledging broad language in *Merrion*, emphasized that *Merrion* had permitted taxation of non-Indian activity on *trust land* within the reservation. The rule now was clear: "An Indian tribe's sovereign power to tax—

whatever its derivation—reaches no further than tribal land.'' 532 U.S. at 653.

Finally, in Nevada v. Hicks, 533 U.S. 353 (2001), the Court held that a tribal court had no jurisdiction over tort claims against state officers for allegedly excessive actions they took in executing a search warrant at the residence of a tribal member on trust land within a reservation. The prelude to the search was interesting. The officers were investigating an alleged off-reservation game violation. They secured two successive search warrants from a state court for the on-reservation search, but the state judge (reflecting a common understanding of tribal sovereignty) made the first search warrant contingent upon tribal court approval. The second search warrant did not contain a similar condition, but in both instances the officers obtained warrants from the tribal court for the searches. The searches found no evidence of crime, but in the second search the officers allegedly damaged some property. The Indian tribal member whose property had been searched and allegedly damaged brought a tort suit in tribal court for trespass, abuse of process, and violation of civil rights pursuant to 42 U.S.C. § 1983. The Supreme Court held that the tribe had no jurisdiction to regulate non-Indian officers for their conduct in conducting a search arising from an alleged off-reservation crime even though the search was of an Indian residence on trust land.

The ownership status of land, in other words, is only one factor to consider in determining whether regulation of the activities of nonmembers is "necessary to protect tribal self-government or to control internal relations." It may sometimes be a dispositive factor. * * * But the existence of tribal ownership is not alone enough to support regulatory jurisdiction over nonmembers.

533 U.S. at 360. The Court then invoked *Strate*'s rule that a tribe's adjudicatory jurisdiction could not exceed its legislative jurisdiction, and held that the tribal court had no jurisdiction over the officers. The Court further held that tribal courts were not courts of general jurisdiction in the sense that they could enforce the provisions of 42 U.S.C. § 1983, which provides a federal cause of action for violation of federal rights by persons acting under color of state law.

Hicks is a very expansive opinion in applying *Montana* to limit tribal sovereign power, and to extend state power, in Indian country. The decision gives no weight to the fact that the plaintiff was a tribal member. It appears to render futile and unnecessary the cooperative arrangements reflected in the state court's requirement in *Hicks* of a tribal warrant, or in tribal-state extradition agreements that have been worked out during the past fifty years. See, e.g., Arizona ex rel. Merrill v. Turtle, 413 F.2d 683 (9th Cir.1969). Since *Hicks*, authorities in some states have continued to honor such cooperative agreements and have not unilaterally asserted state power in Indian country to the degree permitted by *Hicks*. In at least one instance, however, state authorities executed a search warrant against an enterprise of the tribe itself. See Inyo

County, California v. Paiute–Shosone Indians of the Bishop Community, 538 U.S. 701 (2003). In that case, the Supreme Court held that the tribe could not sue in federal court as a "person" under 42 U.S.C. § 1983 to vindicate an intrusion on its sovereign interests; whether any other remedy existed under federal law was left for further consideration in the lower courts. Id.

Hicks is thus the culmination of a series of cases that has reversed the usual presumption regarding sovereignty when the tribe's power over nonmembers is concerned. Instead of presuming that tribal power exists, and searching to see whether statutes or treaties negate that presumption, the Court presumes that tribal power over nonmembers is absent unless one of the *Montana* exceptions applies or Congress has otherwise conferred the power. *Hicks*, 533 U.S. at 359–60; see also South Dakota v. Bourland, 508 U.S. 679, 695 n.15 (1993). *Hicks* also builds on *Strate*'s formulation that a tribe's adjudicative jurisdiction cannot exceed its legislative jurisdiction; indeed, *Hicks* leaves open the question whether the tribe's adjudicative jurisdiction may be *less* than its legislative jurisdiction. Even if the two types of jurisdiction are held to be equal, the limitation of adjudicatory jurisdiction is an anomaly and it is not clear where *Strate* discovered it. Most courts can entertain transitory causes of action, with no requirement that the parties be subject to regulatory or legislative power of the forum state. In any event, the Supreme Court appears to have cemented firmly its view that tribes, as domestic dependent nations, have no authority over non-members unless one of the two *Montana* exceptions applies, and no criminal authority over non-Indians at all.

A thematic question is presented by the Supreme Court's line of cases from United States v. Wheeler, 435 U.S. 313 (1978), through *Montana* to *Hicks*. Sovereign power, even when exercised by democratically elected officials, is typically both coercive and territorial. These Supreme Court decisions, however, emphasize two factors not previously considered to be of jurisdictional importance: tribal membership (as opposed to Indian status) and, to a decreasing degree, land ownership (as opposed to reservation status as Indian country). Each factor inclines toward a view of tribal power that is not necessarily sovereign and governmental. Private clubs may regulate the conduct of members, but that membership-based power is not governmental; the members may resign and the club has no ability to regulate nonmembers. Private landowners can establish rules of behavior for those who wish to remain on their lands, but that power, too, is not governmental. The question raised by the line of cases from *Wheeler* to *Montana* to *Hicks*, which stress membership and, to a lesser degree, rights of land ownership as sources of tribal power, is whether the Supreme Court is evolving, purposefully or not, toward a non-governmental view of tribal power and, if so, how far and fast that evolution will proceed.

On the other hand, a governmental view of tribal power is still dominant in relation to a tribe's control over its own members. *Wheeler*'s actual holding was that an exercise by a tribe of criminal jurisdiction over one of its members was the act of an independent sovereign. 435 U.S. at 327. At least with regard to internal tribal matters (a category that is increasingly being narrowed by the cases applying *Montana*), the governmental theory of tribal power that has its origins in the Cherokee Cases retains some of its vitality.

2.   PREEMPTION OF STATE LAW

Tribal sovereignty has operated to a considerable degree as a shield against intrusions of state law into Indian country. Chief Justice Marshall's view, as described above, was that state laws could simply "have no force" in Indian territory. Worcester v. Georgia, 31 U.S. (6 Pet.) 515, 561 (1832). That rule was modified some fifty years later, however, to permit state law to apply to a crime by a non-Indian against a non-Indian on an Indian reservation. United States v. McBratney, 104 U.S. 621 (1881); Draper v. United States, 164 U.S. 240 (1896). But the Supreme Court has almost always held the line against permitting state law to apply to Indians in Indian country. In Williams v. Lee, 358 U.S. 217 (1959), a unanimous Court ruled that state courts had no jurisdiction over a civil claim by a non-Indian against an Indian for a transaction arising on the Navajo reservation. The Court stated that state law had been permitted to intrude only where "essential tribal relations" were not involved, and that "absent governing Acts of Congress, the question has always been whether the state action infringed on the right of reservation Indians to make their own laws and be governed by them." To permit state court jurisdiction in this instance, said the Court, "would undermine the authority of the tribal courts over Reservation affairs and hence would infringe on the right of the Indians to govern themselves." 358 U.S. at 220, 223.

In McClanahan v. Arizona State Tax Comm'n, 411 U.S. 164 (1973), the Supreme Court made it clear that state law would be permitted to intrude into Indian country only if two conditions were met: (1) there was no interference with tribal self-government; and (2) non-Indians were involved. Thus the Court held that Arizona could not tax the income of an Indian earned on the reservation. In so holding, however, the Court articulated a new approach to the doctrine of tribal sovereignty.

> [T]he trend has been away from the idea of inherent Indian sovereignty as a bar to state jurisdiction and toward reliance on federal preemption. * * * The modern cases thus tend to avoid reliance on platonic notions of Indian sovereignty and to look instead to the applicable treaties and statutes which define the limits of state power. * * *

411 U.S. at 172 (footnote omitted). Reading the inexplicit treaty and statutes with the "tradition of

sovereignty in mind," the Court found that they precluded state taxation.

Even though *McClanahan* reached a result highly protective of tribal sovereignty, it launched a methodology that may often have the opposite effect. By reducing sovereignty to a backdrop and relying on the preemptive effect of federal law to exclude state power, *McClanahan*'s analysis appears to alter the presumption that the tribe has governmental power over all matters affecting the tribe on the reservation, and that the state does not. It seems instead to assume that the state has power unless federal law (including federal Indian policy) has preempted it.

Because Congress is rarely explicit in preempting state law, the preemption analysis following *McClanahan* often involves a weighing and balancing of the competing state and federal interests.

> State jurisdiction is preempted by the operation of federal law if it interferes with or is incompatible with federal and tribal interests reflected in federal law, unless the state interests at stake are sufficient to justify the assertion of state authority.

New Mexico v. Mescalero Apache Tribe, 462 U.S. 324, 334 (1983). Under the previous, more formalistic approach of Williams v. Lee, 358 U.S. 217, 220 (1959), state law simply could not be applied if it interfered with the right of Indians to make their own laws and be governed by them, no matter how important the state interest was. Under the preemption analysis, considered by itself, an extremely important state interest may interfere with and override tribal interests in self-government.

The rule of *Williams v. Lee* that state law may not interfere with tribal self-government remains in effect as an independent test to be applied along with preemption analysis, New Mexico v. Mescalero Apache Tribe, 462 U.S. 324, 334 n.16 (1983), but tribal self-government no longer seems to be generously defined to include everything that affects Indian interests. See Atkinson Trading Co. v. Shirley, 532 U.S. 645, 658–59 (2001). As a consequence, most cases involving the application of state law in Indian country are decided on preemption grounds.

In general, the Supreme Court in applying its preemption analysis has considered tribal self-determination to be a weighty federal interest. It has declined, however, to entertain a presumption that all on-reservation activities affecting the tribes are beyond the reach of state power as a necessary implication of the dormant Indian commerce clause, U.S. Const., Art. I, § 8, cl. 3. Ramah Navajo School Bd., Inc. v. Bureau of Revenue, 458 U.S. 832, 845–46 (1982).

Because preemption analysis is highly fact-specific and depends upon the interplay of the particular statutes, treaties, regulations and interests involved, it is less predictable than a more formalistic prescription for protecting Indian sovereignty. When preemption is employed, generalizations become more than usually suspect, and cases must be analyzed in light of their own facts. Yet, a few patterns have emerged. The states have been categorically precluded from directly taxing reservation lands or reservation Indians. See County of Yakima v. Confederated Tribes and Bands of the Yakima Indian Nation, 502 U.S. 251, 257 (1992); Oklahoma Tax Comm'n v. Chickasaw Nation, 515 U.S. 450 (1995). States also have been largely unsuccessful in taxing non-Indian contractors doing business with tribes on reservations. See, e.g., White Mountain Apache Tribe v. Bracker, 448 U.S. 136 (1980); Ramah Navajo School Bd., Inc. v. Bureau of Revenue, 458 U.S. 832 (1982). They have, however, succeeded in taxing cigarette sales to non-members of the tribes on reservations, and even in requiring the tribal seller to collect and remit the tax. Moe v. Confederated Salish and Kootenai Tribes of Flathead Reservation, 425 U.S. 463 (1976); Washington v. Confederated Tribes of the Colville Indian Reservation, 447 U.S. 134 (1980); Oklahoma Tax Comm'n v. Citizen Band of Potawatomi Indian Tribe, 498 U.S. 505 (1991). The state is not preempted even when the tribe imposes its own cigarette tax. Colville, supra. States have also succeeded in imposing severance taxes on non-Indian oil and gas producers in Indian country, despite a similar tribal tax. Cotton Petroleum Corp. v. New Mexico, 490 U.S. 163 (1989). For a fuller discussion of state taxation, see Chap. IX, Section C.

A state has been held not preempted from regulating liquor sales by a tribal member on reservation; indeed, in reasoning not since repeated, the tribe itself was held to be preempted by the exercise of federal regulation. Rice v. Rehner, 463 U.S. 713 (1983). States have been preempted, however, from regulating hunting and fishing by non-Indians on the reservation when the tribe regulated extensively, New Mexico v. Mescalero Apache Tribe, 462 U.S. 324 (1983), and from regulating high stakes bingo and poker games operated by tribes on reservations, California v. Cabazon Band of Mission Indians, 480 U.S. 202 (1987).

Protection of tribal sovereignty under the preemption analysis of *McClanahan* has therefore been substantial but not unwavering. There is one area in which the Supreme Court appears willing to protect tribal sovereignty from state intrusion without weighing the importance of the state interest. The state courts will not be allowed to exercise civil jurisdiction that interferes with tribal court jurisdiction involving tribal members on the reservation. *Williams v. Lee* governs. See Iowa Mut. Ins. Co. v. LaPlante, 480 U.S. 9, 15 (1987). Although Strate v. A–1 Contractors, 520 U.S. 438, 451–52 (1997), refused to apply a presumption of tribal jurisdiction to nonmember activities on fee land, it did not limit the applicability of *Williams v. Lee* in cases involving members and reservation activity.

The Supreme Court's recent decision in Nevada v. Hicks, 533 U.S. 353 (2001), expanded the reach of state law into Indian country by upholding the power of state officers to execute a search warrant at an Indian residence on Indian trust land within a reservation, when the officers were investigating an alleged off-reservation crime. The Court stated that

"State sovereignty does not end at a reservation's border." 533 U.S. at 361. Although that proposition has long been true with regard to conduct of non-Indians not affecting tribal interests, it ordinarily had not been applied in a situation where state enforcement mechanisms were applied to an Indian in Indian country. *Hicks* does not, however, establish any general power of states to regulate Indians in Indian country; it was essential to the Court's holding that state officers were investigating an off-reservation crime, which fell within the state's jurisdiction.

3. PLENARY POWER OF CONGRESS

Although there may be argument over the extent to which the courts may properly limit tribal sovereignty, there has never been any doubt that Congress is legally free to do so. Talton v. Mayes, 163 U.S. 376, 384 (1896); Santa Clara Pueblo v. Martinez, 436 U.S. 49, 56 (1978). Congress' power over Indian affairs is plenary. It has been deemed to arise from the Indian Commerce Clause or even from the fact of conquest. See United States v. Long, 324 F.3d 475, 479 (7th Cir.2003), cert. denied, ___ U.S. ___, 124 S.Ct. 151 (2003). Plenary power, of course, is subject to constitutional restraint when, for example, Congress deals with recognized Indian property interests, see Babbitt v. Youpee, 519 U.S. 234 (1997). As yet, however, no court has found a constitutionally protectible interest in tribal sovereignty itself, and numerous examples exist of federal statutes limiting it. The Major Crimes Act, 18 U.S.C.A § 1153, is an example of federal intrusion on the tribe's traditional power to punish its own members for crime. See United States v. Kagama, 118 U.S. 375 (1886); Ex parte Crow Dog, 109 U.S. 556 (1883). Public Law 280, 67 Stat. 588, which extended state civil and criminal jurisdiction over certain tribes, and the Civil Rights Act of 1968, 25 U.S.C.A. § 1301 et seq., which imposed most of the restraints of the Bill of Rights on the tribes, were both examples of federal legislation interfering substantially with tribal self-government. Finally, federal statutes terminating the special relationship between the federal government and the tribes have the effect of subjecting virtually all tribal affairs to state jurisdiction and causing the ultimate erosion of tribal government. See Chapter III, Section E, supra.

Although the doctrine of plenary power of Congress over tribal sovereignty has its critics, see Red Lake Band of Chippewa Indians v. Swimmer, 740 F.Supp. 9, 11–12 (D.D.C. 1990), it remains in full strength in the courts, so long as Congress makes its intent to limit sovereignty clear. See, e.g., Fletcher v. United States, 116 F.3d 1315, 1328 (10th Cir.1997). One court has found the Fair Labor Standards Act sufficiently unclear that it would not be applied to tribal off-reservation fish and wildlife police, thus "making federal law bear as lightly on Indian tribal prerogatives as the leeways of statutory interpretation allow." Reich v. Great Lakes Indian Fish & Wildlife Comm'n, 4 F.3d 490, 496 (7th

Cir.1993). Such an approach to statutory interpretation does not, however, negate congressional power. Thus it may be said with accuracy that, however useful tribal sovereignty is as a source of inherent tribal power and as a shield against state intrusion, such sovereignty exists entirely at the sufferance of Congress. Political restraints may, of course, keep Congress from eliminating or greatly diminishing tribal sovereignty, but legal restraints do not.

C. SOVEREIGN IMMUNITY OF THE TRIBES

The principle that tribes enjoy the sovereign's common law immunity from suit is well established, even though the Supreme Court has observed that "it developed almost by accident." Kiowa Tribe of Oklahoma v. Manufacturing Technologies, Inc., 523 U.S. 751, 756 (1998). The immunity applies to activities of the tribe whether on or off the reservation, and whether the activity is deemed governmental or commercial. Id. The immunity extends to agencies of the tribes. Hagen v. Sisseton–Wahpeton Community College, 205 F.3d 1040 (8th Cir.2000). It extends to intertribal councils. Taylor v. Alabama Intertribal Council, 261 F.3d 1032 (11th Cir.2001). It applies in both state and federal court. See Pan American Co. v. Sycuan Band of Mission Indians, 884 F.2d 416 (9th Cir.1989). Tribal immunity extends to claims for declaratory and injunctive relief, not merely damages, and it is not defeated by a claim that the tribe acted beyond its power. Imperial Granite Co. v. Pala Band of Mission Indians, 940 F.2d 1269 (9th Cir.1991). Sovereign immunity also has been held to protect a tribe against enforcement of a federal court subpoena. United States v. James, 980 F.2d 1314, 1319–20 (9th Cir.1992); Catskill Development, L.L.C. v. Park Place Entertainment Corp., 206 F.R.D. 78, 88 (D.D.N.Y. 2002); contra United States v. Velarde, 40 F.Supp.2d 1314 (D.N.M. 1999). It is unclear to what degree immunity protects a tribe from execution of a state search warrant on a tribal enterprise, where the warrant arose from an investigation of off-reservation crime. The Supreme Court held that a tribe could not sue under 42 U.S.C. § 1983 to remedy violation of its sovereign immunity in such a case, but left it to further proceedings in the lower courts to determine whether the tribe had some other remedy under federal law. Inyo County, California v. Paiute–Shoshone Indians of the Bishop Community, 538 U.S. 701 (2003).

Inclusion of a group of Indians on the Federal Register list of recognized tribes (see Chapter I, Section B) is ordinarily sufficient to establish entitlement to immunity, unless the suit in issue concerns the validity of that listing. Cherokee Nation of Oklahoma v. Babbitt, 117 F.3d 1489, 1499 (D.C.Cir. 1997). Even an unrecognized tribe may qualify for immunity if it meets common-law requirements of tribal existence. Koke v. Little Shell Tribe of Chippewa Indians, 315 Mont. 510, 68 P.3d 814 (2003).

Tribal sovereign immunity is a controversial subject, partly because tribal immunity retains its full vitality in an era when other governments are limiting their general immunity. The Supreme Court has noted that the immunity can operate harshly and might need revision, but it has left any change in the doctrine to Congress. *Kiowa*, 523 U.S. at 758–60. Although Congress has occasionally waived tribal immunity for specific purposes, it has made no changes in the overall doctrine. Thus, states that have abandoned their own immunity from tort liability must nevertheless honor the immunity of the tribes. See Morgan v. Colorado River Indian Tribe, 103 Ariz. 425, 443 P.2d 421 (1968).

To mitigate partially the harsh effects of immunity, the Tenth Circuit created an exception permitting suit when tribal remedies are unavailable. Dry Creek Lodge, Inc. v. Arapahoe & Shoshone Tribes, 623 F.2d 682, 685 (10th Cir.1980). The exception was later narrowed to require that the plaintiff be a non-Indian and that the dispute not concern internal tribal issues. See Ute Distribution Corp. v. Ute Indian Tribe, 149 F.3d 1260, 1266 n.8 (10th Cir. 1998). Other circuits have not adopted this "*Dry Creek* exception," see, e.g., R.J. Williams Co. v. Fort Belknap Hous. Auth., 719 F.2d 979, 981 (9th Cir. 1983), and it is extremely doubtful that the exception can be squared with the Supreme Court decisions in Santa Clara Pueblo v. Martinez, 436 U.S. 49, 59 (1978), or *Kiowa*, supra.

Tribes are not immune from suits by the United States. EEOC v. Karuk Tribe Housing Auth., 260 F.3d 1071, 1075 (9th Cir.2001). The United States remains immune, however, from suit in tribal court.

United States v. Yakima Tribal Court, 806 F.2d 853 (9th Cir.1986). States are similarly immune. Montana v. Gilham, 133 F.3d 1133 (9th Cir.1998) (amended opinion).

The fact that a state can tax a tribal activity does not mean that tribal immunity from suit is lost. The Supreme Court in Oklahoma Tax Comm'n v. Citizen Band Potawatomi Indian Tribe, 498 U.S. 505 (1991), rejected a state argument that it should be able to sue a tribe to collect taxes that the state was allowed to impose. The discussion in *Potawatomi* causes some confusion, however, because it does not always differentiate between sovereign immunity of tribes from suit and immunity of tribes and Indians from state taxation in Indian country, which is a matter of preemption.

The fact that a tribe cannot be sued does not defeat all challenges to the exercise of its power. The Supreme Court has held that a tribal officer is not protected by the tribe's immunity from suit for declarative and injunctive relief. Santa Clara Pueblo v. Martinez, 436 U.S. at 59. If the official acts beyond his or her authority, or beyond the authority that the tribe had the power legally to confer, the official may be sued. See Dawavendewa v. Salt River Project, 276 F.3d 1150, 1159–61 (9th Cir.), cert. denied, 537 U.S. 820 (2002); Baker Elec. Co-op, Inc. v. Chaske, 28 F.3d 1466, 1471–72 (8th Cir.1994). Thus a party claiming that a tribe had no power under federal law to impose a tax can sue tribal officials to enjoin enforcement, just as state taxpayers can sue state officials under Ex Parte Young,

209 U.S. 123 (1908). Big Horn County Elec. Coop., Inc. v. Adams, 219 F.3d 944, 954 (9th Cir.2000).

On the other hand, if tribal officials act within the scope of their lawful authority and relief would run against the tribe itself, they share the tribe's immunity from suit; the suit is one against the officials in their official capacity. E.g., Fletcher v. United States, 116 F.3d 1315, 1324 (10th Cir.1997); Linneen v. Gila River Indian Community, 276 F.3d 489, 492 (9th Cir.), cert. denied, 536 U.S. 939 (2002). A plaintiff cannot escape this rule by denominating the suit as one against officers in their individual capacities when relief would amount to specific performance against the tribe. Tamiami Partners v. Miccosukee Tribe of Indians, 177 F.3d 1212, 1225–26 (11th Cir.1999). One circuit, however, has adopted a rule that tribal officials are not immune from suits for declaratory or injunctive relief even if they act within their lawful authority. Comstock v. Alabama and Coushatta Indian Tribes, 261 F.3d 567, 570 (5th Cir.2001); see TTEA v. Ysleta Del Sur Pueblo, 181 F.3d 676, 680–81 (5th Cir.1999). Wholly apart from questions of sovereign immunity, tribal officers may also be immune from liability for damages by reason of their status as judges, or as officers acting in good faith. See Penn v. United States, 335 F.3d 786 (8th Cir.2003); Kennerly v. United States, 721 F.2d 1252, 1259–60 (9th Cir.1983).

It is clear that Congress can waive a tribe's immunity from suit, but that waiver must be clearly expressed. The Supreme Court refused to find a congressional waiver in the Civil Rights Act of 1968, which imposed some of the restrictions of the Bill of Rights upon the tribes. Santa Clara Pueblo v. Martinez, 436 U.S. 49, 58–59 (1978). But when a federal statute, such as the Hazardous Materials Transportation Act, clearly indicates that its enforcement mechanism applies to Indian tribes, tribal sovereign immunity cannot bar enforcement of the statute by a private party. Northern States Power Co. v. Prairie Island Mdewakanton Sioux Indian Community, 991 F.2d 458 (8th Cir.1993). Thus tribes may be sued in federal court under the "citizen suit" provisions of the Resource Conservation and Recovery Act (RCRA). Blue Legs v. U.S. Bureau of Indian Affairs, 867 F.2d 1094 (8th Cir.1989). The Safe Drinking Water Act similarly authorizes suits against persons, expressly incorporating tribes. See Osage Tribal Council v. U.S. Dept. of Labor, 187 F.3d 1174, 1181 (10th Cir.1999). On the other hand, the Americans with Disabilities Act has been held not to waive tribal immunity from suit, even though it is applicable to tribes, because it contains no terms indicating an intent to permit suits against tribes. Florida Paraplegic, Ass'n v. Miccosukee Tribe of Florida, 166 F.3d 1126 (11th Cir.1999); see also Bassett v. Mashantucket Pequot Tribe, 204 F.3d 343, 357–58 (2d Cir.2000) (Copyright Act). Federal officials acting without congressional authorization are not capable of waiving tribal immunity. United States v. United States Fidelity & Guar. Co., 309 U.S. 506, 513 (1940).

There is no longer any doubt that a tribe can waive its own immunity. One method is by contract. See Nenana Fuel Co. v. Native Village of Venetie, 834 P.2d 1229 (Alaska 1992). Although the intention to waive must be clear, the waiver need not include the precise term "sovereign immunity." Sokaogon Gaming Enterprise Corp. v. Tushie–Montgomery Assoc., 86 F.3d 656, 660 (7th Cir. 1996). The Supreme Court has held that a tribe waives its immunity by entering a form construction contract with a clause requiring arbitration of any disputes and agreeing that arbitration awards may be enforced "in any court having jurisdiction thereof." C & L Enterprises, Inc. v. Citizen Band of Potawatomi Indian Tribe of Oklahoma, 532 U.S. 411 (2001). A waiver of immunity arising from an arbitration agreement is limited to arbitration and its enforcement, however; it does not extend to all kinds of litigation that might arise from the subject matter of the contract. See Tamiami Partners, Ltd. v. Miccosukee Tribe of Indians, 63 F.3d 1030, 1048–49 (11th Cir.1995). The question of tribal immunity was held appropriate for tribal court exhaustion in Sharber v. Spirit Mountain Gaming Inc., 343 F.3d 974 (9th Cir.2003).

Many of the tribes have formed tribal corporations under a provision of the Indian Reorganization Act of 1934, 25 U.S.C.A. § 477, which authorized the Secretary of Interior to issue to the tribes corporate charters conferring certain stated powers and "such further powers as may be incidental to the conduct of corporate business." Incorporation by itself does not waive immunity. American Vantage Cos. v. Table Mountain Rancheria, 292 F.3d 1091, 1099 (9th Cir.2002). Many of the charters issued pursuant to the Act conferred the power to "sue and be sued." Some courts have construed the term to constitute a waiver of tribal immunity. See, e.g., Rosebud Sioux Tribe v. A & P. Steel, Inc., 874 F.2d 550 (8th Cir.1989); Fontenelle v. Omaha Tribe, 430 F.2d 143 (8th Cir.1970); Martinez v. Southern Ute Tribe, 150 Colo. 504, 374 P.2d 691 (1962). A majority of courts, however, has held that a mere "sue and be sued" clause does not constitute a waiver. See, e.g., Garcia v. Akwesasne Housing Authority, 268 F.3d 76, 86–87 (2d Cir.2001); Ninigret Development Corp. v. Narragansett Indian Wetuomuck Housing Auth., 207 F.3d 21, 29–30 & n.5 (1st Cir.2000); Dillon v. Yankton Sioux Tribe Housing Auth., 144 F.3d 581 (8th Cir.1998). Similarly, incorporation of a tribal sub-entity under state laws enabling corporations to sue and be sued does not waive immunity. Ransom v. St. Regis Mohawk Educ. & Community Fund, Inc., 86 N.Y.2d 553, 562–64, 635 N.Y.S.2d 116, 121–22, 658 N.E.2d 989, 994–95 (1995). If a tribally-chartered corporation operates independently of the tribal government and does not engage in governmental functions, however, it may not qualify for immunity in the first place because it is not an arm of the tribe. See Dixon v. Picopa Constr. Co., 160 Ariz. 251, 772 P.2d 1104 (1989).

A tribe may also waive its immunity by its conduct, particularly in litigation. By bringing an action, a tribe consents to a full adjudication of the claim it sues upon, United States v. Oregon, 657 F.2d 1009 (9th Cir.1981), and to claims of recoupment or set-off that arise from the transaction sued upon and do not exceed the tribe's claim. Rosebud Sioux Tribe v. A & P Steel, Inc., 874 F.2d 550 (8th Cir.1989); Jicarilla Apache Tribe v. Andrus, 687 F.2d 1324 (10th Cir.1982). A tribe that brings a quiet title action and invites adverse claims waives its immunity to those claims. Rupp v. Omaha Indian Tribe, 45 F.3d 1241 (8th Cir.1995). A tribe, however, does not waive its immunity from counterclaims, even compulsory ones, by bringing an action. Oklahoma Tax Comm'n v. Citizen Band Potawatomi Indian Tribe, 498 U.S. 505, 509 (1991). It also does not waive immunity for other related but collateral claims. Pit River Home and Agr. Co-op. Ass'n v. United States, 30 F.3d 1088, 1100–01 (9th Cir.1994). McClendon v. United States, 885 F.2d 627 (9th Cir.1989). A tribe that becomes a party to federal administrative proceedings does not thereby waive its immunity from suit brought by another party seeking review of the agency decision. Quileute Indian Tribe v. Babbitt, 18 F.3d 1456 (9th Cir.1994); Kescoli v. Babbitt, 101 F.3d 1304 (9th Cir.1996). A tribe does not waive immunity under the Rehabilitation Act merely by accepting funds and agreeing not to discriminate on account of disability. Sanderlin v. Seminole Tribe of Florida, 243 F.3d 1282, 1286–89 (11th Cir.2001).

Most of the lower courts to consider the question have held that a tribe, by conducting gaming under the Indian Gaming Regulatory Act, waives sovereign immunity for the limited purpose of enforcing compliance with the Act. See, e.g., Montgomery v. Flandreau Santee Sioux Tribe, 905 F.Supp. 740 (D.S.D. 1995); Maxam v. Lower Sioux Indian Community of Minnesota, 829 F.Supp. 277 (D. Minn. 1993); but see Davids v. Coyhis, 869 F.Supp. 1401 (E.D. Wis. 1994). The Supreme Court has stated in dictum that immunity is waived by the section of the Act that gives federal courts jurisdiction over state suits to enjoin gaming in violation of a gaming compact, 25 U.S.C.A. § 2710(d)(7)(A)(ii). See *Kiowa*, 523 U.S. at 758. The Tenth Circuit has so held. Mescalero Apache Tribe v. New Mexico, 131 F.3d 1379, 1385 (10th Cir.1997).

CHAPTER VI

INDIAN TREATIES

A. TREATY RIGHTS, PAST AND PRESENT

When Europeans first established colonies in America, they had little choice but to deal with the Indian tribes as the independent nations that they were. Terms of peace and exchanges of land were accordingly accomplished by treaty between the colonial governments and the tribes. After the Revolution, the federal government continued to deal with the tribes by treaty, although it also regulated various aspects of Indian affairs by statute.

From the first treaty with the Delawares in 1787 until the end of treaty-making in 1871, hundreds of agreements were entered between the federal government and various bands and tribes of Indians. Provisions of the treaties differed widely, but it was common to include a guarantee of peace, a delineation of boundaries (often with a cession of specific lands from the tribe to the federal government), a guarantee of Indian hunting and fishing rights (often applying to the ceded land), a statement that the tribe recognized the authority or placed itself under the protection of the United States, and an agreement regarding the regulation of trade and travel of persons in the Indian territory. Treaties also commonly included agreements by each side to punish and compensate for acts of depredation by "bad men" among their own number, a clause that still can support a claim against the United States. See Tsosie v. United States, 825 F.2d 393 (Fed.Cir. 1987).

In the early years of the Republic, the tribes negotiated from positions of some strength, but as time went on the bargaining positions changed drastically and the federal government became able to dictate terms. Even when the tribes possessed some bargaining power, the treaty-making process put them at a disadvantage. Treaties were written in English, and their terms were often explained inexactly to the Indian signatories. The very concepts of land ownership and governmental relations embodied in the treaties were often wholly foreign to the tribal cultures. Moreover, the federal government frequently negotiated with individuals whom it had selected and who were not the traditional leaders of the concerned tribes. All of these factors contributed to overreaching on the part of the federal government.

Nevertheless, important rights were guaranteed to the tribes by treaty, and many of these rights continue to be enforceable. Such enforcement is not subject to the defense of laches. United States v. Washington, 157 F.3d 630, 649 (9th Cir.1998). Rights secured to the tribes by treaty today include beneficial ownership of Indian lands, hunting and fishing rights, and entitlement to certain federal services such as education or health care. This is not to say that all such present rights are secured by treaty; many of them are the product of statute or executive agreement. A substantial number, however, still arise from treaties.

A tribe need not be federally recognized to establish that it is the beneficiary of a treaty. United States v. Suquamish Tribe, 901 F.2d 772 (9th Cir. 1990); Greene v. Babbitt, 64 F.3d 1266, 1270 (9th Cir.1995). It is enough that a group establish that it has preserved an organized tribal structure that it can trace back to the treaty. United States v. Oregon, 29 F.3d 481, amended 43 F.3d 1284 (9th Cir. 1994).

Indian treaties stand on essentially the same footing as treaties with foreign nations. Because they are made pursuant to the Constitution, they take precedence over any conflicting state laws by reason of the Supremacy Clause. U.S.Const., Art. VI, § 2; Worcester v. Georgia, 31 U.S. (6 Pet.) 515 (1832). They are also the exclusive prerogative of the federal government. The First Trade and Intercourse Act, 1 Stat. 137 (1790), forbade the transfer of Indian lands to individuals or states except by treaty "under the authority of the United States." This provision, repeated in later Trade and Intercourse Acts, has become of tremendous importance in recent years because several eastern states negotiated large land cessions from Indian tribes near the end of the eighteenth century. In County of Oneida v. Oneida Indian Nation, 470 U.S. 226 (1985), the Court held invalid a treaty entered in 1795 between the Oneidas and the State of New York. The treaty, which had been concluded without the participation of the federal government, transferred 100,000 acres of Indian lands to the state. The Court held that the tribe still had a viable claim for damages. Similar claims exist in other eastern states; in Maine, the likely invalidity of a 1795 state-tribal treaty clouded land titles covering about sixty percent of the state until legislation settled the issue. See Joint Tribal Council of Passamaquoddy Tribe v. Morton, 528 F.2d 370 (1st Cir.1975); Maine Indian Claims Settlement Act, P.L. 96–420, 94 Stat. 1785 (1980).

Not only is the treaty-making power exclusively federal, it is almost entirely presidential. Although two-thirds of the Senate must concur in any treaty, the initiation of the process and the terms of negotiation are inevitably controlled by the executive branch. (Indeed, there were many instances, especially in California, where executive officials negotiated treaties and acted upon them, despite the failure of the Senate to ratify them, which rendered them legal nullities. See Karuk Tribe v. Ammon, 209 F.3d 1366, 1371 (Fed.Cir.2000)). In the middle of the eighteenth century, Congress and particularly the House of Representatives grew increasingly resentful of being excluded from the direction of Indian affairs. The result was the passage in 1871 of a rider to an Indian appropriations act providing that "No Indian nation or tribe * * * shall be acknowledged or recognized as an independent nation, tribe, or power with whom the United States may contract by treaty * * *." 25 U.S.C.A. § 71. The rider also specified that existing treaty obligations were not impaired. As an attempt to limit by statute the President's constitutional treaty-making power, the rider may well be invalid, but it accomplished its purpose nonetheless by making it clear that no further treaties would be ratified. Indian treaty-making consequently ended in 1871, and formal agreements made with the tribes thereafter were either approved by both houses of Congress or were simply embodied in statutes.

B. CONSTRUCTION OF TREATIES

To compensate for the disadvantage at which the treaty-making process placed the tribes, and to help carry out the federal trust responsibility, the Supreme Court has fashioned rules of construction sympathetic to Indian interests. Treaties are to be construed as they were understood by the tribal representatives who participated in their negotiation. Tulee v. Washington, 315 U.S. 681, 684–85 (1942). They are to be liberally interpreted to accomplish their protective purposes, with ambiguities to be resolved in favor of the Indians. Carpenter v. Shaw, 280 U.S. 363 (1930). Courts "look beyond the written words to the larger context that frames the Treaty, including 'the history of the treaty, the negotiations, and the practical construction adopted by the parties.'" Minnesota v. Mille Lacs Band of Chippewa Indians, 526 U.S. 172, 196 (1999) (quoting Choctaw Nation v. United States, 318 U.S. 423, 432 (1943)).

One of the most important applications of the rules of sympathetic construction is found in Winters v. United States, 207 U.S. 564 (1908), which dealt not with a treaty but with an Indian agreement made in 1888 and ratified by an act of Congress. The tribes involved in that agreement had ceded to the United States a large tract of land to be opened up for settlement, while reserving to themselves other lands, bordered by a flowing stream, which became the Fort Belknap Reservation in Montana. Non–Indian settlers diverted the stream, and the United States brought suit on behalf of the Indians. The settlers argued that lands would not have been ceded for settlement without also ceding the water that would permit them to become fruitful. The United States argued that lands would not have been reserved for the tribes unless water also had been reserved to make the reservation productive. Faced with these plausible contradictory interpretations, the Court chose to construe the agreement from the standpoint of the Indians and to resolve the conflict in their favor. The resulting decision has become the foundation of all Indian water law. See Chapter XIV, Section B, infra.

Interpretation of treaties as the Indians understood them has also preserved extremely important fishing rights. Treaties in the Pacific Northwest that guaranteed Indians the right of "taking fish" at customary stations off-reservation "in common with all citizens of the Territory" were held to guarantee up to half of the harvestable fish; they did not merely guarantee the same rights as those enjoyed by non-Indians. See, e.g., Washington v. Washington State Commercial Passenger Fishing Vessel Ass'n, 443 U.S. 658 (1979). For further discussion of this issue, see Chap. XV, Section C.

In a recent example of sympathetic interpretation, a tribe was held still to enjoy rights to hunt, fish and gather on ceded land under an 1837 treaty that guaranteed such rights "during the pleasure of the President of the United States." Minnesota v. Mille Lacs Band of Chippewa Indians, 526 U.S. 172 (1999). The 1837 treaty rights were held to have survived, among other challenges, a treaty of 1855 that relinquished all "right, title, and interest, of whatsoever nature the same may be" in the ceded lands; the relinquishment did not mention hunting and fishing rights and any ambiguity had to be resolved in favor of the Indians. The treaty right was also held to survive the admission of Minnesota as a state.

If the language of a treaty is clear, however, it will be applied whether or not the outcome is favorable to the Indians. Oregon Dept. of Fish and Wildlife v. Klamath Indian Tribe, 473 U.S. 753, 774 (1985). Thus an income tax exemption will not result from a treaty when there is no language that could reasonably be construed to confer it. Lazore v. C.I.R., 11 F.3d 1180, 1185 (3d Cir.1993). Some courts refuse to find a treaty exception to any federal statute of general application unless the treaty specifically sets it forth. See United States v. Gallaher, 275 F.3d 784, 788–89 (9th Cir.2001). A treaty right to hunt on ceded lands "so long as game may be found thereon" was held to be a transitory right that did not survive the later incorporation of the lands into the State of Wyoming, Crow Tribe of Indians v. Repsis, 73 F.3d 982 (10th Cir.1995), but this ruling is almost certainly not the law after *Mille Lacs Band*, supra. Conditional treaty rights to hunt, fish and gather on ceded land "until it be surveyed and offered for sale by the President" were held to be extinguished when the land was offered for sale, even if not sold. Menominee Indian Tribe v. Thompson, 161 F.3d 449, 459 (7th Cir. 1998). A right to a hunting ground "until the President of the United States, shall deem it expedient to extinguish their title" was extinguished when the tribe later ceded the land. Id. at 460. Similarly, in Montana v. United States, 450 U.S. 544 (1981), the Supreme Court held that a treaty setting aside lands for the Crow Tribe did not convey title to the bed of a river within those lands. The Court relied on the presumption that the United States holds title to navigable waterways in trust for the states, which receive the title upon their admission to the Union on an "equal footing" with other states. In Idaho v. United States, 533 U.S. 262 (2001), however, the Supreme Court held that lake and stream beds, clearly included in an executive order reservation and essential to its purposes, remained in tribal ownership and did not pass to Idaho upon statehood. The Court relied in part on Congress's knowledge of agreements with the tribe that assumed or recited tribal ownership of lake and stream bed, even though those agreements had not been ratified. Subsequent lower court decisions have also applied sympathetic construction and held that the bed of navigable waters is conveyed to a grantee tribe if the tribe was known to be dependent upon fishing at the time of the treaty. E.g., Puyallup Indian Tribe v. Port of Tacoma, 717 F.2d 1251, 1258 (9th Cir.1983); Confederated Salish & Kootenai Tribes v. Namen, 665 F.2d 951 (9th Cir.1982).

The rule that treaties must be construed in a manner to effectuate their purpose sometimes leads to nice questions concerning the scope of that purpose. In Grand Traverse Band of Ottawa and Chippewa Indians v. Director, Mich. Dept. of Nat. Resources, 141 F.3d 635 (6th Cir.1998), the court held that a treaty right to fish commercially in an area of the Great Lakes included a right to transient mooring of fishing vessels at municipal marinas because without such mooring the Indians could not fish commercially. On the other hand, a treaty right to fish was held not to excuse treaty Indians from the prohibition against motor boats in the Boundary Waters Canoe Area Wilderness; the protected act of fishing was differentiated from the process of transportation to the fishing location. United States v. Gotchnik, 222 F.3d 506 (8th Cir.2000).

The rule of sympathetic construction has been carried over from treaties to statutes dealing with Indian matters, as well as to executive orders establishing reservations. See Confederated Tribes of the Chehalis Indian Reservation v. Washington, 96 F.3d 334, 342 (9th Cir.1996). Thus an unrecognized tribe may assert a right to hunt arising from establishment of a reservation by executive order and statute. Timpanogos Tribe v. Conway, 286 F.3d 1195 (10th Cir.2002). The Supreme Court on numerous occasions has adhered to "the general rule that statutes passed for the benefit of the dependent Indian tribes or communities are to be liberally construed, doubtful expressions being resolved in favor of the Indians." Alaska Pacific Fisheries Co. v. United States, 248 U.S. 78, 89 (1918). Indeed, the Court resolved ambiguity in favor of the tribes in construing Public Law 280, a statute that deals with Indians but was not necessarily passed for their benefit. Bryan v. Itasca County, 426 U.S. 373, 392–93 (1976). On the other hand, the Supreme Court rejected a "sympathetic" construction of a statute giving Kansas jurisdiction over major crimes by Indians, partly because it doubted that the statute was passed for the benefit of the Indians. Negonsott v. Samuels, 507 U.S. 99, 110 (1993). The fact that legislation may benefit Indians more than others does not necessarily make the statute one enacted for their benefit. Hoonah Indian Ass'n v. Morrison, 170 F.3d 1223, 1228–29 (9th Cir.1999). Even when all the requisites for invocation of the rule of sympathetic construction appear to be present, the rule simply has been ignored on occasion. See Mountain States Tel. & Tel. Co. v. Pueblo of Santa Ana, 472 U.S. 237 (1985). Of course, when the statute is perfectly clear, the rule simply does not apply and the statute will be enforced according to its terms. Shoshone–Bannock Tribes v. Department of Health and Human Services, 279 F.3d 660 (9th Cir.2002) (amended opinion).

Although the rule of sympathetic construction arose out of a desire to protect the tribes from overreaching by more powerful interests, it continues to apply when a tribe has become wealthy and powerful. See Connecticut v. U.S. Dept. of the Interior, 228 F.3d 82, 92–93 (2d Cir.2000). One circuit court has opined, however, that the rule may operate with less force in construing a statute when the affected tribes were well represented before the Congress that enacted it. United States v. Atlantic Richfield Co., 612 F.2d 1132, 1137 (9th Cir.1980).

The Supreme Court has recently expressed doubt that the canon of sympathetic construction carries as much force when a court is interpreting a statute rather than a treaty. In Chickasaw Nation v. United States, 534 U.S. 84 (2001), the Court declined to construe the Indian Gaming Regulatory Act to grant Indian tribal gaming the same exemption from federal excise taxes enjoyed by the states. The Court relied on the canon of construction that federal tax provisions should not be interpreted to create exemptions that are not clearly expressed. The Court then stated:

Nor can we say that the pro-Indian canon is inevitably stronger–particularly where the interpretation of a congressional statute rather than an Indian treaty is at issue.

Id. at 535–36. Whether this statement is a precursor to future cases in which the Court may find the canon of favorable construction overcome by other canons, particularly with regard to statutes rather than treaties, remains to be seen. In the meantime, it is possible to read *Chickasaw* more narrowly as a reflection of the unusual strength of the presumption against unexpressed exemptions from federal taxation. This strength is illustrated by two Ninth Circuit treaty cases. In the first, a treaty provision guaranteeing "the right, in common with the citizens of the United States, to travel upon all public highways" was held to confer immunity from state truck license and permit fees for treaty Indians hauling goods to market. Cree v. Flores, 157 F.3d 762 (9th Cir.1998). In the second case, the same treaty provision was held not to confer immunity from *federal* vehicle and fuel excise taxes because it contained no "exemptive language"; the standard for judging federal taxability was held to be less sympathetic to tribal treaty activity. Ramsey v. United States, 302 F.3d 1074, 1078–80 (9th Cir. 2002), cert. denied, ___ U.S. ___, 124 S.Ct. 54 (2003).

The usual rule, however, is that the canon of sympathetic construction has more strength than the ordinary canons of statutory interpretation. "[T]he standard principles of statutory construction do not have their usual force in cases involving Indian law." Montana v. Blackfeet Tribe of Indians, 471 U.S. 759, 766 (1985). Two circuits have held that the canon of sympathetic construction also overcomes the rule of deference to an administrative agency's interpretation of a statute that it administers—a rule that is something more than a mere interpretive aid. Ramah Navajo Chapter v. Lujan, 112 F.3d 1455 (10th Cir.1997); Albuquerque Indian Rights v. Lujan, 930 F.2d 49, 59 (D.C.Cir. 1991); contra Williams v. Babbitt, 115 F.3d 657, 663 n.5 (9th Cir.1997). Certainly in the general run of cases the rule of sympathetic construction continues to offer substantial benefit to Indian interests, such as exemption of tribes from state excise taxes, Quinault Indian Nation v. Grays Harbor County, 310 F.3d 645 (9th Cir.2002).

C. ABROGATION OF TREATIES

One of the least understood facts about Indian treaties is that they may be abrogated unilaterally by Congress. Because treaties often contain recitals that they will remain in effect "as long as the grass shall grow" or for some equally eternal length of time, many people assume that any alterations in terms would have to be mutually negotiated by the federal government and the tribes. The law, however, is to the contrary.

Indian treaties as well as international treaties stand on the same footing as federal statutes. Like federal statutes, they can be repealed or modified by later federal statutes. Thus if the United States enters a treaty with a foreign nation and Congress subsequently passes a statute inconsistent with the provisions of the treaty, the statute will control and the treaty is abrogated, at least to the extent of the inconsistency. Whatever may be the implications of the abrogation for purposes of international law, there is no question that the abrogating statute becomes the governing internal law of the United States. Chae Chan Ping v. United States (The Chinese Exclusion Case), 130 U.S. 581 (1889).

The Supreme Court's first application of the same principle to Indian treaties came in The Cherokee Tobacco, 78 U.S. (11 Wall.) 616 (1871), which upheld a federal tax on tobacco sold within Cherokee territory despite a prior treaty that guaranteed an exemption. The decision most often cited for the proposition that Congress may abrogate an Indian treaty, however, is Lone Wolf v. Hitchcock, 187 U.S. 553 (1903). That case involved a treaty with the Kiowas and Comanches which set aside lands to be held communally by the tribes and provided that no further cessions of those lands could be made without the consent of three-fourths of the adult male Indians of the tribes. Years later, Congress passed a statute ceding additional lands without the three-fourths vote of approval. The Court upheld the statute, stating that a treaty could not be given a legal effect that would restrict the future exercise of Congress' plenary power over Indian affairs. The Court elaborated:

> The power exists to abrogate the provisions of an Indian treaty, though presumably such power will be exercised only when circumstances arise which will not only justify the government in disregarding the stipulations of the treaty, but may demand, in the interest of the country and the Indians themselves, that it should do so. When,

therefore, treaties were entered into between the United States and a tribe of Indians it was never doubted that the *power* to abrogate existed in Congress, and that in a contingency such power might be availed of from considerations of governmental policy, particularly if consistent with perfect good faith towards the Indians.

187 U.S. at 566. While it well might be questioned whether the land cession in *Lone Wolf* was consistent with perfect good faith towards the Indians, the outcome left no doubt about Congress's ability to abrogate.

The mere fact that Congress has the *power* to abrogate does not mean, however, that every statute that is potentially inconsistent with a treaty effects an abrogation. If Congress expressly states that it is modifying a particular treaty, then the deed is done and the courts have no room to maneuver. It is far more common for Congress to pass legislation seemingly inconsistent with a treaty without mentioning (or perhaps even considering) the effect that the statute is to have on treaty rights. In such cases, the courts have an opportunity to consider whether the unexpressed intent of Congress was indeed to abrogate, or whether congressional purposes would be better served by implying exceptions to the statute that will prevent impairment of the treaty. The nature of the judicial function in this type of case is similar to that in cases involving a question of implied repeal of a statute or of preemption of state law by a federal statute. The outcome depends in part on the nature and scope of the particular statute involved, and may also depend upon a weighing and balancing of policy issues that exist quite independently of the intent or purposes of Congress. These characteristics make it difficult to reduce decisions of this type to a pattern.

The trust relationship between the federal government and the Indian tribes ought to weigh heavily against implied abrogation of treaties. Indeed, the Supreme Court at one time seemed to suggest that Congress was required to make an abrogation express, see Frost v. Wenie, 157 U.S. 46 (1895), but it no longer adheres to that view. In holding that the Eagle Protection Act abrogated a treaty right of hunting, the Supreme Court rejected a *per se* rule requiring an explicit statement from Congress:

> What is essential is clear evidence that Congress actually considered the conflict between its intended action on the one hand and Indian treaty rights on the other, and chose to resolve that conflict by abrogating the treaty.

United States v. Dion, 476 U.S. 734, 738–740 (1986). Even this requirement may sometimes yield when a congressional statute clearly forbids what a treaty requires, and the policy behind the federal statute is deemed important and likely to be frustrated if exceptions are allowed. Thus a clear congressional ban on hunting in Glacier Park was held to abrogate a tribal hunting right secured by an agreement ratified by Congress, even though there was no evidence that Congress actually considered the conflict between the ban and the agreement. United States v. Peterson, 121 F.Supp.2d 1309 (D. Mont. 2000).

A tribe's treaty right to the "exclusive use and benefit" of all of the land within a reservation, and a right to regulate conduct that may go with it, has been held to be lost with regard to land that passed into non-Indian hands under subsequently enacted Allotment Acts. Brendale v. Confederated Tribes and Bands of the Yakima Indian Nation, 492 U.S. 408, 422–23 (1989) (plurality opinion); Montana v. United States, 450 U.S. 544, 559 & n.9 (1981). Similarly, the taking by the United States of a portion of a reservation for a dam and reservoir was held to abrogate the tribe's treaty right to regulate non-Indian hunting and fishing in the taken area. South Dakota v. Bourland, 508 U.S. 679 (1993). But a tribe's treaty right to "exclusive use and occupancy" of its former reservation has been held to protect it from attempts of the BIA to place land within that reservation in trust for a competing tribe. Citizen Band of Potawatomi Indian Tribe v. Collier, 142 F.3d 1325 (10th Cir.1998).

Where there is room for doubt as to congressional intent, the Supreme Court has sometimes gone to considerable lengths to avoid the destruction of treaty rights. Menominee Tribe v. United States, 391 U.S. 404 (1968), provides the cardinal example. An 1854 treaty set aside lands for the Menominee "to be held as Indian lands are held." The Court, appropriately enough, interpreted this phrase sympathetically to guarantee hunting and fishing rights on the reservation lands. In 1954, Congress passed a Termination Act which provided that in 1962 the special relationship between the Menominee Tribe and the federal government would end and that

> "all statutes of the United States which affect Indians because of their status as Indians shall no longer be applicable to members of the tribe, and the laws of the several States shall apply to the tribe and its members in the same manner as they apply to other citizens or persons within their jurisdiction."

25 U.S.C.A. § 899 (1954), repealed 25 U.S.C.A. § 903a(b) (1973). No mention was made in the Termination Act of the Menominee's treaty hunting and fishing rights. A majority of the Court held that the Termination Act did not abrogate the treaty hunting and fishing rights. It pointed out that Congress in other statutes had carefully preserved Indian treaty rights, and that the Termination Act referred to federal *statutes* becoming inapplicable but said nothing of treaties. In concluding, the majority stated, "[w]e find it difficult to believe that Congress without explicit statement would subject the United States to a claim for compensation by destroying property rights conferred by treaty * * *." 391 U.S. at 412–413. While these remarks cannot now be read as requiring an explicit congressional statement for every abrogation, the *Menominee* case is unquestionably strong authority for the proposition that congressional intent to abrogate a treaty is not easily to be implied.

As the quoted language of the *Menominee* case indicates, abrogation of a treaty may give rise to a claim of compensation when the abrogation destroys a property right. The abrogation itself is effective, but the tribe is entitled to a claim for a "taking" under the Fifth Amendment. See United States v. Creek Nation, 295 U.S. 103 (1935).

CHAPTER VII

CRIMINAL AND CIVIL JURISDICTION IN INDIAN COUNTRY

A. INTRODUCTION

The most complex problems in the field of Indian Law arise in jurisdictional disputes among the federal government, the tribes and the states. To resolve those problems it is essential to know the basic limits of jurisdiction of each of the three contending powers. Although ambiguities still remain in abundance, those limits have been most thoroughly defined in regard to criminal and civil *adjudicatory* jurisdiction, which is discussed in this chapter. The more uncertain area of regulatory jurisdiction is dealt with in Chapter IX, infra. The division of jurisdiction set forth in this chapter is that which prevails in the absence of any federal statute such as Public Law 280, which grants criminal and civil jurisdiction to the states. The effects of Public Law 280 are discussed in Chapter VIII, infra. Other specialized statutes, such as Indian claims settlement acts, may allocate jurisdiction in atypical ways. See, e.g., Rhode Island v. Narragansett Indian Tribe, 19 F.3d 685 (1st Cir.1994); Charles v. Charles, 243 Conn. 255, 701 A.2d 650 (1997). The division of jurisdiction described here also does not apply to some eastern tribes long placed under state jurisdiction for nearly all purposes or recognized only by the state. See, e.g., Seneca v. Seneca, 293 A.D.2d 56, 741 N.Y.S.2d 375 (2002); State v. Velky, 263 Conn. 602, 821 A.2d 752 (2003).

Subject matter jurisdiction of federal, tribal or state courts usually depends heavily upon two issues: (1) whether the parties involved are Indians or, in some applications, tribal members, and (2) whether the events in issue took place in Indian country. The question of who is an Indian is discussed in Chapter I, Section C. What, then, is "Indian country"?

B. INDIAN COUNTRY

After many years of change and development, the concept of Indian country was given its present definition by Congress in 1948. 18 U.S.C.A. § 1151 provides:

[T]he term "Indian country", as used in this chapter, means (a) all land within the limits of any Indian reservation under the jurisdiction of the United States government, notwithstanding the issuance of any patent, and, including rights-of-way running through the reservation, (b) all dependent Indian communities within the borders of the United States whether within the original or subsequently acquired territory thereof, and whether within or without the limits of a state, and (c) all Indian allotments, the Indian titles to which have not been extinguished, including rights-of-way running through the same.

Although this definition is for purposes of the criminal code, it is also used for civil jurisdiction. Alaska v. Native Village of Venetie, 522 U.S. 520, 527 (1998). Whether particular land is Indian country is a question of law. United States v. Roberts, 185 F.3d 1125 (10th Cir.1999).

Subsection (a) includes all of the territory within an Indian reservation. It is most important to note that even land owned by non-Indians in fee simple (i. e., where there has been "issuance of any patent") is still "Indian country" if it is within the exterior boundaries of an Indian reservation. There exist within many reservations large tracts of land long since settled by non-Indians, and even entire towns incorporated by non-Indians under state law, but all of those tracts and towns are Indian country for purposes of jurisdiction. Seymour v. Superintendent, 368 U.S. 351 (1962). As will be seen later in this chapter, the ownership of land within Indian country has recently assumed jurisdictional importance in some circumstances, see, e.g., Montana v. United States, 450 U.S. 544 (1981), but the concept of Indian country is still a major jurisdictional determinant.

Although the mere opening up of a reservation for non-Indian settlement does not remove the newly settled lands from Indian country, a congressional decision to abandon the reservation status of those lands does. In cases where Congress has opened reservations to heavy settlement, there is often a difficult question of fact whether the intent was to permit non-Indians to live and own land on a reservation or whether it was to extinguish a portion of the reservation (to "diminish" the reservation) and open it for settlement as public, non-Indian land. The answers to this fact-bound inquiry have not been very predictable in the past. In Seymour v. Superintendent, 368 U.S. 351 (1962), and Mattz v. Arnett, 412 U.S. 481 (1973), the Supreme Court held that extensive allotment and settlement of the Colville and Klamath River Reservations, respectively, did not end the reservation status of those lands. But in DeCoteau v. District County Court, 420 U.S. 425 (1975), and Rosebud Sioux Tribe v. Kneip, 430 U.S. 584 (1977), the Court found that Congress had terminated ("disestablished") the entire Lake Traverse Reservation and large tracts of land in the Rosebud Reservation, respectively.

In Solem v. Bartlett, 465 U.S. 463 (1984), the Court reviewed these cases and stated that they "have established a fairly clean analytical structure" for determining whether a reservation had been diminished. Most important was the language of the statute: "[e]xplicit reference to cession or other language evidencing the present and total surrender of all tribal interests" was strongly indicative of intent to diminish, and created an almost insurmountable presumption when combined with a commitment to compensate the tribe for the opened land. 465 U.S. at 470–71. Even without language of cession, a diminishment could be found from other factors, although it would not lightly be implied. The other factors were the manner in which the transaction was arranged or considered at the time; subsequent treatment of the area by the concerned governments; and later demographic consequences of the opening. Considering all of these factors in order, the Court in Solem v. Bartlett found that operative statutory language merely providing for sale of the land did not indicate an intent to diminish, even though stray language elsewhere in the statute referred to the opened lands as being in "the public domain" and to the unopened areas as "the reservation thus diminished." 465 U.S. at 475. Contemporaneous circumstances did not show an intent to diminish, and subsequent treatment of the area by the concerned governments was too contradictory to be useful. Finally, relatively few non-Indians had settled on the opened lands, while a majority of present tribal members resided there. Accordingly, the Court held that there had been no diminishment.

Despite *Solem*'s reliance on demographics, that factor should probably not be viewed as sufficient by itself to establish that a surplus land act was intended to diminish a reservation; the demographic results are best seen as one post-event clue to Congress' intent regarding the future of the reservation. See South Dakota v. Yankton Sioux Tribe, 522 U.S. 329, 356 (1998). There are numerous instances of existing reservations containing substantial tracts of fee land heavily populated by non-

Indians. See, e.g., Duncan Energy Co. v. Three Affiliated Tribes of the Fort Berthold Reservation, 27 F.3d 1294, 1297–98 & n.4 (8th Cir.1994); Oliphant v. Suquamish Indian Tribe, 435 U.S. 191, 193 n.1 (1978); see also Oneida Indian Nation of New York v. City of Sherrill, 337 F.3d 139, 163–64 (2d Cir.2003).

In two fairly recent diminishment cases, the Supreme Court applied the factors set forth in Solem v. Bartlett and found that Congress had intended in surplus land acts to diminish, respectively, the Uintah Reservation in Utah and the Yankton Sioux Reservation in South Dakota. Hagen v. Utah, 510 U.S. 399 (1994); South Dakota v. Yankton Sioux Tribe, 522 U.S. 329 (1998). In *Hagen*, the Court rejected a contention that Congress was required clearly to state its intention of modifying the reservation boundaries. Applying the factors of Solem v. Bartlett, the Court found that contemporary understanding and later demographics supported diminishment, and that subsequent treatment of the area by government was not illuminating. Most significant, however, was the operative language of the act directing that surplus lands "be restored to the public domain." That language, said the Court, denoted a congressional intent to end the reservation status of those lands. The Court did not state that this language was conclusive of the issue, but it emphasized the wording so heavily that it seems doubtful that the Court would fail to find diminishment when those words appear in the operative portion of the statute. This conclusion is buttressed by *Yankton Sioux Tribe*, supra, in which the Supreme Court, along with other factors, applied the "almost insurmountable" presumption of diminishment that *Solem* derived from clear statutory language of cession combined with a commitment by the United States to pay for the ceded lands. *Yankton*, 522 U.S. at 344. One court of appeals, however, has subsequently held that a provision in executive orders that lands be restored to the public domain was overridden by strong evidence of executive intent not to diminish the reservation. Confederated Tribes of the Chehalis Indian Reservation v. Washington, 96 F.3d 334 (9th Cir.1996). In addition, the Tenth Circuit, in subsequently dealing with the same reservation involved in *Hagen*, adhered in the interest of finality to its earlier decision that lands of the reservation not directly covered by *Hagen* remained part of the reservation although in part they may have been ordered restored to the public domain. Ute Indian Tribe of Uintah and Ouray Reservation v. Utah, 114 F.3d 1513 (10th Cir.1997).

When a reservation is diminished or disestablished, the area excluded from the reservation is no longer Indian country under subsection (a) of 18 U.S.C.A. § 1151, which refers to "all land within the limits of any Indian reservation." Particular sub-portions of the excluded area, however, may still qualify as Indian country under subsections (b) and (c) of § 1151–as dependent Indian communities or allotments in trust. See Mustang Production Co. v. Harrison, 94 F.3d 1382, 1385 (10th Cir.1996); United States v. Stands, 105 F.3d 1565, 1572 (8th

Cir.1997). One circuit has held that blocks of trust land in a disestablished area may nevertheless qualify as informal "reservation" Indian country under subsection (a) of § 1151. HRI, Inc. v. EPA, 198 F.3d 1224, 1249–54 (10th Cir.2000); see also Oklahoma Tax Comm'n v. Sac and Fox Nation, 508 U.S. 114, 123 (1993).

Subsection (b) of 18 U.S.C.A. § 1151, which incorporates "dependent Indian communities" into the definition of Indian country, is a codification of the Supreme Court's holding in United States v. Sandoval, 231 U.S. 28 (1913). That case involved the New Mexico Pueblos, which held their land in fee simple under Spanish grants and which were not formally designated as reservations. The Court held that the Pueblo lands were Indian country nevertheless, since the Pueblos were wards dependent upon the federal government's guardianship. Id.; see also Indian Country, U.S.A. v. Oklahoma Tax Comm'n, 829 F.2d 967 (10th Cir.1987). The Court later held that the Pueblo lands could not be alienated without the consent of the United States. United States v. Candelaria, 271 U.S. 432 (1926). Dependent Indian communities, then, are Indian country whether or not they are located within a recognized reservation.

The Supreme Court has recently delineated the elements of a dependent Indian community. The case arose in Alaska, where the issue was of extreme importance because of the unique corporate system under which nearly all Native groups held their land. See Chapter XIII, Section C(2). The

Court held that the two essential characteristics of a dependent Indian community were that the land be set aside for the use of Indians, and that the land (not merely the tribe) must be under the superintendence of the federal government. Alaska v. Native Village of Venetie Tribal Government, 522 U.S. 520 (1998). Federal superintendence means that the community must be "sufficiently 'dependent' upon the Federal Government that the Federal Government and the Indians involved, rather than the States, are to exercise primary jurisdiction over the land in question." Id. at 531. Although the Court did not forbid consideration of other factors, such additional factors must not be balanced against or used to dilute the two requirements of federal set-aside and federal superintendence. Id. at 531 n.7.

At least one state court has applied *Venetie* strictly and held that a tract of land within a dependent Indian community is not Indian country unless that specific tract has been set aside by the federal government for use by Indians. Thus a road owned and maintained by the Bureau of Land Management within such a community was held not to be Indian country. New Mexico v. Frank, 132 N.M. 544, 52 P.2d 404 (2002); cf. Cruse v. State, 67 P.3d 920 (Okla.Crim.App.2003). Such a result makes for difficult "checkerboard" enforcement, however. A contrary view requires a court to determine initially the proper "community of reference" before analyzing whether that entire community qualifies under § 1151(b). See HRI, Inc. v. EPA, 198 F.3d 1224, 1248–49 (10th Cir.2000).

Subsection (c) of § 1151 is self-explanatory; it includes within Indian country any allotment that is either still in trust (which necessarily means that it is beneficially owned by an Indian), or is owned in fee by an Indian with a restriction on alienation in favor of the United States. Yankton Sioux Tribe v. Gaffey, 188 F.3d 1010, 1022 (8th Cir.1999). Such allotments are Indian country whether or not they are located within a reservation. Id.

C. HISTORICAL BACKGROUND OF JURISDICTION IN INDIAN COUNTRY

1. INITIAL JURISDICTION OF THE TRIBES AND THE GROWTH OF FEDERAL AUTHORITY

In colonial days, the Indian territory was entirely the province of the tribes, and they had jurisdiction in fact and theory over all persons and subjects present there. Shortly after the Revolution, federal jurisdiction was extended to non-Indians committing crimes against Indians in Indian territory, as part of the overall federal policy of providing a buffer between the non-Indian and Indian populations. 1 Stat. 138 (1790); 1 Stat. 743 (1799); 2 Stat. 139 (1802). Federal jurisdiction was further extended in 1817 to cover crimes by both Indians and non-Indians in Indian country with the notable exception of crimes by Indians against Indians; the latter were left entirely to be dealt with by tribal law or custom. 3 Stat. 383. That 1817 statute extending federal criminal law into Indian country has undergone several revisions and is now codified as 18 U.S.C.A. § 1152; it is commonly known as the General Crimes Act or sometimes the Federal Enclaves Act or the Indian Country Crimes Act. See, generally, Clinton, *Development of Criminal Jurisdiction Over Indian Lands: The Historical Perspective*, 17 Ariz.L.Rev. 951 (1975).

This pattern, emphasizing federal jurisdiction over crimes between non-Indians and Indians while maintaining exclusive tribal jurisdiction over all-Indian crimes, continued until Congress modified it in reaction to the Supreme Court's decision in Ex parte Crow Dog, 109 U.S. 556 (1883). *Crow Dog* involved the conviction of an Indian in territorial court for the murder of another Indian in Indian country. The murder was alleged to have violated the general federal statute against murder, extended to Indian country by the General Crimes Act. The Supreme Court held that there was no jurisdiction, because the General Crimes Act excluded from coverage crimes by an Indian against an Indian. The Court left no doubt of its conviction that in justice the matter should be handled by the tribe:

> It is a case where, against an express exception in the law itself, that law * * * is sought to be extended over aliens and strangers; * * * and to subject them to the responsibilities of civil conduct, according to rules and penalties of which they could have no previous warning; which judges them by a standard made for others, and not for them, which takes no account of the

conditions which should except them from its exactions, and makes no allowance for their inability to understand it.

109 U.S. at 571. The Court's heartfelt defense of tribal jurisdiction did not seem to impress Congress; it reacted to *Crow Dog* by promptly passing the Major Crimes Act, which created federal jurisdiction over seven crimes (including murder) committed by Indians in Indian country, whether the victim were Indian or non-Indian. 23 Stat. 362, 385 (1885). Subsequent amendments have expanded the number of major crimes to fourteen. 18 U.S.C.A. § 1153. To the considerable extent that it covered crimes by Indians against Indians, the Major Crimes Act was the first systematic intrusion by the federal government into the internal affairs of the tribes. The Supreme Court held that this exercise of congressional power was justified by the dependent status of the tribes as wards of the federal government. United States v. Kagama, 118 U.S. 375 (1886).

Despite the Major Crimes Act, the tribes continued to exercise very substantial jurisdiction over Indians in Indian country. Non-major crimes by Indians were within the exclusive jurisdiction of the tribes, and remain so today (assuming, as we do throughout this chapter, that the crime is committed in a state where Public Law 280 does not apply; see Chapter VIII, infra). The tribes also retained jurisdiction to punish minor crimes by Indians against non-Indians, a jurisdiction shared with the federal government under 18 U.S.C.A. § 1152. Many tribes even continued to punish Indians for conduct that constituted a major crime, effectively exercising jurisdiction concurrent with that conferred upon the federal courts by Congress. See Wetsit v. Stafne, 44 F.3d 823 (9th Cir.1995). Federal enforcement was often lax (and virtually nonexistent in the case of larceny, which Congress had included among the major crimes), and the tribes tended to fill the vacuum when federal authorities refused or failed to prosecute. Recently, the Supreme Court decided that tribes as domestic dependent sovereigns had no power to exercise criminal jurisdiction over Indians who were not members of the tribe. Duro v. Reina, 495 U.S. 676 (1990). Congress promptly overturned that ruling, however, recognizing and affirming "the inherent power of Indian tribes * * * to exercise criminal jurisdiction over all Indians * * *." 25 U.S.C.A. § 1301(2). Thus tribal exercise of power over Indians has been and still is extensive.

On the other hand, tribal jurisdiction over non-Indians, embodied in several early treaties, ceased to be exercised as the federal government assumed primary responsibility under the General Crimes Act, 18 U.S.C.A. § 1152. During the periods of removal to reservations and the Allotment Act, the declining power of the tribes left them in no position to enforce their laws against non-Indians. The Law and Order Codes written by the Department of Interior for use in Courts of Indian Offenses covered only crimes by Indians, and tribal codes adopted after passage of the Indian Reorganization Act of 1934 followed the same pattern. In the

1970's, however, several tribes that had become dissatisfied with the state of law enforcement against non-Indians responded by asserting tribal jurisdiction over crimes committed by them. The tribes contended that such jurisdiction was inherent in tribal self-government. The Supreme Court rejected the tribal position in Oliphant v. Suquamish Indian Tribe, 435 U.S. 191 (1978), and held that the tribes lacked criminal jurisdiction over non-Indians. The Court said that to exercise such jurisdiction in the absence of an authorizing statute of Congress would be inconsistent with the status of the tribes as dependent nations. Unless Congress alters the pattern, then, the inherent tribal jurisdiction over crimes is restricted to those committed by Indians.

One additional federal limitation on tribal jurisdiction over internal affairs is found in the Indian Civil Rights Act of 1968, 25 U.S.C.A. § 1301 et seq., more fully described in Chapter XI, infra. The act imposed most of the requirements of the Bill of Rights upon the tribes in the exercise of their jurisdiction. Tribal courts are consequently required to observe due process and enforce other rights analogous to those arising under the First, Fourth, Fifth, Sixth, Eighth and Fourteenth Amendments. Persons held in tribal custody in violation of the provisions of the Act are afforded a right of review in federal court by habeas corpus. The Act also limits the sentences that may be imposed by tribal courts to a maximum of a $5,000 fine and one year in jail for any one crime. 25 U.S.C.A. § 1302(7). For all practical purposes, therefore, tribal courts are limited to misdemeanor jurisdiction in criminal cases. There are no comparable maximum limits placed upon their civil jurisdiction.

2. THE SELECTIVE EXTENSION OF STATE LAW INTO INDIAN COUNTRY

One of the basic premises underlying the constitutional allocation of Indian affairs to the federal government was that the states could not be relied upon to deal fairly with the Indians. Severe limitations upon the exercise of state power in Indian territory therefore seemed implicit in the nation's early Indian policy, but the extent of these limitations was not dealt with authoritatively until John Marshall's decision in the second of the famous Cherokee cases, Worcester v. Georgia, 31 U.S. (6 Pet.) 515 (1832). At the heart of the case lay Georgia's attempt to exercise total jurisdiction within Cherokee territory—to divide that territory among several Georgia counties, to apply Georgia law to all persons within the area, and to prohibit the Cherokees from exercising any governmental powers of their own. Chief Justice Marshall's opinion for the Court totally rejected Georgia's attempt, and characterized the Cherokee territory as one "in which the laws of Georgia can have no force * * *." 31 U.S. (6 Pet.) at 561. Marshall reviewed the history of governmental relations with the Indian tribes, the treaties entered with the Cherokees, and the constitutional provision for congressional regulation of commerce with the Indian tribes. All of these, said Marshall, reinforced the tribal right of self-government and the exclusively federal right to govern relations between the tribe and outsiders. The Georgia laws interfered with these rights and were a nullity.

For fifty years, Marshall's view that state law and power could not intrude into Indian country held sway. Then a major change occurred in United States v. McBratney, 104 U.S. 621 (1881). In that case a non-Indian had been convicted in federal circuit court of murdering another non-Indian on the Ute reservation in Colorado. The Supreme Court, in a highly doubtful construction of the applicable federal statutes, first held that the federal court could exercise criminal jurisdiction only over places within the *exclusive* jurisdiction of the federal government. If the state had any jurisdiction over this crime, then the federal court necessarily had none. The state of Colorado must have jurisdiction, the Court ruled, because Congress had admitted it to the union "upon an equal footing with the original States" and no exception was made for jurisdiction over the Ute reservation. The laws of Colorado therefore extend throughout the state, including the Ute reservation, insofar as they relate to crimes by non-Indians against non-Indians. The federal conviction was accordingly reversed, and the lower court was directed to deliver the defendant to state authorities.

The outcome in *McBratney* was repeated in even more unlikely circumstances some fifteen years later. In Draper v. United States, 164 U.S. 240 (1896), the Supreme Court was presented with virtually the same facts as in *McBratney*, with one exception that ought to have been crucial. The murder of a non-Indian in *Draper* had occurred on the Crow reservation in Montana, and the congressional act enabling Montana's admission to the union provided that the people of Montana forever disclaimed all title to Indian lands and that "said Indian lands shall remain under the absolute jurisdiction and control of the Congress of the United States * * *." 25 Stat. 676, 677 (1889). Despite this language, the Supreme Court ruled that the state and not the federal courts had jurisdiction over the crime involved. While agreeing that the enabling act might have foreclosed state jurisdiction over crimes by or against Indians, the Court stated that Congress could not have intended any result so drastic as the exclusion of state power to punish wholly non-Indian crimes in Indian country.

Despite the dubious statutory and judicial underpinnings for the *McBratney* and *Draper* decisions, they have become firmly entrenched in existing law. New York ex rel. Ray v. Martin, 326 U.S. 496 (1946). Even *Draper's* disregard of the jurisdictional provision in the state's enabling act remains authoritative; the Supreme Court has subsequently explained that the state's disclaimer is of title, not jurisdiction, and the provision for "absolute" federal jurisdiction does not necessarily mean "exclusive" federal jurisdiction! Organized Village of Kake v. Egan, 369 U.S. 60, 68 (1962).

At first glance, *McBratney* and *Draper* might seem to have had a very limited effect on Indian affairs, since they dealt only with crimes where no Indians were involved as either victims or perpetrators. In both theoretical and practical terms, however, the decisions had an enormous and complicating impact on the law of jurisdiction in Indian country, for they made it impossible ever after to deal with questions of state jurisdiction on a purely geographical basis. Marshall's rule in *Worcester* that state law can have no force in Indian country had several virtues, but perhaps the greatest was simplicity. When tribal and state powers were viewed in purely territorial terms, it was necessary only to discover the location of a transaction or occurrence in order to determine which of two competing systems of law and courts had control over it. *McBratney* and *Draper*, on the other hand, require not only a determination of location, but also an inquiry into the nature of the subject matter and the identity of the parties involved in the case. They open the door to judicial balancing of state and tribal interests whenever arguable questions of jurisdiction arise.

The Supreme Court's clearest subsequent articulation of the test of state jurisdiction in Indian country came many years later in a civil case. Williams v. Lee, 358 U.S. 217 (1959), was a suit brought in state court by a non-Indian against an Indian couple for the purchase price of goods sold to the Indians on the Navajo reservation in Arizona. The Supreme Court held that the state courts had no jurisdiction over the action. Justice Black's opinion for the majority laid heavy emphasis upon Worcester v. Georgia and Marshall's proposition that state laws can "have no force" in Indian country, and then added:

Over the years this Court has modified these principles in cases where essential tribal relations were not involved and where the rights of Indians would not be jeopardized, but the basic policy of *Worcester* has remained. * * * Essentially, absent governing Acts of Congress, the question has always been whether the state action infringed on the right of reservation Indians to make their own laws and be governed by them.

358 U.S. at 219–220. The Court also pointed out that Congress in Public Law 280 had provided the sole means for a state to acquire civil and criminal jurisdiction in Indian country and Arizona had not availed itself of that procedure. It is noteworthy that the Court easily assumed that even *concurrent* state jurisdiction would unduly interfere with the powers of the tribal courts.

While the result in Williams v. Lee was highly protective of tribal jurisdiction, the test it announced was capable of being interpreted to permit increased exercise of state power within Indian country. In the subsequent case of Organized Village of Kake v. Egan, 369 U.S. 60 (1962), for example, the Court clearly suggested that state law and state court jurisdiction could be extended to Indians as well as non-Indians in Indian country, so long as there did not seem to be a direct interference with the tribal government itself. This rather expansive view of state power co-existed for several years with the more restrictive approach taken in Williams v. Lee, resulting in considerable uncertainty. This uncertainty was put to rest a decade later in McClanahan v. Arizona Tax Com'n, 411 U.S. 164 (1973), but *McClanahan* also introduced new subtleties to the subject of state jurisdiction in Indian country.

McClanahan involved an attempt by the state of Arizona to collect state income tax on the earnings of an Indian who resided on the Navajo Reservation and whose income was derived entirely from personal services performed on that reservation. The state argued that a tax on the income of an individual Indian did not interfere with tribal government and therefore was permissible under the test of Williams v. Lee, supra. In rejecting that contention, the Court first noted that it was not convinced that an individual income tax avoided infringing upon tribal self-government. But the primary defect in the state's argument, according to the Court, was that the test of Williams v. Lee was never intended to apply to attempted exercises of state jurisdiction over Indians. It was only when the state asserted power over *non-Indians* in Indian country that it was appropriate to balance the state and tribal interests by determining whether or not state jurisdiction would infringe upon tribal self-government. When the state attempted to reach Indians in Indian country, the legality of the state's action had to be determined by reference to applicable federal statutes and treaties, interpreted in light of a history of Indian tribal sovereignty and independence from state law. In the case of the Navajo reservation, those sources made it clear that the state had no power to impose its tax.

The subtlety that *McClanahan* introduced into jurisdictional analysis was its preemption approach. Notions of Indian sovereignty, which had loomed large in Williams v. Lee, were reduced to a "backdrop against which the applicable treaties and federal statutes must be read" to determine whether state law was preempted. 411 U.S. at 172. *McClanahan*'s analysis assumes that state law applies if not preempted, which is a reversal of previous presumptions that state law did not apply to matters affecting Indians in Indian country.

Because federal treaties and statutes rarely preempt state law expressly, preemption analysis often becomes a matter of weighing and balancing the competing interests.

> State jurisdiction is preempted by the operation of federal law if it interferes with or is incompatible with federal and tribal interests reflected in federal law, unless the state interests at stake are sufficient to justify the assertion of state authority.

New Mexico v. Mescalero Apache Tribe, 462 U.S. 324, 334 (1983). In theory at least, this formula permits a state law that serves an extremely important state interest to interfere even with tribal self-government. The previous standard of Williams v. Lee, on the other hand, precluded application of *any* state law that "infringed on the right of reservation Indians to make their own laws and be governed by them." 358 U.S. at 220. The *Williams* rule is still employed as a test for the application of state law in Indian country, 462 U.S. at 334 n.16, but the area of tribal self-government that it absolutely protects is no longer construed to include everything affecting tribal interests. In most current clashes between state law and tribal authority, preemption analysis seems to predominate over the approach of Williams v. Lee. An example is Cotton Petroleum Corp. v. New Mexico, 490 U.S. 163 (1989), upholding the state's right to impose a severance tax on non-Indian oil and gas lessees operating on the reservation, even though the tribe also imposed a severance tax.

The Court now recognizes that in "exceptional circumstances" state law may be applied even to tribes and tribal members in Indian country. California v. Cabazon Band of Mission Indians, 480 U.S. 202, 215 (1987); New Mexico v. Mescalero Apache Tribe, 462 U.S. 324, 331–32 (1983). Such applications have occurred, but they have indeed been exceptional. States have been permitted to tax sales of cigarettes to nonmembers by a tribal shop, and to require the tribal seller to collect and remit the tax (although the state must depend on methods of enforcement other than suing the tribe). Washington v. Confederated Tribes of Colville Indian Reservation, 447 U.S. 134 (1980); Oklahoma Tax Comm'n v. Citizen Band Potawatomi Indian Tribe, 498 U.S. 505 (1991). They have been permitted to regulate liquor sales by a licensed tribal member on-reservation, when federal legislation and the tribe's dependent status had traditionally precluded the tribe from doing so. Rice v. Rehner, 463 U.S. 713 (1983); see Fort Belknap Indian Community v. Mazurek, 43 F.3d 428 (9th Cir.1994). Finally, in a most unusual case (see Chapter XV, Section C), a state has been permitted to regulate Indian fishing for conservation purposes, in places that unexpectedly turned out to be within a reservation. Puyallup Tribe, Inc. v. Department of Game, 433 U.S. 165 (1977).

On the other hand, the Supreme Court still presumes that states are preempted from taxing Indian activities, income, or property in Indian country. See Oklahoma Tax Comm'n v. Sac and Fox Nation, 508 U.S. 114, 126 (1993); Oklahoma Tax Comm'n v. Chickasaw Nation, 515 U.S. 450 (1995). States have been preempted from regulating hunting and fishing by *non-Indians* on trust lands within a reservation, where the tribe and the federal government had extensively regulated. New Mexico v. Mescalero Apache Tribe, 462 U.S. 324 (1983). They have also been preempted from regulating gambling operations conducted by tribes on their reservations. California v. Cabazon Band of Mission Indians, 480 U.S. 202 (1987). Finally, states regularly have been preempted from taxing non-Indian contractors who do business with tribes on the reservations. E.g., White Mountain Apache Tribe v. Bracker, 448 U.S. 136 (1980); Ramah Navajo School Bd., Inc. v. Bureau of Revenue, 458 U.S. 832 (1982).

The preemption doctrine, which is somewhat more fully discussed in Chapter V, Section B, has therefore made it quite difficult to draw bright jurisdictional lines for the application of state law in Indian country. Its primary impact, however, has been in the areas of taxation and regulation, rather than adjudicatory jurisdiction. The Supreme Court, at least until very recently, has been extraordinarily protective of the civil jurisdiction of tribal courts. Thus, in a case brought in federal court, the Supreme Court held that the federal question of a tribal court's jurisdiction over a reservation-based suit against a non-Indian must be determined in the first instance by the tribal court itself. National Farmers Union Ins. Cos. v. Crow Tribe, 471 U.S. 845 (1985). Later, the Court imposed the same requirement in a federal diversity case when the matter in litigation was also the subject of a tribal court action brought by an Indian against non-Indians. The Court stated:

> If state-court jurisdiction over Indians or activities on Indian lands would interfere with tribal sovereignty and self-government, the state courts are generally divested of jurisdiction as a matter of federal law.

Iowa Mut. Ins. Co. v. LaPlante, 480 U.S. 9, 15 (1987). This statement is notable for its absence of weighing and balancing. It applies the more protective test of Williams v. Lee, which it cites. The Court also stated that civil jurisdiction over the activities of non-Indians on reservation lands "presumptively lies in the tribal courts unless affirmatively limited by a specific treaty provision or federal statute." 480 U.S. at 18.

A few years before the decisions in *National Farmers Union* and *LaPlante*, however, the Supreme Court began a line of cases that narrowed tribal jurisdiction over non-Indians, necessarily leaving the states to fill any vacuum. The seminal decision was Montana v. United States, 450 U.S. 544 (1981), which is more fully discussed in Chapter V, Section B. *Montana* held that the tribe, as a domestic dependent sovereign, had no power to regulate nonmember activities on nonmember-owned fee lands. *Montana* did specify two exceptions when a tribe could regulate non-Indian activities on fee-owned reservation lands: (1) a tribe may regulate and tax "the activities of nonmembers who enter consensual relationships with the tribe or its members," and (2) a tribe may regulate conduct of nonmembers that "threatens or has some direct effect on the political integrity, the economic security, or the health or welfare of the tribe." Although the second exception could be read to permit exercise of a broad police power of the tribe over nonmembers, it has been interpreted very narrowly by subsequent Supreme Court decisions.

An example is Strate v. A–1 Contractors, 520 U.S. 438 (1997), which built on *Montana* and narrowed *LaPlante*. *Strate* held that a tribe, by reason of its domestic dependent status, could not exercise civil jurisdiction over a tort suit between nonmembers arising from an accident on a state highway within a reservation. The Court held that a state highway right-of-way, where the tribe had no gatekeeping right, was the equivalent of non-Indian fee land, and that tribes had no jurisdiction over nonmember activities on such land under *Montana*. *Montana*'s second exception was to be read narrowly and did not apply here. The Court in *Strate* then introduced another principle: "As to nonmembers * * * a tribe's adjudicative jurisdiction does not exceed its legislative jurisdiction." Id. at 453. The language in *LaPlante* presumptively placing civil jurisdiction in tribal court was said to stand for "nothing more than the unremarkable proposition" that "where tribes possess authority to regulate activities of nonmembers," jurisdiction presumptively lies in the tribal court. Id. The Supreme Court in *Strate* also reemphasized *Montana*'s narrow description of inherent tribal power: the power to punish members, determine membership, regulate domestic relations among members, and prescribe rules of inheritance for members. Id. at 459. (If this list were to be deemed exhaustive of tribal powers, there would seem to be no occasion for the *LaPlante* presumption of tribal court jurisdiction over nonmembers to operate.) The consequence of the ruling in *Strate* is that state courts have exclusive jurisdiction over suits between nonmembers arising on non-Indian fee or right-of-way lands within a reservation. That result is not a new intrusion of state power into Indian country, because state courts previously had civil jurisdiction over such a suit. What is new is that the state jurisdiction is now exclusive of the tribe, and neither state nor federal courts are required to abstain in favor of tribal courts in such an action. Id. at 459 n.14.

Although *Strate*, like *Montana*, involved activities only of nonmembers (indeed, non-Indians), it phrased the question for decision as whether a tribal court could "entertain a civil action against" nonmembers. 520 U.S. at 442. At least one court of appeals, relying on *Strate*'s narrow view of tribal interests, has subsequently held that tribal courts could not exercise jurisdiction of actions by tribal members against non-Indians arising out of accidents on rights-of-way. Burlington Northern R. Co. v. Red Wolf, 196 F.3d 1059 (9th Cir.1999); Wilson v. Marchington, 127 F.3d 805 (9th Cir.1997). If the actions had been reversed, however, and the tribal members had been the defendants, Williams v. Lee would require the cases to be brought in tribal court. Whether that proposition is threatened by *Strate* when fee lands or state rights-of-way are involved remains to be seen.

Montana was subsequently applied to prevent a tribe from taxing nonmember activity on non-Indian fee land within a reservation. Atkinson Trading Company v. Shirley, 532 U.S. 645 (2001). One month later, the Supreme Court decided Nevada v. Hicks, 533 U.S. 353 (2001), which endorsed a major new intrusion of state authority into Indian country. In that case, state officers investigating off-reservation crime conducted a search of an Indian's residence on trust land within a reservation. The officers had a state search warrant and had also procured a tribal search warrant. During the unsuccessful search, the officers allegedly damaged property and the Indian resident sued in tribal court. The Supreme Court, applying *Strate* and *Montana*, held that the tribal court had no jurisdiction because the tribe had no power to regulate state officers executing process relating to off-reservation crime. Even though the search was of an Indian residence on trust land, regulation of the officers by the tribe was not "essential to tribal self-government or internal relations–to 'the right to make laws and be governed by them.' " Id. at 364. Thus, according to the Supreme Court, this limitation of tribal power was prohibited neither by *Montana*'s second exception nor by Williams v. Lee. Moreover, *Montana*'s limitation of tribal authority was not confined to fee lands or rights-of-way. "The ownership status of land * * * is only one factor to consider in determining whether regulation of the activities of nonmembers is 'necessary to protect tribal self-government or to control internal relations.' " Id. at 360.

Hicks was a surprising decision that upset a number of settled expectations. The state officers, at the insistence of the state court, had secured a tribal search warrant but the opinion in *Hicks* left no doubt that the tribal warrant was wholly unnecessary. If the same reasoning is applied to arrest warrants, state officers will be able enter Indian country and arrest Indians for alleged off-reservation crimes, and the tribe would have no power to regulate the officers' activity. Such a result would render meaningless the extradition arrangements that many tribes have worked out with state authorities. Cf. Arizona ex rel. Merrill v. Turtle, 413 F.2d 683 (9th Cir.1969). Despite the implications of *Hicks*, many state and tribal authorities are continuing to honor consensual agreements governing search and arrest within Indian country.

In summary, then, the recent trend of Supreme Court decisions has been to narrow greatly tribal civil power over nonmembers, leaving states with increased or exclusive jurisdiction over controversies arising from such activity. Tribes retain power to regulate nonmembers' consensual activities with a tribe or its members, and to regulate conduct that threatens the tribe's integrity–a test that is strictly applied to require a substantial threat. The limitation on tribal regulation of nonmember activity has migrated from fee lands, as in *Montana*, to trust lands, as in *Hicks*. It is important, however, to keep in mind that the officers in *Hicks* were investigating off-reservation crime, in which the state had an exclusive interest. The *Montana* analysis is likely to come out differently when a nonmember conducts other activity of lower priority on reservation trust land or with reservation Indians. Certainly *Hicks* cannot be read as conferring a general power on state officers to police Indians in Indian country. That power remains with the tribe in civil matters, and with the tribe and federal government in criminal cases. To reduce these generalizations to more accurate specifics, it is necessary to examine in detail the present division of criminal and civil jurisdiction among the federal government, the tribes, and the states.

D. PRESENT DIVISION OF CRIMINAL JURISDICTION IN INDIAN COUNTRY

1. FEDERAL CRIMINAL JURISDICTION

a. Federal Crimes of Nationwide Applicability

There are some general federal criminal statutes that are effective throughout the nation, and they apply in Indian country to all persons, whether or not Indian. Statutes punishing theft from the United States mail or treason are obvious examples. Other examples include federal narcotics laws, United States v. Brisk, 171 F.3d 514 (7th Cir.1999), the Organized Crime Control Act, see United States v. Funmaker, 10 F.3d 1327 (7th Cir.1993), the Racketeer Influenced and Corrupt Organizations Act (RICO), United States v. Juvenile Male, 118 F.3d 1344 (9th Cir.1997), and the Contraband Cigarette Trafficking Act, Grey Poplars Inc. v. 1,371,100 Assorted Brands of Cigarettes, 282 F.3d 1175 (9th Cir.2002). Such crimes actually have little to do with Indian law, and it need only be noted that federal jurisdiction over them applies in Indian country as it does everywhere else.

In one interesting application of this principle, the Ninth Circuit held that the federal conspiracy statute, 18 U.S.C.A. § 371, was a law of nationwide applicability. United States v. Begay, 42 F.3d 486 (9th Cir.1994). The case was interesting because the predicate crimes that were charged as objects of the conspiracy were kidnapping and various assaults punishable under the Major Crimes Act, 18 U.S.C.A. § 1153. Those predicate crimes were not ones of nationwide applicability; they applied only when the crimes were committed by Indians in Indian country. The court of appeals rejected a contention that linking conspiracy with major crimes impermissibly extended the scope of the Major Crimes Act beyond that intended by Congress. The court also rejected a contention that the government was required to prove that the conspiracy occurred in Indian country. On the other hand, the government was required to prove that the objects of the conspiracy—kidnapping and aggravated assault in violation of the Major Crimes Act— occurred in Indian country. 42 F.3d at 501. A similar issue was raised in United States v. Yankton, 168 F.3d 1096 (8th Cir.1999), in which the court held that the crime of accessory after the fact, 18 U.S.C. § 3, was a crime of general application even though the underlying crime was not. See also Standing Bear v. United States, 68 F.3d 271 (8th Cir.1995), holding that the federal statute proscribing use of a firearm in a crime of violence, 18 U.S.C.A. § 924(c)(1), was one of nationwide applicability, even though the crime in which the firearm was used was murder in violation of the Major Crimes Act. Because a law of nationwide applicability applies in Indian country of its own force, and is not imported by way of the General Crimes Act, 18 U.S.C. § 1152, it is not subject to the exception in the General Crimes Act for crimes committed by an Indian against an Indian. See United States v. Wadena, 152 F.3d 831, 841 (8th Cir.1998); see subsection b, immediately below.

In United States v. Markiewicz, 978 F.2d 786, 800 (2d Cir.1992), the Second Circuit suggested that crimes of nationwide applicability apply to Indian-against-Indian offenses in Indian country only if the offenses are "peculiarly Federal" crimes and the prosecution "would protect an independent federal interest." No other circuit has imposed this requirement. See, e.g., United States v. Begay, 42 F.3d at 500; United States v. Blue, 722 F.3d 383 (8th Cir. 1983). Indeed, it seems to serve little purpose, because virtually any federal criminal statute of nationwide applicability could pass its test. See, e.g., United States v. Boots, 80 F.3d 580, 593–94 (1st Cir.1996).

When a crime consists of violation of a regulatory scheme, it is probably appropriate to determine whether the underlying regulation, which purports to be of universal application, properly applies to Indians in Indian country. See United States v. White, 237 F.3d 170 (2d Cir.2001). Ordinarily a federal statute of general application that is silent as to its applicability to Indians in Indian country applies to them unless the law touches exclusive rights of self-governance in purely internal tribal matters, or would abrogate treaty rights, or unless there is some other proof of intent of Congress not to apply the law to Indians on their reservations. Id. at 173; see United States v. Brisk, 171 F.3d 514 (7th Cir.1999). For most generally applicable federal criminal statutes such as mail theft or assault on a federal officer, that do not involve a regulatory regime, there is little need for such an analysis; the law can simply be applied.

b. Crimes Punishable Under the General Crimes Act, 18 U.S.C.A. § 1152

One of the most important federal criminal statutes applicable in Indian country is the General Crimes Act, 18 U.S.C.A. § 1152, sometimes called the Federal Enclaves Act or, more recently, the Indian Country Crimes Act. Its primary present function is to provide for prosecution of crimes by non-Indians against Indians and of non-major crimes by Indians against non-Indians. It was originally passed by Congress in 1817 in order to permit punishment of all crimes committed by non-Indians in Indian territory, as well as some crimes committed by Indians against non-Indians. At that time, it was assumed that all such crimes were beyond the reach of state law and that some of them were probably also beyond the effective reach of tribal law. In its present form, the General Crimes Act provides as follows:

18 U.S.C.A. § 1152:

Except as otherwise expressly provided by law, the general laws of the United States as to the punishment of offenses committed in any place within the sole and exclusive jurisdiction of the United States, except the District of Columbia, shall extend to the Indian country.

This section shall not extend to offenses committed by one Indian against the person or property of another Indian, nor to any Indian committing any offense in the Indian country who has been punished by the local law of the tribe, or to any case where, by treaty stipulations, the exclusive jurisdiction over such offenses is or may be secured to the Indian tribes respectively.

The effect of the Act is to import into Indian country the entire body of criminal law applicable in areas under exclusive federal jurisdiction. To understand what has been imported, it is necessary to know what law governs areas under exclusive federal jurisdiction and why.

On a nationwide scale, federal criminal statutes are relatively few in number; Congress has always assumed that the basic, comprehensive body of criminal law would be legislated by the states, as indeed it has been. There are, however, some areas of the country, such as federal forts and arsenals, where federal jurisdiction is exclusive and state law does not apply. In the absence of some sort of special legislation, these areas would have been left with an inadequate criminal law structure. Congress accordingly reacted in two ways to solve the problem. First, it passed statutes from time to time providing for the punishment of specific crimes committed in territory under federal jurisdiction.

Thus 18 U.S.C.A. § 1111 provides for the punishment of murder committed within the special maritime and territorial jurisdiction of the United States. Various other crimes were covered in similar fashion, but the result was far from a complete criminal code. Congress consequently took a second approach as early as 1825; it passed what is now known as the Assimilative Crimes Act, 18 U.S.C.A. § 13. That statute provides:

> Whoever within [the special maritime and territorial jurisdiction of the United States] is guilty of any act or omission which, although not made punishable by an enactment of Congress, would be punishable if committed or omitted within the jurisdiction of the State, Territory, Possession, or District in which such place is situated, by the laws thereof in force at the time of such act or omission, shall be guilty of a like offense and subject to a like punishment.

The effect of this provision is to borrow most of state criminal law and to apply it through federal law to areas under federal jurisdiction. Thus a violator of the Assimilative Crimes Act is charged with a federal offense and is tried in federal court, but the crime is defined and the sentence prescribed by state law.

The relevance of the Assimilative Crimes Act to the subject of Indian Law is that the Assimilative Crimes Act is one of the general laws of the United States that is extended to Indian country by the General Crimes Act, 18 U.S.C.A. § 1152. See

Williams v. United States, 327 U.S. 711 (1946). Of course, the other specific federal criminal statutes applicable in areas of exclusive federal jurisdiction, such as 18 U.S.C.A. § 1111 proscribing the crime of murder, are also extended into Indian country by the General Crimes Act.

The primary need filled by the General Crimes Act was that of a body of law to punish non-Indian crime, and it served that purpose. Although the intention of Congress was almost certainly to apply federal law to *all* crimes committed by non-Indians in Indian country, that intention was eventually frustrated by the Supreme Court. In United States v. McBratney, 104 U.S. 621 (1881), and Draper v. United States, 164 U.S. 240 (1896), the Court held that state courts had jurisdiction over crimes by non-Indians against non-Indians, and that the federal government did not. By the same reasoning, victimless crimes by non-Indians similarly ought to be subject to state and not federal law. The Eighth Circuit held to the contrary, however, in a case involving drunken driving and speeding by a non-Indian. United States v. Billadeau, 275 F.3d 692 (8th Cir.2001). In any event, the result of *McBratney* and *Draper* is that, when a non-Indian is prosecuted under the General Crimes Act and there is a victim, the victim must be an Indian. The Indian or non-Indian status of the defendant and victim must be alleged in the indictment and proved at trial. United States v. Prentiss, 256 F.3d 971 (10th Cir. 2001) (en banc).

The General Crimes Act also applies to Indians, but in a more limited fashion than it does to non-Indians. In the first place, the Act itself enumerates three exceptions; it does not apply to the following:

i.   crimes by Indians against Indians;

ii.   crimes by Indians that have been punished by the tribe; and

iii.   crimes over which a treaty gives exclusive jurisdiction to the tribe.

The first exception is the largest, and represents a recognition by Congress at the time of the Act's passage that all-Indian crimes were solely the concern of the tribes in the exercise of their powers of self-government. Although Congress later modified its position by asserting federal jurisdiction over "major crimes" by Indians even when the victim was Indian (see subsection c, immediately below), the General Crimes Act exception remained unchanged and leaves the punishment of the majority of all-Indian crimes to the tribes.

While the first exception to the General Crimes Act refers to crimes by Indians *against* Indians, a fair construction of the whole statute seems to require that victimless crimes by Indians also be excluded from federal jurisdiction. A victimless crime by an Indian is just as much an internal tribal matter as a crime by an Indian against an Indian. For that reason the Supreme Court rejected an attempt by federal authorities to prosecute an Indian for the consensual crime of adultery with another Indian in Indian country. The government contended that the crime was not within the first exception to the General Crimes Act because it could not be considered a crime "against" an Indian. The Supreme Court ruled that there was no jurisdiction, and that to hold otherwise would subject Indians "not only to the statute relating to adultery, but also to many others which it seems most reasonable to believe were not intended by Congress to be applied to them." United States v. Quiver, 241 U.S. 602, 606 (1916); see also Ex parte Mayfield, 141 U.S. 107 (1891).

The correctness of the Supreme Court's position in *Quiver* becomes all the more apparent upon examination of the consequences that would follow if the General Crimes Act were applied to victimless crimes by Indians. Because the Assimilative Crimes Act is one of the "general laws of the United States" imported into Indian country by the General Crimes Act, the full panoply of state law governing victimless crimes would be applied to tribal Indians. The result would be an enormous intrusion on tribal authority over Indian affairs. One much-criticized case that supplies an example is United States v. Sosseur, 181 F.2d 873 (7th Cir.1950). There the General Crimes Act and the Assimilative Crimes Act were applied to convict an Indian of operating slot machines for which he had a tribal license. The court relied in part on the fact that the primary users of the machines were non-Indian tourists, and that may be the best explanation for the decision. If, however, the crime is viewed as a victimless one, the decision seems to impose the requirements of state law quite unnecessarily upon an Indian in Indian country whose conduct is more appropriately governed by the contrary provisions of tribal law. In that sense, the *Sosseur* decision seems inconsistent with the Supreme Court's ruling in *Quiver*, supra. It is also inconsistent, in practical effect, with California v. Cabazon Band of Mission Indians, 480 U.S. 202 (1987), which held state law inapplicable to high-stakes bingo and poker games conducted by tribes on their reservations.

In the same vein as *Sosseur* is the recent decision of the Eighth Circuit in United States v. Thunder Hawk, 127 F.3d 705 (8th Cir.1997). There the defendant Indian was convicted in federal court under the Assimilative Crimes Act of driving under the influence of alcohol. The court held that the crime was not within the exception of § 1152 for crimes by an Indian against an Indian, even though the defendant's driving had caused injuries to his Indian daughter, because the offense requires no victim. The victimless crime was held to fall within the terms of the Assimilative Crimes Act. *Quiver* was distinguished on the ground that it involved domestic relations, "an area traditionally left to tribal self-government." 127 F.3d at 709. The court of appeals also viewed driving under the influence as a public crime against both Indians and non-Indians. It is difficult to see, however, why punishment of Indians for driving under the influence does not fall within the tribe's power of self-government. Indeed, the federal authorities prosecuted Thunder Hawk while a charge for the same offense was pending against him in tribal court!

An appealing argument can even be made that the General Crimes Act and its incorporated Assimilative Crimes Act ought *never* to be applied to Indians (in other words, that not only should victimless crimes by Indians be excluded from those Acts, but also crimes by Indians against non-Indians). The Indian who commits a crime in Indian country is subject to the comprehensive criminal jurisdiction of the tribe and, for a few specified crimes, of the federal government under the Major Crimes Act. There is no criminal law vacuum for the Indian (as there was for the non-Indian) and therefore no need to import a body of criminal law by way of the General Crimes Act and Assimilative Crimes Act. To do so merely displaces tribal law that is far more appropriate for governing the conduct of the Indian. See Clinton, *Criminal Jurisdiction Over Indian Lands: A Journey Through a Jurisdictional Maze*, 18 Ariz.L.Rev. 503, 535–36 (1976). A major difficulty with this argument is presented by the second exception to the General Crimes Act, which excludes prosecution of crimes by Indians that have been punished by the tribe. This exception does not appear to be aimed at crimes against Indians, because they are entirely excluded by the first exception. Nor does it seem likely that it applies to victimless crimes by Indians, which are also wholly internal affairs that ought to be left to the tribe whether or not it chooses to punish them. The most sensible meaning that can be attributed to the second exception is that it applies to crimes by Indians against non-Indians, and that Congress intended to apply the General Crimes Act to such crimes unless they had actually been punished by the tribes. Unless Congress later modified that intention by passage or amendment of the Major Crimes Act (and the legislative history is far from conclusive to that effect), the exception continues to support application of the General Crimes Act to non-major crimes by Indians against non-Indians. In any event, the General Crimes Act and Assimilative Crimes Act have been applied, with varying degrees of attention to their underlying purposes, to such crimes. United States v. John, 587 F.2d 683 (5th Cir.1979); United States v. Burland, 441 F.2d 1199 (9th Cir.1971); cf. United States v. Butler, 541 F.2d 730 (8th Cir.1976). When a crime by an Indian against a non-Indian is one of the enumerated offenses in the Major Crimes Act, however, prosecution must be brought under that Act and not the General Crimes Act. Henry v. United States, 432 F.2d 114 (9th Cir.1970), modified 434 F.2d 1283 (1971); United States v. John, supra.

The third exception to the General Crimes Act, which excludes crimes over which a treaty gives exclusive jurisdiction to a tribe, is of little significance today. Only a few of the early treaties conferred such jurisdiction, and several of those have been abrogated or have ceased to be enforceable because the tribe no longer exercises governmental functions.

c. Crimes Punishable Under the Major Crimes Act, 18 U.S.C.A. § 1153

The Major Crimes Act was passed by Congress in 1885, in reaction to the Supreme Court's holding in Ex parte Crow Dog, 109 U.S. 556 (1883), that federal courts had no jurisdiction over the murder of an Indian by an Indian in Indian territory. In its present form, the Act provides in part as follows:

18 U.S.C.A. § 1153:

(a) Any Indian who commits against the person or property of another Indian or other person any of the following offenses, namely, murder, manslaughter, kidnapping, maiming, a felony under chapter 109A, incest, assault with intent to commit murder, assault with a dangerous weapon, assault resulting in serious bodily injury (as defined in section 1365 of this title), an assault against an individual who has not attained the age of 16 years, arson, burglary, robbery, and a felony under section 661 of this title within the Indian country, shall be subject to the same law and penalties as all other persons committing any of the above offenses, within the exclusive jurisdiction of the United States.

* * *

Chapter 109A, incorporated in the statute, refers to sexual abuse; section 661 deals with theft. Jurisdiction is sufficient under the Major Crimes Act if any part of the offense took place in Indian country. United States v. Van Chase, 137 F.3d 579 (8th Cir.1998).

Although the Major Crimes Act was passed in reaction to a crime by an Indian against an Indian, it applies when an Indian commits any of the specified crimes against anyone. United States v. Bird, 342 F.3d 1045 (9th Cir.2003). The Act's requirement that the crime be "against the person or property of another Indian or other person" has been held, however, to exclude a crime against the federal government (burglary of a BIA building). United States v. Errol D., Jr., 292 F.3d 1159 (9th Cir.2002).

The principal effect of the Major Crimes Act was to permit prosecution of Indians by reference to selected federal criminal statutes applicable in federal reserves. The Indian status of the defendant must be alleged in the indictment. United States v. Belgarde, 148 F.Supp.2d 1104 (D. Mont. 2001). The Act originally covered seven crimes, but the list has been expanded to the present fourteen by a series of amendments. Occasional problems were caused when Congress added to the list crimes for which there was no existing federal definition, but Congress has since amended the Act to provide that the crimes of burglary, incest and any other named major crimes not defined by federal law were to be "defined and punished in accordance with the laws of the State in which such offense was committed." 18 U.S.C.A. § 1153(b); see United States v. Welch, 822 F.2d 460 (4th Cir.1987).

A split in federal circuits arose over whether the Federal Sentencing Guidelines, which originally applied to anyone convicted of "an offense described in any Federal statute," could be applied to an Indian convicted of burglary or incest under the Major Crimes Act, when those federally-undefined offenses were required by that Act to be "punished in accordance with" state law. Compare United States v. Bear, 932 F.2d 1279 (9th Cir.1990), with United States v. Norquay, 905 F.2d 1157 (8th Cir. 1990). Congress put an end to the conflict by amending 18 U.S.C.A. § 3551 so that it expressly applied the Guidelines to persons convicted under the Major Crimes Act. Federal jurisdiction over a major crime has been treated as including jurisdiction to revoke supervised release imposed as punishment for that crime. United States v. Lomayaoma, 86 F.3d 142 (9th Cir.1996).

The Major Crimes Act is supplemented by a jurisdictional statute, 18 U.S.C.A. § 3242, which provides that Indians prosecuted under the Major Crimes Act "shall be tried in the same courts, and in the same manner, as are all other persons committing such offenses within the exclusive jurisdiction of the United States." For the most part this statute merely emphasizes the fact that Major Crimes Act prosecutions are regular federal criminal trials subject to the same procedures as any others. The statute had controlling effect, however, in one important case determining the extent of federal jurisdiction under the Major Crimes Act. In Keeble v. United States, 412 U.S. 205 (1973), an Indian was charged under the Major Crimes Act with assault with intent to commit serious bodily injury. At the close of his trial, he requested the judge to instruct the jury that they might convict him of the lesser included offense of simple assault. The district court refused the instruction on the ground that the Major Crimes Act did not give it jurisdiction over the crime of simple assault, and the court of appeals affirmed. The Supreme Court reversed, holding that an Indian was entitled to an instruction on a lesser included offense because he was entitled to be tried "in the same manner" as a non-Indian under 18 U.S.C.A. § 3242. It follows that the federal court has jurisdiction to impose punishment on the defendant if he is convicted of the lesser offense. United States v. DeMarrias, 876 F.2d 674 (8th Cir.1989). One circuit has held that a federal court continued to have jurisdiction over lesser-included offenses even after the court ordered a judgment of acquittal on the Major Crime charged. United States v. Walkingeagle, 974 F.2d 551 (4th Cir.1992).

Keeble leaves open the question whether an Indian defendant is entitled to plea-bargain and plead guilty in federal court to a reduced charge over which the court would not originally have jurisdiction under the Major Crimes Act. It is possible that such a practice would be viewed as an undue extension of federal authority; on the other hand, forbidding the practice may force an Indian defendant to trial on a Major Crimes charge when he or she otherwise could have bargained for conviction of a lesser offense. A final problem posed by *Keeble* concerns the source to be used by the federal court in defining and punishing the lesser included offense. In Felicia v. United States, 495 F.2d 353 (8th Cir.1974), the court of appeals held that the lesser included offense was to be defined and punished according to state law because the Major Crimes Act mandates such treatment for crimes not defined by federal law. In United States v. John, 587 F.2d 683 (5th Cir.1979), another court of appeals held that the General Crimes Act applied to the lesser included offense. Under the latter approach, the lesser included offense would be defined and punished according to federal statute if there is one and state law if there is not.

Enforcement of the Major Crimes Act (like that of the General Crimes Act) has often been criticized by tribal authorities as being too lax. Overburdened United States Attorneys have often been unenthusiastic about prosecuting the less serious of the major crimes. One solution of the tribes has been to exercise concurrent jurisdiction, which the Major Crimes Act probably permits (see subsection 2, Tribal Criminal Jurisdiction, below). The tribe may prosecute for lesser included or collateral minor offenses encompassed in the same act that constituted a major crime without potential double jeopardy problems, because the tribes and the federal government are separate sovereigns. United States v. Wheeler, 435 U.S. 313 (1978): see Wetsit v. Stafne, 44 F.3d 823 (9th Cir.1995). *Wheeler* and other cases treating constitutional problems arising from the division of criminal jurisdiction in Indian country are discussed in Chapter XI, infra.

d. Other Federal Statutes

There are innumerable other federal statutes affecting criminal jurisdiction on individual reservations or in specially defined areas of Indian country. See, e.g., Kansas Act, 18 U.S.C.A. § 3243; Negonsott v. Samuels, 507 U.S. 99 (1993). It is neither possible nor desirable to catalog them here. The most that can be said is that an early step in dealing with a particular problem of criminal jurisdiction must be a search to determine the existence and scope of any such statutes.

2. TRIBAL CRIMINAL JURISDICTION

In the absence of federal statutes limiting it, tribal criminal jurisdiction over the Indian in Indian country is complete, inherent and exclusive. Ex parte Crow Dog, 109 U.S. 556 (1883). Although Congress has legislated a number of limitations, much remains of the original jurisdiction of the tribes over Indians. It is exercised primarily by tribal courts, which are described in Chapter IV, Section D, supra.

The tribe has exclusive jurisdiction over non-major crimes committed by Indians against Indians in Indian country. Such crimes are specifically excepted from the jurisdiction conferred upon the federal courts by the General Crimes Act, 18 U.S.C.A. § 1152. Similarly, victimless crimes by Indians are matters wholly internal to the tribes, and they too must be regarded as subject to exclusive tribal jurisdiction. United States v. Quiver, 241 U.S. 602, 606 (1916); cf. United States v. Wheeler, 435 U.S. 313 (1978); but see United States v. Thunder Hawk, 127 F.3d 705 (8th Cir.1997); United States v. Sosseur, 181 F.2d 873 (7th Cir.1950).

Non-major crimes by Indians against non-Indians are also unquestionably subject to the jurisdiction of tribal courts, but here the jurisdiction is not exclusive. Federal courts also have jurisdiction over such crimes by virtue of the General Crimes Act, supra. That Act excludes from its coverage Indians who have been punished by their tribes, thus making it clear that the tribes share jurisdiction over these crimes.

"Major crimes" are the fourteen named crimes made subject to federal jurisdiction by the Major Crimes Act, 18 U.S.C.A. § 1153. At least one federal circuit has concluded that tribes have concurrent jurisdiction to punish conduct that also constitutes an offense under the Major Crimes Act. Wetsit v. Stafne, 44 F.3d 823 (9th Cir.1995). The Supreme Court has not decided the question. See Oliphant v. Suquamish Indian Tribe, 435 U.S. 191, 203 n. 14 (1978). The legislative history of the Major Crimes Act strongly supports tribal exercise of concurrent jurisdiction. See Clinton, *Criminal Jurisdiction Over Indian Lands: A Journey Through a Jurisdictional Maze*, 18 Ariz.L.Rev. 503, 559, n. 295 (1976). Moreover, the great majority of tribes for many years have exercised jurisdiction over the crime of theft, which duplicates larceny, a crime rather surprisingly included in the original Major Crimes Act.

The issue whether the tribes have concurrent jurisdiction over major crimes by Indians has been rendered less important by the passage of the Civil Rights Act of 1968, which now limits the jurisdiction of the tribal courts to sentences not exceeding one year's imprisonment and a $5,000 fine or both. 25 U.S.C.A. § 1302(7). Even before passage of the Civil Rights Act, most tribes had left major crimes other than larceny entirely to the federal government; with the Act's sentencing limit they have little incentive to change that pattern. Here as elsewhere tribes may choose to exercise less than their maximum jurisdiction.

Because virtually all federal jurisdictional statutes refer to "Indians" and not "tribal members," it generally had been assumed that tribal jurisdiction over crimes by Indians was not limited to members of the tribe asserting jurisdiction. It has been common practice for tribal courts to exercise authority over members of other tribes who commit crimes within the court's geographical jurisdiction. Doubt was first cast upon this practice by language in the Supreme Court decision of United States v. Wheeler, 435 U.S. 313 (1978), where the Court continually referred to a tribe's inherent criminal jurisdiction over its *members*. Then, in 1990, the Supreme Court decided that tribes as domestic dependent sovereigns had no power to exercise criminal jurisdiction over Indians who were not members of the tribe. Duro v. Reina, 495 U.S. 676 (1990). Congress promptly overturned that ruling, however, providing that tribal powers of self-government included "the inherent power of Indian tribes, hereby recognized and affirmed, to exercise criminal jurisdiction over all Indians * * *." 25 U.S.C.A. § 1301(2). Thus the tribes continue to exercise criminal jurisdiction over nonmember as well as member Indians.

Congress's action raised some interesting questions, however. In order to avoid ex post facto violations, § 1301(2) was held not to be retroactively applicable to permit tribal prosecution of a nonmember Indian for a crime committed before its enactment. Means v. Northern Cheyenne Tribal Court, 154 F.3d 941 (9th Cir.1998). In addition, the statute is phrased as a recognition of pre-existing inherent authority, which raises the question whether Congress is able to overrule the Supreme Court as to what the law has always been. *Means* thought not. Id. at 946. On the other hand if, contrary to its phraseology, § 1301(2) confers new power on the tribes, then a prosecution of a nonmember Indian in the future might be construed as an exercise by the tribe of a delegated federal power. In that event the tribe and the federal government could not prosecute for the same crime without violating the Double Jeopardy Clause. Faced with this question, the Ninth Circuit held that Congress could overturn the Supreme Court's view of the historical powers of tribes because the point was one of federal common law. United States v. Enas, 255 F.3d 662 (9th Cir.2001) (en banc). A tribal prosecution under § 1301(2) was therefore an exercise of inherent tribal sovereignty and dual prosecution was permitted. Four concurring judges of the en banc court took the view that Congress could recognize new inherent power that tribes could exercise as sovereigns and not as federal delegates, but the majority required an inherent power to be one that the tribes once exercised historically. Id. at 670–71. The Eighth Circuit addressed the same double jeopardy question, and originally divided equally on it. See United States v. Weaselhead, 156 F.3d 818 (8th Cir.1998) (en banc). It revisited the issue en banc in United States v. Lara, 324 F.3d 635 (8th Cir.2003), and disagreed with *Enas*. It held that "the distinction between a tribe's inherent and delegated powers is of constitutional magnitude and therefore is a matter ultimately entrusted to the Supreme Court. * * * Once the federal sovereign divests a tribe of a particular power, it is no longer an inherent power and it may only be restored by delegation of Congress's power." Id. at 639. Dual prosecution was therefore forbidden. This interesting conflict in the approach of the Ninth and Eighth Circuits will presumably be put to rest soon; the Supreme Court granted certiorari in *Lara*, ___ U.S. ___, 124 S.Ct. 46 (2003). Lurking in the background of this issue is the question whether, if the Supreme Court views § 1301(2) as a delegation of federal power, it violates the citizenship or equal protection rights of nonmember Indians by treating them differently from non-Indians. *See Duro*, 495 U.S. at 692–94.

In a decision addressing a somewhat analogous question, the Seventh Circuit held that the Menominee Tribe, which had been "terminated" and later "restored" to its former status by Congress, exercised its own inherent power in prosecuting a tribal member after the restoration. United States v. Long, 324 F.3d 475 (7th Cir.2003), cert. denied, ___ U.S. ___, 124 S.Ct. 151 (2003). The restoration was not a new delegation of federal power, and accordingly dual prosecution was permitted.

The jurisdiction of a tribe is generally confined to crimes committed within the geographical limits of its reservation and, presumably, any of its dependent Indian communities. One exception to this rule was established in Settler v. Lameer, 507 F.2d 231 (9th Cir.1974), in which the Yakima tribal court was held to have jurisdiction to punish tribal members who committed game violations in exercise of their off-reservation treaty fishing rights. Certain cases of juvenile delinquency also appear to be an exception to the general rule, but in fact are not. When an Indian juvenile domiciled on a reservation commits criminal acts off-reservation, the tribal court generally exercises jurisdiction to adjudicate delinquency. The reason is that the matter in issue is the status of delinquency, with a locus on the reservation, and not the individual acts committed off-reservation.

It now has been authoritatively established that tribes have no general criminal jurisdiction over non-Indians. Oliphant v. Suquamish Indian Tribe, 435 U.S. 191 (1978). As explained in subsection C(1) of this chapter, *Oliphant* arose from attempts by the tribes in the 1970's to solve some of their law

enforcement problems by asserting criminal jurisdiction over non-Indians. The Suquamish Tribe argued in *Oliphant* that it had inherent but long-
unexercised jurisdiction over non-Indians that had
not been limited by treaty or federal statute. The
Supreme Court agreed that the tribe's power had
not actually been curtailed by treaty or statute, but
held that criminal jurisdiction over non-Indians
would be inconsistent with the status of tribes as
dependent sovereigns. The court also noted that
some of the provisions of federal criminal statutes
seemed inconsistent with the existence of dormant
tribal jurisdiction over non-Indians. For example,
the second exception to the General Crimes Act, 18
U.S.C.A. § 1152, precludes federal prosecution of an
Indian who has been punished by his tribe. If the
tribe had power to punish non-Indians, would they
not have been given similar protection against double punishment? The Major Crimes Act, 18 U.S.C.A.
§ 1153, was passed because Congress did not wish
to leave the punishment of serious crimes entirely
to the tribes. If the tribes had power to punish both
Indians and non-Indians, then why did the Major
Crimes Act provide for federal punishment only of
Indians? The Court in *Oliphant* did not conclude
from these inconsistencies that the General Crimes
Act or Major Crimes Act themselves precluded the
tribes from exercising criminal jurisdiction over
non-Indians. Instead, the Court viewed the Acts as
persuasive evidence that no such jurisdiction existed at the times Congress passed them. The Court's
reasoning has its force, but it is difficult to evaluate

the understanding of Congress during a period when Congress had no reason to focus on the problems that might arise if the tribes elected to exercise jurisdiction over non-Indians. At a much later date, Congress passed the Civil Rights Act of 1968, 25 U.S.C.A. § 1301 et seq., which guaranteed to all persons (not merely Indians) a number of constitutional-type rights against tribal actions that are most likely to occur in the exercise of the tribe's criminal jurisdiction. Federal law accordingly provides opposition as well as support to the decision in *Oliphant*, but the decision in any event is clear: the tribes have no general criminal jurisdiction over non-Indians, and any change in that situation must come from Congress.

One small area of criminal jurisdiction over non-Indians may survive *Oliphant*. It seems likely that a tribal court would still have power to enforce decorum in its courtroom by the use of criminal contempt power against disruptive non-Indians. The exercise of such power may be essential to the very existence of a tribal court, and is therefore not inconsistent with the status of a tribe as a dependent sovereign. The same argument might also be used to support the use of contempt power to enforce subpoenas issued to non-Indians in the course of the tribal court's exercise of its legitimate jurisdiction. Finally, tribes generally retain the power to exclude unwanted persons from their reservations (a power often guaranteed by treaty). The power of exclusion might be viewed as quasi-criminal, and could be exercised against non-Indians at least to the extent that they do not have a federally-conferred right to be on the reservation. See Merrion v. Jicarilla Apache Tribe, 455 U.S. 130, 144–45 (1982); Hardin v. White Mountain Apache Tribe, 779 F.2d 476, 478–79 (9th Cir.1985). The tribe does not have power to exclude federal officials engaged in carrying out their duties. United States v. White Mountain Apache Tribe, 784 F.2d 917 (9th Cir.1986).

3. STATE CRIMINAL JURISDICTION

Outside of Indian country, the state has general criminal jurisdiction over all persons, including Indians. See, e.g., Hagen v. Utah, 510 U.S. 399 (1994). The Supreme Court has recently held that the state's interest in investigating such crimes permits state officers to execute a search warrant at an Indian residence on trust land within a reservation; the tribe cannot regulate the officers' activity. Nevada v. Hicks, 533 U.S. 353. For crimes within Indian country, however, the state's jurisdiction is generally limited to those crimes that do not concern Indians or Indian interests.

The state has exclusive jurisdiction over crimes by non-Indians against non-Indians in Indian country. Even though such crimes would appear to fall within the federal jurisdiction conferred by the General Crimes Act, 18 U.S.C.A. § 1152, the Supreme Court held the state's jurisdiction to be exclusive in United States v. McBratney, 104 U.S. 621 (1881); Draper v. United States, 164 U.S. 240 (1896). While these cases emphasized the inherent right of the states to jurisdiction within their boundaries, the Supreme Court has subsequently adhered to the results but justified them on the ground that Indians were not directly affected. New York ex rel. Ray v. Martin, 326 U.S. 496 (1946).

Victimless crimes committed by non-Indians in Indian country are also within the exclusive jurisdiction of the state, by reason of the same authority. See Solem v. Bartlett, 465 U.S. 463, 465 n.2. It should be emphasized, however, that the crimes should be truly victimless. Crimes against Indian property interests are not victimless.

States traditionally have no criminal jurisdiction in Indian country over crimes by Indians against anyone, or crimes by non-Indians against Indians. Thus a theft of horses by an Indian on a reservation cannot be punished by the state, even though the thief took the horses off-reservation where they were discovered. State v. Speaker, 300 Mont. 115, 4 P.3d 1 (2000). Crimes by Indians are punishable either by the tribe or the federal government and crimes by non-Indians against Indians are punishable exclusively by the federal government. Williams v. United States, 327 U.S. 711 (1946). The Ninth Circuit has recognized a narrow exception to this principle: the state can prosecute Indians for violation of state laws regarding liquor sales in Indian country. Fort Belknap Indian Community v. Mazurek, 43 F.3d 428 (9th Cir.1994). The exception was deemed necessary to effectuate the state power to regulate liquor sales in Indian country, which was recognized in Rice v. Rehner, 463 U.S. 713 (1983).

Another possible exception may occur when the tribe is engaged in litigation in state court and a tribal official commits an act on the reservation that constitutes contempt of an order of the state court. The state court may exercise its civil and, in flagrant cases, its criminal contempt power. See In re Humboldt River Stream System Adjudication, 59 P.3d 1226 (Nev. 2002). The general rule, however, is that the state is excluded from criminal jurisdiction over crimes involving Indians in Indian country.

In the past this rule held true even when the Indians involved were members of tribes other than the one that governed the reservation where the crime took place. As described in subsection 2 immediately above, the Supreme Court held in Duro v. Reina, 495 U.S. 676 (1990), that tribes had no criminal jurisdiction over nonmember Indians, which might have left a jurisdictional vacuum to be filled by the state in such cases. Congress overruled the Court, however, and tribes now have jurisdiction over crimes by nonmember Indians, 25 U.S.C.A. § 1301(2), and the state does not.

4. CHART OF CRIMINAL JURISDICTION IN INDIAN COUNTRY BY PARTIES AND CRIMES

Notes:

i. This chart does not reflect federal crimes applicable to all persons in all places, such as theft from the mails or treason.

ii.   This chart does not apply to Indian country over which the state has taken jurisdiction pursuant to Public Law 280, 18 U.S.C.A. § 1162.

———

Crime by Parties	Jurisdiction	Statutory Authority
a. Crimes by Indians against Indians:		
i. "Major" crimes.	Federal or tribal (concurrent)	18 U.S.C.A. § 1153
ii. Other crimes.	Tribal (exclusive)	
b. Crimes by Indians against non-Indians:		
i. "Major" crimes.	Federal or tribal (concurrent)	18 U.S.C.A. § 1153
ii. Other crimes.	Federal or tribal (concurrent)	18 U.S.C.A. § 1152
c. Crimes by Indians without Victims:	Tribal (exclusive)	
d. Crimes by non-Indians against Indians:	Federal (exclusive)	18 U.S.C.A. § 1152
e. Crimes by non-Indians against non-Indians:	State (exclusive)	
f. Crimes by non-Indians without Victims:	State (exclusive)	

E.   ARREST AND EXTRADITION

Until very recently there has been relatively little authority regarding the powers of the federal, state and tribal police in Indian country. In general, powers of policing and arrest follow the criminal jurisdiction of the three governments in the absence of special arrangements or agreements. For example, federal officers enforce the Major Crimes Act against Indians and the General Crimes Act against both Indians and non-Indians in Indian country. Tribal police enforce tribal laws against Indians and also have sufficient power over non-Indians to exercise the tribal power of exclusion. That power has been held to allow tribal police to investigate a crime committed by a non-Indian, and to turn both the results and the offender over to state authorities. State v. Haskins, 269 Mont. 202, 887 P.2d 1189 (1994). In addition to regular tribal police, many reservations utilize Indian police of the Bureau of Indian Affairs, who have authority to arrest for violations of either federal or tribal law. Finally, state police or county sheriffs and similar state personnel have authority to arrest non-Indians committing crimes against non-Indians or victimless crimes. State officers have no jurisdiction over Indians with regard to crimes committed in Indian country, however.

The Supreme Court recently held that state officers investigating alleged off-reservation crime by an Indian may execute a search warrant at the Indian's residence on trust land within the reservation. Nevada v. Hicks, 533 U.S. 353 (2001). The tribe has no power to regulate the officers' activity. Id. One question that arises after *Hicks* is whether its reasoning would apply equally to an arrest by state officers of an Indian in Indian country for an off-reservation crime. Even though an arrest is arguably much more of an interference with Indian interests than a search, much of the discussion in the *Hicks* majority opinion would seem to apply and permit an arrest without tribal consent. If so, many state-tribal extradition arrangements that have been worked out rather painstakingly over the years, and that courts have honored, would seem to have been rendered largely unnecessary. See, e.g., Benally v. Marcum, 89 N.M. 463, 553 P.2d 1270 (1976); State v. Yazzie, 108 N.M. 677, 777 P.2d 916 (App.1989); Arizona ex rel. Merrill v. Turtle, 413 F.2d 683, 686 (9th Cir.1969). In many cases, however, state, local and tribal authorities continue to abide by their consensual arrangements regarding arrest and execution of criminal process within Indian country even after *Hicks*. In a few instances, arrests by state officers of Indians in Indian country for off-reservation crimes had been permitted before *Hicks*. See, e.g., State ex rel. Old Elk v. District Court, 170 Mont. 208, 552 P.2d 1394, appeal dismissed, 429 U.S. 1030 (1976). Courts had also permitted arrests of Indians by state officers when the offense was committed out of Indian country and a fresh pursuit ended in it. City of Cut Bank v. Bird, 307 Mont. 460, 38 P.3d 804 (2001); State v. Lupe, 181 Ariz. 211, 889 P.2d 4 (App.1994); see United States v. Patch, 114 F.3d 131, 134 (9th Cir.1997).

For crimes committed within Indian country, however, the power to arrest there is still determined by the Indian or non-Indian status of the actor and victim. The difficulties caused by this division of jurisdiction are obvious. In the absence of special arrangements, a state police officer who stops a speeder on a state highway that passes through Indian country will lack authority to arrest if the speeding driver is an Indian, but will retain authority if the driver is a non-Indian. Needless to say, the officer often cannot know in advance which will be the case. For that reason, one court has held that an officer can briefly stop a moving vehicle to ascertain whether a violator is an Indian and, if so, may turn him or her over to tribal police. United States v. Patch, 114 F.3d 131 (9th Cir.1997); see also Duro v. Reina, 495 U.S. 676, 697 (1990). Similarly, tribal police may encounter non-Indians who have committed crimes against non-Indians or victimless crimes, but be without power to arrest them. Those officers, too, have been held to have authority to stop the violator and, if he or she is a non-Indian, to hold the violator for state authorities. State v. Schmuck, 121 Wash.2d 373, 850 P.2d 1332 (1993); see Strate v. A–1 Contractors, 520 U.S. 438, 456 n.11 (1997). The most satisfactory solution to these problems is for the tribal and state officers to cross-deputize, so that each is empowered to arrest for the other government. See, e.g., State v. Waters, 93 Wash.App. 969, 971 P.2d 538 (1999).

Although in City of Farmington v. Benally, 119 N.M. 496, 892 P.2d 629 (App.1995), state charges were dismissed because an arrest had been improperly made by a state officer in Indian country, that result does not always follow. Some courts hold that, when the charge is valid, the manner in which the defendant is brought from Indian country to the court does not affect the court's jurisdiction. See, e.g., Primeaux v. Leapley, 502 N.W.2d 265 (S.D. 1993).

F. PRESENT DIVISION OF CIVIL JURISDICTION IN INDIAN COUNTRY

1. STATE CIVIL JURISDICTION

a. General Civil Litigation

A description of state civil jurisdiction in Indian country is best begun by establishing what the state courts *cannot* do. Williams v. Lee, 358 U.S. 217 (1959), held that state courts had no jurisdiction over a claim by a non-Indian against an Indian when the claim arose in Indian country. The assertion of state jurisdiction in those circumstances would infringe "on the right of reservation Indians to make their own laws and be governed by them." State jurisdiction was permitted only "where essential tribal relations were not involved and where the rights of Indians would not be jeopardized * * *." 358 U.S. at 219–20; see Iowa Mut. Ins. Co. v. LaPlante, 480 U.S. 9 (1987). Moreover, Congress by passing Public Law 280 had provided a method for the states to assume jurisdiction and the state in *Williams* had not availed itself of that method.

It is noteworthy that the opinion in Williams v. Lee drew its jurisdictional line between Indians and non-Indians. It said:

Today the Navajo Courts of Indian Offenses exercise broad criminal and civil jurisdiction which covers suits by outsiders against Indian defendants. No Federal Act has given state courts jurisdiction over such controversies.

358 U.S. at 222. As a consequence of this rationale, courts applying Williams v. Lee for many years thereafter made no distinction between member and nonmember Indians. The Supreme Court, however, first made such a distinction in United States v. Wheeler, 435 U.S. 313 (1978), a criminal double jeopardy case. Then in Washington v. Confederated Tribes of the Colville Indian Reservation, 447 U.S. 134 (1980), the Court permitted a state to impose a sales tax upon Indians on a reservation other than their own. *Colville* stated that the imposition of the tax would not "contravene the principle of tribal self-government, for the simple reason that nonmembers are not constituents of the governing Tribe." 447 U.S. at 162. That language seemed calculated to avoid the impact of Williams v. Lee, supra, insofar as nonmember Indians are concerned. Then, in 1990, the Supreme Court decided that tribes as domestic dependent sovereigns had no power to exercise criminal jurisdiction over Indians who were not members of the tribe. Duro v. Reina, 495 U.S. 676 (1990). Congress promptly overturned that ruling, however, recognizing and affirming "the inherent power of Indian tribes * * * to exercise criminal jurisdiction over all Indians * * *." 25 U.S.C.A. § 1301(2).

That action of Congress presumably settled the matter for purposes of criminal jurisdiction, but the Supreme Court in a subsequent civil case held that tribes had no jurisdiction over a tort action between "nonmembers" arising out of an automobile accident on a state right-of-way through the reservation. Strate v. A–1 Contractors, 520 U.S. 438, 442 (1997). In *Strate*, the distinction was not necessary to the decision, because both parties were non-Indians, but the language of the opinion indicates the Supreme Court's preference for distinguishing between the tribe's power over its own members and its power (or presumptive lack of it) over non-members, Indian or not. Although it is not clear how far the Supreme Court will go in applying that distinction when it is crucial to a jurisdictional decision in a civil case, it is no longer safe to assume that a tribe's civil authority over nonmember Indians is the same as its authority over its members. For that reason, much of the following discussion will refer to "members" as the group over which the tribe has indisputable civil authority. The converse term "nonmembers" is not always employed in opposition to it, however, because of the uncertainty over their jurisdictional status in various contexts. (*Strate* is further discussed under Tribal Court Jurisdiction, subsection 3(a) below).

Strate involved only nonmembers on both sides, but it phrased the question for decision as whether a tribal court could "entertain a civil action against" nonmembers when the claim arose on a state right-of-way. *Strate*, 520 U.S. at 442. "Against" focuses on the defendant's status to determine jurisdiction (as did Williams v. Lee). *Strate* also described tribal interests very narrowly. Consequently, one court of appeals has held that tribal courts could not entertain actions by tribal members against nonmembers when the claims arose on rights-of-way within the reservations. Burlington Northern R. Co. v. Red Wolf, 196 F.3d 1059 (9th Cir.1999); Wilson v. Marchington, 127 F.3d 805 (9th Cir.1997). The state accordingly had jurisdiction. If the tribal members were the defendants, however, Williams v. Lee would require the actions to be brought in tribal court. It is not yet clear whether *Strate* forecasts erosion of that rule for non-Indian fee lands and state rights-of-way.

It should be noted that the rule of Williams v. Lee deprives the state courts of *subject matter* jurisdiction; the Court assumed for purposes of its decision that valid service of process had occurred. As a consequence, the parties cannot confer jurisdiction on the state by consent. Even where the tribal council itself consents to the state's exercising concurrent jurisdiction, the state is precluded from doing so in the absence of a formal assumption of jurisdiction pursuant to Public Law 280 (See Chapter VIII). Kennerly v. District Court, 400 U.S. 423 (1971).

Because *Williams* precludes the state courts from assuming jurisdiction when a non-Indian sues a tribal member (or possibly any Indian) over a claim arising in Indian country, it follows even more strongly that the state has no jurisdiction over such claims when both parties are tribal members. E.g., Fisher v. District Court, 424 U.S. 382, 386 (1976); Sigana v. Bailey, 282 Minn. 367, 164 N.W.2d 886 (1969); Gourneau v. Smith, 207 N.W.2d 256 (N.D. 1973).

One might be tempted to conclude from *Williams* that the state is precluded from taking jurisdiction over claims by tribal members against non-Indians, when the claims arise in Indian country. That conclusion would be incorrect; the Supreme Court has said that nothing in Williams v. Lee prevents the maintenance of such actions in state court, and they have traditionally been brought there. Three Affiliated Tribes of the Fort Berthold Reservation v. Wold Engineering, P.C., 467 U.S. 138, 148 (1984) (*Fort Berthold I*). In the *Fort Berthold* litigation, the State of North Dakota attempted to deny state jurisdiction over actions brought by tribes or tribal Indians unless the tribe had consented to state jurisdiction over all claims arising on its reservation and had waived its sovereign immunity. The Supreme Court, in an unusual application of preemption doctrine, held that Public Law 280 precluded the state from denying jurisdiction in that manner. Three Affiliated Tribes of the Fort Berthold Reservation v. Wold Engineering, 476 U.S. 877 (1986) (*Fort Berthold II*). See Chapter VIII, Section F, infra. Several state decisions have also guaranteed the access of Indian plaintiffs to state court by invoking the equal protection clause. Paiz v. Hughes, 76 N.M. 562, 417 P.2d 51 (1966); Bonnet v. Seekins, 126 Mont. 24, 243 P.2d 317 (1952). In fact, on some reservations the Indian plaintiff has no alternative; a number of tribal codes provide for civil jurisdiction over non-Indian defendants only when they stipulate to it. In summary, then, it is clear that state courts have jurisdiction over suits against non-Indians (and perhaps nonmembers) no matter where the claim arose. Indeed, even when the claim arises in Indian country, state jurisdiction is increasingly becoming exclusive because recent Supreme Court decisions are severely reducing tribal court jurisdiction over cases against nonmembers. See Subsection 2, immediately below. State court process may be served on a non-Indian defendant in Indian country in connection with a state-court suit. See Langford v. Monteith, 102 U.S. 145 (1880); State v. Zaman, 194 Ariz. 442, 984 P.2d 528 (1999).

It is not clear what effect, if any, the exhaustion requirement of Iowa Mut. Ins. Co. v. LaPlante, 480 U.S. 9 (1987), has on state court actions against non-Indians or nonmembers. In *LaPlante*, the Supreme Court ruled that a federal court should stay its hand, in a case where it had diversity jurisdiction, in favor of parallel tribal court proceedings against a non-Indian defendant. At least one circuit court has applied *LaPlante* in a situation where there were no parallel proceedings in tribal court; it has required an Indian plaintiff to exhaust tribal court remedies before bringing a diversity case against a non-Indian in federal court. Wellman v. Chevron U.S.A., Inc., 815 F.2d 577 (9th Cir.1987); see also Crawford v. Genuine Parts Co., 947 F.2d 1405 (9th Cir.1991). If the federal courts in diversity cases must require exhaustion, it is difficult to see why the state courts should not require it as well. At least one has agreed. Drumm v. Brown, 245 Conn. 657, 716 A.2d 50 (1998). There remains a tension, however, between the thrust of *LaPlante*, with its emphasis on deference to tribal court jurisdiction, and *Berthold I*, in which the Supreme Court stated that it failed "to see how the exercise of state-court jurisdiction in this case [brought by an Indian tribe against a non-Indian] would interfere with the right of tribal Indians to govern themselves under their own laws." 467 U.S. at 148. Until that tension is resolved, it is difficult to predict whether the Indian plaintiff will routinely be faced with an exhaustion requirement when suing a non-Indian in state court.

One result of the present division of civil jurisdiction is that the court in which a case is heard will often be determined by who sues first. If a tribal member and a non-Indian (or, possibly, a nonmember Indian) have a dispute centered in Indian country (putting aside disputes arising on fee lands), and the non-Indian wishes to sue, his or her sole remedy is in tribal court, under Williams v. Lee. If the tribal member wishes to sue, he or she may sue in state court (and under some tribal codes will be precluded from suing in tribal court).

If the tribal member does in fact sue in state court, the question arises whether that court has jurisdiction to entertain a counterclaim against him or her. The issue has not been settled, but the most sensible rule would probably be that "compulsory" counterclaims—those arising from the same transaction or occurrence as the main claim—are within the jurisdiction of the state court. The tribal plaintiff conceded as much in *Fort Berthold II*, 476 U.S.

at 891. It is true that under Williams v. Lee the state court seems to lack subject matter jurisdiction for such claims, and that such a deficiency cannot normally be cured by the fiction that a plaintiff in bringing suit "consents" to counterclaims. On the other hand, it seems unacceptably wasteful to litigate the same fact situation twice, and the intrusion upon tribal self-government caused by a counterclaim would seem to be minimal when the controversy is already being litigated in state court. Whether or not the state is allowed to take jurisdiction of compulsory counterclaims, it seems quite clear from Williams v. Lee that it should have no jurisdiction over "permissive" counterclaims against a tribal member that are unrelated to the main claim and that arose in Indian country. The exclusive forum for pursuing the tribal member in regard to those separate matters is tribal court.

State courts also have jurisdiction over claims against Indian defendants (whether the plaintiff is Indian or non-Indian) that arise outside of Indian country, as when an Indian leaves the reservation and enters a commercial transaction to be performed off-reservation. See Smith Plumbing Co. v. Aetna Casualty & Surety Co., 149 Ariz. 524, 531, 720 P.2d 499, 506 (1986). Such cases often present the question whether the state may initiate suit by serving process upon the Indian on the reservation. While the traditional view was that state process did not run to Indians in Indian country, modern decisions have split on this point. For example, such service was upheld in State Securities, Inc. v.

Anderson, 84 N.M. 629, 506 P.2d 786 (1973), but struck down in Francisco v. State, 113 Ariz. 427, 556 P.2d 1 (1976). Authority is similarly divided over the question whether a valid state judgment against an Indian arising from an off-reservation claim can be directly executed in Indian country. Such enforcement was permitted in Little Horn State Bank v. Stops, 170 Mont. 510, 555 P.2d 211 (1976), but denied in Annis v. Dewey County Bank, 335 F.Supp. 133 (D.S.D.1971). Enforcement of such a judgment by garnishing a non-Indian creditor on the reservation was held invalid in Joe v. Marcum, 621 F.2d 358 (10th Cir.1980). See also United States v. Morris, 754 F.Supp. 185 (D.N.M. 1991).

An all-or-nothing approach to these issues of service of process and enforcement of judgments presents a dilemma. The state should have some way of initiating a lawsuit over which it has jurisdiction even if the Indian defendant has returned to Indian country. On the other hand, direct execution of a resulting judgment on the reservation does have substantial potential of interfering with tribal self-government. Joe v. Marcum, supra; but see Natewa v. Natewa, 84 N.M. 69, 499 P.2d 691 (1972). The best solution to the problem of service of process in Indian country is to permit the state to exercise long-arm jurisdiction by mail service as it does over defendants located out of state. See Dixon v. Picopa Constr. Co., 160 Ariz. 251, 772 P.2d 1104 (1989). The least intrusive way to enforce a state judgment would be to sue on it in tribal court (or to enforce it by registration if the tribe permits that expeditious approach). Recognition of judgments is further discussed in Section G, near the end of this Chapter.

b. Divorce

As Williams v. Lee, 358 U.S. 217 (1959), would suggest, state courts have no jurisdiction to grant divorces when both parties are Indians domiciled in Indian country. Whyte v. District Court, 140 Colo. 334, 346 P.2d 1012 (1959); State ex rel. Stewart v. District Court, 187 Mont. 209, 609 P.2d 290 (1980); In re Marriage of Limpy, 195 Mont. 314, 636 P.2d 266 (1981). When both parties are Indians domiciled outside of Indian country, however, the state court does have jurisdiction. United States ex rel. Cobell v. Cobell, 503 F.2d 790 (9th Cir.1974).

As in other civil cases, state courts have jurisdiction to divorce when both parties are non-Indians, even though they are domiciled in Indian country. There is little chance that such jurisdiction can intrude upon tribal self-government.

The question of jurisdiction over divorces between Indian and non-Indian spouses in Indian country is far from settled. Because the domicile and status of the *plaintiff* was once regarded as the sole basis for state jurisdiction in divorce, the states tended to accept jurisdiction over divorces brought by non-Indians but not by Indians when both were domiciled in Indian country. This tendency may continue even in states that now follow the Uniform Marriage and Divorce Act, which bases jurisdiction on the domicile of either the plaintiff or the defendant. With the option of focusing on the status and domicile of either party, state divorce jurisdiction could follow the pattern of other civil cases. In that event, it could be argued that state courts ought not to accept divorces by non-Indians against Indians in such cases because of the possibility of interfering with the jurisdiction of tribal courts. One court has held that the state lacks jurisdiction in such a case, at least when the tribal court had already exercised jurisdiction. Byzewski v. Byzewski, 429 N.W.2d 394 (N.D. 1988). Another court held that the tribe had jurisdiction and expressed no opinion on whether it was exclusive of the state. Sanders v. Robinson, 864 F.2d 630 (9th Cir.1988). It might also be argued by analogy to other civil cases that the Indian has an equal protection right to utilize state court to divorce a non-Indian. There is virtually no authority addressing that question, however. (Further problems arising from divorces between Indians and non-Indians in Indian country are discussed under Tribal Civil Jurisdiction, subsection 2(b), below.)

Because decrees for alimony, child support and child custody pursuant to divorce require *in personam* jurisdiction over the defendant, the jurisdictional rules for such orders are the same as those for general civil litigation, discussed in subsection (a) immediately above.

c. Adoption and Child Custody

Jurisdiction over adoption and custody of Indian children is now governed by the Indian Child Welfare Act of 1978, 25 U.S.C.A. §§ 1901–1963. "Custody" proceedings covered by the Act include foster care placement, termination of parental rights, and pre-adoptive and adoptive placement, but not custody proceedings between parents in connection with divorce. The Act was designed to protect the integrity of the tribes and the heritage of Indian children by inhibiting the practice of removing those children from their families and tribes to raise them as non-Indians. See Mississippi Band of Choctaw Indians v. Holyfield, 490 U.S. 30, 32–37 (1989).

Under the Act, state courts have no jurisdiction over adoption or custody of Indian children who are domiciled or reside within the reservation of their tribe, unless some federal law (such as Public Law 280) confers such jurisdiction. "Domicile" under the Act is a matter of federal law; a legitimate child takes the domicile of its parents and an illegitimate child takes the domicile of its mother. *Holyfield*, 490 U.S. at 43–48. That construction defeats a state rule that children born off-reservation and given up for adoption by their parents were not domiciled on the reservation. The Act also provides that state courts have no jurisdiction over children who are wards of a tribal court, regardless of the domicile or residence of the children. Jurisdiction in these cases lies exclusively with the tribe.

State courts do have jurisdiction over adoption and custody of Indian children not domiciled or residing on their tribe's reservation, Navajo Nation v. Confederated Tribes and Bands of the Yakama Nation, 331 F.3d 1041 (9th Cir.2003), but the Act places important qualifications upon that jurisdiction. In any proceeding for foster care placement of such children or for termination of parental rights, the state court, "in the absence of good cause to the contrary" and in the absence of objection by either parent, must transfer the proceeding to tribal court upon the petition of either parent, the child's Indian custodian, or the tribe. The tribe may decline such a transfer. 25 U.S.C.A. § 1911(b). The states are required to give tribal adoption and custody orders full faith and credit. 25 U.S.C.A. § 1911(d).

The Indian Child Welfare Act also provides priorities for state courts to follow in placement of Indian children, with preference first to the child's extended family, then to members of his or her tribe, then to Indian families generally. Preferences are also given to tribally licensed institutions. The tribe may override these preferences by adopting its own list. 25 U.S.C.A. § 1915. The Act also contains numerous other provisions that should be consulted in connection with any adoption or custody proceeding involving Indian children. The BIA has published guidelines for state courts in administering the Act, which are not binding on the courts but often are applied by them. See, e.g., In the Matter of M.R.G., 314 Mont. 396, 66 P.3d 312 (2003). There is a large and growing body of precedent applying the Act to a multiplicity of child welfare fact situations.

d. Probate

State courts have no jurisdiction over the probate of Indian trust property; such jurisdiction is exclusively federal. In other respects, authority is sparse, but an application of Williams v. Lee, 358 U.S. 217 (1959), would prevent the state from exercising jurisdiction over the probate of non-trust movables of a tribal member (and possibly any Indian) who died domiciled in Indian country.

It also follows that state courts have jurisdiction over non-trust estates of Indians who died domiciled outside of Indian country, and over the estates of non-Indians (and perhaps nonmember Indians) whether or not domiciled in Indian country, at least where the heirs are non-Indian. It might well be argued that where a non-Indian dies domiciled in Indian country and leaves Indian heirs, an exercise of state jurisdiction has the potential of interfering with internal tribal affairs. Many tribes, however, leave such matters to the states (effectively if not legitimately) by providing for probate only of estates of Indian decedents.

State courts also have jurisdiction over probate of any land outside of Indian country, and presumably may exercise ancillary jurisdiction over movables located out of Indian country which are part of the estate of an Indian who died domiciled in Indian country. The state's jurisdiction in the latter case would be ancillary to the primary jurisdiction of the tribe.

2. TRIBAL CIVIL JURISDICTION

a. General Civil Litigation

The civil jurisdiction of tribal courts, unlike their criminal jurisdiction, is subject to no statutory limit on the relief the courts may grant. When a case calls for it, there is nothing to prevent a tribal court from entering a multi-million dollar judgment. Cf. Burlington Northern R. Co. v. Red Wolf, 106 F.3d 868 (9th Cir.1997), vacated, 522 U.S. 801 (1997).

With regard to subject matter, tribal courts have exclusive jurisdiction over a suit by any person against an Indian for a claim arising in Indian country. Williams v. Lee, 358 U.S. 217 (1959). Necessarily, then, the tribe has exclusive jurisdiction over disputes between tribal members arising on the reservation. Jones v. Billy, 798 So.2d 1238 (Miss. 2001). It also has exclusive jurisdiction over wholly internal tribal subject matter, such as membership disputes. Smith v. Babbitt, 100 F.3d 556 (8th Cir.1996). The exclusive jurisdiction recognized by Williams v. Lee had always been assumed to extend to suits against Indians from recognized tribes other than the one upon whose reservation the claim arose, but the Supreme Court in recent years has rendered this assumption unsafe. In Duro v. Reina, 495 U.S. 676 (1990), the Court held that tribal courts could not exercise criminal jurisdiction over nonmember Indians. Congress overruled that decision, 25 U.S.C.A. § 1301(2), but that statute did not address civil jurisdiction. In Washington v. Confederated Tribes of the Colville Indian Reservation,

447 U.S. 134 (1980), the Court permitted a state to impose a sales tax on Indians making purchases on a reservation other than their own. The Court stated that "[f]or most practical purposes those Indians stand on the same footing as non-Indians resident on the reservation." 447 U.S. at 161. Then, in Strate v. A–1 Contractors, 520 U.S. 438 (1997), the Court held that a tribal court had no jurisdiction over a dispute between "nonmembers" arising out of a vehicle accident on a state right-of-way within the reservation. In *Strate*, the nonmembers were non-Indians, but the Court talked only of nonmembers and tribal members in drawing a line of adjudicatory jurisdiction.

The line *Strate* drew is not without its problems. The Court announced a new principle that "a tribe's adjudicative jurisdiction does not exceed its legislative jurisdiction" and stated that, apart from the two exceptions set forth in *Montana*, infra, the civil authority of tribes and their courts did not extend to activities of nonmembers on fee lands. *Strate*, 520 U.S. at 453. One difficulty with this formulation is that, because Congress overruled *Duro*, the tribe does have criminal legislative authority over nonmember Indians in Indian country. 25 U.S.C.A. § 1301(2). Indian country includes fee lands and rights-of-way within a reservation. 18 U.S.C.A. § 1151(a). Thus, the tribal court would not be exceeding the tribe's legislative jurisdiction if it entertained litigation between nonmember Indians arising from an accident on a right-of-way. If *Strate* was referring only to the tribe's *civil* legislative authority, then the tribe's civil jurisdiction appears to be narrower than its criminal jurisdiction—the opposite of the condition the Court has previously said to prevail. See National Farmers Union Ins. Cos. v. Crow Tribe, 471 U.S. 845, 854–55 & nn. 16 & 17 (1985).

In addition to their exclusive jurisdiction over reservation-based claims against tribal members, tribal courts also probably have the power to adjudicate claims against tribal members domiciled or present within their territory even though those claims arose outside of Indian country. Many tribes, however, have chosen not to exercise such jurisdiction.

Much recent litigation has been concerned with the power of tribal courts to entertain claims against non-Indian (or nonmember) defendants that arise in Indian country. For years the tribes made no attempt to exercise that power by compulsion; some tribal codes still provide for such jurisdiction only when the non-Indian defendant stipulates to it. Recently, however, numbers of tribes have revised their codes to permit their tribal courts generally to exercise jurisdiction over non-Indians for reservation-based claims. A non-Indian defendant contested such jurisdiction in National Farmers Union Ins. Cos. v. Crow Tribe, 471 U.S. 845 (1985). The Supreme Court did not resolve the question, but deferred to the tribal court so that it could determine its own jurisdiction in the first instance. The Court made it clear, however, that Oliphant v. Suquamish Indian Tribe, 435 U.S. 191 (1978), which held that the tribes had no criminal jurisdiction over non-Indians, did not control the question of the tribes' civil jurisdiction.

In Iowa Mut. Ins. Co. v. LaPlante, 480 U.S. 9 (1987), the Supreme Court similarly stayed its diversity jurisdiction to permit a tribal court to determine its own jurisdiction over parallel litigation. Here again, the Supreme Court did not actually decide whether the tribal court had power to entertain a case against a non-Indian defendant, but its language was very affirmative:

> Tribal authority over the activities of non-Indians on reservation lands is an important part of tribal sovereignty. * * * Civil jurisdiction over such activities presumptively lies in the tribal courts unless affirmatively limited by a specific treaty provision or federal statute.

Id. at 18.

This passage encouraged many tribes, and numbers of lower courts, to assume that tribal courts could exercise general civil jurisdiction over all reservation-based litigation, particularly if one of the parties was the tribe or a tribal member. The seeds of a narrower view had already been planted, however, in Montana v. United States, 450 U.S. 544 (1981). *Montana* held that an Indian tribe had no authority to regulate hunting and fishing by non-Indians on non-Indian-owned fee land within the reservation. The Court stated that the tribe's domestic dependent sovereignty extended only to self-government and the control of internal relations.

Hunting and fishing by non-Indians on non-Indian fee lands was neither. *Montana* at one point went considerably farther, however, and announced a general proposition that "the inherent sovereign powers of an Indian tribe do not extend to the activities of nonmembers of the tribe." The only exceptions were (1) that a tribe could regulate "activities of nonmembers who enter consensual relationships with the tribe or its members," as through commercial dealings, and (2) that a tribe could exercise "civil authority over the conduct of non-Indians on fee lands within its reservation when that conduct threatens or has some direct effect on the political integrity, the economic security, or the health or welfare of the tribe." *Montana*, 450 U.S. at 565–66.

The Supreme Court carried *Montana* a step farther in 1997, when it held that a tribal court had no jurisdiction over litigation between nonmembers arising out of a vehicle accident on a state highway within a reservation. Strate v. A–1 Contractors, 520 U.S. 438 (1997), mentioned above. The Court narrowed the statement in *LaPlante* that civil jurisdiction over non-Indian activities within a reservation "presumptively lies in the tribal courts"; that statement, according to *Strate*, meant nothing more than that the tribal court presumptively had jurisdiction over those non-Indian activities that the tribe could regulate under *Montana*. The right-of-way, which was open to the public, was the equivalent of non-Indian-owned fee land and the tribe therefore lacked jurisdiction. *Montana*'s exceptions did not apply: the nonmembers were not in a consensual relationship with the tribe or its members, and their activity on the highway did not threaten or have a direct effect on the political integrity, economic security, or health or welfare of the tribe. *Strate*, 520 U.S. at 456–59. The Court also stated that the second *Montana* exception should be read narrowly, in light of *Montana*'s description of tribal authority as the power to punish tribal offenders, to determine membership, and to regulate domestic relations and inheritance for members.

Strate was a forerunner of further restrictions on tribal jurisdiction over nonmembers. It has been applied to preclude tribal court jurisdiction over actions by *tribal members* against nonmembers arising from accidents on rights-of-way. Burlington Northern R. Co. v. Red Wolf, 196 F.3d 1059 (9th Cir.1999); Wilson v. Marchington, 127 F.3d 805 (9th Cir.1997). A consensual relationship between an injured Indian passenger of a car and a nonmember driver was held insufficient to qualify for the first *Montana* exception because it was of a personal rather than commercial nature. Boxx v. Long Warrior, 265 F.3d 771 (9th Cir.2001). *Strate* also stated that it was expressing no view on the governing law or proper forum when such an accident occurs on a tribal road. (The Ninth Circuit later held that a tribal court had jurisdiction over a suit against a nonmember Indian over an accident on a tribal road. McDonald v. Means, 309 F.3d 530 (9th Cir. 2002) (amended opinion)). The major conceptual issue left on the table by *Strate* was whether *Mon-*

tana should be treated as an exception, confined to non-Indian fee lands and their equivalent, to the general sovereignty that a tribe may exercise over its reservation, or whether *Montana* now provides the all-encompassing formula for tribal jurisdiction over nonmembers.

It was not long before the Supreme Court weighed in on that question. Atkinson Trading Co. v. Shirley, 532 U.S. 645 (2001), held that the tribe had no power to tax hotel occupancy by non-Indians on fee land within the Navajo reservation. The Court clearly regarded *Montana* not as an exception to presumed power of a tribe over its reservation but as a "general rule that Indian tribes lack civil authority over nonmembers on non-Indian fee land." Id. at 654. *Montana*'s exceptions were narrowly construed lest they "swallow the rule." Id. at 655. Then, in Nevada v. Hicks, 533 U.S. 353 (2001), the Court for the first time applied to trust land *Montana*'s presumption against tribal authority over nonmembers. The Court held that the tribe had no power to regulate a search by state officers investigating off-reservation crime even though the search was of an Indian-owned residence on tribal trust land. Because the tribe had no legislative jurisdiction over the state officers, the tribal court could not entertain a suit against them brought by the offended tribal member.

With the *Montana* "rule" broadly applicable throughout reservations, the extent of tribal regulation and tribal court jurisdiction over nonmembers is subject to great limitation. If the second *Montana* exception were broadly interpreted, so that most events within a reservation were deemed to affect tribal interests, the *Montana* rule would not cause much of a dent in tribal authority. But *Strate*, *Atkinson* and *Hicks* dictate a narrow interpretation of the second *Montana* exception. The first exception does permit tribal regulation of most sizeable reservation businesses and extractive industries, see FMC v. Shoshone–Bannock Tribes, 905 F.2d 1311 (9th Cir.1990), which will have leases or other consensual arrangements with the tribe, but still leaves much nonmember activity untouched. The recent line of Supreme Court decisions leaves the civil authority of the tribes considerably diminished from what it was understood to be a decade ago.

Hicks also held that tribal courts did not qualify as courts of general jurisdiction, which would permit them to entertain general federal civil claims such as those arising under 42 U.S.C.A. § 1983. According to the Supreme Court, tribal courts could not be courts of general jurisdiction because *Strate* had held that "a tribe's inherent adjudicative jurisdiction over nonmembers is at most only as broad as its legislative jurisdiction." *Hicks*, 533 U.S. at 367. It remains to be seen how much this holding will constrain tribal courts in entertaining federal causes of action. In Sharber v. Spirit Mountain Gaming Inc., 343 F.3d 974 (9th Cir.2003), a federal court was ordered to stay its hand in an action under the Family and Medical Leave Act to permit a tribal court to determine whether it had jurisdiction over such a claim. Tribal courts may be granted jurisdiction to apply other federal law in specific statutes such as the Indian Child Welfare Act, however. See 25 U.S.C.A. § 1911(a).

It will be somewhat anomalous if *Strate, Atkinson* and *Hicks* ultimately hamper the ability of tribal courts to entertain the typical reservation-based claim brought by an Indian plaintiff against a nonmember. When the tribal member is the defendant in such a case, tribal jurisdiction is *exclusive* under Williams v. Lee, 358 U.S. 217 (1959). When the subject of the litigation is exactly the same, but the tribal member is the plaintiff instead of the defendant, the tribal interest is very nearly as strong. It should certainly be strong enough to support concurrent jurisdiction. See Stock West, Inc. v. Confederated Tribes of the Colville Reservation, 873 F.2d 1221, 1228 (9th Cir.1989).

Frequently, when a nonmember (usually a non-Indian) is sued in tribal court, he or she will bring an action in federal court either to challenge the tribal court's jurisdiction or to attempt to litigate the underlying dispute in federal court. In such cases, federal courts have regularly abstained or stayed their proceedings, on the authority of *National Farmers Union* and *LaPlante*, supra, to permit the tribal court to determine in the first instance whether it has jurisdiction. Thus a party seeking in federal court to challenge a tribal court's colorable jurisdiction must first exhaust tribal remedies. Allstate Indemnity Co. v. Stump, 191 F.3d 1071, amended, 197 F.3d 1031 (9th Cir.1999); see also Brown v. Washoe Housing Authority, 835 F.2d

1327 (10th Cir.1988); Bruce H. Lien Co. v. Three Affiliated Tribes, 93 F.3d 1412 (8th Cir.1996). Exhaustion is required in a suit where there is a motion to compel arbitration under the Federal Arbitration Act. Gaming World International, Ltd. v. White Earth Band of Chippewa Indians, 317 F.3d 840, 849–52 (8th Cir.2003). Even the United States has been required to exhaust. United States v. Tsosie, 92 F.3d 1037 (10th Cir.1996). Exhaustion must include any tribal appellate remedies. Kerr–McGee Corp. v. Farley, 115 F.3d 1498 (10th Cir. 1997). Tribal courts, therefore, are frequently called upon to decide in the first instance a question of federal Indian law: whether the tribal court has jurisdiction in a case involving nonmembers. If the tribal court decides it has jurisdiction, it proceeds with the case. If the federal court later agrees that the tribe had jurisdiction, it cannot relitigate the merits of the dispute. *LaPlante*, 480 U.S. at 19. In one case involving a dispute over a reservation boundary, however, a tribal court's decision concerning the location of the boundary necessarily decided both the merits and jurisdiction. In reviewing the jurisdictional question (whether the boundary decision was clearly erroneous), the federal court necessarily revisited the merits. Enlow v. Moore, 134 F.3d 993 (10th Cir.1998).

National Farmers Union set forth some exceptions to the requirement of exhaustion of tribal remedies. Exhaustion is not required when (1) the assertion of tribal jurisdiction is motivated by a desire to harass or is otherwise in bad faith; (2) the challenged tribal exercise of authority is patently violative of express jurisdictional prohibitions, or (3) exhaustion would be futile for lack of an opportunity to challenge the tribal court's jurisdiction. *National Farmers Union*, 471 U.S. at 856 n.21. The Supreme Court has added a gloss that immensely broadens these exceptions, however. In *Strate*, the Court ruled that, in cases concerning nonmembers on fee land subject to *Montana*'s rule precluding tribal court jurisdiction, the "otherwise applicable exhaustion requirement" does not apply because it would serve no purpose except delay. *Strate*, 520 U.S. at 459 n.14. *Hicks* then applied this same exception to the exhaustion requirement when trust land and an Indian plaintiff were involved. *Hicks*, 533 U.S. at 369. Because the most common cases formerly calling for exhaustion were those involving application of *Montana*, the rulings in *Strate* and *Hicks* may have greatly diminished the operation of the exhaustion requirement as a practical matter. Much will depend on whether *Strate* and *Hicks* are viewed as instances when the tribe was *clearly* without jurisdiction under *Montana*, leaving little need for exhaustion, or whether they exemplify a general rule that *Montana* issues are never subject to exhaustion. It is difficult to regard *Strate* and *Hicks* as clear cases of the absence of tribal jurisdiction.

The Supreme Court created another exception to exhaustion in El Paso Natural Gas Co. v. Neztsosie, 526 U.S. 473 (1999). That case involved a highly unusual provision in the Price–Anderson Act that transforms any public liability action arising from nuclear accident into a federal claim removable from state to federal court. The Supreme Court held that this provision for removal as of right indicated an unmistakable congressional preference for a federal forum for this particular kind of case. It was accordingly improper for a lower federal court to require tribal exhaustion of the question whether the tribal court had jurisdiction over the Price–Anderson claims. In so ruling, the Court recited the exhaustion rules of *National Farmers Union* and *LaPlante.* It also stated that its decision was not to be interpreted as precluding tribal courts from addressing federal preemption defenses in the first instance. *Neztsosie,* 526 U.S. at 485 n.7. The *Neztsosie* decision is therefore a relatively narrow one if it remains confined to its own terms.

At least one federal court of appeals has required exhaustion in diversity cases brought by Indian plaintiffs even though there were no proceedings pending in tribal court. Wellman v. Chevron U.S.A., Inc., 815 F.2d 577 (9th Cir.1987); Crawford v. Genuine Parts Co., 947 F.2d 1405 (9th Cir.1991). If the federal courts must defer to tribal courts to avoid undue interference with tribal adjudication of claims by tribal members against nonmembers, it is difficult to see why state courts should not be required to do the same. See Drumm v. Brown, 245 Conn. 657, 716 A.2d 50 (1998). On the other hand, the Supreme Court stated in *Berthold I* that it failed to see how such state court actions interfered with tribal self-government. 467 U.S. at 148. It is likely, therefore, that tribal courts will continue to share any jurisdiction over nonmember defendants with the state courts, with the possibility that some requirement of abstention or exhaustion will one day be imposed on the state courts in favor of the tribes.

Because the tribes until recently have been very cautious in asserting civil jurisdiction, there has been little litigation dealing with service of tribal process. Tribal process is clearly effective when served within tribal territory. Abode service upon absent Indians, and possibly even non-Indians, domiciled within tribal territory should also be permissible. Direct service outside of tribal territory will almost certainly be ineffective to confer jurisdiction by itself. There appears to be no reason, however, why a tribe may not exercise long-arm jurisdiction over absent defendants for claims arising from activities within the tribe's territory. See Red Fox v. Hettich, 494 N.W.2d 638, 645 (S.D. 1993). Service upon the absent defendant can then be effected by mail or some form of substituted service, assuming that the parties or subject matter otherwise qualify for an exercise of tribal jurisdiction.

b. Divorce

The tribal courts have exclusive jurisdiction over divorces between Indians domiciled in Indian country. Whyte v. District Court, 140 Colo. 334, 346 P.2d 1012 (1959); State ex rel. Stewart v. District

Court, 187 Mont. 209, 609 P.2d 290 (1980). They may also have jurisdiction concurrent with the state over divorces between Indians domiciled off-reservation who remain tribal members and submit themselves to the jurisdiction of the tribal court. In other words, membership as well as domicile might suffice as a jurisdictional base for a tribal divorce.

Divorce between Indian and non-Indian spouses domiciled in Indian country presents several unresolved jurisdictional problems. Williams v. Lee and its progeny would suggest that the non-Indian who seeks to divorce an Indian would have to go to tribal court, while an Indian who seeks to divorce a non-Indian would have a right to use the state courts as well as the tribal courts. The analogy to Williams v. Lee is difficult to make, however, because states have traditionally based divorce jurisdiction on the domicile and status of the *plaintiff*. There is accordingly a tendency for state courts to accept jurisdiction of divorce cases brought by non-Indians even though they are domiciled in Indian country and seek a divorce from an Indian. See Byzewski v. Byzewski, 429 N.W.2d 394 (N.D. 1988). Yet such an exercise of jurisdiction is surely just as much an interference with tribal self-government as state jurisdiction was in the ordinary civil case of Williams v. Lee. It would therefore be preferable for such cases to be left to exclusive tribal jurisdiction, but it cannot be said that this preference is presently the law with respect to divorce. The tribe's jurisdiction remains exclusive, however, over the disposition of trust lands in divorce proceedings, In re

Marriage of Wellman, 258 Mont. 131, 852 P.2d 559 (1993), or orders of custody and support requiring personal jurisdiction over the Indian defendant domiciled in Indian country, *Byzewski*, 429 N.W.2d at 400.

Another problem of jurisdiction arises from the fact that a number of tribal codes do not base jurisdiction, as some states still do, on the domicile and status of the plaintiff, but instead treat divorce the same as other civil cases and provide for jurisdiction only over Indian *defendants*. Jurisdiction under those codes extends to non-Indian defendants only if they consent. The result in such cases is that an Indian wishing to divorce an unconsenting non-Indian cannot do so in tribal court. If the state is one that bases jurisdiction solely on the domicile and status of the plaintiff, the state courts are likely to refuse jurisdiction over the same case on the ground that the plaintiff is an Indian domiciled in Indian country. The Indian plaintiff is then without a forum. The best solution for this problem is for such tribes to modify their codes, as some have done, so that their courts can accept cases brought by Indian plaintiffs domiciled in Indian country whether or not the non-Indian defendant consents to jurisdiction. One court of appeals has held that the tribal court has jurisdiction in such a case. Sanders v. Robinson, 864 F.2d 630 (9th Cir.1988).

As in other civil cases, tribal courts probably do not have jurisdiction to divorce when both parties are non-Indian and no Indian interests are involved, even though the parties may be domiciled within the court's geographical territory.

c. Adoption and Child Custody

The Indian Child Welfare Act of 1978, 25 U.S.C.A. §§ 1901–1963, governs adoption and child custody proceedings involving Indian children. There is a large and growing body of precedent applying the Act in various factual circumstances. Custody proceedings subject to the Act include foster care placement, termination of parental rights, and pre-adoptive and adoptive placement, but not parental custody pursuant to divorce. 25 U.S.C.A. § 1903(1); see Comanche Indian Tribe of Okla. v. Hovis, 53 F.3d 298 (10th Cir.1995). Under the Act, tribal courts have exclusive jurisdiction over adoption and custody of Indian children who reside or are domiciled within the reservation of their tribe, unless some federal law (such as Public Law 280) provides to the contrary. 25 U.S.C.A. § 1911(a); see also, Fisher v. District Court, 424 U.S. 382 (1976). "Domicile" under the Act is a matter of federal law; a legitimate child takes the domicile of its parents and an illegitimate child takes the domicile of its mother. Mississippi Band of Choctaw Indians v. Holyfield, 490 U.S. 30, 43–48 (1989). That construction defeats a state rule that children born off-reservation and given up for adoption by their parents were not domiciled on the reservation. Tribes also have exclusive jurisdiction over such proceedings involving any Indian child who is a ward of the tribal court, regardless where the child resides or is domiciled. 25 U.S.C.A. § 1911(a).

Tribal courts also have jurisdiction over adoption and custody of Indian children who are tribal members or who are eligible for membership, even though those children reside or are domiciled outside of the tribe's reservation. This jurisdiction is concurrent with that of the state, but in cases of foster care placement or termination of parental rights, the state court must transfer the case to tribal court upon petition of either parent, the child's Indian custodian, or the tribe unless the state court finds "good cause" for retaining the case or unless either parent objects to the transfer. The tribal court may decline to accept such transfers. 25 U.S.C.A. § 1911(b).

d. Probate

Tribal courts have exclusive jurisdiction over the probate of non-trust movable assets of Indians who die domiciled in Indian country, subject only to whatever ancillary jurisdiction state courts may need to exercise to marshal for the tribal court those movables located outside of Indian country. Here again, the principal authority supporting such exclusive jurisdiction is Williams v. Lee, 358 U.S. 217 (1959). Inheritance is perhaps the most traditional and customary aspect of tribal law, and state jurisdiction would probably represent a very severe intrusion on the right of Indians to manage their internal affairs. Even the narrow description of inherent tribal powers in Montana v. United States, 450 U.S. 544, 564 (1981), includes the power "to prescribe rules of inheritance for members."

Some tribal codes purport to authorize tribal probate jurisdiction over non-trust assets of tribal *members*, even if they die domiciled outside of Indian country. Membership might well support such jurisdiction, but state courts would have concurrent jurisdiction that could cause considerable confusion in the probate of estates. Perhaps for this reason, tribal courts in practice generally confine themselves to probate of estates of Indians who died domiciled on their reservations or restrict their exercise of jurisdiction to movables located on the reservation. Tribal courts generally do not exercise probate jurisdiction over estates of non-Indians. Cf. Hinshaw v. Mahler, 42 F.3d 1178, 1180 (9th Cir. 1994).

Tribal courts have no probate jurisdiction over trust property such as land allotments, which are handled exclusively by the federal government. They also have no jurisdiction over land located outside of Indian country, which is subject to the exclusive jurisdiction of the state where the land lies. As a consequence, tribal probate proceedings rarely involve interests in real estate.

3. FEDERAL CIVIL JURISDICTION

a. General Civil Litigation

The federal role in the adjudication of civil disputes in Indian country is far more limited than its role in criminal matters. The federal courts are not courts of general jurisdiction. There are only two applicable bases of federal jurisdiction in civil suits: federal question and diversity of citizenship.

The federal question jurisdiction of federal courts is the same in Indian country as it is anywhere else. If a claim arises under federal law, then it may be brought under such statutes as 28 U.S.C.A. §§ 1331 or 1343, assuming that the other requirements of those statutes are met. Indian tribes are authorized by 28 U.S.C.A. § 1362 to bring suits as plaintiffs in federal court, but their claims must still arise under federal law. Gila River Indian Community v. Henningson, Durham & Richardson, 626 F.2d 708 (9th Cir.1980). A tribe cannot meet that requirement by suing state officers under 42 U.S.C.A. § 1983, because a tribe does not qualify as a "person" entitled to bring actions under that statute. Inyo County, California v. Paiute–Shoshone Indians of the Bishop Community, 538 U.S. 701 (2003). A tribe's claim based on pre-Revolutionary British treaties that were implemented by a federal Trade and Intercourse Act was held to arise under federal law. Catawba Indian Tribe v. South Carolina, 865 F.2d 1444 (4th Cir.1989) (en banc). The mere fact that a party to a case is an Indian or an Indian tribe does not turn a civil dispute into a federal question, nor does the fact that the controversy arose in Indian country. Schantz v. White Lightning, 502 F.2d 67 (8th Cir.1974). A dispute between two Indian residents of the same state over a contract entered and to be performed on an Indian reservation does not, for example, qualify for federal jurisdiction. TTEA v. Ysleta Del Sur Pueblo, 181 F.3d 676, 681 (5th Cir.1999).

Federal question jurisdiction has assumed increased importance in Indian law since the decision of National Farmers Union Ins. Cos. v. Crow Tribe, 471 U.S. 845 (1985). In that case, a non-Indian brought an action in federal court to enjoin tribal court proceedings in which the non-Indian was a defendant. The Supreme Court held:

> Because petitioners contend that federal law has divested the Tribe of this aspect of sovereignty, it is federal law on which they rely as a basis for the asserted right of freedom from Tribal Court interference. They have, therefore, filed an action "arising under" federal law within the meaning of § 1331.

Id. at 853. As a consequence, anyone asserting an absence of tribal power under federal statute, treaty or the "common law" of federal Indian law has an entree into federal court. The potential of this rule for permitting undue federal interference in the tribal courts was mitigated, however, by the other holding in National Farmers Union: that the federal court must stay its hand and permit the tribal court to rule in the first instance upon the question of its own jurisdiction. Id. at 856. The only exceptions to this requirement occur when tribal jurisdiction is asserted to harass or in bad faith, or the tribal act is patently violative of express jurisdictional prohibitions, or exhaustion would be futile because of lack of opportunity to challenge tribal court jurisdiction. *National Farmers Union*, 471 U.S. at 856 n.21.

The Supreme Court has greatly broadened these exceptions to exhaustion, however, in Strate v. A–1 Contractors, 520 U.S. 438 (1997), and Nevada v. Hicks, 533 U.S. 353 (2001). *Strate* held that, in a case where the application of Montana v. United States, 450 U.S. 544 (1981), precluded tribal court jurisdiction over a nonmember's activities on fee land or its equivalent, exhaustion was unnecessary because it would serve no purpose except delay. *Strate*, 520 U.S. at 459 n.14. *Hicks* then took the same approach in a case where trust land and an Indian plaintiff were involved. Because the typical action brought in federal court to challenge tribal court jurisdiction raises issues under the *Montana* rule, it is possible that *Strate* and *Hicks* have greatly reduced the occasions on which exhaustion will be required of a federal court. See, e.g., Burlington Northern R. Co. v. Red Wolf, 196 F.3d 1059, 1065–66 (9th Cir.1999). *Strate* and *Hicks* can be interpreted to state that exhaustion is unnecessary when the absence of tribal jurisdiction is very clear (although it is hard to find such clarity in those two cases), see Allstate Indem. Co. v. Stump, 191 F.3d 1071, 1073, as amended, 197 F.3d 1031 (9th Cir. 1999), but they also easily can be interpreted to eliminate exhaustion whenever the issue is one of applying the *Montana* presumption against tribal jurisdiction over nonmembers.

The Supreme Court created another exception to exhaustion in El Paso Natural Gas Co. v. Neztsosie,

526 U.S. 473. That case involved an unusual provision of the Price–Anderson Act that transformed any public liability action arising from a nuclear incident into a federal case removable from state to federal court. The Supreme Court held that this provision indicated a strong congressional preference for a federal forum which rendered it inappropriate to leave to a tribal court the question whether it had jurisdiction over such claims. *Neztsosie* set out the usual rules of exhaustion from *National Farmers Union* and Iowa Mut. Ins. Co. v. LaPlante, 480 U.S. 9 (1987), and also stated that its decision was not to be interpreted as precluding tribal courts from entertaining federal preemption defenses. *Neztsosie*, 526 U.S. at 485 n.7.

There undoubtedly will still be some cases in which exhaustion is appropriate under any standard. One circuit has analogized abstention for tribal exhaustion to abstention under Colorado River Water Conservation Dist. v. United States, 424 U.S. 800 (1976), which must be narrowly construed in light of the federal court's unflagging obligation to exercise jurisdiction. Garcia v. Akwesasne Housing Auth., 268 F.3d 76, 80 (2d Cir.2001). Another circuit, however, has expressly rejected that view, Bank One, N.A. v. Shumake, 281 F.3d 507, 514–15 (5th Cir.2002), and a narrow approach to tribal exhaustion has not been in evidence in the great majority of decisions. See Duncan Energy Co. v. Three Affiliated Tribes of the Fort Berthold Reservation, 27 F.3d 1294, 1300 (8th Cir.1994). The requirement of exhaustion of tribal remedies applies even when no tribal court proceedings are pending. Smith v. Moffett, 947 F.2d 442 (10th Cir.1991). It applies in favor of Courts of Indian Offenses as well as tribal courts. Tillett v. Lujan, 931 F.2d 636 (10th Cir.1991). The rule applies to tribal members. Kerr–McGee Corp. v. Farley, 115 F.3d 1498 (10th Cir. 1997). It applies to cases where there is a motion to compel arbitration under the Federal Arbitration Act. Gaming World Int'l, Ltd. v. White Earth Band of Chippewa Indians, 317 F.3d 840 (8th Cir.2003). A tribal waiver of sovereign immunity for a class of claims does not waive the exhaustion requirement. Davis v. Mille Lacs Band of Chippewa Indians, 193 F.3d 990 (8th Cir.1999). Even the United States has been forced to exhaust when it sued tribal members for grazing violation penalties. United States v. Plainbull, 957 F.2d 724 (9th Cir.1992). One court of appeals, however, excused a tribe from having to exhaust when it sought to characterize the action as arising off-reservation and no tribal court proceedings were pending. Altheimer & Gray v. Sioux Mfg. Co., 983 F.2d 803 (7th Cir.1993). A plaintiff is not required to exhaust when no tribal court was in existence at the time suit was filed. Comstock Oil & Gas Inc. v. Alabama and Coushatta Indian Tribes of Texas, 261 F.3d 567 (5th Cir.2001). Exhaustion includes exhaustion of tribal appellate remedies. Kerr–McGee Corp. v. Farley, 115 F.3d 1498 (10th Cir.1997). Exhaustion of appellate remedies will not be required if there is no functioning tribal appellate court. Johnson v. Gila River Indian Community, 174 F.3d 1032 (9th Cir.1999).

If, during exhaustion, the tribal court decides that it has jurisdiction, it presumably will proceed to decide the merits of the case. The objecting party may then return to federal court, where the federal court will review de novo the federal question of the tribe's jurisdiction, being "guided" but not controlled by the tribal court's views. It will review the tribe's jurisdictional factual findings only for clear error. FMC v. Shoshone–Bannock Tribes, 905 F.2d 1311 (9th Cir.1990). If the federal court decides that the tribal court had jurisdiction, it will not relitigate the tribal decision on the merits. See Iowa Mut. Ins. Co. v. LaPlante, 480 U.S. 9, 19 (1987). The only exception occurs when the tribal court jurisdictional decision is so intertwined with the merits that one cannot be reviewed without the other. See Enlow v. Moore, 134 F.3d 993 (10th Cir.1998).

Several federal statutes confer jurisdiction on the federal courts to adjudicate disputes involving beneficial rights in trust property. See, e.g., 25 U.S.C.A. §§ 345–346, 28 U.S.C.A. § 1353. This jurisdiction is exclusive.

Diversity of citizenship is a basis for federal jurisdiction under 28 U.S.C.A. § 1332 when the amount in controversy exceeds $75,000. Because Indians are citizens of the states where they reside whether or not the residence is in Indian country, the requisite diversity does not exist between a reservation Indian and a non-Indian domiciled in the same state. An Indian tribe that is not incorporated is not a citizen of any state and cannot be sued in federal court on the basis of diversity. American Vantage Companies v. Table Mountain Rancheria, 292 F.3d 1091 (9th Cir.2002). The presence of such a tribe as a party destroys the requisite total diversity. Ninigret Development Corp. v. Narragansett Indian Wetuomuck Housing Auth., 207 F.3d 21 (1st Cir. 2000). A tribe may, however, charter a tribal corporation that becomes a citizen of the state of its principal place of business for purposes of diversity jurisdiction. See Gaines v. Ski Apache, 8 F.3d 726 (10th Cir.1993).

For a number of years it was assumed that the diversity jurisdiction of federal courts in Indian country was limited to suits that could be brought in state court, but the Supreme Court decided to the contrary in Iowa Mut. Ins. Co. v. LaPlante, 480 U.S. 9 (1987). In that case, an insurance company that was being sued in tribal court brought a diversity action in federal court, seeking a declaration that its policy did not cover the disputed claim. As the defendant in the federal action was an Indian, the Supreme Court assumed that the state courts would have no jurisdiction over the case, and the insurance company did not contend otherwise. Id. at 13 n.4. The Supreme Court held that the requisites of diversity jurisdiction were nevertheless present, but that the federal court should stay its hand until the tribal court determined its own jurisdiction. If the tribal court ruled that it had jurisdiction and decided the merits of the insurance dispute, the jurisdictional ruling could be challenged in federal court, but "proper deference to the tribal court system precludes relitigation" of the merits as resolved in tribal court. Id. at 19. One circuit court has even held, in a case where no tribal proceedings were pending, that an Indian plaintiff must exhaust tribal court remedies before bringing a diversity case against a non-Indian in federal court. Wellman v. Chevron U.S.A., Inc., 815 F.2d 577 (9th Cir.1987).

b. Divorce; Adoption and Child Custody; Probate

Federal courts exercise no divorce, adoption or child custody jurisdiction. They also exercise no probate jurisdiction, but probate of Indian trust properties is the sole responsibility of the federal government and is administered by the Department of Interior. 25 U.S.C.A. § 372. The decisions of the Secretary are "final and conclusive," but may be judicially reviewed for conformity with the Constitution. Kicking Woman v. Hodel, 878 F.2d 1203 (9th Cir.1989).

4. CHART OF CIVIL JURISDICTION IN INDIAN COUNTRY BY PARTIES AND SUBJECT MATTER

Notes:

i. This chart does not apply to Indian country over which the state has assumed jurisdiction pursuant to Public Law 280, 25 U.S.C.A. § 1322, 28 U.S.C.A. § 1360.

ii. In all instances where state jurisdiction is shown, federal jurisdiction may be acquired if the parties meet requirements of diversity of citizenship and amount.

iii. Where subject matter of claim particularly affects Indian interests, normal state jurisdiction may be precluded.

---

a. General Civil Litigation:

Plaint.	Defend.	Source of Claim	Jurisdiction
Indian	Indian	Indian country	Tribal (exclus.)
		Non–Indian country	Tribal or state (concurr.)
Non–Indian	Indian	Indian country	Tribal (exclus.)
		Non–Indian country	State; possibly tribal (concurr.)
Indian	Non–Indian	Indian country exc. non-Indian fee lands	Tribal (if code allows); State (concurr.)
		Indian country non-Indian fee lands	State; possibly tribal (concurr.)
		Non–Indian country	State (exclus.)
Non–Indian	Non–Indian	Indian country	State; possibly tribal (concurr.)
		Non–Indian country and Indian country fee lands	State (exclus.)

b. Divorce:

Plaint.	Defend.	Domicile of Parties	Jurisdiction
Indian	Indian	Indian country	Tribal (exclus.)
		Non–Indian country	State; Tribal if code allows (concurr.)

Plaint.	Defend.	Domicile of Parties	Jurisdiction
Non–Indian	Indian	Indian country	State (probable); Tribal (concurr.)
		Non–Indian country	State (exclus.)
Indian	Non–Indian	Indian country	Tribal (exclus.)
		Non–Indian country	State (exclus.)
Non–Indian	Non–Indian	Anywhere	State (exclus.)

c.   Adoption and Child Custody (non-Divorce) (Consult 25 U.S.C.A. § 1911):

Proceeding	Domicile or Residence of child	Jurisdiction
Adoption and all custody	Indian country	Tribal (exclus.)
Adoption or adoptive placement	Non–Indian country	Tribal or State (concurr.)
Foster care or termination of parental rights	Non–Indian country	Tribal preferred; State (concurr.)

d.   Probate

Decedent	Decedent's Domicile	Property	Jurisdiction
Indian	Indian country	Trust assets	Federal (exclus.)
		Land out of Indian country	State (exclus.)
		Movables	Tribal (primary)
	Non–Indian country	Trust assets	Federal (exclus.)
		Land out of Indian country	State (exclus.)
		Movables	State (primary); Possibly Tribal (concurr.)
Non–Indian	Anywhere	All assets	State (exclus.)

G.   RECOGNITION OF JUDGMENTS; FULL FAITH AND CREDIT

The division of civil jurisdiction among the tribes, the states and the federal government occasionally gives rise to questions of the enforceability of tribal judgments in state and federal courts and the enforceability of state judgments in tribal courts (federal judgments can be enforced on their own authority in Indian country or out). The Constitution requires each state to give full faith and credit to the judgments of other *states*, U.S.Const., Art. IV, § 1, but this clause in terms does not apply to the judgments of tribes. The Supreme Court has noted however, that tribal court judgments have "in some circumstances" been regarded as entitled to full faith and credit. Santa Clara Pueblo v. Martinez, 436 U.S. 49, 65, n. 21 (1978). Some state courts have simply given full faith and credit. E.g., In re Buehl, 87 Wash.2d 649, 555 P.2d 1334 (1976). Others, while denying the applicability of the full faith and credit clause, have nevertheless given full effect to tribal judgments or decrees as a matter of "comity". E.g., In re Lynch's Estate, 92 Ariz. 354, 377 P.2d 199 (1962); Matter of Marriage of Red Fox, 23 Or.App. 393, 542 P.2d 918 (1975); Wippert v. Blackfeet Tribe, 201 Mont. 299, 654 P.2d 512 (1982). Federal courts have done the same. See, e.g., AT & T Corp. v. Coeur d'Alene Tribe, 295 F.3d 899, 903 (9th Cir.2002). A few states have legislated or adopted court rules on the subject; South Dakota, for example, permits recognition of tribal judgments as a matter of comity if a list of conditions is met, including impartiality of the tribal proceedings. S.D. Cod. Laws 1–1–25; see Red Fox v. Hettich, 494 N.W.2d 638 (S.D.1993). Other state statutes or rules vary greatly in the degree to which they condition recognition of tribal court judgments. For a discussion of the many factors that may enter a decision of recognition of judgments when state and tribal courts have pursued parallel litigation with opposite results, see Teague v. Bad River Band of Lake Superior Tribe of Chippewa Indians, 265 Wis.2d 64, 665 N.W.2d 899 (2003).

The federal statute implementing the full faith and credit clause, 28 U.S.C.A. § 1738, requires all courts within the United States to honor the judgments of courts of "territories." Despite some argument over the matter, it is probable that tribal court judgments do not fall within that terminology. See Ragsdale, *Problems in the Application of Full Faith and Credit for Indian Tribes*, 7 N.Mex.L.Rev. 133 (1977); but see Jim v. CIT Financial Services Corp., 87 N.M. 362, 533 P.2d 751 (1975). One state court, however, has held that the Navajo Nation qualifies as a "territory" for purposes of the Uniform Act to Secure the Attendance of Witnesses from Without a State. Tracy v. Superior Court of Maricopa County, 168 Ariz. 23, 810 P.2d 1030 (1991).

The Indian Child Welfare Act of 1978 requires every tribal, state and federal court to give full faith and credit to tribal judgments in Indian child custody proceedings, as defined by the Act. 25 U.S.C.A. § 1911(d).

Neither the Constitution nor federal statutes appear to require tribal courts to give full faith and credit to state court judgments. As a matter of practice, however, many tribal courts regularly give full effect to state court judgments, presumably also as a matter of "comity."

H. CHOICE OF LAW

Disputes over civil jurisdiction often presume that the law to be applied to the case will differ with the court that decides it. The presumption is often but not always correct. Many tribal codes require the tribal courts to apply, in order: (1) federal law, (2) tribal ordinances and customs not in conflict with federal law and, in matters not covered by the first two categories, (3) state law. Because very few tribes have comprehensive codes or bodies of common law dealing with civil matters, state law is likely to govern a large proportion of the civil cases, particularly those of a nature likely to involve non-Indian parties.

State courts applying normal choice of law principles should frequently apply tribal law to issues arising in Indian country. As indicated in the preceding paragraph, this practice may result in the ultimate application of state law anyway. There are important cases, however, where tribal law leads to a different result from state law, and all too often the tribal law is overlooked. On the other hand, there have been rare but notable instances where state courts have been sensitive to possible application of tribal law. E.g., Jim v. CIT Fin. Serv. Corp., 87 N.M. 362, 533 P.2d 751 (1975).

Federal statutes also impose choice-of-law requirements on state courts in special circumstances.

The Indian Child Welfare Act specifies preferences for placement of Indian children for foster care or adoption and provides that if the child's tribe chooses to establish a different order of preferences they will apply in state court, with certain qualifications. 25 U.S.C.A. § 1915. In addition, Public Law 280 requires state courts exercising jurisdiction over Indian country to apply tribal ordinances and customs "if not inconsistent with any applicable civil law of the State." 28 U.S.C.A. § 1360(c). Finally, the Federal Tort Claims Act provides for federal government liability in tort "under circumstances where the United States, if a private person, would be liable to the claimant in accordance with the law of the place where the act or omission occurred." 28 U.S.C. § 1346(b)(1). In Cheromiah v. United States, 55 F.Supp.2d 1295 (D.N.M. 1999), the court held in a malpractice action based on events at an Indian Health Service hospital that the "law of the place" was tribal law, thereby avoiding a state law cap on malpractice recovery. This result seems to make sense if, as the court found, a non-Indian person in the place of the United States could be sued in tribal court under the applicable rules of Montana v. United States, 450 U.S. 544 (1981). See Section F(2)(a), supra. In a later, very similar case, however, another district court expressly disagreed with *Cheromiah* and held that the law of the place was the law of the state. Bryant v. United States, 147 F.Supp.2d 953 (D.Ariz. 2000). The issue accordingly remains in doubt.

In two large areas of jurisdictional dispute—criminal law and divorce—choice of law plays no part. Tribal and state courts alike follow the general rule that the forum applies its own substantive law in each of these fields.

CHAPTER VIII

PUBLIC LAW 280: A FEDERAL GRANT OF JURISDICTION TO THE STATES

A. INTRODUCTION

Congress has the power to change the division of jurisdiction among the federal, tribal and state governments. On many occasions it has passed statutes affecting jurisdiction over specific tribes or even over all tribes within a given state. In 1953, however, Congress adopted a more general approach. In what is commonly known as Public Law 280, 67 Stat. 588, Congress gave five (later six) states extensive criminal and civil jurisdiction over Indian country, and permitted all other states to acquire it at their option. In the states where Public Law 280 applies, then, it radically shifts the balance of jurisdictional power toward the states and away from the federal government and the tribes. It does not, however, confer total jurisdiction on the states, nor does it alter the trust status of Indian lands or terminate the trust relationship between the tribes and the federal government. It does not end the sovereign immunity of the tribes. California v. Quechan Tribe of Indians, 595 F.2d 1153 (9th Cir.1979); Trudgeon v. Fantasy Springs Casino, 71 Cal. App.4th 632, 84 Cal.Rptr.2d 65 (1999).

From its inception Public Law 280 engendered criticism from both the states and the tribes. State governments resented the fact that they were given the duty of law enforcement without the means to pay for it; Congress neither appropriated funds for that purpose nor rendered Indian lands taxable by the states. The tribes, on the other hand, resented the fact that state jurisdiction was thrust upon them without their consent and they particularly objected to the provision that additional states could acquire jurisdiction without even consulting the concerned tribes. The ultimate result of these criticisms was a group of amendments to Public Law 280 that were passed as part of the Indian Civil Rights Act of 1968. These amendments permitted states to retrocede jurisdiction to the federal government, and also provided that no states in the future could assume jurisdiction without tribal consent. As a consequence, there has been almost no expansion of Public Law 280 jurisdiction since 1968. In the number of states where it is still in effect, however, Public Law 280 presents jurisdictional questions of considerable complexity.

B.   CRIMINAL JURISDICTION

The basic outlines of Public Law 280 are established in those sections that confer jurisdiction on six named states—the "mandatory" states—by operation of the Law itself. Variations that occurred in other states which later elected to assume Public Law 280 jurisdiction—the "optional" states—will be discussed below (Section F).

While Public Law 280 conferred both criminal and civil jurisdiction on the mandatory states, the criminal provision was clearly the most important to Congress. Non–Indians living on or near reservations believed that law enforcement in Indian country had broken down, and urged state jurisdiction as a remedy. See Goldberg, *Public Law 280: The Limits of State Jurisdiction Over Reservation Indians*, 22 U.C.L.A.L.Rev. 535, 541 (1975). That jurisdiction was provided by the following section of Public Law 280:

18 U.S.C.A. § 1162(a):

Each of the States or Territories listed in the following table shall have jurisdiction over offenses committed by or against Indians in the areas of Indian country listed opposite the name of the State or Territory to the same extent that such State or Territory has jurisdiction over offenses committed elsewhere within the State or Territory, and the criminal laws of such State or Territory shall have the same force and effect within such Indian country as they have elsewhere within the State or Territory:

State or Territory of	Indian country affected
Alaska [added in 1958]	All Indian country within the State except [the Annette Islands with regard to the Metlakatla Indians]
California	All Indian country within the State
Minnesota	All Indian country within the State, except Red Lake Reservation
Nebraska	All Indian country within the State
Oregon	All Indian country within the State, except the Warm Springs Reservation
Wisconsin	All Indian country within the State

The effect of this section is clear from its wording; it gives the named states the same power to enforce their regular criminal laws inside Indian country that they had always exercised outside of it. The states already possessed jurisdiction over wholly non-Indian crimes within Indian country, see Chapter VII, Section D3, supra; Public Law 280 filled in all the remaining gaps by extending state power to crimes "by or against Indians."

At the same time that Public Law 280 extended the authority of the six listed states into Indian country, it provided that the General Crimes Act (18 U.S.C.A. § 1152) and the Major Crimes Act (18 U.S.C.A. § 1153) no longer applied in those areas.

18 U.S.C.A. § 1162(c). Federal authority to enforce those two statutes was therefore wholly supplanted by that of the mandatory states in the areas over which they were granted jurisdiction. (Federal power to enforce federal laws of national applicability remained, of course. United States v. Stone, 112 F.3d 971 (8th Cir.1997)). The repeal of the Major Crimes Act and General Crimes Act did not, however, extend to the optional states that later assumed jurisdiction. See United States v. High Elk, 902 F.2d 660 (8th Cir.1990); cf. Negonsott v. Samuels, 507 U.S. 99 (1993); United States v. Cook, 922 F.2d 1026 (2d Cir.1991). In those states, the federal government and the states may both punish conduct that falls within the scope of the Major Crimes or General Crimes Acts. Cf. *Negonsott*, 507 U.S. at 105; State v. Hoffman, 116 Wash.2d 51, 68, 804 P.2d 577, 586 (1991).

The effect of Public Law 280 on tribal criminal law was less clear; the Act made no mention of it. One court of appeals upheld a tribe's exercise of criminal jurisdiction over a member, even though Public Law 280 had granted criminal jurisdiction for such a crime (vehicular homicide) to the state. Walker v. Rushing, 898 F.2d 672 (8th Cir.1990). The court reasoned that a tribe enjoys inherent sovereignty over its members unless clearly limited by Congress, and that Public Law 280 contained no such clear limitation. An amendment to Public Law 280 referred to the criminal jurisdiction earlier given to the mandatory states as "exclusive," but the legislative history is unclear and that term may

simply mean exclusive of federal, not tribal, jurisdiction. See 18 U.S.C. § 1162(c). In any event, implementation of Public Law 280 usually has marked
the end of tribal criminal jurisdiction, either because of a lack of need or a lack of resources to
maintain a tribal criminal justice system parallel to
that of the state. Tribes may, however, choose to
exercise authority in those areas from which Public
Law 280 excludes the states, notably the regulation
of hunting and fishing guaranteed by treaty or
statute. 78 Interior Dec. 101, 103 (1971).

Public Law 280 expressly declines to authorize
states to interfere with hunting and fishing rights,
or to take certain actions affecting Indian trust
lands. See Section E, below. States also have been
held to lack general powers of taxation and regulation in Indian country. See Bryan v. Itasca County,
426 U.S. 373 (1976). The latter limitation, which
affects both the civil and criminal jurisdiction of the
states, is of considerable importance and is discussed in Section D, below.

C. CIVIL JURISDICTION

The grant of civil jurisdiction was added to Public
Law 280 as an afterthought, and there is consequently little legislative history concerning it. See
Goldberg, supra, at 542–543. The grant covered the
same areas of Indian country within the same six
mandatory states as did the grant of criminal jurisdiction: California, Minnesota (except the Red Lake
Reservation), Nebraska, Oregon (except the Warm

Springs Reservation), Wisconsin (except the Menominee Reservation), and, as added in 1958, Alaska (except the Annette Islands). The civil grant was in the following terms:

28 U.S.C.A. § 1360(a):

Each of the States listed * * * shall have jurisdiction over civil causes of action between Indians or to which Indians are parties which arise in the areas of Indian country listed * * * to the same extent that such State has jurisdiction over other civil causes of action, and those civil laws of such State that are of general application to private persons or private property shall have the same force and effect within such Indian country as they have elsewhere within the State * * *.

Like the parallel grant of criminal jurisdiction, this civil section filled in the greatest existing gap in state jurisdiction. Williams v. Lee, 358 U.S. 217 (1959), had denied the state power to adjudicate civil actions against Indians that arose in Indian country; Public Law 280 expressly conferred that power. The state's adjudicatory power was not made total, however. 28 U.S.C.A. § 1360(b) provided that nothing in the grant should confer jurisdiction upon the states "to adjudicate, in probate proceedings or otherwise, the ownership or right to possession of [trust] property or any interest therein." The same section declined to grant the state power to encumber trust property or to interfere with treaty rights—a disclaimer that is common to both the civil and criminal grants and that is discussed in Section E below.

The grant of civil jurisdiction to the states in § 1360 did not deprive tribal courts of concurrent jurisdiction if they chose to exercise it. Native Village of Venetie I.R.A. Council v. Alaska, 944 F.2d 548, 559–62 (9th Cir.1991); Teague v. Bad River Band of Lake Superior Tribe of Chippewa Indians, 236 Wis.2d 384, 402, 612 N.W.2d 709, 717 (2000). In *Venetie*, the state argued that state jurisdiction under Public Law 280 must be exclusive, or Congress would not have provided in the Indian Child Welfare Act that tribes subject to Public Law 280 could petition the Secretary to "reassume" jurisdiction over child custody proceedings pursuant to the Act. See 25 U.S.C.A. § 1918(a). The court of appeals held, however, that § 1918(a) was not rendered unnecessary or meaningless if the tribes already had general concurrent jurisdiction; the grant of jurisdiction under the Indian Child Welfare Act was broader than concurrent-it could give the tribe exclusive or primary jurisdiction. See § 1918(b)(2); see also Chapter VII, Section F(1)(c), F(2)(c), supra. Thus the Village of Venetie was held to have concurrent jurisdiction over child custody even though it had not petitioned for broader jurisdiction under the Indian Child Welfare Act. *Venetie*, 944 F.2d at 561–62.

One controversy that arose from the language of the grant of civil jurisdiction to the states in 28 U.S.C.A. § 1360 concerned the applicability of local law. The question was whether a county or city ordinance qualifies as one of the "civil laws of [the] State that are of general application to private persons or private property" and that are to have the same force and effect in Indian country as they have "elsewhere within the State." One view of the statutory language is that it simply requires that a law or ordinance be of general application within its intended geographical jurisdiction. That view permits a county to extend its "general" laws to Indian country lying within its boundaries. See Rincon Band of Mission Indians v. County of San Diego, 324 F.Supp. 371 (S.D.Cal.1971), aff'd on other grounds, 495 F.2d 1 (9th Cir.1974). A contrary view of the statutory language is that it refers only to the generally applicable laws of the *state*, and not those of the state's local subdivisions. That is the view which has been adopted by the Court of Appeals for the Ninth Circuit, largely on the ground that Congress could not have intended the severe interference with tribal self-government that would result from imposing detailed local regulations upon Indians in Indian country. Santa Rosa Band v. Kings County, 532 F.2d 655 (9th Cir.1975); Segundo v. City of Rancho Mirage, 813 F.2d 1387, 1390 (9th Cir.1987). The Supreme Court has not ruled squarely on this issue, but has expressed doubt that Public Law 280 authorizes the application of local laws to the reservations. California v. Cabazon Band of Mission Indians, 480 U.S. 202, 212 n.11 n. 11 (1987).

D. EXCEPTION FOR TAXATION
AND REGULATION

One further issue that arose from Public Law 280's grant of civil jurisdiction overshadows all others and has important implications for criminal jurisdiction as well. The civil grant is one of power over "civil causes of action." This language would appear to mean that the state simply acquired adjudicatory jurisdiction—the power to decide cases—and not the entire power to legislate and regulate in Indian country. On the other hand, the statutory grant also provides that the "civil laws of [the] State shall have the same force and effect within such Indian country as they have elsewhere within the State." That language might arguably confer full legislative jurisdiction on the state. The true meaning of the statute was vigorously disputed until the Supreme Court resolved the matter adversely to the states in Bryan v. Itasca County, 426 U.S. 373 (1976).

Bryan involved the attempt of a Minnesota county to assess a state and local property tax against personal property owned by an Indian in Indian country over which the state had been granted jurisdiction by Public Law 280. The personal property involved was not trust property, and the state argued that it therefore became subject to the general "civil laws" of the state, including its tax laws. The Supreme Court concluded that the primary purpose of the civil provisions of Public Law 280 was to provide a state forum for the resolution of disputes. Viewed in that light, the provision that the civil laws of the state should have effect in Indian country simply "authorizes application by the state courts of their rules of decision to decide such disputes." 426 U.S. at 384.

The effect of the Court's decision is to confine the civil grant of Public Law 280 to adjudicatory jurisdiction only. The Court in *Bryan* was quite explicit:

[N]othing in its legislative history remotely suggests that Congress meant the Act's extension of civil jurisdiction to the States should result in the undermining or destruction of such tribal governments as did exist and a conversion of the affected tribes into little more than " 'private, voluntary organizations,' " * * *—a possible result if tribal governments and reservation Indians were subordinated to the full panoply of civil regulatory powers, including taxation, of state and local governments.

426 U.S. at 388. It followed that Minnesota's attempted taxation was not authorized by Public Law 280. Whatever powers of taxation or regulation states have in Indian country, see Chapter IX, must be derived from some other source; Public Law 280 confers no such authority.

The *Bryan* principle was applied to the area of criminal law in California v. Cabazon Band of Mission Indians, 480 U.S. 202 (1987). In that case, tribes were operating high-stakes bingo and poker games on their reservations. California sought to apply its penal law prohibiting bingo games unless

they were conducted by charitable organizations
and offered prizes not exceeding $250 per game.
Riverside County sought to apply its ordinance forbidding gambling on card games, with exceptions if
municipalities licensed them. A major issue was
whether the state and county laws were "criminal
laws" applicable to Indian country under Public
Law 280, or were "regulations" excepted from Public Law 280 by the rule of *Bryan*. The Supreme
Court, in ruling for the tribes, accepted the distinction made by the court of appeals between state
"criminal/prohibitory" laws and state "civil/regula-
tory" laws:

> [I]f the intent of a state law is generally to
> prohibit certain conduct, it falls within Pub. L.
> 280's grant of criminal jurisdiction, but if the
> state law generally permits the conduct at issue,
> subject to regulation, it must be classified as
> civil/regulatory and Pub. L. 280 does not author-
> ize its enforcement on an Indian reservation. The
> shorthand test is whether the conduct at issue
> violates the State's public policy.

480 U.S. at 209. The Court then accepted the view
of the court of appeals that the statute and ordinance were regulatory. The Supreme Court pointed
out that California allowed or, in the case of its
lottery, encouraged various forms of gambling, and
that the County permitted card gambling if municipalities authorized it. 480 U.S. at 210–11. The Supreme Court also said that the fact "that an other-

wise regulatory law is enforceable by criminal as well as civil means does not necessarily convert it into a criminal law within the meaning of Pub.L. 280." Id. at 211. *Bryan*, therefore, significantly narrows the criminal as well as the civil effect of Public Law 280.

The distinction between criminal/prohibitory and civil/regulatory laws continues to arise in a variety of settings, with results not entirely predictable. A law providing for the civil commitment of sexually violent persons was held to be criminal/prohibitory. In re Commitment of Burgess, 262 Wis.2d 354, 665 N.W.2d 124 (2003). The distinction is subject to manipulation by the manner in which the issue is presented. For example, a state law prohibiting driving after the suspension of a license could be viewed as a mere regulation of driving, an activity that is regulated rather than prohibited, or as a criminal, public-policy-driven prohibition against driving after suspension of a license. The latter view was adopted (at least for a repeat offender) and the state law enforced against a tribal member in St. Germaine v. Circuit Court for Vilas County, 938 F.2d 75 (7th Cir.1991); accord State v. Busse, 644 N.W.2d 79 (Minn.2002). A similar result has been reached with regard to driving while intoxicated. State v. Couture, 587 N.W.2d 849 (Minn.App.1999). On the other hand, where a state had reduced speeding from a criminal offense to a "traffic infraction," the law was held to be regulatory. Confederated Tribes of the Colville Reservation v. Washington, 938 F.2d 146 (9th Cir.1991). The general run of traffic laws (excluding reckless or drunken driving) has been held civil/regulatory in at least one state. State v. Stone, 572 N.W.2d 725 (Minn. 1997). Some cases seem to turn on the strength of a state's interest, even though it remains difficult to determine whether that interest lies in regulation or prohibition. A state law regulating classes of fireworks, and prohibiting dangerous fireworks except in the hands of licensed and trained persons, with violation a misdemeanor, was held to be criminal/prohibitory in Quechan Tribe v. McMullen, 984 F.2d 304 (9th Cir.1993). One state appellate court even ruled that state hunting regulations were criminal/prohibitory. Jones v. State, 936 P.2d 1263, 1266–67 (Alaska App.1997).

In larger perspective, however, *Bryan's* restriction of state legislative and regulatory authority helped to preserve the vitality of tribes' law-making powers. Public Law 280 had provided that tribal ordinances or customs were to be given full force and effect in the decision of civil controversies by state courts, 28 U.S.C.A. § 1360(c), but this provision was limited to ordinances or customs "not inconsistent with any applicable civil law of the State." Because most states have relatively complete bodies of civil law, the statute did not leave much room for tribal law to operate. The *Bryan* case leaves open to the tribe a much larger legislative role dealing with regulation and taxation.

E. OTHER EXCEPTIONS TO STATE JURISDICTION UNDER PUBLIC LAW 280

Both the grant of criminal jurisdiction and that of civil jurisdiction in Public Law 280 contain the following exceptions:

Nothing in this section shall authorize the alienation, encumbrance, or taxation of any real or personal property, including water rights, belonging to any Indian or any Indian tribe, band, or community that is held in trust by the United States or is subject to a restriction against alienation imposed by the United States; or shall authorize regulation of the use of such property in a manner inconsistent with any Federal treaty, agreement, or statute or with any regulation made pursuant thereto * * *.

18 U.S.C.A. § 1162(b); 28 U.S.C.A. § 1360(b). The two principal effects of these limitations are to preserve the trust status of Indian property and to protect Indian treaty rights.

The provisions negating any grant of power to the states to alienate or tax trust property are reinforced by a provision in the civil grant that nothing therein "shall confer jurisdiction upon the State to adjudicate, in probate proceedings or otherwise, the ownership or right to possession of such property or any interest therein." 28 U.S.C.A. § 1360(b). These provisions have not in themselves been the source of much litigation; the states were previously excluded from such actions and the statute merely maintained the status quo. There has been controversy, however, over what kinds of state activity may constitute an "encumbrance" of Indian lands. If the term is read very broadly, it may preclude the state from enforcing any of its laws—even criminal laws—that would diminish the value of Indian lands. See Snohomish County v. Seattle Disposal Co., 70 Wash.2d 668, 425 P.2d 22 (1967). At the other extreme, "encumbrance" can be interpreted to refer only to matters that directly threaten the Indians' land title. See Rincon Band of Mission Indians v. County of San Diego, 324 F.Supp. 371 (S.D.Cal.1971), aff'd on other grounds, 495 F.2d 1 (9th Cir.1974).

The most reasonable definition of "encumbrance" probably lies between the two extreme views. The term cannot include all criminal legislation that might directly or indirectly affect the utility value of Indian lands, but it also ought not to be restricted to traditional liens upon the land. State zoning laws, for example, have been held to be encumbrances within the meaning of Public Law 280. Santa Rosa Band v. Kings County, 532 F.2d 655, 667 (9th Cir.1975). The controversy over the meaning of the term may tend to decline in importance because Public Law 280 can no longer be viewed as authorizing general state regulation of tribes or tribal members in Indian country, whether or not the regulation constitutes an encumbrance of trust lands. Bryan v. Itasca County, 426 U.S. 373 (1976).

State and local land use regulation is also inhibited by the limitation that nothing in the criminal or civil grants of jurisdiction "shall authorize regulation of the use of [trust] property in a manner inconsistent with any Federal treaty, agreement, or statute or with any regulation made pursuant thereto * * *." 18 U.S.C.A. § 1162(b); 28 U.S.C.A. § 1360(b). The Secretary of Interior has issued a regulation excluding state and local land use regulation of any trust land leased from Indians or Indian tribes, except insofar as the Secretary specifically adopts such regulations. 25 C.F.R. § 1.4. The regulation was attacked as unauthorized, but a court of appeals upheld it as applied to lands purchased by the Secretary for Indians under 25 U.S.C.A. § 465, and suggested that the regulation generally may be authorized by the congressional grant to the Secretary of broad authority over Indian affairs in 25 U.S.C.A. § 2. Santa Rosa Band v. Kings County, 532 F.2d 655, 665–67 and n. 19 (9th Cir.1975).

Another provision in the grant of criminal jurisdiction in Public Law 280 states that nothing in the grant "shall deprive any Indian or any Indian tribe, band, or community of any right, privilege, or immunity afforded under Federal treaty, agreement, or statute with respect to hunting, trapping, or fishing or the control, licensing, or regulation thereof." 18 U.S.C.A. § 1162(b). This restriction simply leaves the states in the same position with regard to treaty hunting and fishing rights that they occupy in the absence of Public Law 280. That position is the subject of much litigation and is discussed in Chapter XV, below.

In at least two cases dealing with termination of the federal trust relationship, however, the language of Public Law 280 has assumed special significance with respect to hunting and fishing. In Menominee Tribe v. United States, 391 U.S. 404 (1968), the Supreme Court held that a federal statute terminating the trust relationship between the federal government and the Menominee Tribe did not extinguish treaty rights to hunt and fish. Tribal members could therefore hunt and fish free of general state regulation even though the Termination Act provided that "the laws of the several States shall apply to the tribe and its members in the same manner as they apply to other citizens or persons within their jurisdiction." 25 U.S.C.A. § 899, repealed, P.L. 93–197, § 3(b), 87 Stat. 770 (1973). The Court relied heavily on the fact that Public Law 280, which came from the same committees of Congress and was amended at about the same time as the Termination Act, expressly excluded any grant of power to the states to interfere with treaty hunting and fishing rights. Reading the two statutes in pari materia, the Supreme Court concluded that Congress could not have intended termination to cause the loss of the Menominees' treaty rights. The same reasoning subsequently was employed to preserve the treaty hunting and fishing rights of the terminated Klamath Tribe. Kimball v. Callahan, 493 F.2d 564 (9th Cir.1974), and Kimball v. Callahan, 590 F.2d 768 (9th Cir.1979).

F. ASSUMPTION OF JURISDICTION BY THE OPTIONAL STATES

In addition to conferring criminal and civil juris-diction on six named states, Public Law 280 author-ized all other states to assume such jurisdiction over Indian country if they chose. P.L. 280, § 7, 67 Stat. 588, 590 (1953). Under this provision there have been total or partial assumptions of jurisdiction by the following states: Arizona, Florida, Idaho, Iowa, Montana, Nevada, North Dakota, Utah and Wash-ington. The manner in which these optional states assumed jurisdiction varied greatly, ranging from total assumptions of both criminal and civil jurisdic-tion, Fla. Stat. Ann. § 285.16, to a very limited assumption for the purposes of regulating only air pollution, Ariz. Rev. Stat. Ann. § 49–561, repealed Laws 2003, Ch. 238, § 4. Other states assumed jurisdiction only over certain reservations, e.g., Mont.Code Ann. §§ 2–1–301 to 306, or over certain offenses or claims, Wash.Rev.Code § 37.12.010. In some cases, the assuming state required consent of the tribes, but Public Law 280 did not require it.

There was considerable doubt about the validity of partial assumptions of jurisdiction under Public Law 280 as it was originally passed, because it authorized the optional states to assume jurisdic-tion "as provided for in this act." Because the mandatory states were given total jurisdiction, an argument could be made that optional states had to assume all civil or criminal jurisdiction or none. Otherwise the states might simply assume advanta-geous portions of jurisdiction and leave the most expensive or difficult enforcement problems to the tribes or the federal government. See Goldberg, Public Law 280: *The Limits of State Jurisdiction Over Reservation Indians*, 22 U.C.L.A.L.Rev. 535, 548–49, 553–55 (1975). In 1968 Congress eliminated all doubt about the validity of partial assumptions of jurisdiction made after that date; it amended Public Law 280 to permit the states to assume "such measure of jurisdiction over any or all of such offenses committed within such Indian country or any part thereof" and "such measure of jurisdiction over any or all such civil causes of action arising within such Indian country or any part thereof" as the state might choose to acquire with the consent of the tribes. 25 U.S.C.A. §§ 1321(a), 1322(a). There still remained a question whether partial assumptions of jurisdiction occurring before 1968 were valid, but the Supreme Court largely settled the issue in Washington v. Confederated Bands and Tribes of the Yakima Indian Nation, 439 U.S. 463 (1979). In that case the Court upheld an incredibly complicated partial assumption of jurisdiction by the State of Washington that had occurred in 1963. The Court reasoned that the selective assumption was authorized by § 7 of Public Law 280, which permitted the optional states to assume jurisdiction "in such manner" as the people of the State, by legislative action, bound themselves to assume. P.L. 280, § 7, 67 Stat. 588, 590 (1953). Subsequently, however, the Eighth Circuit held that South Dakota's narrow assumption in 1961 of jurisdiction only over highways was invalid as inconsistent with the purposes of Public Law 280. Rosebud Sioux Tribe v. South Dakota, 900 F.2d 1164 (8th Cir.1990). *Rosebud* is probably unique, however, because of South Dakota's long and involved history of abortive attempts to assume Public Law 280 jurisdiction. See id. at 1166–68.

The *Yakima* case also settled another major controversy that had surrounded the assumption of jurisdiction by some of the western states. These states had clauses in their constitutions disclaiming all title to Indian lands and providing that such lands should "remain under the absolute jurisdiction and control of the congress of the United States * * *." E.g., Wash.Const. Art. XXVI. These disclaimers had been required by the relevant congressional enabling acts as conditions of admission to the Union. As a consequence, they could not be amended without the consent of Congress. Congress expressly gave its consent in § 6 of Public Law 280 "to the people of any State to amend, where necessary, their State constitution or existing statutes, as the case may be, to remove any legal impediment to the assumption of civil and criminal jurisdiction in accordance with the provisions of this Act." P.L. 280, § 6, 67 Stat. 588, 590 (1953). Several of the disclaimer states, however, simply assumed jurisdiction under Public Law 280 by statute, without bothering to amend their constitutions. This omission raised substantial questions about the validity of the assumptions of jurisdiction. In the *Yakima* case, the Supreme Court concluded that Congress had not intended to require such an amendment if state law itself did not require it. Washington's assumption of jurisdiction was therefore upheld.

Perhaps the greatest criticism of Public Law 280 was that it permitted the states to assume jurisdiction without the consent of the concerned tribes. Congress reacted to this criticism in the Indian Civil Rights Act of 1968 by amending Public Law 280 to provide that no states could assume jurisdiction thereafter without the consent of the tribe or tribes concerned. 25 U.S.C.A. §§ 1321(a), 1322(a). This consent may be obtained only by a majority vote of the adult Indians of the tribe in a special election. 25 U.S.C.A. § 1326. As a result of this provision, there has been only one assumption of jurisdiction under Public Law 280 since 1968—that of Utah—and Utah bound itself to retrocede that jurisdiction whenever a tribe requests it by a majority vote at a special election. Utah Code Ann. § 63–36–15. It is not likely that many states will agree to such a provision, and the result is that the 1968 amendments have largely halted further expansion of Public Law 280 jurisdiction. The 1968 amendments are not retroactive, however; they do not invalidate those assumptions of jurisdiction made without Indian consent prior to 1968 nor do they affect the jurisdiction originally conferred on the mandatory states. United States v. Hoodie, 588 F.2d 292 (9th Cir.1978).

The existence of the optional provisions of Public Law 280 has had an important collateral effect. The Supreme Court has held that Public Law 280 provides the exclusive method by which states may acquire jurisdiction over Indian country, and that conclusion has resulted in the invalidation of less formal acquisitions of state power. In Kennerly v. District Court, 400 U.S. 423 (1971), a tribal council had by resolution provided that civil jurisdiction over suits against Indians should be concurrent in the state and the tribe. The state court exercised jurisdiction in such a case, but the Supreme Court reversed, holding that the state could not acquire jurisdiction without following the requirements of Public Law 280 as amended by the 1968 Indian Civil Rights Act. See also *Fort Berthold I* and *II*, 467 U.S. 138 (1984) and 476 U.S. 877 (1986). Subsequently, the failure of the State of Arizona to assume general Public Law 280 jurisdiction was used by the Supreme Court to reinforce its conclusion that the state had no power to tax income earned by an Indian in Indian country. McClanahan v. Arizona State Tax Com'n, 411 U.S. 164 (1973).

G. RETROCESSION OF JURISDICTION BY A STATE TO THE FEDERAL GOVERNMENT

In further response to criticism of Public Law 280 by both tribes and states, Congress in its 1968 amendments provided a method for states to return Public Law 280 jurisdiction to the federal government. The United States was authorized "to accept a retrocession by any State of all or any measure of the criminal or civil jurisdiction" acquired by that state pursuant to the mandatory or optional provisions of Public Law 280. 25 U.S.C.A. § 1323(a). The President thereupon designated the Secretary of the Interior to exercise the discretionary power of the United States to accept retrocessions of jurisdiction. Exec. Order 11435, 33 Fed.Reg. 17339 (1968).

Notably absent from the retrocession provision is any mechanism for requiring tribal consent or permitting tribal initiative for retrocession. The original option is entirely that of the retroceding state, although the Secretary of the Interior may exercise discretion in accepting or rejecting the proposed retrocession. If the affected tribes wish to influence the process, they must do so by political means directed at the state or the Secretary.

The few questions that have arisen over retrocession have concerned the state's method of retroceding and the effect of the Secretary's acceptance. For example, the Governor of Washington retroceded jurisdiction over the Suquamish Port Madison Reservation by proclamation, without any action by the state legislature. The Secretary accepted it, and the courts examining it have held that the validity of the retrocession is a question of federal law and that validity was established by the Secretary's acceptance. Oliphant v. Schlie, 544 F.2d 1007 (9th Cir.1976), rev'd on other grounds, 435 U.S. 191; United States v. Lawrence, 595 F.2d 1149 (9th Cir.1979). A different question arose when Nebraska by legislative act offered to retrocede jurisdiction over the Omaha and Winnebago Reservations. The Secretary accepted the retrocession of the Omaha

Reservation, but not the Winnebago. Nebraska contended that the retrocession was invalid because the Secretary's acceptance deviated from the state's offer. That contention was rejected and the retrocession of jurisdiction over the Omaha Reservation was held valid. Omaha Tribe of Nebraska v. Village of Walthill, 460 F.2d 1327 (8th Cir.1972).

A question has been raised whether retrocession is the only method a state may use to confer enforcement authority on tribal officers. In State v. Manypenny, 662 N.W.2d 183 (Minn.App.), review granted (Aug. 19, 2003), a tribal officer arrested a non-Indian on a reservation over which the state had not retroceded jurisdiction. The officer acted pursuant to a state-tribal agreement authorizing him to enforce state laws on the reservation. The court upheld the arrest, holding that a state need not retrocede jurisdiction in order to enter such a cooperative agreement.

The provisions of Public Law 280 for assumption and retrocession of jurisdiction played what can only be described as a bizarre part in Three Affiliated Tribes of the Fort Berthold Reservation v. Wold Engineering, 467 U.S. 138 (1984) and Fort Berthold Reservation v. Wold Engineering, 476 U.S. 877 (1986) (*Fort Berthold I* and *II*). In that case the State of North Dakota, apparently in reliance on Public Law 280, attempted to disclaim jurisdiction over actions brought in state court by tribes or tribal Indians, unless the tribe consented generally to state jurisdiction. In *Fort Berthold I*, the Supreme Court understandably held that state courts had jurisdiction over such cases before Public Law 280 was passed and that, in essence, Public Law 280 simply had nothing to do with the case. 467 U.S. at 150. The Court nevertheless remanded to the state supreme court because that court's jurisdictional ruling might have been based on an erroneous view that Public Law 280 governed.

On remand, the Supreme Court of North Dakota adhered to the view that the state courts had no jurisdiction. It held that, under state law, such cases could be brought only if the tribe consented to full state jurisdiction on its reservation, and if the tribe waived its sovereign immunity. The United States Supreme Court then reversed. *Fort Berthold II*, 476 U.S. 877 (1986). It held that the scheme provided by Public Law 280 for the assumption of civil jurisdiction (which did not include the assumption of the jurisdiction the state courts already had over suits by Indians against non-Indians), and for the retrocession of only that jurisdiction assumed pursuant to Public Law 280, preempted the state from disclaiming jurisdiction in the manner it had. Thus Public Law 280, which had no effect one way or another on jurisdiction over cases brought in state court by Indians against non-Indians, was held to preempt the state's denial of such jurisdiction. Whatever the analytical difficulties, the result in *Berthold II* is clear: Indian plaintiffs are guaranteed access to state courts for suits against non-

Indians. See also State v. Zaman, 190 Ariz. 208, 946 P.2d 459 (1997). That outcome is consistent with that reached by several state courts on equal protection grounds. E.g., Paiz v. Hughes, 76 N.M. 562, 417 P.2d 51 (1966); Bonnet v. Seekins, 126 Mont. 24, 243 P.2d 317 (1952).

CHAPTER IX

TAXATION AND REGULATION IN INDIAN COUNTRY

A. INTRODUCTION

A distinction is drawn in the field of Indian Law between governmental power to tax or regulate and the power to adjudicate. This division is significant because the two kinds of jurisdiction are not always coextensive. Public Law 280, for example, gives certain states the power to adjudicate civil controversies arising in Indian country but does not authorize those states to exercise their full powers of taxation or regulation there. Bryan v. Itasca County, 426 U.S. 373 (1976). Tribal powers to adjudicate and to regulate are more nearly congruent now, because in Strate v. A–1 Contractors, 520 U.S. 438 (1997), the Supreme Court ruled that "as to nonmembers, a tribe's adjudicative jurisdiction does not exceed its legislative jurisdiction." Id. at 453. The Supreme Court has left open the question "whether a tribe's adjudicatory jurisdiction over nonmember defendants *equals* its legislative jurisdiction." Nevada v. Hicks, 533 U.S. 353, 358 (2001).

When the question is one of state power, even when Public Law 280 does not apply, the Supreme Court tends to treat issues of taxation and regulation somewhat differently from questions of adjudicatory jurisdiction. At least until recently, state exercise of adjudicatory jurisdiction has been subjected to a rigorous application of the test of Williams v. Lee, 358 U.S. 217 (1959): absent governing acts of Congress, the state may not exercise jurisdiction if it would interfere with the "right of reservation Indians to make their own laws and be ruled by them." Id. at 220. In theory, at least, this test precludes state interference with tribal self-government no matter how important the state's interest may be. It still clearly precludes the exercise of state adjudicatory jurisdiction over reservation-based claims against tribal members.

When the state seeks to extend its power of taxation or regulation to Indian country, however, the emphasis changes. Although the Supreme Court has stated that the rule of Williams v. Lee still applies, e.g., White Mountain Apache Tribe v. Bracker, 448 U.S. 136, 142 (1980), the *Williams* test tends to be subordinated. The Supreme Court is likely "to avoid reliance on platonic notions of Indian sovereignty and to look instead to the applicable treaties and statutes" to determine whether they preempt state law. McClanahan v. Arizona State Tax Comm'n, 411 U.S. 164, 172 (1973). This preemption test is more fully discussed in Chapter III, Section B, and Chapter VII, Section C(2), above. It appears to presume that state law applies unless federal law or policy excludes it. Preemption analysis injects both flexibility and unpredictability into questions of taxation and regulation because the result in each case depends upon a fact-specific balancing of the competing interests. See, e.g., New Mexico v. Mescalero Apache Tribe, 462 U.S. 324, 334 (1983).

Despite the uncertainties inherent in the preemption analysis now being applied, there have been enough decisions in the area of taxation to permit a fairly complete description of the taxing powers of the federal government, the states, and the tribes. Fish and game regulation has also been the subject of extensive litigation, and the topic is sufficiently distinctive that it is treated separately in Chapter XV, below. The law governing other kinds of regulation is less complete, but is growing rapidly as issues of environmental and economic regulation increasingly find their way to court.

B. FEDERAL TAXATION IN INDIAN COUNTRY

The federal taxing power does not depend on geography, and it is fully effective in Indian country with regard to both Indians and non-Indians. Congress can choose to exempt Indians or tribes from taxation, but the exemption must be clearly expressed. Thus federal excise and occupational taxes were held to be applicable to tribal gaming operations; an exemption from "reporting and withholding" was not sufficient to exempt from the taxes themselves. Chickasaw Nation v. United States, 534 U.S. 84 (2001). Similarly, no exemption from federal fuel taxes was implied from a treaty granting the right "to travel the public highways without restriction" to bring goods to market. Ramsey v. United States, 302 F.3d 1074 (9th Cir.2002). Although the treaty had made the treaty Indians exempt from *state* vehicle taxes, the standard for finding an exemption from federal taxes was stricter. Id.

Contrary to a common misconception, Indians are not exempt from federal income tax by reason of being Indians or because their income is earned in Indian country. Superintendent of Five Civilized Tribes v. Commissioner, 295 U.S. 418 (1935). There are, however, certain kinds of income of Indians that Congress has elected not to tax. Perhaps the most important is income from individually allotted land that remains in trust. The General Allotment Act of 1887 provided for tribal lands to be allotted to individual Indians in trust for a period of years, after which the lands were to be conveyed to the allottees in fee "free of all charge or incumbrance whatsoever." 25 U.S.C.A. § 348. This provision has been interpreted to prevent taxation of income or capital gains "derived directly" from allotted land while it remains in trust. Squire v. Capoeman, 351 U.S. 1 (1956). This exemption applies to rents and royalties as well as income from sale of crops or minerals from the land. Rev.Rul. 56–342, 1956–2 Cum.Bull. 20. Gain from the sale of livestock raised and grazed on allotted trust land has also been ruled exempt. Rev.Rul. 62–16, 1962–1 Cum.Bull. 7. On the other hand, income from the operation of a motel or a smokeshop on allotted land has been held to derive from labor and the use of capital improvements rather than directly from the land itself, and has accordingly been held taxable. Critzer v. United States, 597 F.2d 708 (Ct.Cl.1979); Dillon v. United States, 792 F.2d 849 (9th Cir.1986). Similarly, when exempt income is reinvested, the reinvestment income is subject to taxation. Superintendent of Five Civilized Tribes v. Commissioner, 295 U.S. 418 (1935).

Income from trust lands allotted under other allotment acts is exempt from federal taxation even though those acts do not contain the same protective language as the General Allotment Act. Stevens v. Commissioner, 452 F.2d 741 (9th Cir.1971). When allotted land is removed from trust and a fee patent is issued to the allottee, income from the land (like the land itself) becomes fully taxable. Choteau v. Burnet, 283 U.S. 691 (1931). Income of an Indian from trust land leased from the tribe has been held taxable on the ground that the individual Indian had no present or potential ownership interest and the tax could not therefore be a charge or burden on the land. Holt v. Commissioner, 364 F.2d 38 (8th Cir.1966); United States v. Anderson, 625 F.2d 910 (9th Cir.1980).

C. STATE TAXATION IN INDIAN COUNTRY

1. STATE TAXATION OF TRIBES AND TRIBAL MEMBERS

State powers of taxation are severely limited in Indian country, particularly where Indian interests are affected. It has long been settled that the states have no power to tax Indian trust lands, whether held tribally or in allotments. The Kansas Indians, 72 U.S. (5 Wall.) 737 (1866). This exclusion was required by Congress to be written into the constitutions of several western states as conditions of their admission into the Union. The states are also without power to tax other kinds of Indian trust property. Congress may change these rules, and on rare occasion has done so. In 1924, Congress authorized the states to tax royalties from mineral leases of Indian trust lands. 25 U.S.C.A. § 398. In the absence of an explicit provision, however, the usual rule controls, and the state may not tax such receipts. Thus tribal royalties from leases entered after 1938 are not taxable by the states, because the 1939 Indian Mineral Leasing Act contained no such authorization. Montana v. Blackfeet Tribe, 471 U.S. 759 (1985).

At times the immunity of tribes from state taxation in Indian country has been thought to arise from the general doctrine of federal-state intergovernmental immunity—a doctrine that has enjoyed an unstable career. In truth, however, Indian immunities from state taxation arise from federal policies quite distinct from those relating to traditional intergovernmental immunity, and the Supreme Court has recognized that the Indian policy must be evaluated on its own merits. McClanahan v. Arizona State Tax Com'n, 411 U.S. 164, 169–170 (1973). In fact, the exclusion of the states from taxation of Indian property does not even depend on federal trust status of the property; in the absence of congressional authorization, states lack the power to tax even non-trust property when it is owned by a tribal member and has its situs on that tribe's reservation. Bryan v. Itasca County, 426 U.S. 373 (1976); Moe v. Confederated Salish & Kootenai Tribes, 425 U.S. 463 (1976). Thus a state may not impose vehicle excise and registration fees upon Indians who live and garage their vehicles in Indian country. Oklahoma Tax Comm'n v. Sac and Fox Nation, 508 U.S. 114 (1993). Similarly, a state may not impose motor fuel excise taxes in Indian country when their legal incidence falls upon the tribe or its members. Oklahoma Tax Comm'n v. Chickasaw Nation, 515 U.S. 450 (1995).

States are preempted by federal law and policy from taxing the reservation income of tribal members domiciled on the tribe's reservation, as the Supreme Court held in the pivotal decision of McClanahan v. Arizona State Tax Com'n, 411 U.S. 164 (1973); see also Oklahoma Tax Comm'n v. Sac and Fox Nation, 508 U.S. 114 (1993). Among the statutes that the Court relied upon in *McClanahan* was the Buck Act, 4 U.S.C.A. § 105 et seq., which extended state taxing power into federal reserves but provided that nothing in the applicable sections of the Act should "be deemed to authorize the levy or collection of any tax on or from any Indian not otherwise taxed." 4 U.S.C.A. § 109. The Court also pointed out that it was very difficult to see how the state could impose or collect its tax when it lacked civil and criminal adjudicatory jurisdiction over Indians in Indian country. The Court has subsequently observed that the policies in favor of immunity of tribes and members from state taxation are so strong, and the corresponding state interest so weak, that they need not be rebalanced in each new case; a *per se* rule against such taxation is applied. California v. Cabazon Band of Mission Indians, 480 U.S. 202, 215 n.17 (1987); see also Oklahoma Tax Comm'n v. Chickasaw Nation, 515 U.S. 450, 458 (1995).

The General Allotment Act, however, has been held to authorize the states to tax fee land within a reservation, whether owned by Indians or non-Indians; the congressional intent was to permit the land to become alienable and taxable when a fee patent was issued. County of Yakima v. Confederated Tribes and Bands of the Yakima Indian Nation, 502 U.S. 251 (1992). Thus, when a tribe reacquires in fee simple land that was formerly allotted and patented under the Allotment Act, the state may tax the lands. Cass County, Minnesota v. Leech Lake Band of Chippewa Indians, 524 U.S. 103 (1998). In *Cass County*, the Supreme Court held that "[w]hen Congress makes Indian reservation land freely alienable, it manifests an unmistakably clear intent to render such land subject to state and local taxation." Id. at 115. The tribe can escape taxation of reacquired lands by successfully petitioning the Secretary to accept a transfer of the lands to be held in trust by the United States for the tribe. Id.; see 25 U.S.C.A. § 465. The permission to tax derived from the process of allotment is limited to taxation of the patented allotted land only; it does not authorize taxation in Indian country of other activities such as the *sale* of those lands by the tribe or its members. *Yakima*, 502 U.S. at 268–70. The state also may not impose a compensating use tax triggered by a transfer of land by the tribe. Quinault Indian Nation v. Grays Harbor County, 310 F.3d 645 (9th Cir.2002).

In an interesting twist on *Cass County*, the Second Circuit held that reservation land that had long ago been conveyed in violation of the Trade and Intercourse Act, and had been repurchased by the tribe in the open market, remained exempt from state taxation. Oneida Indian Nation v. City of Sherrill, New York, 337 F.3d 139 (2d Cir.2003). Because the land had never properly been removed from reservation status, it retained its tax-free status.

Outside of Indian country, every Indian is subject to state jurisdiction and if he or she engages in taxable activity there, the state can impose its tax unless a treaty precludes it. A treaty guaranteeing tribal members the "right, in common with citizens of the United States, to travel upon all public highways" conferred an exemption from state truck license and weight fees for off-reservation travel to markets. Cree v. Flores, 157 F.3d 762 (9th Cir. 1998). Such provisions are exceptional, however. The state can tax income of a tribal member domiciled outside of Indian country even if the income is earned from employment by the tribe on the reservation. Oklahoma Tax Comm'n v. Chickasaw Nation, 515 U.S. 450 (1995). Even an Indian tribe is subject to state taxation if it undertakes to operate a business outside of Indian country. Mescalero Apache Tribe v. Jones, 411 U.S. 145 (1973).

2. STATE TAXATION OF NONMEMBERS

At the time *McClanahan* and prior cases restricting state taxation were decided, it was assumed that the restriction imposed upon the state was against taxing *any* Indian in Indian country, regardless of the tribal affiliation of that Indian. In 1980, however, the Supreme Court drew a sharp distinction between members of the tribe that governed a given reservation and other Indians not members of that tribe. In Washington v. Confederated Tribes of Colville Indian Reservation, 447 U.S. 134 (1980), the Court held that the State of Washington could impose cigarette and sales taxes on sales made to nonmember Indians in Indian country. The Court stated:

> Federal statutes, even given the broadest reading to which they are reasonably susceptible, cannot be said to pre-empt Washington's power to impose its taxes on Indians not members of the Tribe. * * * [T]he mere fact that nonmembers resident on the reservation come within the definition of "Indian" for purposes of the Indian Reorganization Act of 1934 * * * does not demonstrate a congressional intent to exempt such Indians from state taxation.

Nor would the imposition of Washington's tax on these purchasers contravene the principle of tribal self-government, for the simple reason that nonmembers are not constituents of the governing Tribe. For most practical purposes those Indians stand on the same footing as non-Indians resident on the reservation.

447 U.S. at 160–61. The Court repeated this ruling in Oklahoma Tax Comm'n v. Citizen Band Potawatomi Indian Tribe, 498 U.S. 505, 512–13 (1991). It is clear, therefore, that the Court now treats nonmember Indians the same as non-Indians for tax purposes.

The state has long been allowed to impose taxes on the property of non-Indians located within Indian country. Utah & Northern Ry. v. Fisher, 116 U.S. 28 (1885); Thomas v. Gay, 169 U.S. 264 (1898). It has also been permitted to tax reservation income of non-Indians domiciled on Indian reservations. Kahn v. Arizona State Tax Com'n, 16 Ariz.App. 17, 490 P.2d 846 (1971), appeal dismissed, 411 U.S. 941 (1973); see Oklahoma Tax Comm'n v. Chickasaw Nation, 515 U.S. 450, 467 (1995). The state may also tax a nonmember Indian's income earned on the host reservation or outside of Indian country. LaRock v. Wisconsin Dept. of Revenue, 241 Wis.2d 87, 621 N.W.2d 907 (2001); Esquiro v. Department of Revenue, State of Oregon, 328 Or. 37, 969 P.2d 381 (1998). There are, however, important limitations on the general power of states to levy taxes in Indian country. The primary limitation is that the state may not tax when the subject matter is preempted by federal law.

The seminal preemption case is Warren Trading Post Co. v. Arizona Tax Com'n, 380 U.S. 685 (1965). There the Supreme Court held that Arizona could not tax the gross receipts of a non-Indian trading post on the Navajo Reservation. The Court pointed out that Indian traders had to be federally licensed and were subject to extensive federal regulation. These regulations took the business of Indian trading "so fully in hand that no room remains for state laws imposing additional burdens upon traders." 380 U.S. at 690. Although this expansive language suggests that no state regulation of any kind could be imposed on Indian traders, the Supreme Court has since rejected that implication in holding that Indian traders could be required to collect and remit state sales taxes collected from nonmember purchasers of cigarettes. Department of Taxation and Finance v. Milhelm Attea & Bros., Inc., 512 U.S. 61 (1994).

The Supreme Court has quite regularly invalidated state taxes imposed on non-Indian contractors engaged in sales or services to the tribes in Indian country. In White Mountain Apache Tribe v. Bracker, 448 U.S. 136 (1980), the Court struck down state taxes on non-Indians cutting timber on a reservation and delivering it to the tribal sawmill. The taxes were a motor carrier license tax based on gross receipts and a fuel use tax. They were held to be preempted by extensive federal regulations applying to timber operations in Indian country. See also Hoopa Valley Tribe v. Nevins, 881 F.2d 657 (9th Cir.1989). The Court in *Bracker* observed that "[t]he unique historical origins of tribal sovereignty make it generally unhelpful to apply to federal enactments regulating Indian tribes those standards of pre-emption that have emerged in other areas of the law." 448 U.S. at 143. In a contemporaneous case, the Supreme Court held invalid a state gross receipts tax applied to the sale of machinery in Indian country by a non-Indian dealer whose permanent place of business was off-reservation. The Court ruled that the sale was preempted by federal statutes regulating Indian trading, which applied to the sale. Central Machinery Co. v. Arizona State Tax Com'n, 448 U.S. 160 (1980). Similarly, the Court has struck down a gross receipts tax imposed on a non-Indian contractor building a school for an Indian school board on the reservation. Ramah Navajo School Board v. Bureau of Revenue, 458 U.S. 832 (1982). The Court stated that "ambiguities in federal law should be construed generously, and federal pre-emption is not limited to those situations where Congress has explicitly announced an intention to pre-empt state activity." Id. at 838. When a nonmember company contracts with the *federal government* to perform work on a reservation, however, the state can tax impose a gross receipts tax on its activities. Arizona Dept. of Revenue v. Blaze Construction Co., 526 U.S. 32 (1999).

The line of cases from *Bracker* to *Ramah* seems to be at odds with the Supreme Court's later statement in Cotton Petroleum Corp. v. New Mexico, 490 U.S. 163, 175 (1989), that "[u]nder current doctrine, * * * a State can impose a nondiscriminatory tax on private parties with whom the United States or an Indian tribe does business, even though the financial burden of the tax may fall on the United States or tribe." This statement must be taken in context, however. It concludes a discussion of the rise and fall of the intergovernmental immunity doctrine, and points out that all that remains of that doctrine is a prohibition against state taxes imposed directly on the federal government or the tribes. The quoted statement does not purport to describe preemption. Indeed, *Cotton Petroleum* undertakes a preemption analysis after its discussion of intergovernmental immunities. It concludes that New Mexico may impose a severance tax on a non-Indian corporation producing oil and gas on a reservation, even though the tribe also imposes a severance tax. In so holding, *Cotton Petroleum* does weigh the competing interests in a manner more favorable to the state than was the case in *Bracker* and *Ramah*, but it does not overrule those cases. It distinguishes them partly on the grounds that federal policies were more pronounced in *Bracker* and *Ramah*, that the state in those cases provided virtually no services except taxation, and that the burden of the tax fell directly on the tribes. *Cotton Petroleum*, 490 U.S. at 183–87. *Cotton Petroleum* also distinguished its summary affirmance of the Ninth Circuit's decision holding the Montana coal severance tax preempted, see Crow Tribe of Indians

v. Montana, 819 F.2d 895 (9th Cir.1987), aff'd, 484 U.S. 997 (1988), by pointing out that the Montana tax was extraordinarily high. *Cotton Petroleum*, 490 U.S. at 186 n.17.

Thus, although *Cotton Petroleum* tilts more toward the states than the Supreme Court's earlier preemption cases, it does not represent a total change in direction. It does re-emphasize some propositions that were already manifest in prior Supreme Court or lower court decisions. For example, some indirect burden on the tribe has often been permitted. A state has been allowed to impose a "possessory interest" tax on non-Indian lessees of Indian trust lands, even though the effect may be to reduce the amount of rental the Indians are able to obtain for their land. Agua Caliente Band of Mission Indians v. County of Riverside, 442 F.2d 1184 (9th Cir.1971); Fort Mojave Tribe v. County of San Bernardino, 543 F.2d 1253 (9th Cir.1976).

In permitting dual taxation, *Cotton Petroleum* echoed Washington v. Confederated Tribes of the Colville Indian Reservation, 447 U.S. 134 (1980), in which both the tribe and the state imposed a tax on cigarettes sold by tribal shops in Indian country. The Court in *Colville* stated:

There is no direct conflict between the state and tribal schemes, since each government is free to impose its taxes without ousting the other. Although taxes can be used for distributive or regulatory purposes, as well as for raising revenue, we see no nonrevenue purposes to the tribal taxes at issue in these cases, and, as already noted, we perceive no intent on the part of Congress to authorize the Tribes to pre-empt otherwise valid state taxes.

447 U.S. at 159. It is therefore clear that the mere existence of a tribal tax does not preempt a state tax even when the result is double taxation that places those who deal with tribes at a disadvantage. See also Fort Mojave Tribe v. County of San Bernardino, 543 F.2d 1253 (9th Cir.1976). *Colville's* language does suggest, however, that when the tribal tax has regulatory purposes that are hindered by a state tax, the state tax may be invalid for interfering with tribal self-government.

Cases like *Colville* involving state cigarette taxes probably go farthest in permitting imposition of state taxes. *Colville* held that sales by a tribe to non-Indians and nonmember Indians were taxable by the state, but that sales to tribal members were not. The state could require the tribal organization to affix state tax stamps to packages of cigarettes and to keep records of exempt and non-exempt sales. None of these provisions was found to interfere with tribal self-government or to be federally preempted. A major reason for the result was that the Court viewed tribal cigarette sales to nonmembers as a "magnet" operation, in which the tribe adds no reservation-based value to the product but markets its tax exemption to purchasers who would otherwise buy elsewhere. *Colville*, 447 U.S. at 155. See also Moe v. Confederated Salish and Kootenai Tribes, 425 U.S. 463 (1976). The same taxes were

upheld in Oklahoma Tax Comm'n v. Citizen Band
Potawatomi Indian Tribe, 498 U.S. 505 (1991), but
the Court also held that the tribe retained its sovereign immunity from suit to collect the taxes. The
states are therefore left with a substantial remedy
problem when the cigarette seller is the tribe. The
Court stated that it has never held individual tribal
officers immune from damage suits by the state, id.
at 514, but those officers sued in their individual
capacities are unlikely to have deep pockets. The
officers may not be sued in their official capacities;
they share the immunity of the tribe when acting
within the scope of their official duties. Hardin v.
White Mountain Apache Tribe, 779 F.2d 476, 479
(9th Cir.1985). The most effective solution for the
states is to enforce the tax against those who supply
the cigarettes to the tribes. See *Potawatomi*, 498
U.S. at 514; Department of Taxation and Finance v.
Milhelm Attea & Bros., Inc., 512 U.S. 61 (1994).

The principle of the cigarette cases has been
applied to permit states to impose taxes on sales
and rentals by non-Indian businesses to non-Indians at a shopping mall on a reservation. Salt River
Pima–Maricopa Indian Community v. Arizona, 50
F.3d 734 (9th Cir.1995). The court permitted the
tax because "the Community's activities did not
contribute to the value of the goods sold, and * * *
Arizona provides most of the governmental services
used by the non-Indian taxpayers." Id. at 736. Similarly, Arizona was permitted to impose a transaction tax on ticket sales for entertainment events
conducted by non-Indians for non-Indians at a res-

ervation lake and concert site. Gila River Indian Community v. Waddell, 91 F.3d 1232 (9th Cir.1996). State services and activities connected with the events predominated over those of the tribe. On the other hand, where a tribe had invested significant funds and effort in constructing and operating off-track betting facilities (and the federal government had regulated gaming in the tribe's interest), a state tax was held to be preempted; the tribe was not "merely serving as a conduit for the products of others." Cabazon Band of Mission Indians v. Wilson, 37 F.3d 430, 435 (9th Cir.1994).

The state has also largely succeeded in taxing vehicle fuel sales to nonmembers, whether by a tribe or a nonmember retailer. See Prairie Band Potawatomi Nation v. Richards, 241 F.Supp.2d 1295 (D.Kan. 2003); Kaul v. Kansas Dept. of Revenue, 266 Kan. 464, 970 P.2d 60 (1998). Where the purchaser was a school operated by a tribe under contract with the federal government pursuant to the Indian Self–Determination and Education Assistance Act, however, a tax on off-reservation fuel distributors was preempted by that Act because it made tribal operation of the school more expensive than government operation. Ramah Navajo School Board, Inc. v. New Mexico Taxation & Revenue Dept., 127 N.M. 101, 977 P.2d 1021 (N.M.App. 1999).

Although all of these cases depend largely or entirely upon preemption analysis, the rule of Williams v. Lee, 358 U.S. 217 (1959)—that the states may not interfere with the right of reservation Indians to make their own laws and be governed by them—has been held to be an additional, independent limitation on the states' power to tax. E.g., White Mountain Apache Tribe v. Bracker, 448 U.S. 136, 142 (1980); Ramah Navajo School Board v. Bureau of Revenue, 458 U.S. 832, 837 (1982). So stated, the rule would doubtless curb any attempt of the states to tax the sovereign functions of the tribes. Where the tax is upon nonmembers, however, the absolute prohibition of Williams v. Lee tends to recede into the background while the courts engage in the balancing of interests called for by the preemption approach that they prefer. Id. When that process results in the preemption of the state tax, the rule of Williams v. Lee is sometimes then invoked as additional support for the result. E.g., Crow Tribe v. Montana, 819 F.2d at 902–03.

D. TRIBAL TAXATION

Even though taxation is one of the most basic powers of self-government, most tribes have only recently begun to exercise it. Tribes always have been assumed to have power to tax their own members, but traditional Indian hostility to taxation and the obvious poverty of a large part of the tribal population forestalled attempts to tax. It is still true that there are few tribal taxes aimed primarily at the member population. Although tribal taxes targeted at non-Indians are nothing new, see Morris v. Hitchcock, 194 U.S. 384 (1904), they have increased in recent years, partly because tribes have heightened revenue needs and partly because tribes are attempting to compensate for what they regard as unfairly low current rates of return from leases or licenses granted to non-Indian enterprises in the past.

The new taxes initially met with considerable success. In Washington v. Confederated Tribes of Colville Indian Reservation, 447 U.S. 134 (1980), the Court upheld the imposition of a tribal cigarette tax on non-tribal purchasers, indicating that federal courts had long acknowledged the power of tribes to tax non-Indians entering the reservation to engage in economic activity. That power was not inconsistent with the tribes' domestic dependent status. No federal statute had taken the power away. Indeed, where the tribe had a significant interest in the subject matter, its power to tax was probably confirmed by the Indian Reorganization Act of 1934, 25 U.S.C.A. § 476. *Colville* also indicated that a legitimate tribal tax is not preempted by a state tax on the same subject matter: "[E]ven if the State's interests were implicated by the tribal taxes, * * * it must be remembered that tribal sovereignty is dependent on and subordinate to only the Federal Government, not the States." 447 U.S. at 154.

This broad view of tribal taxing power was reaffirmed in Merrion v. Jicarilla Apache Tribe, 455 U.S. 130 (1982), which upheld a tribal severance tax applied to non-Indian lessees who mined oil and gas on the reservation. The lessees contended that the tribal power to tax was based entirely on the right of the tribe to exclude nonmembers from the reservation, and that the power could not be exercised against lessees whose leases conferred a right of entry. The Supreme Court held that the power of exclusion was sufficiently broad to support the tax, but it also rejected the lessees' limited view of the tribal taxing power.

> The power does not derive solely from the Indian tribe's power to exclude non-Indians from tribal lands. Instead, it derives from the tribe's general authority, as sovereign, to control economic activity within its jurisdiction, and to defray the cost of providing governmental services. * * *

455 U.S. at 137. Shortly thereafter, the Supreme Court held that the Navajo Tribe could impose a possessory interest tax and a business activity tax without the approval of the Secretary. Kerr–McGee Corp. v. Navajo Tribe, 471 U.S. 195 (1985).

The broad language of *Merrion* seemed to suggest that a tribe was free to tax non-Indian activity anywhere within its reservation, but the Supreme Court has recently withdrawn sharply from that position. In Atkinson Trading Co. v. Shirley, 532 U.S. 645 (2001), the Court held that the Navajo tribe could not impose a hotel occupancy tax on guests of a hotel operated by a nonmember on fee land within the reservation. "An Indian tribe's sovereign power to tax–whatever its derivation–reaches no further than tribal land." Id. at 653. The decision represented a further development of the Supreme Court's jurisprudence derived from Montana v. United States, 450 U.S. 544 (1981), and *Mon-*

tana's presumption that "tribes lack civil authority over the conduct of nonmembers on non-Indian fee land within a reservation." Id. at 647. The tribe lacked jurisdiction to tax even though the hotel benefited from tribal police and fire protection. The Court held that the taxed activity did not fall within either of *Montana*'s exceptions. Although the hotel operator was licensed as an Indian trader, that consensual relationship did not have a sufficient nexus with the hotel guests whose occupancy was taxed. The activity did not fall within the second exception because operation of the hotel did not threaten or have "some direct effect on the political integrity, the economic security, or the health or welfare of the tribe." Id. at 657 (quoting *Montana*).

The effect of *Atkinson* is to remove from the reach of tribal taxation much nonmember economic activity that takes place on reservations. The effect is even more severe when Strate v. A–1 Contractors, 520 U.S. 438 (1997), is added in. In the past, a tribe's property interest in a railroad right-of-way had been held sufficient to permit the tribe to tax it. Burlington Northern R. Co. v. Blackfeet Tribe, 924 F.2d 899 (9th Cir.1991). *Strate*, however, held that rights-of-way, over which the tribe has no gatekeeping function, are the jurisdictional equivalent of fee land so far as nonmember conduct is concerned. Thus the Ninth Circuit has now held that tribes can be enjoined from taxing utilities' rights-of-way, and *Burlington Northern* has been overruled. Big Horn County Elec. Co-op v. Adams, 219 F.3d 944, 953 (9th Cir.2000). The Ninth Circuit has ordered further discovery, however, to determine whether the operation of a railroad had a sufficient harmful effect on tribal interests to fall within *Montana*'s second exception and permit tribal taxation of railroad property. Burlington Northern Santa Fe R. Co. v. Assiniboine and Sioux Tribes of the Fort Peck Reservation, 323 F.3d 767 (9th Cir.2003).

Of course, many non-Indian activities, such as oil, gas, and coal production, are taxable both because they take place on trust land and because they are subject to a consensual arrangement with the tribe. Indeed, the power to tax such nonmember business activity is not confined to the tribe's reservation, but extends to trust allotments of tribal members, which are also Indian country. See Mustang Production Co. v. Harrison, 94 F.3d 1382 (10th Cir. 1996).

Non–Indian businesses seeking to challenge in federal court a tribe's power of taxation regularly have been required first to exhaust tribal court remedies. See, e.g., Reservation Telephone Cooperative v. Three Affiliated Tribes of the Fort Berthold Reservation, 76 F.3d 181 (8th Cir.1996). Exhaustion has been required even when the challenge is to imposition of a business activity tax off-reservation, but on trust land. Texaco, Inc. v. Hale, 81 F.3d 934 (10th Cir.1996). When the tribe seeks to tax nonmember activity on fee land that does not fall within a *Montana* exception, however, no exhaustion is required because the lack of tribal authority is plain. *Atkinson*, 520 U.S. at 459 n.14.

E. FEDERAL REGULATION
IN INDIAN COUNTRY

The federal power to regulate Indian affairs is plenary; it is limited only by the constitutional restraints applicable to all federal activity. In the exercise of this power, the federal government may wholly preempt the regulatory power of both the states and the tribes.

No attempt will be made here to canvass the numerous federal statutes and regulations operative in Indian country. Land use is probably the area most thoroughly regulated by the federal government, but many other subjects are affected as well.

Because federal power over Indian affairs is plenary, questions of the applicability of general federal legislation in Indian country depend upon the intention rather than the power of Congress. In most cases, Congress does not state whether it intends its legislation to apply to tribes or Indians or Indian country, and courts are consequently called upon to decide that question. Generalizations are particularly suspect in this area because each piece of legislation has its own subject matter that affects Indian interests in its own particular way. The process is or ought to be one of balancing tribal interests in exemption against the federal interest in applicability. The most widely accepted rule is that set forth in Donovan v. Coeur d'Alene Tribal Farm, 751 F.2d 1113, 1116 (9th Cir.1985):

A federal statute of general applicability that is silent on the issue of applicability to Indian tribes will not apply to them if: (1) the law touches "exclusive rights of self-governance in purely intramural matters"; (2) the application of the law to the tribe would "abrogate rights guaranteed by Indian treaties"; or (3) there is proof "by legislative history or some other means that Congress intended [the law] not to apply to Indians on their reservations...."

Results under this test and its predecessors have varied. A provision of the Federal Power Act authorizing power companies to condemn lands was held to permit condemnation of fee lands owned by the Tuscarora Tribe. Federal Power Com'n v. Tuscarora Indian Nation, 362 U.S. 99 (1960). No implied requirement of tribal consent is read into the licensing provisions of that Act. Escondido Mut. Water Co. v. La Jolla Band of Mission Indians, 466 U.S. 765 (1984). The Employee Retirement Income Security Act (ERISA) has been held to apply to tribes. Lumber Industry Pension Fund v. Warm Springs Forest Products Industries, 939 F.2d 683 (9th Cir. 1991); Smart v. State Farm Ins. Co., 868 F.2d 929 (7th Cir.1989). The National Environmental Protection Act has been held applicable to Indian country. Davis v. Morton, 469 F.2d 593 (10th Cir.1972).

The Resource Conservation and Recovery Act (RCRA) expressly provides for application to Indian tribes, and it abrogates tribal sovereign immunity. Blue Legs v. BIA, 867 F.2d 1094 (8th Cir.1989); Backcountry Against Dumps v. EPA, 100 F.3d 147 (D.C.Cir.1996).

On the other hand, statutes (other than ERISA) that would regulate the relation between tribes and their employees have generally been ruled inapplicable. The National Labor Relations Act has been held not to apply to an Indian tribe itself as an on-reservation employer, Fort Apache Timber Co., 226 N.L.R.B. 503, 93 L.R.R.M. 1296 (1976). Where the tribe chartered a tribal organization to provide health services off-reservation, however, the National Labor Relations Act was held not plainly inapplicable, so that the NLRB's subpoenas could be enforced. NLRB v. Chapa De Indian Health Program, Inc., 316 F.3d 995 (9th Cir.2003). One circuit has held that the NLRA did not preempt tribal authority to enact a "right-to-work" ordinance; the tribe enjoyed the same ability allowed the states by the Act. NLRB v. Pueblo of San Juan, 276 F.3d 1186 (10th Cir.2002) (en banc). Title VII of the Civil Rights Act of 1964 expressly excepts Indian tribes from coverage. 42 U.S.C. § 2000e(b). Plaintiffs may not nullify this exception by suing tribes or tribal officials for discrimination under 42 U.S.C. § 1981. Taylor v. Alabama Intertribal Council, 261 F.3d 1032 (11th Cir.2001). The Age Discrimination in Employment Act (ADEA), which has no such exception, has been ruled to be inapplicable as an undue interference, respectively, with treaty or inherent rights of tribal self-government. EEOC v. Cherokee Nation, 871 F.2d 937 (10th Cir.1989); EEOC v. Karuk Tribe Housing Authority, 260 F.3d 1071 (9th Cir.2001). One federal circuit has held that the Occupational Safety and Health Act

(OSHA) does not apply to a tribal business because it would conflict with treaty-secured rights to exercise sovereignty and exclude nonmembers. Donovan v. Navajo Forest Products Industries, 692 F.2d 709 (10th Cir.1982). Two other circuits, however, concluded that OSHA did apply and was not an undue abrogation of the tribe's right of exclusion, whether founded in treaty or inherent sovereignty. U.S. Dep't of Labor v. OSHA, 935 F.2d 182 (9th Cir. 1991); Donovan v. Coeur d'Alene Tribal Farm, 751 F.2d 1113 (9th Cir.1985); Reich v. Mashantucket Sand & Gravel, 95 F.3d 174 (2d Cir.1996). Even when a treaty expressly conflicts with a federal statute of general application, the statute will apply if Congress appears to have intended to override treaty rights. Thus the Bald Eagle Protection Act applies to Indians and abrogates their treaty rights to take bald eagles. United States v. Dion, 476 U.S. 734 (1986).

When a federal regulation rather than a statute is involved, its validity depends upon its being within the statutory authority Congress conferred upon the regulating agency. For example, controversy has arisen over the authority of the Secretary of Interior to issue the regulation in 25 C.F.R. § 1.4, which purports to exclude all state and local zoning or land use regulations from being applied to trust lands leased from any tribe. The regulation was held beyond the Secretary's authority in Norvell v. Sangre de Cristo Dev. Co., 372 F.Supp. 348 (D.N.M. 1974), rev'd for lack of jurisdiction, 519 F.2d 370 (10th Cir.1975), and Rincon Band of Mission Indi-

ans v. County of San Diego, 324 F.Supp. 371
(S.D.Cal.1971), aff'd on other grounds, 495 F.2d 1
(9th Cir.1974). It was upheld as to lands purchased
by the Secretary for Indians under 25 U.S.C.A.
§ 465 in Santa Rosa Band v. Kings County, 532
F.2d 655, 665–67 (9th Cir.1975), and it was also
suggested there that the regulation may be within
the Secretary's general authority over Indian affairs
granted by 25 U.S.C.A. § 2. Id. at 667 n. 2.

F.   STATE REGULATION IN
INDIAN COUNTRY

Questions of state power to regulate in Indian
country, like questions of state power to tax, are
generally treated as issues of preemption:

> State jurisdiction is pre-empted by the operation
> of federal law if it interferes or is incompatible
> with federal and tribal interests reflected in fed-
> eral law, unless the state interests at stake are
> sufficient to justify the assertion of state authori-
> ty.

New Mexico v. Mescalero Apache Tribe, 462 U.S.
324, 334 (1983). This test, with its fact-specific
weighing and balancing, probably yields even more
unpredictable results in the field of regulation than
it does in that of taxation. As in tax cases, preemption analysis is sometimes buttressed by reference
to the rule of Williams v. Lee, 358 U.S. 217 (1959),
that state law may not interfere with the right of
reservation Indians to make their own laws and be
governed by them. The primary tool, however, is

preemption analysis, perhaps because the standard of Williams v. Lee does not lend itself to a balancing process.

Until quite recently, it was assumed that the states were utterly without power to regulate Indians in Indian country. The Supreme Court even cautioned against applying the test of Williams v. Lee in such situations because that test, now viewed as highly protective of tribal sovereignty, might permit undue extension of state power. McClanahan v. Arizona State Tax Com'n, 411 U.S. 164, 179–80 (1973). The state fared no better under a preemption analysis. "When on-reservation conduct involving only Indians is at issue, state law is generally inapplicable, for the State's regulatory interest is likely to be minimal and the federal interest in encouraging tribal self-government is at its strongest." White Mountain Apache Tribe v. Bracker, 448 U.S. 136, 144 (1980). It is not surprising, then, that state traffic safety laws and motor vehicle safety responsibility laws have been held inapplicable to Indians in Indian country, even though the Indians may be using state highways there. United States v. Harvey, 701 F.2d 800, 805 (9th Cir.1983); Wauneka v. Campbell, 22 Ariz.App. 287, 526 P.2d 1085 (1974). Indeed, state vehicle registration and titling laws were held preempted in one case by tribal regulations for licensing vehicles of the tribe and its resident members even when those vehicles leave the reservation and travel elsewhere in the state. Prairie Band of Potawatomi Indians v. Wagnon, 276 F.Supp.2d 1168 (D.Kan.2003). State hazardous waste regulations are similarly inapplicable to Indians in Indian country. Washington v. United States, 752 F.2d 1465, 1467–68 (9th Cir.1985). The state is also precluded from imposing land use regulations on formerly allotted fee land that is still in Indian hands within a reservation, even though the free alienability of such lands would subject them to state property taxation. Gobin v. Snohomish County, 304 F.3d 909 (9th Cir.2002), cert. denied, ___ U.S. ___, 123 S.Ct. 1488 (2003).

The usual absence of state power to regulate tribal members in Indian country is clearly emphasized in Bryan v. Itasca County, 426 U.S. 373 (1976). There the Supreme Court held that, even when state civil jurisdiction had been extended into Indian country by Public Law 280, the state lacked power to tax property held by a tribal member there. The Court pointed to the destruction of tribal governments likely to result "if tribal governments and reservation Indians were subordinated to the full panoply of civil regulatory powers including taxation, of state and local governments." 426 U.S. at 388.

A few small cracks have begun to appear, however, in the barrier that precludes the states from regulating Indians in Indian country. One is that the states may be as free to regulate "nonmember Indians"—Indians of tribes other than that which beneficially owns the reservation—as they are to regulate non-Indians. "For most practical purposes those [nonmember] Indians stand on the same footing as non-Indians resident on the reservation."

Washington v. Confederated Tribes of Colville Indian Reservation, 447 U.S. 134, 161 (1980). In civil cases, the Supreme Court now draws its jurisdictional lines between tribal members and nonmembers, rather than between Indians and non-Indians. See Strate v. A–1 Contractors, 520 U.S. 438 (1997).

The Supreme Court has acknowledged "that in exceptional circumstances a State may assert jurisdiction over the on-reservation activities of tribal members." New Mexico v. Mescalero Apache Tribe, 462 U.S. 324, 331–32 (1983). More recently, in permitting state officers investigating off-reservation crime to execute a search warrant at an Indian residence on trust land, the Supreme Court stated: "When * * * state interests outside the reservation are implicated, States may regulate the activities even of tribe members on tribal land * * *." Nevada v. Hicks, 533 U.S. 353, 362 (2001). Thus, the preemption test for state regulation is more lenient toward the states than the test for state taxation; the states are subject to a virtually *per se* rule against taxation of tribes or Indians in Indian country. California v. Cabazon Band of Mission Indians, 480 U.S. 202, 215 n.17 (1987). It should be emphasized, however, that the occasions when states have been permitted to regulate Indians in Indian country have been rare and truly exceptional. In one instance the State of Washington was allowed to regulate on-reservation fishing of salmon and steelhead trout. Puyallup Tribe, Inc. v. Department of Game, 433 U.S. 165 (1977) (*Puyallup III*). That case is more fully described in Chapter XV; it is enough to note here that the decision was one in a series that dealt with the sharing of off-reservation fishing between Indian treaty fishermen and non-Indians. It was unexpectedly discovered late in the litigation that some of the fishing stations were actually on-reservation. Another instance in which state regulations may reach tribal members on the reservation occurs when the state taxes sales of cigarettes to non-Indians; the state may require the tribal seller to collect and remit the tax. Washington v. Confederated Tribes of the Colville Indian Reservation, 447 U.S. 134 (1980).

One exceptional subject in which states can regulate tribal members on the reservation is that of liquor sales. In Rice v. Rehner, 463 U.S. 713 (1983), the Supreme Court upheld a state licensing requirement as applied to a tribal Indian who sold liquor pursuant to a license from the tribe. Part of the Court's rationale was based upon 18 U.S.C.A. § 1161, which permits sales of liquor in Indian country only "in conformity both with the laws of the State * * * and with an ordinance duly adopted by the tribe * * *." The Court also engaged, however, in a most unusual preemption analysis. It held that extensive federal regulation for more than a century, with no tradition of tribal authority over liquor sales, preempted the *tribe* from any ability to exclude the operation of state law. This approach is the reverse of the usual preemption analysis. Ordinarily, a long history of federal regulation will preempt the *state* from exercising regulatory power over a tribe. Nor is this unusual preemption analysis the only surprising facet of Rice v. Rehner; the opinion even goes so far as to hold that the tribes lost their inherent power to regulate liquor as a consequence of their domestic dependent status! 463 U.S. at 726. Despite its expansive approach, *Rice* probably does not represent a significant modification of the usual rule that states may not regulate tribal members in Indian country. The long history of federal prohibition of liquor in Indian country almost certainly confines the *Rice* ruling to its subject matter. See also Fort Belknap Indian Community v. Mazurek, 43 F.3d 428 (9th Cir.1994); Potawatomi Indian Tribe v. Oklahoma Tax Comm'n, 975 F.2d 1459 (10th Cir.1992).

Fears of the tribes that they would be unable to escape state regulation of non-traditional activities were significantly allayed in California v. Cabazon Band of Mission Indians, 480 U.S. 202 (1987). That case involved high-stakes bingo and poker games conducted by tribes on their reservations. The state and one of its counties sought to impose their more restrictive regulations on the games, which catered entirely to non-Indian players. After holding that the state laws were regulatory, and thus not extended into California Indian country by Public Law 280, the Supreme Court held that the state laws were preempted. Although it rejected any *per se* rule that state law could not apply to tribal operations, the Court held that federal and tribal interests in tribal self-development and self-sufficiency outweighed any state interest in discouraging organized crime. The Court placed heavy emphasis on the encouragement and approval of the gambling enterprises by federal authorities.

Two federal statutes may permit the application of state law to tribal members in narrow areas. One authorizes states to apply workers' compensation laws to all lands owned or held by the United States. 40 U.S.C. § 290. One state court has relied on this statute in applying its compensation laws to a tribal member operating a business on a reservation. Idaho ex rel. Industrial Comm'n v. Indian Country Enterprises, Inc., 130 Idaho 520, 944 P.2d 117 (1997). Another, unusual federal statute provides that the Secretary of the Interior, under such rules as he may prescribe, shall permit the states to enforce sanitation and quarantine regulations and, if the tribe consents, compulsory educational laws in Indian country. 25 U.S.C.A. § 231. The Secretary has never issued regulations so permitting, and the state power has accordingly been unexercised except where the tribe has approved application of school attendance laws.

Despite these actual or potential exceptions, the opportunities for state law to apply to tribal members in Indian country are extremely limited. Accordingly, much current controversy between the states and the tribes centers on regulation of activities of nonmembers on the reservation. In these cases, preemption analysis is applied in its conventional form. The more the federal government and the tribe have taken control of an activity, the more likely is the state to be preempted.

The prime example is New Mexico v. Mescalero Apache Tribe, 462 U.S. 324 (1983), which concerned non-Indian hunting and fishing on the reservation. The tribe, in conjunction with the federal government, had undertaken substantial development of game and fish resources, to provide a source of tribal income from non-Indian hunters and fishermen. The state had not contributed to game and fish development on the reservation, so its stake was correspondingly low. The Supreme Court held that the state was preempted from applying its regulations to the non-Indian hunting and fishing. Game and fish regulation, which is more fully discussed in Chapter XV, is perhaps especially likely to be preemptive because dual regulation is impracticable; the more restrictive regulation necessarily governs.

State regulation of nonmembers in Indian country is least likely to be preempted when the activity takes place on, or involves, fee lands owned by nonmembers. In Montana v. United States, 450 U.S. 544 (1981), the Supreme Court held that a tribe could not regulate hunting and fishing by non-Indians on non-Indian-owned fee land. To the extent that the tribe is excluded, state regulation is in little danger of being preempted. The same principle applies to state highway rights-of-way as to fee lands. See Strate v. A–1 Contractors, 520 U.S. 438 (1997). It also applies to land condemned for a dam and reservoir project that remained within the reservation but had been broadly opened to the public. South Dakota v. Bourland, 508 U.S. 679 (1993).

With regard to zoning of nonmember fee lands within a reservation, the Supreme Court reached an unusual compromise in Brendale v. Confederated Tribes and Bands of the Yakima Indian Nation, 492 U.S. 408 (1989). The compromise resulted from a split vote of the Justices and the lack of a majority position. The state was permitted to zone fee lands within an "open" part of the reservation, which had largely passed into nonmember ownership, and the tribe was permitted to zone the smaller proportion of fee lands within the "closed" part of the reservation that retained its primarily tribal flavor. The distinction between "open" and "closed" portions of Indian country had not previously been accorded jurisdictional significance.

G.   TRIBAL REGULATION

The power of the tribes to regulate parallels their power to tax, both in its general scope and in the fact that it has been sparingly exercised (except for criminal jurisdiction over Indians). Like tribal taxation, tribal regulation is certain to increase with the growing economic development of the reservations. The tribe clearly has power to regulate tribal members in Indian country, and may even regulate them outside of Indian country when important tribal interests are at stake. Thus a tribe may regulate off-reservation treaty fishing by its members. Settler v. Lameer, 507 F.2d 231 (9th Cir.1974). The Navajo Tribe was held to have authority to order its members to remove structures they had erected on

Hopi lands, in a case arising out of the Hopi–Navajo partition. Sidney v. Zah, 718 F.2d 1453 (9th Cir. 1983).

Tribes also have substantial power to regulate nonmembers engaged in activity in Indian country that affects Indian interests. See Washington v. Confederated Tribes of Colville Indian Reservation, 447 U.S. 134, 152 (1980). For example, a tribe has been permitted to regulate on-reservation repossession of motor vehicles by off-reservation dealers. Babbitt Ford, Inc. v. Navajo Indian Tribe, 710 F.2d 587 (9th Cir.1983). In recent decades, however, the Supreme Court has substantially narrowed the regulatory authority of tribes over nonmembers. This process began on fee lands within the reservation, but has recently expanded in some circumstances to trust land. In Montana v. United States, 450 U.S. 544 (1981), the Court held that a tribe could not regulate hunting and fishing by non-Indians on non-Indian-owned fee land. The tribe lacked inherent sovereign power to regulate non-Indian activities on fee land with but two exceptions noted. "A tribe may regulate, through taxation, licensing, or other means, the activities of nonmembers who enter consensual relationships with the tribe or its members, through commercial dealings, contracts, leases, or other arrangements." Id. at 565. And a tribe may retain power to regulate conduct that "threatens or has some direct effect on the political integrity, the economic security, or the health or welfare of the tribe." Id. at 566. For purposes of applying *Montana*, state highway rights-of-way are equivalent to non-Indian-owned fee lands. Strate v. A–1 Contractors, 520 U.S. 438 (1997). Thus a tribe cannot enforce against nonmembers its affirmative action law with regard to employment on a state-owned right-of-way crossing the reservation. Montana Dept. of Transportation v. King, 191 F.3d 1108 (9th Cir.1999). Land condemned for a dam and reservoir project that remained within the reservation but had been broadly opened to the public is also the equivalent of fee land. South Dakota v. Bourland, 508 U.S. 679 (1993).

In Nevada v. Hicks, 533 U.S. 353 (2001), the Supreme Court held that tribes lacked authority to regulate the activities of state officers investigating off-reservation crime when they searched an Indian residence on trust land within the reservation. *Montana*'s presumption against tribal regulation of nonmembers was thus permitted to operate for the first time on trust land. The Court ruled that a preclusion of tribal power to regulate this activity was consistent both with *Montana* and with the right of Indians to make their own laws and be governed by them. Id. at 362. *Hicks* undoubtedly represents a substantial narrowing of tribal regulatory authority, but it should not be read too categorically or without reference to the state law enforcement interest that it involved. For example, nonmembers who are free to hunt without tribal regulation on nonmember-owned fee lands within a reservation under *Montana* are certainly not entitled to hunt the remainder of the reservation, trust lands and all, without being subject to tribal regulation.

Montana's first exception for consensual activity undoubtedly permits regulation of many major non-Indian industries in Indian country; they are almost certain to be engaged in consensual activity with the tribe or its members. Thus a tribe was held to have power to regulate a bingo enterprise because its non-Indian operator had entered a joint venture with a tribal member. United States ex rel. Morongo Band of Mission Indians v. Rose, 34 F.3d 901 (9th Cir.1994). A tribe was held to have sovereign authority to enact a "right-to-work" law when the only cited instance of its application was to a lumber company operating on lands leased from the tribe. NLRB v. Pueblo of San Juan, 276 F.3d 1186, 1193 (10th Cir.2002) (en banc). There are many more modest activities of nonmembers, however, that may not be consensual. *Montana*'s second exception could be interpreted to permit tribal regulation of all activity significantly affecting tribal interests, but that exception was given a narrow interpretation in Strate v. A–1 Contractors, 520 U.S. 438 (1997). *Strate* stated that the exception must be read with *Montana*'s description of inherent tribal powers in mind: the power to determine membership, to regulate domestic relations among members, and to prescribe rules of inheritance for members. That is an exceptionally limited description of tribal self-government, however; the area that the tribe is entitled to protect almost certainly must encompass other functions. Tribal health and safety regulations come to mind. See Cardin v. De la Cruz, 671 F.2d 363 (9th Cir.1982). There is no doubt, however, that the Supreme Court currently interprets tribal self-government narrowly for purposes of the second *Montana* exception. See *Hicks*, supra, and Atkinson Trading Co. v. Shirley, 532 U.S. 645 (2001). The Eighth Circuit also interpreted *Montana*'s second exception narrowly, before *Strate*, in upholding a finding that non-Indian hunting did not have a "direct effect on the political integrity, the economic security, or the health or welfare of the Tribe as a whole," even though non-Indians may have harassed cattle grazing on tribal lands, failed to close pasture gates or let down wires on fences, and had taken deer that reduced the numbers available to tribal members. South Dakota v. Bourland, 39 F.3d 868 (8th Cir. 1994).

Even after *Montana*, tribes were able to enforce zoning regulations against non-Indian fee owners within a reservation. Knight v. Shoshone and Arapahoe Indian Tribes, 670 F.2d 900 (10th Cir.1982). The Supreme Court subsequently addressed the zoning issue, however, in Brendale v. Confederated Tribes and Bands of the Yakima Indian Nation, 492 U.S. 408 (1989), and reached a mixed result, because of the Court's lack of a majority position. The state was permitted to zone fee lands within an "open" part of the reservation, which had largely passed into nonmember ownership, and the tribe was permitted to zone the smaller proportion of fee lands within the "closed" part of the reservation that retained its primarily tribal flavor. In a more specialized case, the Hoopa Valley Tribe was held to have the power to regulate logging by a nonmember on reservation fee land because the power had been delegated by Congress in the Hoopa–Yurok Settlement Act, 25 U.S.C.A. § 1300i et seq. Bugenig v. Hoopa Valley Tribe, 266 F.3d 1201 (9th Cir.2001).

Brendale and *Strate* have not prevented tribes from retaining considerable power to regulate non-Indians on fee lands with regard to water pollution. In 1987, Congress amended the Clean Water Act to permit the Environmental Protection Agency to treat tribes as states for purposes of establishing water quality standards. The Agency approves tribal standards only after a determination that the potential impact of regulated activities on the health and welfare of the tribe is serious and substantial. Under this system, a tribe's regulation of non-Indians on fee land was upheld as falling within *Montana*'s second exception. Montana v. U.S. Environmental Protection Agency, 137 F.3d 1135 (9th Cir.1998); see also City of Albuquerque v. Browner, 97 F.3d 415 (10th Cir.1996). The tribe may exercise its EPA-delegated authority to regulate water quality even though the state owns the underlying lakebed. Wisconsin v. EPA, 266 F.3d 741 (7th Cir.2001).

Tribes have power to regulate, concurrently with the states, non-Indian liquor sales by reason of a federal statute, § 18 U.S.C. 1161. United States v. Mazurie, 419 U.S. 544 (1975); Rice v. Rehner, 463 U.S. 713, 730–31 (1983). The authority is solely statutory because *Rice* held, in a rather puzzling passage, that the tribes' domestic dependent status deprived them of self-government in liquor regulation. 463 U.S. at 726. The statutory authority is more expansive than the inherent tribal regulatory authority limited in Montana v. United States, 450 U.S. 544 (1981), because it extends without qualification to non-Indian liquor transactions on non-Indian-owned fee lands within the reservation. City of Timber Lake v. Cheyenne River Sioux Tribe, 10 F.3d 554 (8th Cir.1993).

One limitation upon tribal regulation of non-Indians is a practical one; tribal courts have no criminal jurisdiction over non-Indians. Oliphant v. Suquamish Indian Tribe, 435 U.S. 191 (1978). This fact deprives the tribes of one of the most common methods of enforcing regulatory measures. As a result, tribes are attempting to enforce their regulatory ordinances by the use of civil recoveries or, when nonmember fee lands or rights-of-way are not involved, by the power of exclusion.

An ultimate limitation of tribal power to regulate either Indians or non-Indians is federal preemption; Congress clearly has the power to oust the jurisdiction of the tribe or to condition its exercise, as it has done in the Indian Civil Rights Act of 1968 (see Chapter XI).

CHAPTER X

INDIAN GAMING

A. INTRODUCTION

Indian gaming is a startling economic phenomenon. In the space of a few years, it has become the largest single revenue-producing activity for Indian tribes. That is not to say that every tribe is able to share in the economic benefits; a great many tribes are not geographically situated to conduct a profitable gaming operation. Other tribes have declined to engage in gaming for moral or traditional reasons. For those who are engaged in large commercial gaming operations, however, the returns have been enormous. Those tribes are quite aware that this favorable economic condition could change. Indian gaming might reach a saturation point. Competition from non-Indian gaming could increase as pressure builds on the states to authorize more statewide gaming. For at least the near future, however, those tribes with substantial gaming operations are understandably inclined to view gaming as the first tribal economic program that has really worked.

The present system of regulation of Indian gaming grew out of the division of jurisdiction among the federal government, the states, and the tribes that has been described in Chapters VII–IX, but from those fundamental materials Congress fashioned a structure that is unique. The governing federal statute, the Indian Gaming Regulatory Act of 1988 (IGRA), 25 U.S.C.A. §§ 2701–2721, occupies the field of Indian gaming regulation, but also provides for the application of state law to a significant degree. The Act requires compacts between the tribes and states to govern the scope and conduct of Indian casino-type gaming, and those compacts may further allocate jurisdiction between tribe and state. The Act requires states that meet certain criteria to bargain in good faith to arrive at such compacts. In order to enforce that duty, the Act authorized tribes to bring an action in federal court against states that failed to comply. That key provision for the enforcement of the duty to bargain was struck down, however, by the Supreme Court in Seminole Tribe v. Florida, 517 U.S. 44 (1996). *Seminole* held that Congress lacked the power under the Indian Commerce Clause to abrogate the states' Eleventh Amendment immunity from suit in federal court. Thus the complex scheme devised by Congress became substantially skewed. To understand where the law of Indian gaming now stands, it is necessary first to review its initial status, and then to examine the changes wrought by the Regulatory Act, *Seminole* and decisions following in their wake.

B. CALIFORNIA v. CABAZON BAND
OF MISSION INDIANS

During the late 1970's and early 1980's, a number of tribes began operating commercial bingo or poker games on their reservations, in a manner that did not conform to state law. In most cases, such operations were supported by tribal ordinances that had been approved by the Secretary of the Interior. States in which these operations took place attempted to enforce their laws regulating or prohibiting the tribal bingo or card operations. Such an attempt by California and one of its counties reached the Supreme Court in California v. Cabazon Band of Mission Indians, 480 U.S. 202 (1987).

California was (and is) a Public Law 280 state, with the consequence that its criminal laws had been extended to Indians in Indian country, but its regulatory and legislative authority had not. See Chapter VIII, Section D. The primary issue in *Cabazon Band*, therefore, was whether California's law prohibiting bingo games unless they were conducted by charitable organizations and limited pots to $250, and the county's ordinance prohibiting poker games, were "criminal/prohibitory" or "civil/regulatory" in nature. The Supreme Court described the distinction as follows:

[I]f the intent of a state law is generally to prohibit certain conduct, it falls within Pub. L. 280's grant of criminal jurisdiction, but if the state law generally permits the conduct at issue, subject to regulation, it must be classified as

civil/regulatory and Pub. L. 280 does not authorize its enforcement on an Indian reservation. The
shorthand test is whether the conduct at issue
violates the State's public policy.

480 U.S. at 209. The Supreme Court held that the
laws were civil/regulatory. California's public policy
did not forbid gambling: the state operated its own
lottery, authorized pari-mutuel betting on horse
races, and permitted many organizations to conduct
bingo and card games. The county, too, permitted
municipalities to authorize card games otherwise
prohibited by the county ordinance. The fact that
California's regulations were enforced by misdemeanor penalties did not change their nature.
"[T]hat an otherwise regulatory law is enforceable
by criminal as well as civil means does not convert
it into a criminal law within the meaning of Pub. L.
280." 480 U.S. at 211.

The Supreme Court in *Cabazon Band* then held
that the case did not present the "exceptional circumstances" permitting a state to regulate Indians
in Indian country absent congressional authorization. The Court took account of the strong federal
support for Indian gaming operations, in the form
of the Secretary's approval of tribal ordinances,
approval of gaming management contracts under 25
U.S.C. § 81, and the granting of various federal
development loans. The Court rejected the state's
argument that the tribes were marketing a tax
exemption as they did in the case of cigarette sales.
The tribes did not simply resell a product; they
built facilities and provided services to their pa-

trons. The only significant state interest, that of preventing organized crime from infiltrating gaming, was not real or substantial enough to overcome the strong federal interest in the promotion of tribal economic activity in the form of gaming.

After this decision in *Cabazon Band*, tribal bingo and card operations grew apace. Some of the tribes undertook to branch out into other forms of gaming. In states that were not subject to Public Law 280, the tribes believed themselves to be in a particularly strong position; even if state law were deemed to be criminal/prohibitory, it could not be applied against the tribe or its members. On the other hand, the states were not without their weapons. State criminal law could be applied against the nonmember customers, so long as gambling was viewed as a victimless crime. See State ex rel. Poll v. Montana Ninth Judicial Dist. Ct., 257 Mont. 512, 851 P.2d 405 (1993). Immunity from state law would do the tribes little good if the states stood ready to arrest their customers. Also lurking in the background was the threat of federal enforcement of the Organized Crime Control Act, 18 U.S.C. § 1955, which prohibits gambling operations in violation of state law, see United States v. Farris, 624 F.2d 890 (9th Cir.1980), and the Johnson Act, 15 U.S.C. §§ 1171–1178, which prohibits gambling machines within Indian country. See Citizen Band Potawatomi Indian Tribe v. Green, 995 F.2d 179 (10th Cir.1993).

Congress ultimately responded to the situation by enacting the Indian Gaming Regulatory Act of 1988.

Although that Act built upon some of the reasoning of *Cabazon Band*, it also provided novel responses to the competing regulatory claims of the federal government, the states, and the tribes.

C. THE INDIAN GAMING REGULATORY ACT OF 1988

1. THE ACT

The Indian Gaming Regulatory Act (IGRA), 25 U.S.C.A. §§ 2701–2721, 18 U.S.C.A. § 1166, divides Indian gaming (meaning gaming by federally recognized tribes) into three classes, with different regulatory results for each class. Class I gaming consists of social games for prizes of minimal value or traditional forms of Indian gaming connected with tribal ceremonies or celebrations. § 2703(6). Class I gaming is within the exclusive jurisdiction of the tribes and is not regulated by the Act. § 2710(a). Class I gaming is not of legal or economic significance.

Class II gaming consists first of bingo, "whether or not electronic, computer, or other technologic aids are used in connection therewith," including "pull tabs, lotto, punch boards, tip jars, instant bingo, and other games similar to bingo." § 2703(7)(A)(i). "Lotto" in that application means a board game played with counters, similar to bingo, and not a lottery operation like that conducted by several states under the name of "Lotto." Oneida Tribe of Indians v. Wisconsin, 951 F.2d 757 (7th Cir.1991). Keno does not qualify as being "similar to bingo." Shakopee Mdewakanton Sioux Community v. Hope, 16 F.3d 261 (8th Cir.1994). Also included in Class II are card games either explicitly authorized by state law, or not prohibited by state law and played anywhere within the state, but only if the card games are played in conformity with state regulations regarding hours of play and limits on wagers or pot sizes. § 2703(7)(A)(ii). Explicitly excluded from Class II gaming are banked card games (where players play against the house and not just each other), such as baccarat, chemin de fer, and blackjack, as well as "electronic or electromechanical facsimiles of any game of chance or slot machines of any kind." § 2703(7)(B). (Card games already in operation in Michigan, the Dakotas, and Washington were grandfathered, but only for the existing "nature and scope" of those games. § 2703(7)(C); see United States v. Sisseton–Wahpeton Sioux Tribe, 897 F.2d 358 (8th Cir.1990)). Class II gaming is within the jurisdiction of the tribes, but is subject to other restrictions of the Act. Notably, a tribe may engage in Class II gaming "within a State that permits such gaming for any purpose by any person, organization or entity * * *" but it must be authorized by a tribal ordinance. This restriction is reflective of the rationale in *Cabazon Band*; if a state permits bingo or unbanked card games for any purpose, its public policy cannot be offended by this type of gambling.

Class II gaming is subject to regulation and oversight by a National Indian Gaming Commission of three members, established by the Act. §§ 2704–

2708. Tribal gaming ordinances for both Class II and III gaming are subject to approval by the Commission Chairman, according to certain criteria set by the Act. The Commission also has certain duties of inspection and oversight of Class II gaming, unless it has granted the tribe a certificate of self-regulation. The Act specifies the purposes for which Class II gaming revenues may be used, and requires approval of the Secretary for any plan to distribute per capita payments to tribal members. § 2710(b)(3). The latter requirement apparently is made applicable to Class III revenues by § 2710(d)(1)(A)(ii) and (2)(A). Ross v. Flandreau Santee Sioux Tribe, 809 F.Supp. 738, 741 n.2 (D.S.D.1992).

Class III gaming is defined as "all forms of gaming that are not class I gaming or class II gaming." § 2703(8). In practice, Class III includes the staples of the typical casino, such as slot machines, craps, roulette, and banked card games such as blackjack. In order to conduct Class III gaming, a tribe must first meet the two requirements for Class II gaming-that it has an approved authorizing ordinance, and is "located in a State that permits such gaming for any purpose by any person, organization, or entity." It then must meet the additional requirement that its Class III gaming be "conducted in accordance with a Tribal–State compact entered into by the Indian tribe and the State * * * that is in effect." § 2710(d)(1). A compact takes effect when notice of its approval by the Secretary is published in the Federal Register. § 2710(d)(3)(B).

If the Secretary fails to approve or disapprove a compact within 45 days after it is submitted for approval, the compact is considered approved "but only to the extent the compact is consistent with the provisions of" IGRA. § 2710(d)(8)(C). The Act specifies that the Johnson Act, forbidding the use or possession of gambling devices in Indian country, does not apply to gaming under a compact that is in effect in a state in which gambling devices are legal. § 2710(d)(6). Signing of a compact does not avoid the effect of the Johnson Act if the state otherwise prohibits gambling devices entirely. Citizen Band Potawatomi Indian Tribe v. Green, 995 F.2d 179 (10th Cir.1993).

The Act provides that compacts may include provisions relating to "the application of the criminal and civil laws and regulations of the Indian tribe or the State" concerning the gaming activity, "the allocation of criminal and civil jurisdiction between the State and the Indian tribe" necessary to enforce such laws and regulations, remedies for breach of contract, and other matters concerning the gaming operation. § 2710(d)(3)(B). There is accordingly an unprecedented degree of freedom on the part of the parties to allocate jurisdiction over Class III gaming under the umbrella of the federal Act.

The Act provides that, upon request of a tribe, a state shall negotiate in good faith with the tribe to enter such a compact. § 2710(d)(3). If the state fails to bargain in good faith, the tribe has a cause of action in federal court. (This latter provision is the one rendered largely ineffectual by the decision in

Seminole Tribe, discussed in subsection 2, immediately below). If the court finds that the state failed to bargain in good faith, it can order the state and tribe to conclude a compact within 60 days. § 2710(d)(6)(B)(iii). If the parties do not reach agreement within 60 days, they submit their last best offers to a court-appointed mediator, who chooses one of the two proposed compacts. If the state does not consent to that proposal, it is submitted to the Secretary, who then issues "procedures" consistent with the selected proposal for the conduct of Class III gaming on the reservation in question. Although no provision of the Act expressly grants a cause of action to enforce a compact, such a claim has been held to arise under the Act and therefore may be brought in federal court under federal question jurisdiction. Cabazon Band of Mission Indians v. Wilson, 124 F.3d 1050 (9th Cir. 1997).

IGRA provides for and regulates gaming "on Indian lands." § 2710(a), (d). The term includes lands within a reservation and individual or tribal trust lands over which the tribe "exercises governmental power." § 2703(4); Kansas v. United States, 249 F.3d 1213 (10th Cir.2001). A tribe must have such lands to have standing to initiate the bargaining process. Match-E-Be-Nash-She-Wish Band of Pottawatomi Indians v. Engler, 304 F.3d 616 (6th Cir. 2002). One tribe that had a gaming compact entered a contract, which the Commission approved, for a "National Indian Lottery" in which ticket purchases could be made by telephone from outside the tribe's reservation. The Ninth Circuit held that such a lottery could not be attacked collaterally, but did not rule on its ultimate legality. AT & T Corp. v. Coeur d'Alene Tribe, 295 F.3d 899 (9th Cir.2002). It is therefore unclear whether the lottery qualifies under IGRA as gaming "on Indian lands." Cf. Missouri ex rel. Nixon v. Coeur D'Alene Tribe, 164 F.3d 1102 (8th Cir.1999).

Finally, the Act forbids gaming on lands away from the tribe's reservation and acquired by the Secretary for the tribe after 1988. § 2719. There are exceptions to this prohibition for lands within or contiguous to the tribe's existing reservation, for initial reservations of newly recognized tribes or restored lands of restored tribes, and for lands acquired in settlement of land claims. A "restored" tribe need not be a tribe that whose former trust relationship was terminated and restored; recognition or "acknowledgment" is sufficient. Grand Traverse Band of Ottawa and Chippewa Indians v. United States Attorney, 198 F.Supp.2d 920 (W.D.Mich.2002). Acquired trust lands qualify as "restored" if they were of cultural or historical significance to the tribe and were within land it formerly ceded. Id. Lands also qualify if the congressional intent in authorizing acquisition was to put the tribe at least partially back in a position it once enjoyed–to make restitution for past wrongs– even if the land was not part of a former reservation. City of Roseville v. Norton, 348 F.3d 1020 (D.C.Cir.2003). Courts defer to the Secretary's discretion on this issue. See Oregon v. Norton, 271

F.Supp.2d 1270 (D.Or.2003). There is a further exception to the prohibition on gaming on lands acquired after 1988: the Secretary, after consultation with appropriate tribal, state and local officials, may approve such gaming on newly-acquired lands if he or she determines that it would be in the best interest of the tribe and its members, and would not be detrimental to the surrounding community, but only if the governor of the state concurs. This provision was the subject of a rather celebrated claim that improper political influence led to the denial of the request of three small Wisconsin tribes to come within the exception. See Sokaogon Chippewa Community v. Babbitt, 214 F.3d 941 (7th Cir. 2000). The Act's provision for a "governor's veto" with regard to this exception has been upheld against claims by a tribe that such interference with the Secretary's power was unconstitutional as a violation of the Appointments Clause, the separation of powers, or the non-delegation doctrine, or was a breach of trust responsibility. Confederated Tribes of Siletz Indians v. United States, 110 F.3d 688 (9th Cir.1997); Lac Courte Oreilles Band of Lake Superior Chippewa Indians v. United States, 259 F.Supp.2d 783 (W.D.Wis.2003). Approval of the Secretary for gaming on newly acquired lands is required under § 2719 even if the tribe and state have entered an approved compact governing Class III gaming there. Keweenaw Bay Indian Community v. United States, 136 F.3d 469 (6th Cir.1998). The entire issue is of great importance to tribes that are not otherwise geographically well situated for gaming operations.

Some tribes, particularly those who participated in the eastern land settlement claims, are subject to special legislative exemptions from the applicability of IGRA, and care must be taken to examine the statutes governing any particular tribe. See, e.g., Passamaquoddy Tribe v. Maine, 75 F.3d 784 (1st Cir.1996); Ysleta del Sur Pueblo v. Texas, 36 F.3d 1325 (5th Cir.1994); Narragansett Indian Tribe v. National Indian Gaming Comm'n, 158 F.3d 1335 (D.C.Cir.1998); 25 U.S.C.A. § 941*l* (Catawba Tribe Restoration Act).

2. COMPACTS AND *SEMINOLE TRIBE*

Much of the contention over Class III gaming has centered on the tribal-state compact process. Major difficulties ensued early on because the governors of some states entered such compacts and were later held to have lacked authority under state law to contract. (That problem still arises today. See Saratoga County Chamber of Commerce, Inc. v. Pataki, 100 N.Y.2d 801, 766 N.Y.S.2d 654, 798 N.E.2d 1047, cert. denied, ___ U.S. ___, 124 S.Ct. 570 (2003)). Several compacts in New Mexico were held invalid for that reason, despite Secretarial approval. See Pueblo of Santa Ana v. Kelly, 104 F.3d 1546 (10th Cir.1997). Although the compacts had been "entered into," they were signed by the state governor without authority and therefore were not "in effect" as required by § 2710(d)(1)(C) for legalized

Class III gaming. See also Narragansett Indian Tribe v. State, 667 A.2d 280 (R.I.1995); cf. Kickapoo Tribe of Indians v. Babbitt, 43 F.3d 1491 (D.C.Cir. 1995). The problem in New Mexico was ultimately solved by agreement on new compacts, properly executed.

The most severe jolt to the IGRA scheme came from the Supreme Court in Seminole Tribe v. Florida, 517 U.S. 44 (1996). The provision of the Indian Gaming Regulatory Act that was at issue there was § 2710(d)(7), which authorized a tribe to bring an action in federal court against a state that refused to bargain in good faith for a state-tribal gaming compact. The Supreme Court earlier had held that states were protected by the Eleventh Amendment from being sued without their consent by tribes in federal court. Blatchford v. Native Village of Noatak, 501 U.S. 775 (1991). In § 2710(d)(7) of IGRA, however, Congress had clearly indicated its intention to waive the states' Eleventh Amendment immunity, and Congress had been held to have that power under the Interstate Commerce Clause in Pennsylvania v. Union Gas Co., 491 U.S. 1 (1989). In a decision having ramifications far beyond the field of Indian law, the Supreme Court in *Seminole* held that Congress lacked the power to abrogate state Eleventh Amendment immunity under either the Indian or the Interstate Commerce Clause. *Union Gas* was overruled. The Eleventh Amendment restricted the judicial power granted to the federal courts under Article III of the Constitution. Congress could not enlarge that restricted judicial power by statute enacted pursuant to the Commerce Clauses. Congress's abrogation of state Eleventh Amendment immunity in the Indian Gaming Regulatory Act was therefore unconstitutional.

The Court in *Seminole* then addressed the argument that, even if the state could not be sued, a suit for injunctive relief could be maintained against the governor or other state officials under the doctrine of Ex Parte Young, 209 U.S. 123 (1908). *Young* employs the fiction that a state officer acting in violation of federal law does not really act for the state, and therefore can be enjoined. The Supreme Court in *Seminole*, however, held that it would be inappropriate to assume that Congress intended to permit the *Young* alternative, because it had set out a complex set of remedial procedures in IGRA that included no such option. The Court pointed out that it was not holding that Congress was without power to authorize a *Young* remedy; it was merely holding that Congress had not so intended in IGRA. 517 U.S. at 75 n.17. (The Court in a later case again resisted easy invocation of the *Young* remedy. Idaho v. Coeur d'Alene Tribe, 521 U.S. 261 (1997)). One court of appeals, however, has permitted suit under *Young* when the plaintiff seeks prospective relief against a continuing violation of federal law. Mille Lacs Band of Chippewa Indians v. Minnesota, 124 F.3d 904, 913–14 (8th Cir.1997), aff'd on other grounds, 526 U.S. 172 (1999).

Seminole presents debatable issues far beyond Indian law. For present purposes, however, it is enough to emphasize that *Seminole* opened a gaping hole in the system established by Congress in IGRA. The Act gave state laws a reach that they otherwise did not have; state laws relating to gambling were extended into Indian country. The compensation for the tribes was that they could force the states to bargain for a compact permitting Class III gaming. After *Seminole*, the tribes could force the states no longer. Although some states might continue to bargain, and one or two might even waive their Eleventh Amendment immunity, many states were likely simply to hold the line and refuse to bargain. The fact that a state may have bargained in the past did not waive its Eleventh Amendment immunity. Ponca Tribe of Oklahoma v. Oklahoma, 89 F.3d 690, 691 n.2 (10th Cir.1996). Without compacts, there could be no legal Class III gaming.

The question for the tribes, then, was whether there was any other viable route to the approval of new gaming operations. One alternative, mentioned by the Supreme Court in *Seminole* without an expression of opinion as to its validity, is that which had been adopted by the Eleventh Circuit in the decision the Supreme Court reviewed in *Seminole*. The Eleventh Circuit relied on the Regulatory Act's severability clause, and held that the remaining procedures regarding compacts continued in force. Seminole Tribe of Florida v. Florida, 11 F.3d 1016, 1029 (11th Cir.1994). Under that alternative, a tribe may proceed as follows:

> One hundred and eighty days after the tribe first requests negotiations with the state, the tribe may file suit in district court. If the state pleads

an Eleventh Amendment defense, the suit is dismissed, and the tribe, pursuant to 25 U.S.C. § 2710(d)(7)(B)(vii), then may notify the Secretary of the Interior of the tribe's failure to negotiate a compact with the state. The Secretary then may prescribe regulations governing class III gaming on the tribe's lands.

Id. at 1029.

This alternative would be the most efficient from the standpoint of the tribes, but there was considerable controversy between Congress and the Secretary of the Interior over the desirability of this solution. Ultimately, the Secretary adopted regulations along the lines suggested by the Eleventh Circuit. When a tribe is unable to secure the negotiation of a compact and sues to compel good faith bargaining, and the state successfully invokes its Eleventh Amendment immunity, the tribe may petition the Secretary to prescribe procedures to govern Indian gaming by the tribe. 25 C.F.R. § 291.3. The tribe's petition proposes procedures and the state may propose alternatives. §§ 291.4(j), 291.7. If the state does, the matter is referred for mediation. § 291.9. Whether the state opposes the petition or not, the Secretary has the power to approve or disapprove proposed procedures according to criteria that assure conformity with IGRA.

Although this route to Class III gaming seems in theory to be an effective one for a tribe that is unable to force a state to bargain, in practice it has not been productive as yet. Whether administrative hesitancy comes from doubts concerning whether the procedure will survive challenges in court, or from political difficulties in forcing class III gaming on the states, the fact remains that the route of direct secretarial issuance of gaming procedures has not proved a solution to the problem posed by *Seminole*.

An alternative for the tribes at the time of *Seminole* might have been to sue the states in state court to force bargaining, but the Supreme Court closed that door not long after *Seminole*. In Alden v. Maine, 527 U.S. 706 (1999), the Supreme Court held that Congress had no power to waive a state's sovereign immunity in *state* court. Yet another approach is for the tribes to induce the United States to sue recalcitrant states on their behalf. The Eleventh Amendment immunity of the states does not extend to actions brought by the United States on behalf of a tribe. See Arizona v. California, 460 U.S. 605, 614 (1983). One district court held that the United States had a fiduciary duty to bring such a claim, Chemehuevi Indian Tribe v. Wilson, 987 F.Supp. 804 (N.D. Cal. 1997), but another held to the contrary, United States v. 1020 Electronic Gambling Machines, 38 F.Supp.2d 1213 (E.D. Wash. 1998). It is unlikely that the tribes will be able to overcome the traditional discretion of the United States concerning when or whether to bring an action. See Shoshone Bannock Tribes v. Reno, 56 F.3d 1476 (D.C.Cir.1995).

For some time after *Seminole*, tribal gaming remained in considerable disarray. Many tribes already had compacts, and they conducted relatively secure gaming operations, although they remained concerned over what would happen when the compacts expired after their agreed term of years. Others, including several tribes in California, conducted casino-type gaming without compacts, under a threat of federal enforcement that was slow in coming. See In re Indian Gaming Related Cases, 331 F.3d 1094, 1103 (9th Cir.2003).

In the end, much of the remedy for the stalemate turned out to be both political and financial. Tribal gaming has enjoyed substantial popular support in many places. One Arizona tribe succeeded in an innovative state-law approach to the problem posed by *Seminole*. The state governor refused to negotiate after having entered sixteen compacts with other tribes. The tribe proposed, and the voters adopted, an initiative requiring the governor to enter the "standard form" compact enjoyed by the other tribes if negotiations failed. The state supreme court held the initiative to be enforceable against the governor, and to be consistent with IGRA. Salt River Pima–Maricopa Indian Community v. Hull, 190 Ariz. 97, 945 P.2d 818 (1997). Subsequently, when the existing compacts in Arizona approached expiration, a further initiative election dictated the entry of new compacts. Some other states have also followed the path of initiatives or referenda to approve tribal gaming directly or to waive the state's sovereign immunity relating to the IGRA compact process. California passed a "standard form" compact initiative that was declared in violation of the state constitution (except for its waiver of state immunity). Hotel Employees and Restaurant Employees Internat'l Union v. Davis, 21 Cal.4th 585, 88 Cal.Rptr.2d 56, 981 P.2d 990 (1999). The legislature and voters subsequently amended the state constitution expressly to permit Indian tribal casino-type gaming. See Cal. Const. Art. IV, 19(f); *Gaming Related Cases*, 331 F.3d at 1103 & n.11. The amendment was held not to violate either IGRA or the Equal Protection Clause. Flynt v. California Gambling Control Comm'n, 104 Cal.App.4th 1125, 129 Cal.Rptr.2d 167 (2002), cert. denied, ___ U.S. ___, 124 S.Ct. 398 (2003); Artichoke Joe's v. Norton, ___ F.3d ___ 2003 WL 22998116 (9th Cir.2003).

One of the incentives for states to enter compacts is the prospect of negotiating a share of tribal gaming revenues to be paid to the state. The Act provides that nothing in the section governing Class III gaming shall be interpreted to permit a state or any of its subdivisions to impose "any tax, fee, charge, or other assessment upon any Indian tribe or upon any other person or entity authorized by an Indian tribe to engage in a class III activity." § 2710(d)(4). A demand by a state for direct taxation of a tribe or its land was evidence of the state's refusal to bargain in good faith. § 2710(d)(7)(B)(iii)(II). Under these provisions, a state's bald insistence on a share of tribal gaming revenues would be viewed as a forbidden attempt to tax.

Although after *Seminole* the question whether the state is attempting to tax Indian gaming is unlikely to arise in litigation, the Secretary still has to approve a tribal-state compact before it takes effect. 25 U.S.C.A. 2710(d)(3)(B). This requirement offers an opportunity for the Secretary to police possible overreaching by the states in violation of IGRA's no-tax clause. The primary means for the states to receive a share of revenues without violating the no-tax clause is to offer a quid pro quo for a share of gaming revenues. That quid pro quo ordinarily is a promise of a degree of monopoly ("exclusivity") for Indian tribal gaming. See *Gaming Related Cases*, 331 F.3d at 1100. If the state agrees to prohibit casino-type gaming other than by Indian tribes, then payment by the tribes of a reasonable share of revenues is deemed to be a payment for exclusivity and not a tax. The state may also exact (or the tribes may offer) other conditions without violating IGRA, so long as the state gives value, normally in the form of some degree of monopoly. Thus, California compacts that granted a tribal monopoly of casino-type gaming were permitted to include provisions requiring the gaming tribes to share revenues with non-gaming tribes, to pay the state a share of revenues for various purposes related to gaming (including gambling addiction treatment programs), and to require the tribe to adopt a labor ordinance and permit labor organizing and, if the union won elections, collective bargaining with regard to employees of casinos or related establishments. *Gaming Related Cases*, supra. (The most recent round of Arizona compacts also provides for revenue sharing with non-gaming or remote tribes by allocating slot machine rights to those tribes that can then be licensed to the gaming tribes.)

The anti-tax clause has had some other effects. Although it does not directly *prohibit* the state from taxing Indian gaming, the Act has been held to preempt California from collecting a business license tax on the portion of off-track wagers placed in tribal gaming facilities on-reservation. Cabazon Band of Mission Indians v. Wilson, 37 F.3d 430 (9th Cir.1994). Although the tax fell on the non-Indian racing association, it clearly burdened the Bands and was inconsistent with the IGRA's goal of promoting the tribes' economic welfare. Id.; cf. Indian Country, U.S.A. v. Oklahoma Tax Comm'n, 829 F.2d 967 (10th Cir.1987). The anti-tax clause refers, of course, only to state taxes. Federal wagering and occupation excise taxes apply to tribal gaming. Chickasaw Nation v. United States, 534 U.S. 84 (2001); see Chap. IX, Section B, supra.

3. CLASS II AND CLASS III GAMING

IGRA requires that Class II and Class III gaming be located in a state that "permits such gaming" by anyone. § 2710(b)(1)(A),(d)(1)(B). This requirement means that if a state chooses, as Utah has, to allow no gambling at all for any purpose anywhere within the state, then the tribes in that state may not conduct either Class II or Class III gaming. Almost no other states are that pure, however; most permit some form of gambling by some persons. The issue then arises whether the state's permission of some gambling that falls within Class II or Class III satisfies the entire condition for *all* kinds of tribal gambling within that class. The answers have varied. In Sycuan Band of Mission Indians v. Roache, 54 F.3d 535, 539 (9th Cir.1994), the Ninth Circuit, relying on the rationale of *Cabazon Band*, asserted that, if California permits any type of Class II gaming, the tribe may conduct Class II gaming. The Second Circuit made a similar ruling with regard to Class III gaming: if the state permits some types of Class III gaming, it has a duty to negotiate with a tribe a Class III compact that is not limited to the games the state otherwise permits. Mashantucket Pequot Tribe v. Connecticut, 913 F.2d 1024 (2d Cir.1990); see also Lac du Flambeau Band of Lake Superior Chippewa Indians v. Wisconsin, 770 F.Supp. 480 (W.D. Wis. 1991), app. dism., 957 F.2d 515 (7th Cir.1992). Otherwise, the state could impose unilaterally its full system of regulation, by negotiating only for games it permits. The Eighth and Ninth Circuits, however, have ruled that the state has no duty to negotiate with the tribe over particular types of Class III games that state law prohibits. Cheyenne River Sioux Tribe v. South Dakota, 3 F.3d 273 (8th Cir.1993); Rumsey Indian Rancheria of Wintun Indians v. Wilson, 64 F.3d 1250 (9th Cir.1994), amended, 99 F.3d 321 (1996). The state must actually prohibit the game, however, not merely regulate it. *Rumsey*, 64 F.3d at 1259 n.5; cf. United States v. Sisseton–Wahpeton Sioux Tribe,

897 F.2d 358 (8th Cir.1990). Nothing prevents a state from changing its public policy to prohibit a particular type of gaming, thereby eliminating its duty to negotiate. Coeur d'Alene Tribe v. State, 842 F.Supp. 1268 (D. Idaho 1994), aff'd, 51 F.3d 876 (9th Cir.1995).

There has been a considerable amount of litigation over whether particular games fall within Class II or Class III. One source of ambiguity is the provision allowing as a Class II game bingo "whether or not electronic, computer, or other technologic aids are used in connection therewith" including punch boards, pull-tabs and certain other games. It is to be contrasted with the exclusion from Class II of any "electronic or electromechanical facsimiles of any game of chance or slot machines of any kind." § 2703(7). In United States v. 103 Electronic Gambling Devices, 223 F.3d 1091 (9th Cir.2000), the government sought to condemn electronic bingo "MegaMania" games played by computer by many players in different locations, on the theory that they were not true bingo games but were gambling devices prohibited by the Johnson Act. The Johnson Act prohibits gambling devices on Indian land, 15 U.S.C.A. 1175(a), unless there is a valid tribal-state gaming compact. IGRA, § 2710(d)(6). The government contended that the games were not bingo because they were banked—the players played against the house—and players paid for each draw. The Ninth Circuit rejected the government's arguments, holding that games that meet IGRA's three requirements for bingo are legal class II games. 223

F.3d at 1096. The three requirements are that the players play for prizes with cards bearing numbers or other designations, that the numbers are covered when drawn or electronically determined, and the first player to cover a designated pattern on a card wins. § 2703(7)(A). The Tenth Circuit subsequently reached the same conclusion as the Ninth. United States v. 162 MegaMania Gambling Devices, 231 F.3d 713 (10th Cir.2000).

Several disputes have arisen over electronic pull-tab games. One type was played in a coin machine with a computer program limiting choices to the specified number of chances on the pre-determined board; the issue was whether the game was simply a pull-tab or punchboard game using a permissible electronic or computer ''aid,'' or was an ''electronic facsimile'' of a game of chance or ''slot machine'' excluded from Class II. The District of Columbia and Ninth Circuits held that the games were Class III facsimiles of games of chance. Cabazon Band of Mission Indians v. National Indian Gaming Comm'n, 14 F.3d 633 (D.C.Cir.1994); Sycuan Band of Mission Indians v. Roache, 54 F.3d 535 (1994). A video ''Pick 6'' lotto game met the same fate in Spokane Indian Tribe v. United States, 972 F.2d 1090 (9th Cir.1992).

A more direct ruling on the relationship between the Johnson Act and IGRA came in another pull-tab case, involving machines that dispensed paper tabs that could then be read and displayed electronically by machine (although the paper tab remained controlling for confirmation of a prize). The Johnson

Act issue was created by the fact that IGRA expressly provides that the Johnson Act does not apply to gaming under a compact (i.e., Class III gaming), § 2710(d)(6), but is silent regarding its applicability to Class II gaming. Presented with that question, the Tenth Circuit held that "if a piece of equipment is a technologic aid to an IGRA Class II game, its use, sale, possession or transportation is then necessarily not proscribed" by the Johnson Act. Seneca–Cayuga Tribe v. National Indian Gaming Comm'n, 327 F.3d 1019, 1035 (10th Cir.2003), pet. for cert. filed, Nov. 21, 2003. The court then eliminated another ambiguity by accepting the view of the Commission that IGRA permitted technologic aids to be used for pull-tabs as well as bingo, and held that the pull-tab machines were Class II aids, not gambling devices or Class III facsimiles. The same result was reached in Diamond Game Enterprises, Inc. v. Reno, 230 F.3d 365 (D.C.Cir.2000). A different tack was taken by the Eighth Circuit, which held that a tribe engaged in Class II gaming had to comply not only with IGRA but also with the Johnson Act. United States v. Santee Sioux Tribe, 324 F.3d 607 (8th Cir.2003). The court went on to hold, however, that the electronic pull-tab game was not a "gambling device" within the meaning of the Johnson Act, and was a Class II technologic aid.

4. ENFORCEMENT

A central feature of IGRA is its unique criminal jurisdictional provision, 18 U.S.C.A. § 1166. That section extends all state laws pertaining to gambling, including but not limited to criminal provisions, into Indian country. "State laws" include state decisional law authorizing injunctive relief against illegal gaming enterprises. United States v. Santee Sioux Tribe, 135 F.3d 558 (8th Cir.1998). The statute excepts from the definition of "gambling" any Class I gaming, any Class II gaming regulated by the Commission, and any Class III gaming under a compact approved by the Secretary that is in effect. Finally, § 1166 provides that the United States has exclusive jurisdiction to enforce those state gambling laws extended to Indian country unless the tribe, by compact, consents to the state's exercise of that jurisdiction. IGRA is sufficiently pervasive, however, that it leaves no room for the Assimilative Crimes Act to import state law to be applied to an Indian gaming operation. United Keetoowah Band of Cherokee Indians v. Oklahoma, 927 F.2d 1170 (10th Cir.1991).

The fact that the federal government's criminal jurisdiction is exclusive in the absence of a compact providing otherwise has been of great practical importance in certain instances. In some states where there was a standoff between tribe and state, and the tribes operated casinos without compacts, the state could not prosecute because the right to prosecute was exclusively federal. Sycuan Band of Mission Indians v. Roache, 54 F.3d 535 (9th Cir.1994). In California, for example, numbers of tribes continued to operate Class III games for substantial periods of time without compacts, because federal authorities were reluctant to shut the operations down. See, e.g., Cabazon Band of Mission Indians v. Wilson, 124 F.3d 1050 (9th Cir.1997). That tolerant attitude did not prevail at all times and places, however, and does not continue today. Operation of casinos in Indian country without a compact has resulted in convictions under the Organized Crime Control Act, 18 U.S.C. § 1955, which prohibits operation of a gambling business in violation of state law, and the Johnson Act, 18 U.S.C. § 1175, which prohibits use of a gambling device in Indian country. United States v. E.C. Investments, Inc., 77 F.3d 327 (9th Cir.1996); United States v. Cook, 922 F.2d 1026 (2d Cir.1991).

IGRA authorizes the Chairman of the Regulatory Commission to issue orders of temporary closure of gaming activities for substantial violations of the Act, and the Commission may make such orders permanent. 25 U.S.C. §§ 2705(a)(1), 2713(b)(1), 2706(a)(5). Such orders may extend to all gaming, not just particular games. United States v. Seminole Nation of Oklahoma, 321 F.3d 939 (10th Cir.2002). The orders are subject to administrative review by the Commission and then to review in court under the Administrative Procedure Act; the administrative remedies must be exhausted first. In re Sac & Fox Tribe of the Mississippi in Iowa/Meskwaki Casino Litigation, 340 F.3d 749 (8th Cir.2003). Upon a suit by the Attorney General, a closure order may be enforced by injunction in federal court upon a showing of irreparable harm or state decisional law authorizing such a remedy, imported into the Regulatory Act by 18 U.S.C.A. § 1166(a). Id.; United

States v. Santee Sioux Tribe, 135 F.3d 558 (8th Cir.1998). A district court in California has held that the United States may maintain a suit for injunction of non-compact gaming without a Commission order, but has required a showing that the state bargained in good faith. United States v. Santa Ynez Band of Chumash Mission Indians, 983 F.Supp. 1317 (C.D.Cal.1997).

IGRA provides a cause of action for a tribe or state to enjoin Class III gaming carried on in violation of any tribal-state compact. § 2710(d)(7)(A). This provision waives tribal sovereign immunity for such suits. See Mescalero Apache Tribe v. State of N.M., 131 F.3d 1379 (10th Cir.1997). This provision does not, however, give a state a right to enjoin gaming conducted on Indian lands *without* a compact; such a construction would improperly extend all of state regulatory enforcement into Indian country. See Florida v. Seminole Tribe, 181 F.3d 1237 (11th Cir.1999); Cabazon Band of Mission Indians v. Wilson, 124 F.3d 1050, 1059–60 (9th Cir.1997). Thus, when a compact permits only simulcast horse race gaming, and says nothing of slot machines or other Class III gaming, the state cannot obtain an injunction against slot machines under § 2710(d)(7)(A) on the theory that the Class III gaming is "in violation" of a compact. *Cabazon Band*, 124 F.3d at 1059–60. In addition, IGRA creates no private right of action that would permit the state to sue the tribal chairman to enjoin Class III gaming without a compact. *Seminole Tribe*, 181 F.3d at 1250. When casino-type gaming is being carried on *off* of Indian lands, however, the state may sue to enjoin the operation. Missouri ex rel. Nixon v. Coeur D'Alene Tribe, 164 F.3d 1102 (8th Cir.1999). When there is a compact, section 2710(d)(7)(A) preempts the jurisdiction of a tribal gaming commission to determine whether a particular form of gaming violates the compact; the state is not required to exhaust that tribal remedy and is not bound by the tribal commission's ruling that slot machines were permitted by a compact. Crow Tribe of Indians v. Racicot, 87 F.3d 1039 (9th Cir.1996).

Tribes have generally been unsuccessful in invoking IGRA to prevent state bodies from revealing under state law public records relating to tribal gaming operations, which may include some financial information. See, e.g., Confederated Tribes of Siletz Indians v. Oregon, 143 F.3d 481 (9th Cir. 1998); Confederated Tribes of the Chehalis Reservation v. Johnson, 135 Wash.2d 734, 958 P.2d 260 (1998).

When private parties seek to sue a tribe or its officials for violation of IGRA, the results are mixed. Tribal members have had some success in challenging a distribution of per capita payments for failure to comply with the Act's requirement of secretarial approval. In those cases, courts have held that the tribe, by engaging in gaming under the Act, waived its immunity for suits seeking only injunctive or declaratory relief requiring compliance with the Act. They also have held that the plaintiffs had standing, and assumed or decided that the Act provides a private right of action to persons claiming improper distribution. See Ross v. Flandreau Santee Sioux Tribe, 809 F.Supp. 738 (D.S.D.1992); Maxam v. Lower Sioux Indian Community of Minnesota, 829 F.Supp. 277 (D.Minn.1993); but see Davids v. Coyhis, 869 F.Supp. 1401 (E.D. Wis. 1994); Montgomery v. Flandreau Santee Sioux Tribe, 905 F.Supp. 740 (D.S.D. 1995). On the other hand, when a challenge to distribution was actually a challenge to a tribe's decisions regarding membership, the tribal court had exclusive jurisdiction. Smith v. Babbitt, 100 F.3d 556 (8th Cir.1996); see also Sac & Fox Tribe of the Mississippi in Iowa/Meskwaki Casino Litigation, 340 F.3d 749 (8th Cir.2003). One group of tribal members, however, was able to challenge in federal court under the Administrative Procedure Act the approval of a tribal adoption ordinance by the Interior Board of Indian Appeals; the ordinance diluted the members' right to gaming proceeds. Feezor v. Babbitt, 953 F.Supp. 1 (D.D.C.1996).

Others seeking to sue on an implied right of action for violations of IGRA have had little success. A management contractor has been held to have no private right of action under the Act to compel the tribe to license the contractor's employees. Tamiami Partners, Ltd. v. Miccosukee Tribe of Indians of Florida, 63 F.3d 1030, 1049 (11th Cir.1995). In an analogous case the Tenth Circuit squarely held that IGRA contains no private right of action at all for an individual seeking compliance with its provisions. Hartman v. Kickapoo Tribe Gaming Comm'n,

319 F.3d 1230 (10th Cir.2003). A tribal member who opposed gaming has also been held to have no standing to challenge a gaming compact properly entered between a tribe and the state. Willis v. Fordice, 850 F.Supp. 523 (S.D.Miss.1994), aff'd, 55 F.3d 633 (5th Cir.1995). One gambler was successful in raising violation of a gaming compact as a matter of defense; the compact prohibited credit gambling, so the gambler's debt was held illegal and void. CBA Credit Services v. Azar, 551 N.W.2d 787 (N.D.1996). A gambler suing because he lost in an illegal game is likely to be barred by state public policy, however. See Kelly v. First Astri Corp., 72 Cal.App.4th 462, 84 Cal.Rptr.2d 810 (1999).

Ordinary tort suits against casinos tend to be unsuccessful unless provision is made for them in a compact. Engaging in casino operations does not waive a tribe's sovereign immunity. Trudgeon v. Fantasy Springs Casino, 71 Cal.App.4th 632, 84 Cal.Rptr.2d 65 (1999); Gallegos v. Pueblo of Tesuque, 132 N.M. 207, 46 P.3d 668 (2002), cert. dism., 536 U.S. 990 (2002).

5. MANAGEMENT CONTRACTS

IGRA requires gaming management contracts to be approved by the Commission Chairman, and defines management contracts to include all collateral contracts relating to gaming. § 2711(a)(1), (3); Catskill Development, L.L.C. v. Park Place Entertainment Corp., 217 F.Supp.2d 423 (S.D.N.Y. 2002). The Commission did not begin to function for sever-

al years after the enactment of IGRA; in the meantime management contracts were held to require
Secretarial approval as contracts "in consideration
of services for said Indians relative to their lands"
under 25 U.S.C. § 81, see United States ex rel.
Morongo Band of Mission Indians v. Rose, 34 F.3d
901 (9th Cir.1994). Other "collateral contracts"
such as slot machine leases related to gaming did
not require such approval under the Secretary's
regime, but would under that of the Commission.
United States ex rel. Mosay v. Buffalo Bros. Mgt.,
Inc., 20 F.3d 739 (7th Cir.1994).

Now that the Commission is in place, a management contract (including contracts collateral to it)
or any modification of it that is not approved by the
Chairman of the Commission is void. 25 C.F.R.
§§ 533.7, 535.1(f); see Turn Key Gaming, Inc. v.
Oglala Sioux Tribe, 164 F.3d 1092 (8th Cir.1999).
This provision has engendered litigation over
whether particular contracts were in fact management contracts. A combination of a consulting
agreement, a construction and loan agreement, and
a participation agreement was held to be a management contract, void for lack of approval, when together the agreements bound the tribe to follow the
"consultant's" recommendations. United States v.
Casino Magic Corp., 293 F.3d 419 (8th Cir.2002).
The Commission's review of management contracts
is limited to ensuring that they comply with the
provisions of IGRA; it does not extend to the question whether the tribal chairman had authority to
contract–a matter for the tribal court to decide in

the first instance. Bruce H. Lien Co. v. Three Affili-
ated Tribes of the Fort Berthold Reservation, 93
F.3d 1412 (8th Cir.1996); see also Gaming World
Intern., Ltd. v. White Earth Band of Chippewa
Indians, 317 F.3d 840 (8th Cir.2003). The tribe may
waive its sovereign immunity in such contracts, as
by an arbitration clause. See C & L Enterprises,
Inc. v. Citizen Band Potawatomi Indian Tribe, 532
U.S. 411 (2001).

Claims based on management contracts have generally been held to arise under federal law for
purposes of federal jurisdiction. The Eleventh Circuit has held that management contracts are so
central to the gaming operation that they implicitly
incorporate IGRA and its regulations. See Tamiami
Partners, Ltd. v. Miccosukee Tribe, 177 F.3d 1212
(11th Cir.1999); see also *Gaming World*, 317 F.3d at
848–49. A state-law suit based on a breach of a
management contract is thus preempted. Great
Western Casinos, Inc. v. Morongo Band of Mission
Indians, 74 Cal.App.4th 1407, 88 Cal.Rptr.2d 828
(1999). Similarly, IGRA completely preempts the
field of licensing of Indian gaming to the degree
that a complaint concerning licensing may be removed to federal court. Gaming Corp. of America v.
Dorsey & Whitney, 88 F.3d 536 (8th Cir.1996).
Actions on other purely routine contract matters
that do not affect the tribe's operation of gaming or
its compliance with IGRA do not raise federal questions, however. *Gaming World*, 317 F.3d at 848;
American Vantage Cos. v. Table Mountain Rancheria, 103 Cal.App.4th 590, 126 Cal.Rptr.2d 849, cert.

denied, ___ U.S. ___, 124 S.Ct. 105 (2003). Thus, a suit between two management companies over a failed joint venture to pursue tribal gaming contracts was not preempted by IGRA because it did not affect the tribe or its interests in gaming. Casino Resource Corp. v. Harrah's Entertainment, Inc., 243 F.3d 435 (8th Cir.2001).

As all of these cases indicate, litigation in the field of Indian gaming is increasing at a rapid pace. All the developments cannot be catalogued here. The major boundaries seem to have been marked out, however, and the compact process is operating with some stability in a large number of states. Many issues remain to be resolved, but the chaos of a few years ago has largely subsided and the gaming tribes have reason for optimism, at least in the near future.

CHAPTER XI

INDIVIDUAL RIGHTS AND INDIAN LAW

A. RIGHTS OF INDIANS

1. INDIANS AND THE FEDERAL GOVERNMENT

In their relation to the federal government, Indians are entitled to the same constitutional rights as anyone else. The protections of the Bill of Rights extend to "persons," and nothing about their status removes Indians from that category.

There is one major constitutional distinction in the manner in which the federal government deals with Indians. Congress and the courts have created an entire body of law dealing with Indians as such. This treatment has led to challenges under the equal protection principles of the Fifth Amendment. These challenges have been uniformly rejected by the Supreme Court. In Morton v. Mancari, 417 U.S. 535 (1974), the Court upheld a statutory "Indian preference" in hiring by the Bureau of Indian Affairs. The Court relied upon the statute's purpose, and the BIA's special role, in aiding Indian self-government, and rejected the claim of unconstitutional discrimination in the following manner:

Literally every piece of legislation dealing with Indian tribes and reservations, and certainly all legislation dealing with the BIA, single out for special treatment a constituency of tribal Indians living on or near reservations. If these laws, derived from historical relationships and explicitly designed to help only Indians, were deemed invidious racial discrimination, an entire Title of the United States Code [25 U.S.C.A.] would be effectively erased and the solemn commitment of the Government toward the Indians would be jeopardized. * * *

In a footnote, the Court added:

The preference is not directed towards a "racial" group consisting of "Indians"; instead, it applies only to members of "federally recognized" tribes. This operates to exclude many individuals who are racially to be classified as "Indians." In this sense, the preference is political rather than racial in nature. * * *

417 U.S. at 552–53 & n. 24.

Equal protection claims have also arisen from the fact that the division of criminal and civil jurisdiction in Indian country often depends upon Indian status of the parties. These claims, too, have been unsuccessful. The most notable example is United States v. Antelope, 430 U.S. 641 (1977). In that case Indian defendants had killed a non-Indian while committing a felony in Indian country. They were prosecuted for first degree murder under federal law, which in those circumstances required no proof of premeditation. Had they been non-Indians, they would have been prosecuted under state law, which required proof of premeditation. The Supreme Court held that this disparity did not violate equal protection because the division of criminal jurisdiction by Indian status was an outgrowth of the entire legal structure dealing with Indians. Relying on *Mancari*, supra, the Court noted that "respondents were not subjected to federal criminal jurisdiction because they are of the Indian race but because they are enrolled members of the Coeur d'Alene Tribe." 430 U.S. at 646. Moreover, the federal criminal law treated equally all those who were subject to it. See also Fisher v. District Court, 424 U.S. 382, 390–91 (1976); United States v. Male Juvenile, 280 F.3d 1008, 1016–17 (9th Cir.2002).

As both *Mancari* and *Antelope* indicate, separate classification of Indians is permissible even when the classification is not tied to tribal self-government. The employment preference in *Mancari*, for example, was not limited to Indians who were members of the tribes being served by the BIA office in question. See also Johnson v. Shalala, 35 F.3d 402 (9th Cir.1994). Similarly, the federal government has been allowed to favor Indian and Alaska Native firms in awarding construction contracts, even though self-government was not involved and the preferences were not limited to members of the tribes for whom the projects were being constructed. American Federation of Government Employees v. United States, 330 F.3d 513 (D.C.Cir.), pet. for cert. filed, 72 U.S.L.W. 3171 (U.S. Sept. 4, 2003);

Alaska Chapter, Associated General Contractors v. Pierce, 694 F.2d 1162 (9th Cir.1982). It was sufficient that the classification was rationally related to Congress' trust responsibility toward the Indians generally. Id. at 1166–1170. The same analysis would support the Indian preference exception to the employment discrimination provisions of the Civil Rights Act of 1964 (Title VII), 42 U.S.C.A. § 2000e–2(i). One court of appeals has suggested, however, that the *Mancari* principle shields from equal protection attack only those statutes that affect uniquely Indian interests. Williams v. Babbitt, 115 F.3d 657 (9th Cir.1997). It has also held that the Indian employment preference mandated by the Indian Self–Determination and Education Assistance Act did not create a private right of action enabling an individual employment applicant to sue in federal court. Solomon v. Interior Regional Housing Auth., 313 F.3d 1194 (9th Cir.2002).

Enforcement of the right of free exercise of religion often takes a distinctive turn when Indians are involved. Many Indian religious beliefs and practices center on particular places or objects. The places may be on federal lands outside of any reservation. The objects may be eagle feathers or peyote. In these cases, federal management or regulation may interfere substantially with religious uses. In recognition of this problem, Congress in 1978 passed an unusual statute called the "American Indian Religious Freedom Act." It provides that

it shall be the policy of the United States to protect and preserve for American Indians their inherent right of freedom to believe, express, and exercise the traditional religions of the American Indian, Eskimo, Aleut, and Native Hawaiians, including but not limited to access to sites, use and possession of sacred objects, and the freedom to worship through ceremonials and traditional rites.

42 U.S.C.A. § 1996. An Executive Order directs agencies administering federal lands to accommodate access to and ceremonial use of Indian religious sites to the extent practicable and not inconsistent with essential agency functions. Exec. Order No. 13007, 61 Fed. Reg. 26771 (1996). While the Act states the sense of Congress, it confers no judicially enforceable private right of action. Lyng v. Northwest Indian Cemetery Protective Ass'n, 485 U.S. 439, 455 (1988). Indians who seek to block federal (or state) action on religious grounds accordingly must usually prove a violation of the First Amendment Free Exercise Clause. Such controversies, when they come to court, are not truly Indian Law cases, even though they have a distinct Indian flavor. Their resolution depends upon general principles of First Amendment free exercise of religion, and not upon Indian status.

Several controversies have involved attempts by government to develop its public lands in a manner that adversely affects Indian religious practices. Initially, the lower courts resolved such controversies by balancing the governmental interest in developing the particular project against the burden it placed on Indian religion. The balancing nearly always came out in favor of the government. The courts rejected, for example, Indian attempts to prevent the government from inundating sacred places upstream from federal dams. Badoni v. Higginson, 638 F.2d 172 (10th Cir.1980); Sequoyah v. TVA, 620 F.2d 1159 (6th Cir.1980). They also rejected attempts to prevent expansion of a ski area on a sacred mountain in a national forest, Wilson v. Block, 708 F.2d 735 (D.C.Cir.1983), and the establishment of a state park in sacred ground, Crow v. Gullet, 706 F.2d 856 (8th Cir.1983).

In Lyng v. Northwest Indian Cemetery Protective Ass'n, 485 U.S. 439 (1988), the Supreme Court went even further. It held that, so long as the government did not coerce individuals into violating their religious beliefs or penalize their religious activity by denying them rights or benefits available to others, the government was free to develop its own property without regard to its interference with religious practices. Balancing was not appropriate. At issue was a proposal to improve a road and conduct logging operations in a region of national forest sacred to Yurok, Karok and Tolowa Indians. In rejecting the Indians' challenge, the Court stated:

> Even if we assume [that the road] will "virtually destroy the Indians' ability to practice their religion" * * *, the Constitution simply does not provide a principle that could justify upholding respondents' legal claims. However much we might wish that it were otherwise, government

simply could not operate if it were required to satisfy every citizen's religious needs and desires.

Id. at 1326–1327. This ruling presumably puts an end to free exercise challenges to governmental development projects. For example, *Lyng* was applied to defeat a free exercise challenge to the Forest Service's approval of a uranium mine near the Grand Canyon. See Havasupai Tribe v. United States, 752 F.Supp. 1471, 1484–86 (D.Ariz.1990), aff'd, 943 F.2d 32 (9th Cir.1991).

A somewhat different free exercise question is presented when an Indian claims that governmental action interferes with individual religious practices. Such claims are now greatly affected by the Supreme Court's decision in Employment Division v. Smith, 494 U.S. 872 (1990), discussed below. In the past, they led to a balancing of governmental and individual religious interests that produced mixed results. A right of Indian males to wear long hair for religious reasons was upheld against a prison regulation, Teterud v. Burns, 522 F.2d 357 (8th Cir.1975), but rejected in favor of a school dress code, New Rider v. Board of Education, 480 F.2d 693 (10th Cir.1973). A free exercise claim of Indian prisoners of the right to wear headbands in a prison dining hall was defeated in Standing Deer v. Carlson, 831 F.2d 1525 (9th Cir.1987). Indians fared better out of the prison context. A Native American was held to be entitled to keep two black bears for religious purposes without paying a state permit fee. Black Hawk v. Pennsylvania, 225 F.Supp.2d 465 (M.D.Pa.2002). Use of peyote by members of the Native American Church during church ceremonies was frequently protected from the reach of criminal drug laws. E.g., 21 C.F.R. § 1307.31 (1987); People v. Woody, 61 Cal.2d 716, 40 Cal.Rptr. 69, 394 P.2d 813 (1964); State v. Whittingham, 19 Ariz.App. 27, 504 P.2d 950 (1973); see Peyote Way Church of God, Inc. v. Smith, 742 F.2d 193 (5th Cir.1984).

Some statutes and regulations incorporate exceptions to accommodate Indian religious interests in varying degrees. The federal Bald and Golden Eagle Protection Act, which prohibits the taking of eagles or the possession of eagle parts, authorizes exceptions "for the religious purposes of Indian tribes." 16 U.S.C.A. § 668a. Although a permit is required under the exception, that fact does not render the Act facially unconstitutional. United States v. Hugs, 109 F.3d 1375 (9th Cir.1997). The circuits are split on whether the limitation of such permits to members of recognized tribes violates the religious rights of those excluded. The limitation was upheld in Gibson v. Babbitt, 223 F.3d 1256 (11th Cir.2000), and United States v. Antoine, 318 F.3d 919 (9th Cir.2003); it was struck down in United States v. Hardman, 297 F.3d 1116 (10th Cir.2002) (en banc). An informal policy of not enforcing the Migratory Bird Treaty Act against members of recognized tribes was held insufficient to support a selective prosecution claim by a member of an unrecognized tribe in United States v. Eagleboy, 200 F.3d 1137 (8th Cir.1999).

In Employment Division v. Smith, 494 U.S. 872 (1990), the Supreme Court was presented with the question whether exceptions to peyote laws were required by the Free Exercise Clause. The case was brought by drug and alcohol abuse counselors who had been discharged for religious use of peyote and had been denied unemployment compensation. After ascertaining that the religious use of peyote was prohibited by Oregon's criminal laws, the Supreme Court held against the discharged workers. The Court ruled that, if the object of a generally applicable law is not to prohibit or burden religion, its incidental effect upon religion cannot give rise to a free exercise claim. Id. at 878–79. Again, no balancing of interests was appropriate.

Congress reacted to *Smith* by enacting the Religious Freedom Restoration Act, 42 U.S.C.A. § 2000bb et seq. The Act prohibited government from substantially burdening a person's exercise of religion unless it can show that the burden furthers a compelling governmental interest and is the least restrictive means of furthering that interest. § 2000bb–1. The Supreme Court, however, held the Restoration Act unconstitutional in its application to the states and their subdivisions, ruling that Congress lacked the power under the Fourteenth Amendment to expand the constitutional right of free exercise by statute. City of Boerne v. Flores, 521 U.S. 507 (1997). With regard to states, then, *Smith* remains the controlling authority. The Religious Freedom and Restoration Act retains its vitality, however, in its application to federal activities.

See, e.g., *Hardman*, 297 F.3d at 1126; Guam v.
Guerrero, 290 F.3d 1210 (9th Cir.2002). In response
to *City of Boerne*, Congress again reacted, this time
with the Religious Land Use and Institutionalized
Persons Act, 42 U.S.C.A. § 2000cc et seq. As an
exercise of the spending power, this statute reim-
poses strict scrutiny on land use regulation and
prison administration that substantially burdens religious exercise, when the challenged action is by a
government receiving federal assistance.

For some years, Indian tribes have complained of
the disturbance of Indian graves, and of the removal of remains and cultural artifacts from tribal
control. Congress responded to these concerns by
enacting the Native American Graves Protection
and Repatriation Act of 1990, 25 U.S.C.A. § 3001–
3013, 18 U.S.C.A. § 1170. The Act first establishes
the ownership of cultural items excavated or discovered on federal or tribal land after November 16,
1990. The Act also applies to land transferred by
the federal government to the states under the
Water Resources Development Act. See Crow Creek
Sioux Tribe v. Brownlee, 331 F.3d 912 (D.C.Cir.
2003). Native American remains and associated funerary objects belong, first, to lineal descendants. If
the descendants cannot be identified, then those
remains and objects, along with unassociated funerary objects, sacred objects, and objects of cultural
patrimony, belong, in order of preference, to the
tribe on whose land the remains or objects were
found, or the tribe having the closest cultural relationship to them, or to the tribe that aboriginally

occupied the area unless another tribe can show a stronger cultural relationship. § 3002. The Act then requires each federal agency and every museum or institution receiving federal funds and holding such items to prepare an inventory of Indian remains and associated funerary objects, and a summary of unassociated funerary objects, sacred objects, and objects of cultural patrimony. §§ 3003, 3004. The Act then provides for repatriation of these items upon request of the appropriate descendant or tribe. § 3005. The repatriation provision, unlike the ownership provision, applies to remains or objects discovered at any time, even before the effective date of the Act, whether or not discovered on tribal or federal land. Pueblo of San Ildefonso v. Ridlon, 103 F.3d 936 (10th Cir.1996). The repatriation provisions have resulted in the return of very large numbers of remains and cultural and religious objects from museums to tribes.

A criminal provision of the Act prohibits trafficking in Native American human remains, or in Native American "cultural items." 18 U.S.C.A. § 1170. Although this provision may have been aimed at museums, it applies to individual traders. United States v. Kramer, 168 F.3d 1196 (10th Cir.1999). Cultural items are defined elsewhere in the Act to include "cultural patrimony," which means "an object having ongoing historical, traditional, or cultural importance central to the Native American group or culture itself, rather than property owned by an individual Native American, and which, therefore, cannot be alienated * * * by any individual regardless of whether or not the individual is a member of the Indian tribe * * *.'' 25 U.S.C.A. § 3001(3)(D). This provision has been held not to be unconstitutionally vague as applied to trafficking in Navajo Yei B'Chei, imperfectly translated as ceremonial masks. United States v. Corrow, 119 F.3d 796 (10th Cir.1997); accord United States v. Tidwell, 191 F.3d 976 (9th Cir.1999).

One rather celebrated case that has arisen under the Act concerns a human skeleton over 9000 years old, found in the State of Washington. The remains were found on land in control of the Army Corps of Engineers, which gave notice of intention to deliver the remains to a group of Columbia River tribes for burial. A number of scientists and a pre-Christian European church brought an action to halt the transfer, contending that there was a dispute whether the remains were ethnologically related to current Indian tribes or, indeed, to any Indians at all. The scientists also claimed a first amendment right to study the remains. After the parties engaged in considerable pulling and hauling, the district court held that the remains were not Native American within the meaning of the Act, and that evidence did not support the Secretary's determination that they had the necessary relationship to the claimant bands. The scientists were allowed to study the remains. Bonnichsen v. United States, 217 F.Supp.2d 1116 (D.Or.2002).

The greatest limitation in the protection offered by the discovery and excavation portions of the Act is that they apply only to tribal and federal lands and some lands transferred by the federal government. Thus a tribe had no remedy under the Act when a municipality allegedly built a golf course on a tribal burial ground. See Castro Romero v. Becken, 256 F.3d 349 (5th Cir.2001). Some state statutes can provide protection, however. See Lummi Nation v. Golder Associates, Inc., 236 F.Supp.2d 1183 (W.D.Wash.2002).

2. INDIAN CITIZENSHIP

Although most constitutional rights may not be denied to any "person," the right to vote and some other benefits may be restricted to citizens. Political participation in both federal and state government therefore depends substantially on citizenship.

Congress in 1924 conferred national citizenship on all Indians born in the United States. 8 U.S.C.A. § 1401(a)(2). Before that time, individual Indians could become citizens in a number of ways. The General Allotment Act, as well as some special allotment statutes, conferred citizenship upon Indians who received allotments. General Allotment Act, ch. 119, § 6, 24 Stat. 388, 390 (1887). That Act also provided citizenship for Indians who took up residence apart from their tribes and "adopted the habits of civilized life." Id.

While the 1924 statute makes all native-born Indians United States citizens, it is the Fourteenth Amendment that makes them citizens of the states where they reside as well. The status of Indians as citizens of the United States and of the individual states does not interfere with the Indians' relationship to their tribes or with the trust relationship between the tribes and the federal government. Winton v. Amos, 255 U.S. 373 (1921); United States v. Nice, 241 U.S. 591 (1916).

3. INDIANS AND THE STATE GOVERNMENTS

The Fourteenth Amendment is the most important guarantee against infringement of civil liberties by the states. Its due process and equal protection clauses protect all "persons" and its rarely used privileges and immunities clause protects "citizens." Indians clearly qualify on both counts, but historically states have often been reluctant to accord Indians those rights enjoyed under state law by non-Indians. These attitudes still linger, but the courts have made it clear that state discrimination against Indians because of their status is without support of law.

One area in which states have attempted to discriminate is in the furnishing of state services. The states attempt to justify the discrimination on the grounds that tribal Indians do not contribute substantially to the tax revenues of the state and that they are the special responsibility of the federal government. Both of these arguments have failed. States usually do not base services to their non-Indian citizens on proof of taxpaying status, and the federal government does not undertake to supply all needs for Indians. States have accordingly been forbidden to exclude Indians from public schools, e.g. Piper v. Big Pine Sch. Dist., 193 Cal. 664, 226 P. 926 (1924), from general relief services, Acosta v. County of San Diego, 126 Cal.App.2d 455, 272 P.2d 92 (1954), or from indigents' health services, County of Blaine v. Moore, 174 Mont. 114, 568 P.2d 1216 (1977); see McNabb v. Bowen, 829 F.2d 787, 794–95 (9th Cir.1987). A town's refusal to supply sewer services to Indian trust land was held to be a violation of equal protection in Fallon Paiute–Shoshone Tribe v. City of Fallon, 174 F.Supp.2d 1088 (D.Nev.2001).

Voting by Indians was resisted by the states for many years on various grounds. One was non-payment of state taxes by Indians in Indian country, even though taxpayer status was not required of non-Indian voters. Another was that, as wards of the federal government, Indians were under guardianship and not legally competent to vote—an argument that misconstrues the federal wardship of the tribes and runs counter to the federal Citizenship Act of 1924. A third ground was that residence in Indian country was not residence within the state for voting purposes—also an argument that had been rejected in other contexts (particularly those dealing with state power over non-Indians in Indian country). All of these state arguments have been discredited in court, and Indians are now entitled to vote in every state. See Harrison v. Laveen, 67 Ariz. 337, 196 P.2d 456 (1948); Montoya v. Bolack, 70 N.M. 196, 372 P.2d 387 (1962).

There has also been state resistance to Indians' holding state office. The fear has been expressed that Indians who were not subject to taxation in Indian country but who were eligible for state services might choose to inaugurate expensive service programs to be paid for entirely by non-Indian taxpayers. The same incentives, however, apply to any elected officeholder who is poor and therefore does not pay state taxes. In Shirley v. Superior Court, 109 Ariz. 510, 513 P.2d 939 (1973), the Supreme Court of Arizona rejected arguments that the Indian officeholder was disqualified by not being subject to state taxes or service of process. In office-holding as in other areas, then, the Indian has the same rights in relation to the state as the non-Indian.

4.   INDIANS AND THE TRIBES

a.   The Constitution and the Tribes

Indians stand in an entirely different constitutional posture with regard to their tribes than they do with regard to the federal or state governments. The differences arise both from the structure of the federal Constitution and the nature of the tribes.

Nearly all of the civil liberties set forth in the Constitution are stated in terms of protection against governmental action. The Bill of Rights is a list of prohibitions against the federal government. The Fourteenth Amendment provides that no "State" shall deny due process or equal protection of the laws. The Indian tribes, however, are not the federal government nor are they states or subdivisions of either. It is therefore normally not possible for any person, Indian or non-Indian, to invoke the Bill of Rights or the Fourteenth Amendment against a tribe. See Talton v. Mayes, 163 U.S. 376 (1896). Thus, in Native American Church v. Navajo Tribal Council, 272 F.2d 131 (10th Cir.1959), a court of appeals held that the First Amendment Free Exercise Clause does not apply to a tribe through the Fourteenth Amendment because "Indian tribes are not states. They have a status higher than that of states." Id. at 134.

There were a few cases in the nineteen-sixties holding that tribal courts were so infused with federal influence that the Fifth Amendment applied to their actions. See Colliflower v. Garland, 342 F.2d 369 (9th Cir.1965); Settler v. Yakima Tribal Court, 419 F.2d 486 (9th Cir.1969). This approach was repudiated, however, by United States v. Wheeler, 435 U.S. 313 (1978), which held that the double jeopardy provision of the Fifth Amendment was not infringed when an Indian was convicted in federal court after having been convicted of a lesser included offense in tribal court. The Supreme Court reiterated that the tribe in punishing its members was exercising its own independent sovereignty that did not derive from the federal government. The second prosecution therefore did not offend the double jeopardy clause, as it would have if the tribal prosecution had been deemed wholly or partly federal.

This controversy was reawakened recently after the Supreme Court held that tribes had no criminal jurisdiction over nonmember Indians. Duro v. Reina, 495 U.S. 676 (1990). Congress responded by enacting 25 U.S.C.A. § 1301(2), which "recognized and affirmed" the inherent criminal jurisdiction of the tribes over nonmember Indians. The Ninth Circuit held that the statute did not delegate federal power to the tribal government, but merely recognized inherent power. As a consequence, dual prosecution by the federal and tribal authorities did not violate the Double Jeopardy Clause. United States v. Enas, 255 F.3d 662 (9th Cir.2001) (en banc). The Eighth Circuit, however, held that § 1301(2) amounted to a new delegation of federal power triggering double jeopardy, and the Supreme Court has granted review. United States v. Lara, 324 F.3d 635 (8th Cir.2003), cert. granted, ___ U.S. ___, 124 S.Ct. 46 (2003). It therefore remains to be seen whether a nonmember Indian can invoke the provisions of the federal Constitution when prosecuted in tribal court.

Apart from the specialized case of § 1301(2), the freedom of the tribes from constitutional restraints against governmental action remains well supported. Not all constitutional guarantees are limited to governmental action; the Thirteenth Amendment prohibition of slavery applies to all persons and entities including Indians and Indian tribes. Today, however, the most important civil liberties are those set forth in the Bill of Rights and the Fourteenth Amendment and they are by their own terms unenforceable against the tribes. In 1968, Congress found this situation unacceptable and decided to intervene by statute. The result was the Indian Civil Rights Act.

b. The Indian Civil Rights Act of 1968

The Indian Civil Rights Act of 1968, 25 U.S.C.A. § 1301 et seq., was passed by Congress in order to impose most of the provisions of the Bill of Rights upon the tribes. The principal guarantees of the Act are found in 25 U.S.C.A. § 1302 which provides:

§ 1302   Constitutional rights

No Indian tribe in exercising powers of self-government shall—

(1) make or enforce any law prohibiting the free exercise of religion, or abridging the freedom of speech, or of the press, or the right of the people peaceably to assemble and to petition for a redress of grievances;

(2) violate the right of the people to be secure in their persons, houses, papers, and effects against unreasonable search and seizures, nor issue warrants, but upon probable cause, supported by oath or affirmation, and particularly describing the place to be searched and the person or thing to be seized;

(3) subject any person for the same offense to be twice put in jeopardy;

(4) compel any person in any criminal case to be a witness against himself;

(5) take any private property for a public use without just compensation;

(6) deny to any person in a criminal proceeding the right to a speedy and public trial, to be informed of the nature and cause of the accusation, to be confronted with the witnesses against him, to have compulsory process for obtaining witnesses in his favor, and at his own expense to have the assistance of counsel for his defense;

(7) require excessive bail, impose excessive fines, inflict cruel and unusual punishments, and in no event impose for conviction of any one offense any penalty or punishment greater than imprisonment for a term of one year and a fine of $5,000, or both;

(8) deny to any person within its jurisdiction the equal protection of its laws or deprive any person of liberty or property without due process of law;

(9) pass any bill of attainder or ex post facto law; or

(10) deny to any person accused of an offense punishable by imprisonment the right, upon request, to a trial by jury of not less than six persons.

The Act thus imposes on the tribes most of the Bill of Rights verbatim. There are notable exceptions, however. Clause (1) protects the free exercise of religion, but has no provision prohibiting the establishment of religion by a tribe. This omission was in conscious recognition of the fact that in some of the tribes, especially the Pueblos, government and religion and all the rest of life are inextricably interwoven. Divorcement of religion from government would have altered those tribes beyond recognition; Congress did not wish to go that far so long as the free exercise of religion by individuals was protected. Another point at which the protection of the Act falls short of that of the Constitution is clause (6), which provides the right of an accused to have counsel "at his own expense." The Constitution requires state and federal governments to supply counsel to indigents at government expense when the prosecution may result in imprisonment. Argersinger v. Hamlin, 407 U.S. 25 (1972). Fears of saddling the tribes with an excessive financial burden and the shortage of lawyers in Indian country apparently influenced Congress. See Tom v. Sutton, 533 F.2d 1101 (9th Cir.1976). The limited right to counsel under the Act has been held to render inapplicable to tribal court the rule of Massiah v. United States, 377 U.S. 201 (1964), which makes inadmissible a confession taken in the absence of defense counsel from a defendant who has been charged. United States v. Doherty, 126 F.3d 769 (6th Cir.1997).

From its passage the Indian Civil Rights Act has engendered controversy. Tribal governments tended to see the Act as an undue federal intrusion into tribal affairs. Some individual Indians and many non-Indians saw the Act as a valuable protection against arbitrary tribal action. The extent to which the Act intrudes upon tribal government is partially dependent upon the manner in which it is interpreted. Several courts have stated that guarantees of due process and equal protection should be applied flexibly and adapted to the tribal context. E.g., Wounded Head v. Tribal Council of Oglala Sioux Tribe, 507 F.2d 1079, 1082–83 (8th Cir.1975); Randall v. Yakima Nation Tribal Court, 841 F.2d 897, 900 (9th Cir.1988). It is accordingly not safe to assume that, in the limited circumstances in which federal courts now apply the Act, the guarantees of the Indian Civil Rights Act will be enforced in exactly the same way as their counterparts in the Constitution. On the other hand, federal courts are most familiar with due process and equal protection law generated in a non-Indian context, and there is likely to be some tendency to apply that law to the tribes without modification. One court of appeals, for example, held that the equal protection clause of the Civil Rights Act required application of the one person, one vote rule in tribal elections. White Eagle v. One Feather, 478 F.2d 1311 (8th Cir.1973). Another held that the search and seizure provisions of the Act are identical to those of the Fourth Amendment. United States v. Strong, 778 F.2d 1393, 1395 (9th Cir.1985). A third, while acknowledging that due process concepts generally must be applied with sensitivity to their tribal context, held that when tribal court procedures parallel those of Anglo–Saxon law, there was no need to weigh tribal interests. Randall v. Yakima Nation Tribal Court, 841 F.2d 897 (9th Cir.1988). Thus due process was violated when a tribal appellate court dismissed an appeal on the ground that the trial court had failed promptly to address a request for in forma pauperis status. Id.

Three developments have limited the degree to which the Indian Civil Rights Act acts as a federal intrusion upon tribal autonomy. The first is the widespread adoption of the rule that a party aggrieved by tribal action must first exhaust tribal remedies before invoking the aid of the federal courts (even though exhaustion is not normally required under other federal civil rights statutes). E.g., O'Neal v. Cheyenne River Sioux Tribe, 482 F.2d 1140 (8th Cir.1973); McCurdy v. Steele, 506 F.2d 653 (10th Cir.1974). Thus one court of appeals upheld the dismissal of a confrontation clause claim in a habeas petition, because it had not been raised before the tribal court of appeals. Selam v. Warm Springs Tribal Correctional Facility, 134 F.3d 948 (9th Cir.1998). Such a result is supported by a strong tradition of exhaustion in the federal law of habeas corpus, now the only means of federal review of tribal court action.

A second limitation upon federal intrusion into tribal autonomy arises from the reluctance of some federal courts to delve into "internal tribal matters" even though federal law might arguably permit intervention. See, e.g., Prairie Band of Pottawatomie Tribe v. Udall, 355 F.2d 364 (10th Cir.1966); Tewa Tesuque v. Morton, 498 F.2d 240 (10th Cir. 1974). The doctrine has perhaps been most often invoked in regard to questions of eligibility for tribal membership or office. See Groundhog v. Keeler, 442 F.2d 674 (10th Cir.1971).

The third and by far the most important limitation upon federal authority under the Indian Civil Rights Act arises from the decision of the Supreme Court in Santa Clara Pueblo v. Martinez, 436 U.S. 49 (1978). That case involved a rule of the Pueblo making ineligible for membership the children born to female members married to a person outside the tribe. In contrast, children of marriages of male members to spouses outside the tribe were eligible. A female member of the Pueblo whose children were excluded by the rule brought suit against the tribe and its Governor, alleging a violation of the equal protection clause of the Indian Civil Rights Act. The Supreme Court did not reach the merits of her claim, but dismissed the suit on procedural grounds of great significance.

First, the Court held that the tribe was immune from suit as a sovereign. This ruling was counter to numerous lower court decisions that had held the Indian Civil Rights Act to be a congressional waiver of tribal sovereign immunity to the extent necessary to enforce the provisions of the Act. The fact that the tribe was held immune in *Santa Clara* did not end that particular case, because injunctive relief was being sought and the tribal Governor was still a defendant. In some instances, however, the tribe may be an indispensable party, and tribal immunity will be a complete bar to suit. In addition, the existence of tribal immunity severely restricts (and in a practical sense eliminates) the availability of damages as a remedy.

The Supreme Court in *Santa Clara* then went on to make an even more important procedural ruling. In § 1303 of the Civil Rights Act, Congress had provided:

> The privilege of the writ of habeas corpus shall be available to any person, in a court of the United States, to test the legality of his detention by order of an Indian tribe.

25 U.S.C.A. § 1303. The Supreme Court in *Santa Clara* held that this section furnished the exclusive federal remedy under the Act. This ruling, too, was contrary to numerous lower federal court decisions in which remedies had been liberally implied in order to effectuate the substantive provisions of the Act. In support of its decision, the Supreme Court emphasized the desire of Congress not to intrude unnecessarily upon tribal self-government. The Court pointed out that remedies other than habeas corpus (especially in civil cases) were likely to lead to federal court interference with tribal affairs.

The effect of this ruling in *Santa Clara* was to eliminate the jurisdictional base upon which most decisional law under the Indian Civil Rights Act had rested. Because the remedy of habeas corpus is available only to test the legality of detention by a tribe, its use will necessarily be confined almost entirely to reviewing actions of the tribal courts or police in criminal cases. Violations of equal protection or takings of property without compensation, for example, are unlikely to result in detention and consequently may not be remedied in federal courts. See Crowe v. Eastern Band of Cherokee Indians, Inc., 584 F.2d 45 (4th Cir.1978). One circuit has carved out an exception to the *Santa Clara* rule and has permitted a non-Indian corporation that was denied a tribal forum to bring an Indian Civil Rights Act claim in federal court. Dry Creek Lodge, Inc. v. Arapahoe and Shoshone Tribes, 623 F.2d 682 (10th Cir.1980). The tribal remedy must actually have been sought and refused. White v. Pueblo of San Juan, 728 F.2d 1307, 1312 (10th Cir.1984). At least one other circuit, however, has held that *Santa Clara* simply forecloses any relief other than habeas corpus in federal court under the Indian Civil Rights Act. R.J. Williams Co. v. Fort Belknap Housing Authority, 719 F.2d 979, 981 (9th Cir. 1983).

One of the more interesting cases to arise under the federal habeas corpus jurisdiction of the Indian Civil Rights Act was Poodry v. Tonawanda Band of Seneca Indians, 85 F.3d 874 (2d Cir.1996). There certain tribal members had been informed by tribal officials that they were guilty of attempting to overthrow the tribal government and were therefore banished forever from the reservation and stripped of all rights of membership. The Second Circuit held that banishment was a severe punishment, involving a sufficient restraint on liberty to qualify as "detention" and permit federal review by habeas corpus under the Act, § 1303. Id.; see also Penn v. United States, 335 F.3d 786, 789 (8th Cir.2003).

The same approach was unsuccessful, however, in a later case in which the plaintiffs alleged that, among other things, they had been terminated from employment, banned from various businesses, stricken from membership roles, and prohibited from speaking with certain tribal members. These actions did not amount to detention. Shenandoah v. United States Dept. of Interior, 159 F.3d 708 (2d Cir.1998). Another court has held that banishment from the reservation of a tribe other than the member's own, because of a criminal conviction, did not amount to detention. Alire v. Jackson, 65 F.Supp.2d 1124 (D.Or.1999). A nonmember may assert a violation of the Indian Civil Rights Act as a defense, however, to a federal action seeking enforcement of an order of exclusion. Santa Ynez Band of Mission Indians v. Torres, 262 F.Supp.2d 1038 (C.D.Cal.2002).

More commonly, however, *Santa Clara* results in a narrow federal review confined to the typical criminal sentence of imprisonment. The *Santa Clara* decision has been highly controversial. It unquestionably reduces the degree of federal interference in tribal self-government, but it also leaves many potential violations of federal law without a federal remedy. Alternatives of an action against tribal officers pursuant to Bivens v. Six Unknown Agents, 403 U.S. 388 (1971), or 42 U.S.C. § 1983 are unavailable because those remedies run, respectively, against federal and state actors, not tribal ones. Dry v. United States, 235 F.3d 1249 (10th Cir.2000). Enforcement of most of the rights incorporated into the Indian Civil Rights Act is therefore left entirely to the tribal courts. Some tribal court systems are reasonably well equipped for the task; others are not. In either case, the effectuation of the non-criminal portions of the Indian Civil Rights Act lies exclusively with them.

B. RIGHTS OF NON–INDIANS

Non–Indians, like Indians, cannot invoke the Bill of Rights or the Fourteenth Amendment against tribal action, because the tribes are neither the federal government nor states. It is perhaps not surprising, therefore, that the first case arising under the Indian Civil Rights Act involved an attempt by a non-Indian to invoke the protections of the Act against tribal action. Dodge v. Nakai, 298 F.Supp. 26 (D.Ariz.1969). The court there held that non-Indians were entitled to the protection of the Act, which extends most of its guarantees to "persons" affected by tribal action. 25 U.S.C.A. § 1302.

Two recent Supreme Court decisions combine, however, to reduce severely the number of occasions upon which non-Indians will be in a position to seek the protection of the Indian Civil Rights Act in federal court. The first decision is Oliphant v. Suquamish Indian Tribe, 435 U.S. 191 (1978). In that case, the Supreme Court held that, because of the domestic dependent status of the tribes, tribal courts had no criminal jurisdiction over non-Indians. See Chapter VII, Section D(2), supra. The second decision is Santa Clara Pueblo v. Martinez, 436 U.S. 49 (1978), discussed in the previous section. There the Court held that habeas corpus was the sole remedy by which enforcement of the Indian Civil Rights Act could be obtained in federal court. The result of that ruling is that federal court enforcement of the Act is confined almost entirely to review of tribal criminal matters. Because *Oliphant* prevents the tribes from exercising criminal jurisdiction over non-Indians, there will be little opportunity for non-Indians to bring Indian Civil Rights Act cases in federal court. Non–Indians seeking to enforce their rights under the non-criminal portions of the Act will have to rely, as the Indians must, upon tribal courts. If the tribe refuses to provide a forum, one circuit will permit the claim to be raised in federal court. Dry Creek Lodge, Inc. v. Arapahoe and Shoshone Tribes, 623 F.2d 682 (10th Cir.1980); but see R.J. Williams Co. v. Fort Belknap Housing Authority, 719 F.2d 979, 981 (9th Cir.1983), both discussed in the preceding section.

Of course, when federal or state rather than tribal action is challenged by non-Indians, the Constitution and the federal courts are available to supply relief when it is due. Non–Indians have attacked federal and state governmental action on equal protection grounds when Indians were singled out for special treatment, but those attacks have not generally been successful. In Morton v. Mancari, 417 U.S. 535 (1974), the Supreme Court upheld an employment preference for Indians in the Bureau of Indian Affairs. Similar preferences had existed in federal statutes since 1834. The Court held that the preference was not invidious race discrimination, but instead was a political classification designed to encourage Indian tribal self-government and to fulfill the special federal responsibility to Indians. The statutory preference consequently did not offend the equal protection principles of the Fifth Amendment.

In Livingston v. Ewing, 601 F.2d 1110 (10th Cir.1979), a court of appeals rejected an equal protection challenge to policies of the Museum and City of Santa Fe permitting only Indians to sell artifacts under the portal of the museum on the town square. The discrimination against non-Indians was held not to be stigmatizing, and the classification was held justified by the state interest in preserving historical and ethnological interest in fine arts.

Other notable statutory provisions affect the status of non-Indians in the context of individual rights. One is Title VII of the Civil Rights Act of 1964, which outlaws employment discrimination based on race, color, religion, sex or national origin, but which has an express exception for employers who publicly discriminate in favor of Indians "living on or near a reservation." 42 U.S.C.A. § 2000e–2(i). Another is 25 U.S.C.A. § 194, which provides that in trials involving title to property where an Indian is on one side and a "white person" on the other, "the burden of proof shall rest upon the white person, whenever the Indian shall make out a presumption of title in himself from the fact of previous possession or ownership." That statute was applied by the Supreme Court in Wilson v. Omaha

Indian Tribe, 442 U.S. 653 (1979), but no equal protection challenge was before the Court. The circuit court had rejected such a challenge on the strength of *Morton v. Mancari*. Omaha Indian Tribe v. Wilson, 575 F.2d 620, 631 n. 18 (8th Cir.1978). A different court of appeals has suggested, however, that *Mancari* shields from equal protection attack only those statutes affecting uniquely Indian interests; it stated that a serious equal protection problem would be presented by a governmentally-mandated monopoly of the reindeer industry by Alaska Natives. Williams v. Babbitt, 115 F.3d 657 (9th Cir.1997).

CHAPTER XII

INDIAN LANDS

A. INTRODUCTION

Indian lands may be held in a variety of ways, each of which presents its own problems and advantages. Two points must be made at the outset of any review of the subject. The first is that the term "Indian lands" refers to those lands that are held by Indians or tribes under some restriction or with some attribute peculiar to the Indian status of its legal or beneficial owners. Today any Indian can purchase real property (such as a residence in Phoenix or Chicago) in the public market and thereby acquire a fee title that is freely disposable. That real property is not "Indian land."

The second point is that the ownership pattern of Indian lands, which is the subject of this chapter, is a matter separate from the questions of what constitutes a reservation and what is meant by Indian country. The latter concepts, which are particularly important for jurisdictional purposes, are discussed in Chapter VII, Section B.

The unique statutory system under which Alaska Natives hold their land is discussed, along with other Alaska Native matters, in Chapter XIII.

B. ABORIGINAL TITLE

In the first of several Trade and Intercourse Acts, 1 Stat. 137 (1790), Congress provided that non-Indians could not acquire lands from Indians except by treaty entered pursuant to the federal Constitution. While providing a measure of protection for existing Indian landholdings, that legislation made no attempt to characterize the nature of the Indian interest in those lands. It remained for Chief Justice Marshall and the Supreme Court to define the title by which Indian tribes held land, and to determine the incidents of that title.

The Supreme Court's definition came in the case of Johnson v. McIntosh, 21 U.S. (8 Wheat.) 543 (1823). There the Court held that Indian tribes were incapable of conveying their land directly to individuals even before passage of the Trade and Intercourse Acts. In reaching its decision, the Court explored at length the legal relation between the European colonizers of America, the Indian tribes, and the land. Chief Justice Marshall concluded that discovery conferred upon the European sovereign a title good against all other European governments. The United States succeeded to that title to the extent that it was held by the British. As for the Indians:

They were admitted to be the rightful occupants of the soil, with a legal as well as just claim to retain possession of it, and to use it according to their own discretion; but their rights to complete sovereignty, as independent nations, were necessarily diminished, and their power to dispose of the soil at their own will, to whomsoever they pleased, was denied by the original fundamental principle, that discovery gave exclusive title to those who made it.

21 U.S. (8 Wheat.) at 574. The United States was accordingly free to grant to others land held by Indian tribes, but the grantee took title subject to the Indian "right of occupancy." Most important from the standpoint of the Indians, however, was Marshall's point that the United States, and *only* the United States, could extinguish the Indian right of occupancy, "either by purchase or conquest." Id. at 587.

Although Marshall softened his language somewhat in the later *Cherokee Cases*, supra Chapter II, Section C, and shifted his emphasis from conquest to purchase as the preferred method of extinguishment, his formulation of Indian land title in Johnson v. McIntosh has remained essentially intact. Indian tribes that occupied and used land to the exclusion of others (except for mere temporary incursions) had an interest denoted as a "right of occupancy." This right later came to be known as "original Indian title" or, more frequently today, as "aboriginal title." That title cannot be compromised by anyone except the federal government. Oneida Indian Nation v. County of Oneida, 414 U.S. 661 (1974). The federal government can extinguish aboriginal title by purchase, which is the usual method, or simply by taking it. Such a taking will not be "lightly implied." United States v. Santa Fe Pacific

R. Co., 314 U.S. 339, 354 (1941); see County of Oneida v. Oneida Indian Nation, 470 U.S. 226, 247–48 (1985). If aboriginal title is not extinguished, a conveyance of fee to a purchaser transfers no more than a reversion that matures only when aboriginal title ends. Catawba Indian Tribe v. South Carolina, 865 F.2d 1444, 1448 (4th Cir.1989). A taking by the federal government of lands held by aboriginal title (usually referred to as an "extinguishment" of aboriginal title) does not give rise to any right of compensation under the Fifth Amendment. Tee–Hit–Ton Indians v. United States, 348 U.S. 272 (1955). In this respect aboriginal title is to be distinguished from "recognized title," discussed in Section D, below. A taking by the federal government of land held by aboriginal title may, however, provide the basis for a claim under the Indian Claims Commission Act of 1946. See Section E, below.

There have been many disputes over whether aboriginally held land has been taken. The federal intent to extinguish title must be clear, but can take various forms. It has been stated that the creation and acceptance of an Indian reservation by treaty constitutes a relinquishment and extinguishment of aboriginal title outside of the reservation. Menominee Indian Tribe v. Thompson, 161 F.3d 449, 462 (7th Cir.1998); see United States v. Santa Fe Pacific R. Co., 314 U.S. 339, 357–58 (1941). That rule does not always hold, however; the circumstances may indicate a different intent of the parties. Cf. Oneida Indian Nation v. New York, 194 F.Supp.2d 104, 139–41 (N.D.N.Y.2002). Treatment of the land in a manner wholly inconsistent with continued tribal occupancy suffices to extinguish title. Thus, military action removing the Indians from the land, followed by inclusion of the land in a National Forest and active federal management of the land for forest purposes, was sufficient to establish a taking in United States v. Gemmill, 535 F.2d 1145 (9th Cir. 1976). Ambiguous acts such as inclusion of the land in a federal grazing district may be insufficient to establish a taking, however. See United States v. Dann, 706 F.2d 919 (9th Cir.1983), rev'd on other grounds, 470 U.S. 39 (1985). Payment by the United States of a tribe's claim for taking of land establishes that the aboriginal title has been extinguished. Western Shoshone Nat'l Council v. Molini, 951 F.2d 200 (9th Cir.1991).

Virtually all of the cases dealing with aboriginal title, from Johnson v. McIntosh onward, have viewed such title as being that of the tribe, rather than its individual members. Similarly, the Trade and Intercourse Acts have been held to protect tribal title, so that those Acts cannot be invoked by individual Indians suing on their own behalf. James v. Watt, 716 F.2d 71 (1st Cir.1983). It can easily be argued that the very concept of aboriginal title requires that the title be tribal.

In Cramer v. United States, 261 U.S. 219 (1923), however, the Supreme Court held that individual Indians may also claim a right of occupancy that predates competing claims of record title acquired by non-Indians. Id. at 227. The Court later characterized this right of occupancy as "individual aboriginal title," United States v. Dann, 470 U.S. 39, 50 (1985). The Ninth Circuit subsequently held that individual Indians (or their lineal ancestors) could acquire aboriginal title to land by settling on it before it was withdrawn from settlement, and could acquire aboriginal grazing rights by grazing cattle prior to withdrawal of the land from open grazing by enactment of the Taylor Grazing Act of 1934. The individual aboriginal grazing rights were limited to the numbers and type of livestock being grazed at the time of the withdrawal, however. United States v. Dann, 873 F.2d 1189 (9th Cir. 1989). Individual aboriginal title does not arise as part of tribal aboriginal title; it must arise separately on its own. Id. Individual aboriginal title must be maintained, directly or by lineal ancestors, continuously from a time before the land was withdrawn. United States v. Kent, 945 F.2d 1441 (9th Cir.1991).

C. THE EASTERN LAND CLAIMS

In recent times, several eastern tribes have asserted land claims based on aboriginal title. In Oneida Indian Nation v. County of Oneida, 414 U.S. 661 (1974), the Oneidas brought a claim for lands ceded to the State of New York by the tribe without the consent of the federal government, in violation of the Trade and Intercourse Act of 1790, 1 Stat. 137. The lower courts held that the tribe did not assert a federal claim and dismissed for lack of jurisdiction. The Supreme Court reversed. Although the Oneidas had entered treaties with the federal government before ceding the disputed lands to the state, the Supreme Court did not rely on those treaties as having created "recognized title" in the Oneidas. Instead, the Court discussed at length the nature of aboriginal (original Indian) title and held that a tribe relying upon it clearly asserted a federal claim. Later, the Court held that the Oneidas retained a federal common law right to sue on their claim, and that the right was not barred by limitations or laches. County of Oneida v. Oneida Indian Nation, 470 U.S. 226 (1985). State condemnation of land of the Seneca Nation was similarly held to violate the Trade and Intercourse Acts. See Seneca Nation of Indians v. New York, 26 F.Supp.2d 555 (W.D.N.Y.1998), aff'd on other grounds, 178 F.3d 95 (2d Cir.1999).

Other eastern tribes brought claims based on aboriginal title that was not the subject of any federal treaty. One notable example was the Passamaquoddy Tribe, which claimed large areas of Maine that had been deeded to the state (then Massachusetts) by a treaty in which the federal government did not participate and which it did not ratify. See Joint Tribal Council of Passamaquoddy Tribe v. Morton, 528 F.2d 370 (1st Cir.1975). Despite a long history of dealing with the state rather than the federal government, the tribe was held to be entitled to federal trust services in pursuing its claims based on aboriginal title. Id. The controversy culminated in passage of the Maine Indian Claims Settlement Act, 25 U.S.C.A. § 1721 et seq., which extinguished the Indians' aboriginal title and provided federal funds for purchase of lands for three Maine tribes. Other such claims have been similarly resolved. E.g., Rhode Island Indian Claims Settlement Act, 25 U.S.C.A. § 1701 et seq.; Florida Indian Land Claims Settlement Act, 25 U.S.C.A. § 1741 et seq.; Connecticut Indian Land Claims Settlement Act, 25 U.S.C.A. § 1751 et seq. Claims settlement acts should be carefully scrutinized whenever questions arise concerning tribes covered by them; the acts frequently provide for jurisdictional and other arrangements quite different from those that would prevail in the absence of such legislation.

All of the eastern claims are based on one of the fundamental principles of aboriginal title: tribal rights to the land may be conveyed or extinguished only by the federal government. A prima facie case for an aboriginal land claim has been held to consist of the following elements: (1) that the claimant is an Indian tribe, (2) that the land is tribal land, (3) that the United States never consented to its alienation, (4) that the trust relationship between the tribe and the United States has not been terminated or abandoned. Golden Hill Paugussett Tribe v. Weicker, 39 F.3d 51, 56 (2d Cir.1994). The last element must be regarded with caution, however. Recognition for purposes of an aboriginal claim does not invariably equate to recognition for all other purposes. Thus a tribe whose constitution had been revoked by federal action still retained the tribal existence necessary to pursue an aboriginal title claim. See Catawba Indian Tribe v. South Carolina, 718 F.2d 1291 (4th Cir.1983), rev'd on other

grounds, 476 U.S. 498 (1986). One circuit has held
that, although the Trade and Intercourse Acts apply
to the state, the state retains its Eleventh Amendment immunity against suit on such a claim; suit
against a state would have to be brought by the
United States. Ysleta Del Sur Pueblo v. Laney, 199
F.3d 281 (5th Cir.2000). One solution is to secure
the joinder of the United States in claims against a
state. See Canadian St. Regis Band of Mohawk
Indians v. New York, 278 F.Supp.2d 313 (N.D.N.Y.
2003). A tribe also remains free to sue a private
party or local government entity over land acquired
in violation of the Acts. The requirement of federal
approval for transfer of Indian land has been held
by the Second Circuit to have arisen with the establishment of federal power under the Constitution;
during the period of the Articles of Confederation
states could purchase Indian land within their borders and thereby extinguish aboriginal title without
the consent of the Confederal Congress. Oneida
Indian Nation v. State of New York, 860 F.2d 1145
(2d Cir.1988). At least one circuit has ruled that,
once land has become freely alienable, as by sale to
a non-Indian of a former allotment, its repurchase
in fee by the tribe does not render it subject to the
Trade and Intercourse Acts. Lummi Indian Tribe v.
Whatcom County, Washington, 5 F.3d 1355 (9th
Cir.1993); see also Cass County Joint Water Resource Dist. v. 1.43 Acres of Land, 643 N.W.2d 685
(N.D.2002). The Supreme Court has never addressed this issue, however. See Cass County,

Minnesota v. Leech Lake Band of Chippewa Indians, 524 U.S. 103, 115 n.5 (1998).

Recent eastern aboriginal title claims often have involved huge tracts of land. The very size of the claims makes them tactically difficult to pursue, because the option is always open to the federal government, at least in theory, to extinguish without compensation the aboriginal title upon which the claims are based. Although any such action would be a drastic method of defeating tribal claims, fear of the possibility has provided a substantial incentive for tribes to settle their claims rather than pursuing them to final judgment.

In the western states, Indian lands were customarily ceded by treaty with the United States. Land claims based on aboriginal title accordingly are rarely found there outside of the framework of the Indian Claims Commission Act. One exception was a claim asserted by a band of Western Shoshone in Nevada; the Supreme Court held that the tribal claim was defeated by the payment of funds into trust for the Tribe, in satisfaction of an award of the Claims Commission. United States v. Dann, 470 U.S. 39 (1985).

D. RECOGNIZED TITLE

Recognized title is title to Indian lands that has been recognized by federal treaty or statute. A treaty may, for example, recognize tribal title by describing a particular land area as being reserved to the tribe. That parcel may or may not have been part of the aboriginal territory of the tribe. Recognition of title is a question of intent, and is sometimes the subject of great controversy. See Northwestern Bands of Shoshone Indians v. United States, 324 U.S. 335 (1945). Where a reservation is expressly set out by treaty or statute, however, there is little question that the tribe has recognized title.

The primary advantage of recognized title is its relative permanence. Recognized title is "property" within the meaning of the Fifth Amendment, so that its taking by the federal government gives rise to a right of compensation. United States v. Creek Nation, 295 U.S. 103 (1935). Moreover, interest may be charged against the federal government for a Fifth Amendment taking, a fact of great importance when the taking may have occurred a century before judgment. See United States v. Sioux Nation, 448 U.S. 371 (1980). Where the tribe's land title is recognized, a taking of timber or mineral rights is also compensable under the Fifth Amendment, because the tribe's interest in the land is presumed to include timber and minerals in the absence of an expression to the contrary in the governing treaty or statute. United States v. Shoshone Tribe, 304 U.S. 111 (1938).

Although most reservations in existence today were either established or confirmed by treaty or statute, there are some reservations that were created in whole or part by presidential executive orders. Executive orders do not establish recognized title, and lands set aside by that method may be taken by the federal government without compensation. Sioux Tribe v. United States, 316 U.S. 317 (1942); Hynes v. Grimes Packing Co., 337 U.S. 86, 103 (1949); Karuk Tribe v. Ammon, 209 F.3d 1366 (Fed.Cir.2000). Of course, territory originally reserved by executive order may subsequently be recognized by statute so as to create a compensable property right in the occupying tribe. Since 1919 (1918 in the case of Arizona and New Mexico), reservations have been required to be created by statute and not executive order. 43 U.S.C.A. § 150; 25 U.S.C.A. § 211.

E. INDIAN CLAIMS

The fact that aboriginal title was not viewed as a compensable property right was only one of the obstacles standing in the way of tribes that sought redress for injuries suffered at the hands of the federal government. The United States could not be sued without its consent. The Court of Claims had been established to permit litigation of certain types of suits against the government but claims based on violation of Indian treaties were excluded from its jurisdiction in 1863. Act of March 3, 1863, ch. 92, § 9, 12 Stat. 765, 767. On various occasions, Congress enacted statutes permitting claims suits by particular tribes, but these acts were often narrowly construed by the courts in a manner that defeated recovery. See Northwestern Bands of Shoshone Indians v. United States, 324 U.S. 335 (1945).

Dissatisfaction with the existing method of handling claims led to passage of the Indian Claims

Commission Act of 1946, 25 U.S.C.A. §§ 70–70v. The Act established the Indian Claims Commission to hear suits brought by tribes, bands or other identifiable groups of Indians. Appeal was permitted to the Court of Claims and by certiorari to the Supreme Court. The Act was liberal in defining the scope of permissible claims. In addition to regular claims in law or equity (including those in tort), the Act authorized recovery for the following:

25 U.S.C.A. § 70a:

* * *

(3) claims which would result if the treaties, contracts, and agreements between the claimant and the United States were revised on the ground of fraud, duress, unconscionable consideration, mutual or unilateral mistake, whether of law or fact, or any other ground cognizable by a court of equity;

(4) claims arising from the taking by the United States, whether as the result of a treaty of cession or otherwise, of lands owned or occupied by the claimant without the payment for such lands of compensation agreed to by the claimant; and

(5) claims based upon fair and honorable dealings that are not recognized by any existing rule of law or equity.

The Act solved a number of problems. Takings of land held by aboriginal title became compensable, as did any number of other unfair actions of the

federal government, whether or not arising from a
treaty. The sovereign immunity of the United
States was waived. The defense of laches, which had
sometimes presented an insuperable barrier to recovery, was also waived. Id.

The intent of Congress in passing the Act had
been to settle once and for all the claims arising
from the government's historical dealings with the
Indians. As a result, an award under the Act defeats
any further tribal claim of an aboriginal right to
occupy the lands for which compensation was set
aside. United States v. Dann, 470 U.S. 39 (1985).
The Act empowered the Commission to hear claims
accruing prior to August 13, 1946; those accruing
later must be brought to the Court of Federal
Claims and their permissible scope is much narrower (claims arising under federal law or executive
order or otherwise cognizable if brought by non-
Indians, 28 U.S.C.A. § 1505; see United States v.
Mitchell, 445 U.S. 535, 538–40 (1980)). Large numbers of claims were adjudicated by the Commission
during its life, which ended in 1978, and substantial
relief was granted to many tribes and Indian
groups.

It should not be assumed, however, that compensation under the Act was total. One of the most
serious limitations was that the usual rule was
applied forbidding the award of interest against the
United States except for Fifth Amendment takings.
See United States v. Sioux Nation, 448 U.S. 371,
387 & n. 16 (1980). An award for land measured by
nineteenth century values without interest falls

many times short of restoring a tribe to the position it would have occupied had it retained the lost land. The Act also permitted the government to offset certain payments made to the claimant tribe in the past, but these deductions were sharply limited in comparison with prior practice and could be allowed only if the Commission found that the entire course of dealings between the government and the tribe warranted it. 25 U.S.C.A. § 70a.

F. INDIAN LANDHOLDING TODAY

Lands presently set aside for Indians, whether by treaty, statute or executive order, may be held in various patterns of tenure. Nearly all of the land is in trust, with the United States holding naked legal title and the Indians enjoying the beneficial interest. The beneficial ownership of the Indians usually does not include ownership of beds of navigable waters, see Montana v. United States, 450 U.S. 544, 551 (1981), unless Congress made very clear its intent to convey such an interest, see Idaho v. United States, 533 U.S. 262 (2001). Within the typical trust arrangement of land tenure, differences exist in the nature of the beneficial holdings. In a few cases where land is held for tribes with a restraint on alienation, even the usual trust title is absent.

When a tribe purchases fee land, there is no restraint on alienability. Lummi Indian Tribe v. Whatcom County, Washington, 5 F.3d 1355 (9th Cir.1993). Thus a state may condemn tribally-owned fee land that is not part of a reservation or aboriginal holding. Cass County Joint Water Resource Dist. v. 1.43 Acres of Land, 643 N.W.2d 685 (N.D.2002). The Secretary of the Interior is authorized, however, to acquire lands in trust for the benefit of Indians. 25 U.S.C. § 465; 25 C.F.R. §§ 151.10–151.12. This power has frequently been exercised in recent years, and is recognized as a viable means of a tribe's protecting land that it has acquired in fee, often as a recovery of reservation land that was lost to non-Indians. See Cass County, Minn. v. Leech Lake Band of Chippewa Indians, 524 U.S. 103, 114–15 (1998); Connecticut ex rel. Blumenthal v. United States Dept. of Interior, 228 F.3d 82 (2d Cir.2000). The Secretary may accept land in trust for a tribe when it is within a reservation, is already owned by the tribe, or when the Secretary determines that "acquisition is necessary to facilitate tribal self-determination, economic development, or Indian housing." 25 C.F.R. § 151.3.

1. COMMUNALLY HELD LAND

One method by which large tracts of reservation land is held, particularly in the Southwest, is communal tribal ownership. The United States holds the legal title, and the undivided beneficial interest is held by the tribe as a single entity. There are two major advantages to this type of ownership. The first is that the land base of the tribe is given maximum protection because of the continuity of beneficial ownership. The second is that management of the land is relatively easy when decisions over leasing and development can be made by a single owner, even though that owner must go through its own form of institutional decision-making. Changes in the use or in the distribution of benefits from use of the land do not infringe any legally protectible rights of individual tribal members. United States v. Jim, 409 U.S. 80 (1972). Although communal ownership is relatively trouble-free when it is exercised by a single tribe, joint exercise has occasionally led to large difficulties. Land communally but jointly held by both the Hopi and Navajo tribes has been the subject of dispute for decades, leading to an equally disputed partition. See, e.g., Masayesva for and on Behalf of Hopi Tribe v. Hale, 118 F.3d 1371 (9th Cir.1997).

2. ASSIGNMENTS

When land is communally held by the tribe, individual members may simply share in the enjoyment of the entire property without having any claim at all to an identifiable piece of land. In practice, however, tribal members usually require some method of knowing that it is permissible for them to erect a residence on a given spot, to graze stock in a particular area, or to engage in other activities requiring a relatively fixed location. This need is customarily met by the tribe's conferring a license upon the individual to use particular land. That license may go by many names, but it is commonly referred to as an "assignment." The terms of assignments may vary greatly in duration and scope. They often expire after a term of years without any guaranteed right of renewal, and they usually are personal to the assignee. In practice, however, there is a pronounced tendency to renew an assignment once given and to permit descendants to acquire the assignment of a deceased assignee. When the United States purchased land in trust for a tribe and issued "land certificates" to individuals for particular parcels, the certificates were held to be assignments of land that remained in tribal ownership, rather than allotments of beneficial title to the individuals. Cermak v. Babbitt, 234 F.3d 1356 (Fed. Cir.2000).

3. ALLOTMENTS

The allotment system of landholding is in total contrast to communal ownership by the tribe. Under various statutes, particularly the General Allotment (Dawes) Act of 1887, 25 U.S.C.A. § 331 et seq., Congress provided for Indian lands to be allotted to individual Indians. Tribally held lands were consequently divided into small farm-sized tracts to be held by individuals. The land was to remain in trust for a certain period, usually 25 years, and then was to become a totally alienable and taxable fee interest in the hands of the Indian, who often sold it. Once the land becomes freely alienable in this manner, it remains taxable by the state even if it is repurchased by the tribe or an individual Indian. Cass County, Minnesota v. Leech Lake Band of

Chippewa Indians, 524 U.S. 103 (1998); In re Kaul, 269 Kan. 181, 4 P.3d 1170 (2000). Reservation allotments that have become alienable fee land in the hands of Indians are not, however, subject to state land-use laws. Gobin v. Snohomish County, 304 F.3d 909 (9th Cir.2002). Many allotments did pass out of trust status under allotment acts, and most of that land is no longer in Indian hands. See, e.g., Cross v. State of Washington, 911 F.2d 341 (9th Cir.1990). In many cases, however, trust periods were extended by statute and in 1934 the Indian Reorganization Act indefinitely extended the trust period of all allotments still in trust or under restraints on alienation. 25 U.S.C.A. § 462. The Act also provided that no further lands were to be allotted. 25 U.S.C.A. § 461. There was, however, a great amount of Indian land allotted and still in trust or under restraint at the time of the Reorganization Act, and large numbers of allotments consequently remain today.

The legal title to most existing allotments is held by the United States, with the entire beneficial interest being in the individual allottees. Some allottees were issued patents in fee, however, with a restraint on alienation. The two types of allotments are treated identically. See United States v. City of Tacoma, 332 F.3d 574 (9th Cir.2003). Decisions concerning the use or disposition of such land accordingly must be made by the allottees, not the tribe, with the concurrence of the United States. Indeed, the tribe has been held not to have a right of action to enforce restrictions in an Allotment Act against non-Indian purchase in excess of a certain acreage. Crow Tribe of Indians v. Campbell Farming Corp., 31 F.3d 768 (9th Cir.1994). The bare trust title of the United States does not create a duty on its part to manage the land's resources. United States v. Mitchell, 445 U.S. 535 (1980) (*Mitchell I*). Comprehensive statutes and regulations do, however, establish duties of the federal government to manage timber resources of allotted lands, and violations of those duties are compensable. United States v. Mitchell, 463 U.S. 206 (1983) (*Mitchell II*). Statutes restricting the sale of trust land without prior approval of the Secretary were held to apply to invalidate the sale of a prime skeleton of a Tyrannosaurus Rex (named "Sue") that was excavated from an individual trust allotment; the fossil in place qualified as land. Black Hills Inst. of Geologic Research v. South Dakota School of Mines and Tech., 12 F.3d 737 (8th Cir. 1993). Allotments may not be condemned by local governments or utilities without the consent of the United States, despite statutory language in 25 U.S.C.A. § 357 that seems to state to the contrary. *City of Tacoma*, supra; United States v. Pend Oreille County Pub. Util. Dist. No. 1, 135 F.3d 602 (9th Cir.1998). The existing restraints on alienation of allotments are not supplemented, however, by the Trade and Intercourse Acts, which have been held to apply only to tribal, not allotted land. San Xavier Development Auth. v. Charles, 237 F.3d 1149 (9th Cir.2001).

The allotment system has led to immense practical problems. Allotted lands may be disposed of by a will approved by the Secretary of Interior, 25 U.S.C.A. § 373, but in most cases wills are not executed. In the absence of a will, the interest of a deceased allottee descends according to the law of intestate succession of the state where the allotment is located. 25 U.S.C.A. § 348. The result of this system of descent operating on trust land is that over a period of generations the beneficial interest of many allotments has come to be shared by as many as a hundred allottees. Productive use of the lands is then a near impossibility because the consent of all allottees is necessary for leasing. Intestacy also results in allotted land passing to non-Indians, which removes it from trust status altogether and creates "checkerboard" patterns of Indian and non-Indian land that further complicate proper land use. Because state courts cannot adjudicate the status of trust lands, allotments create difficulties in distribution of assets upon divorce. See Landauer v. Landauer, 95 Wash.App. 579, 975 P.2d 577 (1999).

To combat the problems caused by fractionated allotments, Congress passed the Indian Land Consolidation Act, 96 Stat. 2517 (1983). It provided, among other things, that an undivided interest representing less than 2% of an allotted tract and yielding less than $100 annual income, could not pass by intestacy or devise, but escheated to the tribe. The Supreme Court, however, held the provision to be an unconstitutional taking of property in violation of the Fifth Amendment. Hodel v. Irving, 481 U.S. 704 (1987). While *Irving* was pending, Congress amended the Act in 1984 to require the income of less than $100 annually to persist over five years, to permit devise and descent of fractional interests to other holders of fractional interests in the same land, and to permit the tribe to adopt alternative remedies with the approval of the Secretary. Once again, however, the Supreme Court held the Act unconstitutional. Babbitt v. Youpee, 519 U.S. 234 (1997); see also Dumarce v. Norton, 277 F.Supp.2d 1046 (D.S.D.2003). A remedy therefore remains elusive. Other statutes that provide for forced purchase of fractional interests by or for the tribe may represent a more viable approach to the problem. See 25 U.S.C.A. §§ 607, 608; Hunger v. Andrus, 476 F.Supp. 357 (D.S.D.1979). In the meantime, allotments continue to cause grave problems for those reservations that are partly or entirely subject to them.

4. NEW MEXICO PUEBLOS

Although the New Mexico Pueblos hold their lands communally, their title is virtually unique. Most of the Pueblo lands were acquired in fee under Spanish rule. When New Mexico Territory was acquired by the United States as a result of the Mexican War, the Treaty of Guadalupe Hidalgo, 9 Stat. 922 (1848), guaranteed property rights acquired under the Spanish and Mexican governments. See Mountain States Tel. & Tel. Co. v.

Pueblo of Santa Ana, 472 U.S. 237 (1985). The Pueblos accordingly own most of their lands in fee, rather than having the United States hold the legal title for them.

The practical effects of the Pueblos' distinctive form of ownership are now minimal. The Pueblos are in a trust relationship with the federal government, United States v. Sandoval, 231 U.S. 28 (1913), and their lands cannot be alienated without the consent of the United States, United States v. Candelaria, 271 U.S. 432 (1926). Water rights are reserved for Pueblo lands in the same manner as they are for other Indian lands. New Mexico v. Aamodt, 537 F.2d 1102 (10th Cir.1976).

G. LEASING OF INDIAN LANDS

Indian lands, whether tribally held or allotted, may be leased with the approval of the Secretary of the Interior. 25 U.S.C.A. § 415. Permissible duration varies with the nature of the lease and the location of the land, but the most common limit is 25 years. On some reservations, 99 year leases are permitted. Id. Particular leases may be affected by various statutes and regulations too numerous to set forth here. Notable among them are the Omnibus Indian Mineral Leasing Act, 25 U.S.C.A. § 396a–g; the National Environmental Policy Act (NEPA), 42 U.S.C.A. § 4321 et seq.; and portions of the Surface Mining Control and Reclamation Act of 1977, 30 U.S.C.A. § 1300(c).

Supervision of leasing is one of the most extensive reservation activities of the Bureau of Indian Affairs, and it has sometimes been a controversial one. See United States v. Navajo Nation, 537 U.S. 488 (2003). Leases may be granted for such purposes as farming, grazing, housing and industrial developments, timber cutting, mining, and oil and gas exploration and production. Some of these uses are almost certain to cause major intrusions into the social structure of the landholding tribe. Under the Secretary's regulations and tribal leases approved by the Secretary, the lessee's interest is subject to foreclosure. See Red Mountain Machinery Co. v. Grace Investment Co., 29 F.3d 1408 (9th Cir.1994). Numbers of leases in the past seem to have provided abnormally low financial returns to the tribes. On occasion this fact has led to damage recoveries for violation of trust responsibility, see United States v. Mitchell, 463 U.S. 206 (1983), but in other cases no duty was found to exist giving rise to compensable claims, see United States v. Navajo Nation, supra. (Major litigation is also under way concerning alleged BIA mismanagement of individual Indian money accounts derived from allotment income. See Cobell v. Norton, 260 F.Supp.2d 110 (D.D.C.2003)). These and other cases concerning the trust responsibility are discussed in Chapter III, Section C. On the other hand, when the Secretary denied approval of a subsidiary agreement in order to cause mineral leases to terminate, solely for the purpose of permitting Indian lessors to negotiate more favorable lease terms, the Tenth Circuit held the Secretary's action to be an abuse of discretion. Woods Petroleum Corp. v. Department of Interior, 47 F.3d 1032 (10th Cir.1995). In view of the conflicting interests represented in leasing of Indian lands, leasing decisions are almost certain to be a continuing subject of dispute.

CHAPTER XIII

ALASKA NATIVES

A. INTRODUCTION

Federal policy toward Alaska Natives (Indians, Eskimos and Aleuts), evolved under very different conditions from those prevailing in what are now the lower forty-eight states, with distinctive legal consequences. The Treaty of Cession by which the United States purchased Alaska from Russia in 1867 provided that the inhabitants who chose to remain, "with the exception of uncivilized native tribes," would be entitled to the rights of citizens. "The uncivilized tribes will be subject to such laws and regulations as the United States may, from time to time, adopt in regard to aboriginal tribes of that country." 15 Stat. 539, 542. Despite this opening, there was very little federal attention paid to the Alaska Natives for many decades thereafter. The Alaska Organic Act of 1884 similarly looked to future legislation: "[T]he Indians or other persons in said district shall not be disturbed in the possession of any lands actually in their use or occupation or now claimed by them but the terms under which such persons may acquire title to such lands is reserved for future legislation by Congress." 23 Stat. 24, 26. That future legislation, too, was slow in coming, although some statutes were enacted that contained similar provisos protecting Native possession.

Totally absent from Alaska were many of the events that shaped Indian law to the south during the eighteenth century. There was no federal policing of jurisdictional lines between the federal government, the tribes, and the local governments. There was consequently little judicial attention paid to that subject. There was no substantial pressure from non-Indian settlers desiring land occupied by the Natives. There were accordingly no military encounters and no removal. Perhaps most important, there were no treaties describing land claimed under aboriginal title, ceding parts of it, and securing recognized title to remaining portions. With no contest over most land, there was no need to define either the nature or the extent of Alaska Native land claims. The territorial court, after some uncertainty, did hold, however, that Alaska Natives were wards of the federal government, and that the lands they occupied were not subject to purchase by third parties. United States v. Berrigan, 2 Alaska 442 (1905).

For the reasons just stated, most Alaska Natives did not become occupants of reservations. The only statutory reservation was that of the Annette Islands, established in 1891 for Metlakatla Indians who had recently migrated from British Columbia. 25 U.S.C.A. § 495. That reservation was held to include adjacent waters by implication. Alaska Pacific Fisheries v. United States, 248 U.S. 78 (1918).

Although other "reserves" were established in varying sizes (often quite small) by executive order during the first decades of the twentieth century, the legality and status of those reserves was never clearly established. In 1934, Congress enacted the Indian Reorganization Act ("IRA"), which authorized the Secretary of the Interior to establish new reservations. 25 U.S.C.A. § 467. Two years later, most of the Reorganization Act was made expressly applicable to Alaska, and Native groups not yet recognized were authorized to organize to adopt constitutions and by-laws. 25 U.S.C.A. § 473a. Pursuant to the authority conferred by the Act, the Secretary ultimately succeeded in establishing six IRA reservations: Venetie, Karluk, Akutan, Diomede, Unalakleet, and Wales. The Supreme Court held, however, that a reservation so established was temporary in nature, and could be revoked by Congress without payment of compensation. Hynes v. Grimes Packing Co., 337 U.S. 86 (1949). In any event, the great majority of Alaska Natives continued to live outside of reservations on land they long had occupied. The boundaries of their occupancy and the nature of their tenure remained uncertain.

Alaska Natives other than Aleuts were authorized to acquire homestead allotments by the Alaska Native Allotment Act of 1906. 34 Stat. 197. The Act was amended to make Aleuts eligible in 1956. The Act was repealed by the Alaska Native Claims Settlement Act in 1971, but pending applications were protected. Allotment claims therefore continue to be litigated. See Alaska v. Babbitt, 75 F.3d 449 (9th

Cir.1995). To qualify for an allotment, a Native must have used the land in his own right, not just as a child under a parent's supervision. Akootchook v. United States, 271 F.3d 1160 (9th Cir.2001). Many of the protected pending claims were later granted legislatively by the Alaska National Interest Lands Conservation Act (ANILCA). See 43 U.S.C.A. § 1634(a); cf. Alaska v. Babbitt, 38 F.3d 1068 (9th Cir.1994). Alaska Natives could also acquire townsite plots under the Alaska Native Townsite Act of 1926, 44 Stat. 629, repealed in 1976. That statute provided for Native communities to place township lands into trusteeship, from which individual townsite plots could be conveyed to individual Natives. Both types of individual title were subject to restraints on alienation. A Native community did not have to be incorporated to be eligible. Aleknagik Natives Ltd. v. United States, 886 F.2d 237 (1989).

With Natives living in scattered locations and attracting little federal attention, it is not surprising that state courts more or less regularly exercised jurisdiction over them. Perhaps in recognition of this fact, Alaska was added in 1958 to the list of mandatory states covered by Public Law 280. See Chapter VIII, supra. Alaska was thereby given criminal and civil adjudicatory jurisdiction over "All Indian country within the Territory." 72 Stat. 545. The criminal provision was subsequently amended in 1970 to provide that the Metlakatla Indian Community of the Annette Islands could exercise jurisdiction over offenses in Indian country in the same manner as tribes not covered by Public Law 280.

See 18 U.S.C.A. § 1162(a). The result of the amendment was that both the tribe and the state exercised concurrent criminal jurisdiction. Booth v. State, 903 P.2d 1079 (Alaska App.1995).

None of these land tenure or jurisdictional provisions, however, purported to address the question of the nature and extent of Native Alaskan aboriginal land claims. Their nature was finally illuminated in Tee–Hit–Ton Indians v. United States, 348 U.S. 272 (1955). That case dealt with a claim by the Tee–Hit–Ton group of Tlingit Indians for the taking of timber by the United States from land to which the Tee–Hit–Tons claimed aboriginal title. The Supreme Court held that the Alaska Indians' title was of the same nature as the aboriginal title, or right of occupancy, once held by the Indians to the south. Such title was good against third parties, but was subject to extinguishment by the federal government without compensation. Thus the nature, but by no means the extent, of the Alaska aboriginal holdings was made clear.

The Alaska Statehood Act provided that Alaska disclaimed all right and title "to any lands or other property (including fishing rights), the right or title to which may be held by any Indians, Eskimos, or Aleuts * * * or is held by the United States in trust for said natives." 72 Stat. 339 (1958). The Act also authorized the State to select huge tracts from the vacant public lands within the former Territory. It soon became clear that the question of competing aboriginal land claims would have to be addressed. Impending development of oil production and pipeline facilities added greatly to the impetus. The result was the Alaska Native Claims Settlement Act.

B. ALASKA NATIVE CLAIMS SETTLEMENT ACT (ANCSA)

In the Alaska Native Claims Settlement Act of 1971, 43 U.S.C.A. §§ 1601–1628, Congress not only provided for the extinguishment of Alaskan aboriginal title; it also created a unique system of landholding that has ramifications well beyond the field of land tenure. The Act and its numerous amendments are many-faceted and very detailed; only the major provisions will be dealt with here.

First, the Act extinguished "[a]ll aboriginal titles, if any, and claims of aboriginal title in Alaska based on use and occupancy, including submerged land underneath all water areas, both inland and offshore, and including any aboriginal hunting or fishing rights that may exist." 43 U.S.C.A. § 1603. It is noteworthy that the Act did not acknowledge whether or not such aboriginal title existed; it simply extinguished such title "if any." It also extinguished all claims based on aboriginal title, including pre-Act claims of trespass. § 1603(c); United States v. Atlantic Richfield Co., 612 F.2d 1132 (9th Cir.1980). The Act did not proceed on the theory of the Indian Claims Commission Act, which provided a means for tribes to prove the existence of their particular aboriginal title and to be compensated for its taking, measured by the value of the right. ANCSA instead extinguished and, as discussed below, compensated without regard to the value of particular claims.

The extinguishment of aboriginal claims "in Alaska" is almost certainly confined to claims within the geographical boundaries of the State, extending three miles into the sea from its coastline. See Amoco Production Co. v. Village of Gambell, 480 U.S. 531, 552 (1987). There have been suggestions that Alaska Native groups could still successfully claim aboriginal hunting and fishing rights in the outer continental shelf. See Village of Gambell v. Hodel, 869 F.2d 1273 (9th Cir.1989), dismissed as moot, 999 F.2d 403 (9th Cir.1993). The paramount rights of the federal government were held to preclude an *exclusive* claim of aboriginal rights to hunt and fish the outer continental shelf, however. Native Village of Eyak v. Trawler Diane Marie, 154 F.3d 1090 (9th Cir.1998). Whether other claims may survive remains to be seen.

In part payment for the extinguishment of aboriginal title, the Act established an Alaska Native Fund of more than $962,500,000, of which $462,500,000 was to be appropriated and $500,000,000 was to come from mineral lease payments. For the rest of the compensation, Native groups were authorized to select approximately 40 million acres of federal public land, to be held under the unique system established by the Act. Selections were to be made from lands withdrawn in or near Native villages; the withdrawal included lands so described that had been "selected by" but not "patented to, the State under the Alaska Statehood Act." This withdrawal also was held to cover lands selected but not patented to the State under the Alaska Mental Health Enabling Act, which predated but was reconfirmed in the Statehood Act. Tyonek Native Corp. v. Secretary of Interior, 836 F.2d 1237 (9th Cir.1988). Two million acres were authorized to be withdrawn by the Secretary to convey cemetery sites to regional corporations, and lands to Native groups not qualifying as villages, to Natives in specified towns who formed urban corporations, and to individual Natives occupying homesites of up to 160 acres. § 1613(h); see Haynes v. United States, 891 F.2d 235 (9th Cir.1989). "Native groups" are communities composed of less than 25 Natives who are in a majority in their locality. § 1602(d). Thus establishment of the boundaries of a "locality" often determines whether members of the Native group are in a majority. Relative proximity of residents, compared to less densely populated surroundings, and sharing of common interests in services or facilities are factors in determining that an area constitutes a locality. Minchumina Natives, Inc. v. U.S. Dep't of Interior, 60 F.3d 1363 (9th Cir.1995). Members enrolled in another village do not qualify as members of the group, but do qualify as residents of the locality for purposes of determining a majority. Chugach Alaska Corp. v. Lujan, 915 F.2d 454 (9th Cir.1990).

The Act provided for the establishment under state law of regional and village corporations in which enrolled Natives would receive corporate stock. Alaska was to be divided into twelve regions, "composed as far as practicable of Natives having a common heritage and sharing common interests," each region to have its own regional corporation. The Act proposed the regions, composed of existing Native associations, with modification permitted for good cause. A thirteenth regional corporation was also authorized, and later established, for non-resident Natives. 43 U.S.C.A. § 1606. The Act also provided for each Native village entitled to receive lands to incorporate, with its articles of incorporation subject to approval of the Regional corporation for its region. § 1607. The village corporations were permitted to select 22 million acres from land where they were located and adjoining areas in proportion to the population of the village; regional corporations were entitled to select lands from an additional 16 million acres, which they then were to reallocate to villages within their regions. § 1611. After these selections, patents to the surface estates were to be issued to the village corporations. Upon receipt of patents, the village corporations are required to convey to certain occupants and governments tracts actually occupied as residences, businesses or municipalities (with allowance for expansion), and certain federal operations. § 1613. That process would still leave the village corporations with large tracts of surface estate. The regional corporations are then given the subsurface rights in all of those lands (with certain exceptions when subsurface rights were already reserved). Most of the revenues received by the regional corporations from the subsurface estates are shared with all twelve of the geographic regional corporations according to their populations. § 1606(i). Disputes over the meaning of the revenue-sharing provision were settled by agreement among the regions; an individual shareholder was held to have no right of action under ANCSA or claim under state law to challenge the arrangement. Oliver v. Sealaska Corp., 192 F.3d 1220 (9th Cir.1999).

The Native corporations receive title to their estates in fee. The Act imposed no restraint on alienation of those lands by their corporate owners, but it did restrain alienation of Natives' corporate stock for twenty years. In the absence of such controlling provisions of ANCSA, the corporations were subject to state corporation law, such as the requirement that distributions to shareholders be equal. See Hanson v. Kake Tribal Corp., 939 P.2d 1320 (Alaska 1997). The ANCSA Amendments of 1987 (actually enacted in 1988) permitted the corporations to extend the restraints on alienation of their stock beyond the original term. Pub. L. 100–241, 101 Stat. 1788. In addition, Native corporations were authorized to transfer their assets to state-chartered trusts, which had no power to transfer lands and which were not subject to the rule against perpetuities. The trusts are "to promote the health, education, and welfare of its beneficiaries." 43 U.S.C.A. § 1629e(b)(1). The provision of ANCSA authorizing the trusts partially preempts state corporation law and permits unequal distributions, such as old-age benefit payments, by the trust. Broad v. Sealaska Corp., 85 F.3d 422 (9th Cir.1996). "Elder" stock distributions are also authorized. Sierra v. Goldbelt, 25 P.3d 697 (Alaska 2001). The 1987 ANSCA amendments also modified the Alaska National Interest Lands Conservation Act to protect undeveloped Native fee lands from property taxation and from certain types of foreclosure and involuntary transfer. 43 U.S.C.A. § 1636. The power to transfer lands voluntarily remains, however. This ability to alienate, as well as the corporate ownership, distinguishes Alaska Native landholding from all other Indian land tenure.

ANCSA also revoked all reserves previously established in Alaska, except for the Annette Islands Reserve. Enrolled members of the Metlakatla Indian community of the Annette Islands Reserve were excluded from benefits under ANCSA. § 1618(a). Corporations of villages occupying reserves revoked by the Act were given the option of taking fee title to the surface and subsurface estates of the prior reserves. If the corporation chose that option, however, it and its members became ineligible for other benefits under ANCSA, including land selections and distribution of funds or stock in regional corporations. § 1618(b).

One goal of ANCSA that clearly has not been realized is that of accomplishing the settlement "without litigation." § 1601(b). The Act's complicated land selection and ownership system, divided between regional and village corporations, raised many questions requiring judicial resolution. The land surrounding villages that was withdrawn by ANCSA for Native selection was withdrawn "subject to valid existing rights." § 1610(a)(1). This clause has been interpreted to protect expectancies, such as a municipality's segregation of land for future subdivision, and a state lessee's option to purchase the land in the future upon certain conditions. Aleknagik Natives Ltd. v. United States, 806 F.2d 924 (9th Cir.1986); Seldovia Native Ass'n, Inc. v. Lujan, 904 F.2d 1335 (9th Cir.1990).

Some disputes have arisen from the reconveyance provision, which among other things requires village corporations receiving surface estates to reconvey without consideration to Natives or non-Natives occupying the tracts "as a primary place of residence, or as a primary place of business, or as a subsistence campsite, or as headquarters for reindeer husbandry." § 1613(c)(1). The village corporation, in determining whether to reconvey to a particular occupant, acts as a federal delegee and is subject to due process requirements of notice to the prospective claimant. Ogle v. Salamatof Native Ass'n, Inc., 906 F.Supp. 1321 (D.Alaska 1995). The reconveyance clause creates a statutory duty, but does not create a fiduciary or trust relationship between the village and the occupant entitled to reconveyance. Id. Predictable issues have arisen over qualified uses. The City of Ketchikan was unsuccessful in claiming that the largest of its four power plants was the city utility's "primary place of business." Nor could the city's utility qualify under another clause providing for reconveyance to non-profit organizations. City of Ketchikan v. Cape Fox Corp., 85 F.3d 1381 (9th Cir.1996). A cabin site used by hunting guides qualified, however, as a primary place of that business. Hakala v. Atxam Corp., 753 P.2d 1144 (Alaska 1988). Occupancy of a cabin as a primary residence qualified even if the occupancy was under a use permit from the Forest Service. Buettner v. Kavilco, Inc., 860 F.2d 341 (9th Cir.1988).

Another source of dispute is the division between surface and subsurface estates. The issue first arose with regard to sand and gravel on land entirely owned by a regional corporation. If sand and gravel were part of the surface estate, then revenues from their extraction belonged entirely to the regional corporation owning the land. If sand and gravel were part of the subsurface estate, then 70% of the revenues had to be shared with other regional corporations. § 1606(i). The sand and gravel were held to be part of the subsurface estate. Chugach Natives, Inc. v. Doyon, Ltd., 588 F.2d 723 (9th Cir. 1978). The same result was reached when the surface estate belonged to a village corporation and the subsurface to a regional corporation. Tyonek Native Corp. v. Cook Inlet Region, Inc., 853 F.2d 727 (9th Cir.1988). Later cases, however, recognize that the surface estate sometimes cannot be developed at all without exploitation of sand and gravel on the spot. Consequently, when there is no other practical source for those materials, an equitable servitude is imposed on the subsurface estate owner. The subsurface owner cannot unreasonably deny the surface owner access to sand and gravel necessary for surface development. The surface owner must, however, pay a reasonable price for the sand and gravel; the purchaser has the burden of demonstrating that the price demanded by the subsurface owner is unreasonable. Koniag, Inc. v. Koncor Forest Resource, 39 F.3d 991 (9th Cir.1994); Shee Atika v. Sealaska Corp., 39 F.3d 247 (9th Cir.1994).

C. GOVERNMENTAL STATUS OF NATIVE ORGANIZATIONS

The unique legal organization of Alaska Native organizations has raised questions whether they enjoy all of the governmental prerogatives of tribes in the lower forty-eight states. The issues concern their relationship to the federal government and the degree of their sovereignty for purposes of self-government, governmental control over their lands, and sovereign immunity. On these questions, the federal courts and the Supreme Court of Alaska have frequently reached different results. The Supreme Court of the United States, however, recently has made clear that Alaska Native groups cannot govern ANCSA corporately-held land as "Indian country." Alaska v. Native Village of Venetie, 522 U.S. 520 (1998).

The fact that there is no Indian country (except for the Annette Islands) in Alaska may have affected the validity of a borough ordinance containing a Native American hiring preference. The case came

before the Ninth Circuit, which certified a question
to the Alaska Supreme Court to determine whether
the preference was permissible under state law. The
Alaska Supreme Court held that the preference
violated the state constitution's equal protection
clause. Malabed v. North Slope Borough, 70 P.3d
416 (Alaska 2003). It distinguished the hiring preference of the Bureau of Indian Affairs upheld in
Morton v. Mancari, 417 U.S. 535 (1974), on the
ground that the borough had no special duty or
interest in furthering Indian self-government, as
the BIA did. Nor did the state constitution create
any special categories for Alaska Natives. "To the
extent that the Alaska Constitution implies any-
thing concerning the state's relations with Alaska
Natives, then, it mirrors the constitutional drafters'
well-recognized desire to treat Alaska Natives like
all other Alaska citizens." 70 P.3d at 422. Upon
receiving the Alaska Supreme Court's answer to its
certified question, the Ninth Circuit then held that
the preference was invalid because no federal law,
particularly including Title VII's exception for Indian preference, 42 U.S.C. § 2000e–2(i), preempted
the state's equal protection clause. Malabed v.
North Slope Borough, 335 F.3d 864 (9th Cir.2003).
The court noted that § 2000e–2(i) excepted preferences to Indians "living on or near a reservation,"
which the Alaska Natives did not. In a more broadly
applicable case, the Ninth Circuit held that the
Indian employment preference clause of the Indian
Self–Determination and Educational Assistance Act
of 1975, 25 U.S.C.A. § 450(e), did not provide a

private right of action for a disappointed Alaska
Native applicant for employment. Solomon v. Interi-
or Regional Housing Authority, 313 F.3d 1194 (9th
Cir.2002).

1. FEDERAL TRUST RELATIONSHIP

In 1918, the Supreme Court had no difficulty
accepting the proposition that establishing a reserve
for Alaska Natives served "a recognized public purpose–that of safe-guarding and advancing a dependent Indian People dwelling within the United
States." Alaska Pacific Fisheries v. United States,
248 U.S. 78, 88 (1918). Those are terms of trust
relationship. Although ANCSA declares that settlement should occur without *"creating* a * * *
lengthy wardship or trusteeship," § 1601(b)(emphasis added), it did not state that it was terminating
any such relationship. It probably did not expressly
preserve the relationship either. ANCSA states that
it shall not diminish "any obligation of the United
States * * * to protect and promote the rights or
welfare of Natives *as citizens of the United States or
Alaska,*" § 1601(c)(emphasis added), but the final
clause can be read to limit the statement to little
more than a guarantee of equal protection. One
circuit observed that ANCSA "arguably precludes
the existence of a general trust responsibility to the
Eskimoes." North Slope Borough v. Andrus, 642
F.2d 589, 612 n.151 (D.C.Cir.1980). The Ninth Circuit, in which Alaska lies, appeared to recognize a
federal trust responsibility comparable to that toward other Indians, even after passage of the Alas-

ka Native Claims Settlement Act. Alaska Chapter, Associated General Contractors v. Pierce, 694 F.2d 1162, 1168–69 n. 10 (9th Cir.1982). That court later clearly embraced this position in Yukon Flats School Dist. v. Native Village of Venetie Tribal Gov't, 101 F.3d 1286 (9th Cir.1996), rev'd on other grounds, 522 U.S. 520 (1998). The Federal Circuit, however, has held that ANCSA created no trust relationship between Natives and the federal government and appears to recognize the existence of none. Bay View, Inc. v. United States, 278 F.3d 1259 (Fed.Cir.2001).

Congress has included Alaska Natives in post-ANCSA legislation in various ways that could be seen as implementing, if not establishing, a trust relationship. The Indian Self–Determination and Education Assistance Act of 1975, which permits tribes to contract to administer federal Indian programs, defines "Indian tribe" to include "any Alaska Native village or regional or village corporation as defined in or established pursuant to [ANCSA] which is recognized as eligible for the special programs and services provided by the United States to Indians because of their status as Indians." 25 U.S.C.A. § 450b(e)(as amended); see Cook Inlet Native Ass'n v. Bowen, 810 F.2d 1471 (9th Cir.1987). A similar definition appears in the Tribally Controlled Community College Assistance Act, 25 U.S.C.A. § 1801(2), and the Indian Health Care Improvement Act, 25 U.S.C.A. § 1603(d), although the significance of the latter inclusion is tempered by the fact that the same section extends coverage of the Act to terminated Indians, with whom there is no trust relationship. § 1603(c). The Indian Child Welfare Act, however, begins with a recitation of the "special relationship between the United States and the Indian tribes and their members and the Federal responsibility to Indian people" and then includes as tribes Alaska Native villages as defined in ANCSA. 25 U.S.C.A. § 1903(8).

Congress made clear that recognition of Indian tribes was a prerogative of the Secretary of the Interior when it required the Secretary to publish "a list of all Indian tribes which the Secretary recognizes to be eligible for the special programs and services provided by the United States to Indians because of their status as Indians." 25 U.S.C.A. § 479a–1. The Secretary now includes more than 200 Alaska Native organizations in the list of tribes recognized as having the immunities and privileges of "acknowledged Indian tribes by virtue of their government-to-government relationship with the United States* * *." 67 Fed. Reg. 46328 (July 12, 2002). In the light of this recognition by the Executive Branch, as well as the congressional statutes referred to above, there is at least a substantial argument for the existence of a trust relationship between the recognized Alaska Native organizations and the federal government.

2. INDIAN COUNTRY

One of the major uncertainties overhanging Alaska Native governmental power was the question whether Native lands held pursuant to ANCSA were "Indian country." See Chapter VII, Section B, supra. The issue was one of great jurisdictional importance. If Native villages occupied their lands as Indian country, they presumably would be able to exercise all of the powers of reservation tribes in the lower forty-eight states. See Chapter VII, supra. Moreover, the State of Alaska would be precluded from exercising general regulatory jurisdiction within that same territory. See Chapter VIII, Section D, supra.

"Indian country" is defined by 18 U.S.C. § 1151 to encompass (a) land within Indian reservations, (b) "dependent Indian communities," and (c) allotments under Indian title. The only reservation left in Alaska after the enactment of ANCSA is the Annette Islands Reserve of the Metlakatla Indians; that reserve is indisputably Indian country. There are also Native allotments in Alaska, but they usually have not been a source of jurisdictional controversy. One exception is Jones v. State, 936 P.2d 1263 (Alaska App.1997), in which the court expressed doubt that Alaska Native allotments could qualify as Indian country. The prime jurisdictional question, however, has been whether lands held by Native entities under ANCSA comprise "dependent Indian communities."

The Supreme Court answered that question in the negative in Alaska v. Native Village of Venetie Tribal Government, 522 U.S. 520 (1998). The issue arose when the Village attempted to impose a tax on a contractor building a state school on fee land held by the Village pursuant to ANCSA. The Village held the land without restrictions on alienation. The Supreme Court held that, for land to be a dependent Indian community, it had to have been set aside by the federal government for the use of Indians, and had to be under the superintendence of the federal government. Lands held by the Village pursuant to ANCSA failed to meet both requirements. ANCSA's transfer of lands to state-chartered corporations, without restraints on alienation, did not set the land aside for use of the Natives; the corporations or the Village could transfer the land out of Native ownership at any time. Active supervision of the lands, not of the tribe, was the requirement, and the federal government must supervise the land essentially as a guardian. Thus lands held by the Alaska Native groups pursuant to ANCSA did not qualify as Indian country. The Village's attempt to tax the contractor accordingly failed. As a consequence of this *Venetie* decision, Alaska Native villages are left without any jurisdiction based on territorial power, and the State of Alaska is left with adjudicatory, regulatory, and legislative jurisdiction over ANCSA-held lands.

3. TRIBAL SELF–GOVERNMENT

Questions then arise concerning the degree to which Alaska Native entities may exercise governmental power without a territorial basis. Even without Indian country, over 200 Native entities remain federally recognized governmental bodies. Indeed, in 1994, the requirements for federal acknowledgment were modified to make clear that occupation of a particular territory was not a prerequisite. See 59 Fed.Reg. 9280, 9286–87; 25 C.F.R. § 83.7. What powers do these governments have after *Venetie*? The answers are not entirely clear, but some insight may be gained from events preceding the Supreme Court's decision. In 1988, the Alaska Supreme Court took the position that most villages and Native groups in Alaska were "not self-governing or in any meaningful sense sovereign." Native Village of Stevens v. Alaska Management & Planning, 757 P.2d 32, 34 (Alaska 1988). The exception was the Metlakatla Indian Community of the Annette Islands Reserve. Id.; see Atkinson v. Haldane, 569 P.2d 151 (Alaska 1977).

At about the same time, the Ninth Circuit took a more individualized and fact-bound approach to the sovereign power of any particular village. Although it agreed with the Alaska Supreme Court that organization under section 16 of the Indian Reorganization Act, 25 U.S.C.A. § 476, did not automatically establish sovereignty, it held that sovereignty could be established by a showing of federal recognition or, failing that, by other historical factors. Alaska v. Native Village of Venetie, 856 F.2d 1384, 1387 (9th Cir.1988); Native Village of Tyonek v. Puckett, 957 F.2d 631, 635 (9th Cir.1992). The Ninth Circuit further defined its position in Native Village of Venetie I.R.A. Council v. Alaska, 944 F.2d 548 (9th Cir.1991). It rejected early views that Alaska Native groups simply did not qualify as independent sovereigns, see In Re Sah Quah, 31 F. 327 (D. Alaska 1886), and held that "[i]f the native villages of Venetie and Fort Yukon are the modern-day successors to sovereign historical bands of natives, the villages are to be afforded the same rights and responsibilities as are sovereign bands of native Americans in the continental United States." *Venetie*, 944 F.2d at 559. The Alaska Supreme Court, however, refused to accept the reasoning of *Venetie I.R.A.*, and adhered to its view in *Stevens* that "Congress intended that most Alaska Native groups not be treated as sovereigns." Matter of F.P., 843 P.2d 1214, 1215 (Alaska 1992). The Alaska Supreme Court earlier, however, had recognized a Native group organized under section 16 of the IRA, 25 U.S.C. § 476, as a "tribe" for the limited purpose of protecting its land under that provision from foreclosure by a city for nonpayment of taxes. Matter of City of Nome, 780 P.2d 363 (Alaska 1989); see also Hydaburg Cooperative Ass'n v. Hydaburg Fisheries, 925 P.2d 246 (Alaska 1996).

All of these cases, however, were decided before the Department of the Interior revised its list of entities entitled to receive federal benefits. Prior to 1988, the intent of the Department in including an Alaskan entity on its list had not been made clear, see Harrison v. State, 791 P.2d 359, 364 n.8 (Alaska App.1990). In 1988 the list was expanded to include all Alaskan entities entitled to receive federal funds or services even if they were not regarded as "tribes" by the Department. In 1993, however, the Department recognized the ambiguity caused by its actions and published a narrower list of "villages and regional tribes [that] have functioned as political entities exercising governmental authority and are, therefore acknowledged to have 'the immunities and privileges available to other federally acknowledged Indian tribes by virtue of their status as Indian tribes * * *.' " 58 Fed.Reg. 54364, 54365 (1993). The Department stated its intent to clarify that the listed tribes "have the same governmental status as other federally acknowledged Indian tribes * * * with a government-to-government relationship with the United States * * *." Id. at 54366. Because recognition of a tribe by the Executive Branch is generally a nonjusticiable political question, judicial acceptance of the sovereign status of the listed villages was likely to follow. See Atkinson v. Haldane, 569 P.2d at 163.

The issue of tribal non-territorial power was framed acutely in a series of child custody proceedings. First, the Supreme Court of Alaska held that tribal courts had no jurisdiction to adjudicate child custody because exclusive jurisdiction over such matters was granted to the state courts by Public Law 280. Native Village of Nenana v. State, Dep't of Health & Social Services, 722 P.2d 219 (Alaska 1986). Next, the Ninth Circuit held to the contrary, ruling that a Native Village as a sovereign entity had inherent authority to make child custody determinations for its members. Native Village of Venetie I.R.A. Council v. Alaska, 944 F.2d 548 (9th Cir.1991). It relied on United States v. Wheeler, 435 U.S. 313, 322 & n. 18 (1978), which described the inherent power of tribal self-government as including the power to regulate domestic relations among tribal members. The Ninth Circuit also endorsed the view that Public Law 280 did not deprive tribes of concurrent civil jurisdiction. See Chapter VIII, Section C, supra. The Supreme Court of Alaska subsequently refused to accept the Ninth Circuit's view, see Matter of F.P., 843 P.2d 1214 (Alaska 1992), leaving the federal and state courts in conflict on this question.

The Alaska Supreme Court thereafter undertook a major examination of the status of Alaska Native self-government in John v. Baker, 982 P.2d 738 (Alaska 1999). The case involved a custody battle between unmarried parents who were Alaska Native members of different villages. A tribal court of one of the villages had entered a decision after which the state court was asked to rule. The Alaska Supreme Court held that the Indian Child Welfare Act did not apply because the custody dispute between unmarried parents fell by implication within the exception for custody in divorce cases. It also held that Public Law 280 did not apply to give the state court jurisdiction because Public Law 280 extended state jurisdiction into "Indian country" and after the Supreme Court decision in *Venetie*, it was clear that there was no Indian country in Alaska (Annette Islands excepted). The Alaska Supreme Court then went on to hold: (1) it would defer to the federal recognition of Alaska Native entities as sovereign tribes; (2) as tribes, these entities retain sovereign power to regulate internal domestic affairs; (3) retention by the tribes of child custody matters was consistent with ANCSA and other federal statutes; (4) general Indian law decisions after ANCSA suggest that the Alaska tribes retain non-territorial sovereignty that includes power over child custody disputes; (5) Alaska courts could exercise concurrent jurisdiction because there was no Indian country from which the state might be excluded; (6) the tribe could apply its own law to custody disputes; and (7) the state court should accord comity to the tribal court decision.

The *John* case represents a major development, and it leaves the Alaska Court more closely in line with federal court decisions. There seems little reason to doubt that, under the reasoning of *John* and the authorities it cites, several other inherent powers of tribal self-government set forth in *Wheeler* may be exercised by Native governments without a territorial base. The basis of jurisdiction emphasized in *Wheeler* is tribal membership, and it supports such matters of internal self-governance as determination of membership, regulation of domestic relations among members, and regulation of inheritance. *Wheeler*, 435 U.S. at 322 n.18. It may also support jurisdiction to enforce civil ordinances regarding members' transfer of tribal artifacts. See Chilkat Indian Village v. Johnson, 870 F.2d 1469 (9th Cir.1989). Membership might even support the other attribute of inherent sovereignty set forth in *Wheeler*–the power to exercise criminal jurisdiction over tribal members. See Duro v. Reina, 495 U.S. 676, 693 (1990). The point is problematical, however, because criminal jurisdiction normally has a territorial element. Finally, Native villages ought to be able to exercise whatever governmental powers might be necessary to administer programs made available or delegated to them by the federal government in recognition or implementation of the federal-tribal government-to-government relationship.

With regard to nonmembers, *John* implicitly permits at least some jurisdiction because one of the two parents involved in that case was a member of a village other than the one whose tribal court decided the case. The consensual relationship of the parents can support the result because it clearly has a nexus to the subject of the controversy. See Atkinson Trading Co. v. Shirley, 532 U.S. 645, 656 (2001); see also *Duro*, 495 U.S. at 688; Montana v. United States, 450 U.S. 544, 565 (1981). It is clear, however, that without Indian country jurisdiction, Native villages may not exercise governmental authority, such as taxation, over nonconsensual activities of nonmembers on ANCSA-held lands. Venetie, supra; Alyeska Pipeline Service Co. v. Kluti Kaah Native Village, 101 F.3d 610 (9th Cir.1996). The villages or their corporations do enjoy the usual rights of landowners, of course, but those prerogatives do not derive from governmental status.

D. HUNTING AND FISHING

Hunting and fishing has always been of extreme importance to Alaska Natives. The subject early attracted the attention of the Supreme Court in Alaska Pacific Fisheries v. United States, 248 U.S. 78 (1918). The Court there held that Congress, in setting aside a reserve for the Metlakatla Indians "the body of lands known as the Annette Islands" included by implication the adjacent waters, because the fishery was the Indians' primary means of subsistence. The Court returned to the subject in Metlakatla Indian Community v. Egan, 369 U.S. 45 (1962), which upheld the power of the Secretary of the Interior to authorize the use of fish traps by Indians in those waters in contravention of state law.

In the companion case of Organized Village of Kake v. Egan, 369 U.S. 60 (1962), the Court reached a different result when the Secretary attempted to authorize the use of fish traps by Village fishermen in waters not part of any reserve. The Court held that the Secretary was not authorized to issue any such permits. One point in issue was the effect of the clause in the Alaska Statehood Act providing that the State "forever disclaim[ed] all right and title * * * to any lands or other property (including fishing rights), the right or title to which may be held by any Indians, Eskimos, or Aleuts" and that such lands or property "shall be and remain under the absolute jurisdiction and control of the United States * * *." 72 Stat. 339 (1958). The Court held that the reference to fishing rights was intended neither to recognize nor to extinguish any aboriginal or possessory rights held by the Natives; it was intended merely to maintain the status quo. The provision for "absolute jurisdiction and control" by the United States "was a disclaimer of proprietary rather than governmental interest." 369 U.S. at 69. Moreover, "absolute jurisdiction" did not necessarily mean "exclusive jurisdiction." Id. at 68. Consequently, the State could exercise jurisdiction and control over the Native fishing, and thus could ban the fish traps.

Alaska Native hunting and fishing thus generally proceeded under state regulation. There were, of course, no treaties and therefore no treaty hunting or fishing rights to be asserted. Any uncertainty concerning the nature and extent of aboriginal rights to hunt and fish were ended in 1971 with the passage of the Alaska Native Claims Settlement Act. It extinguished "any aboriginal hunting or fishing rights that may exist." 43 U.S.C.A. § 1603(b). Because the extinguishment was of aboriginal title "in Alaska," it left a possibility that Natives could claim aboriginal rights beyond the three-mile limit from shore. See Village of Gambell v. Hodel, 869 F.2d 1273 (9th Cir.1989), dismissed as moot, 999 F.2d 403 (9th Cir.1993). The doctrine of federal paramountcy over state sovereignty precludes, however, an exclusive aboriginal right to hunt and fish the outer continental shelf. Native Village of Eyak v. Trawler Diane Marie, Inc., 154 F.3d 1090 (9th Cir.1998). In any event, within the State no pre-existing rights remained and any distinctive treatment of Native hunting and fishing out of Indian country therefore had to be a creature of statute or regulation.

One federal statute that has a substantial impact on Native hunting and fishing is the Alaska National Interest Lands Conservation Act ("ANILCA"), 16 U.S.C.A. § 3101 et seq., enacted in 1980. ANILCA provides, among other things, a system for managing huge amounts of land withdrawn by the federal government for various public purposes. One of the stated purposes of the Act is "to provide the opportunity for rural residents engaged in a subsistence way of life to continue to do so." § 3101(c). The Act was clearly intended to protect subsistence uses of Alaska Natives, but its coverage was broadened to rural residents because of objections that the state constitution might prohibit subsistence preferences based exclusively on Native status.

ANILCA declares "nonwasteful subsistence uses of fish and wildlife" to be the priority consumptive uses of those resources on the public lands of Alaska. § 3112(2). When there are insufficient populations of fish or game to meet subsistence requirements, priority among subsistence users is based on three criteria: whether the subsistence use is a "mainstay of livelihood," local residency, and availability of alternative resources. § 3114. "Subsistence use" means the "customary and traditional uses by rural Alaska residents * * * for direct personal or family consumption as food, shelter, fuel, clothing, tools, or transportation; for the making and selling of handicraft articles out of nonedible byproducts * * *; for barter, or sharing for personal or family consumption; and for customary trade." § 3113. Customary trade may include cash sales, and a ban on such sales has been held to violate ANILCA. United States v. Alexander, 938 F.2d 942 (9th Cir.1991). "Public lands" include not only federal lands, but lands selected by Alaska under the Statehood Act and by Native corporations under ANCSA. § 3102(3). "Public lands" consequently includes a huge proportion of Alaska. It does not, however, include the continental shelf beyond the three mile limit of the State boundary. Amoco Production Co. v. Village of Gambell, 480 U.S. 531 (1987). Public lands also do not include navigable waters over which the federal government reserves only a navigational servitude. Alaska v. Babbitt, 72 F.3d 698, 702–03 (9th Cir.1995). There is a conflict of authority over the status of waters (including navigable waters) reserved as appurtenant to federally reserved lands. The Ninth Circuit has held that such waters are public lands within the meaning of ANILCA. Id. at 703–04. The Supreme Court of Alaska has held that they are not. Totemoff v. State, 905 P.2d 954, 964 (Alaska 1995).

ANILCA provides for the Secretary of the Interior to divide public lands into regions, to create local advisory committees, and to make rules to preserve the priority of subsistence uses of fish and wildlife. § 3115(a),(b),(c). These provisions are rendered inoperative, however, if the State "enacts and implements laws of general applicability that are consistent with the subsistence preference. § 3115(d). In other words, if the State wishes to avoid federal regulation of hunting and fishing on public lands, it must enact a general system of fish and game regulations that protect and give priority to subsistence uses of rural residents." Given the choice between federal regulation or self-regulation with federal oversight, Alaska chose the latter. Kenaitze Indian Tribe v. Alaska, 860 F.2d 312, 314 (9th Cir.1988). Alaska thus enacted laws providing a subsistence use priority for rural residents, but its narrow definition of "rural" was held to be inconsistent with ANILCA. Id. More substantial difficulties followed when the Supreme Court of Alaska held that confining the priority to rural residents violated the state constitution. McDowell v. State, 785 P.2d 1 (Alaska 1989). The State's laws were then declared to be out of compliance with ANILCA and the federal government consequently began regulating fish and game on public lands. See Native Village of Quinhagak v. United States, 35 F.3d 388, 390 (9th Cir.1994). Although a good argument can be made that the scheme of ANILCA renders such federal regulation exclusive, the Supreme Court of Alaska subsequently held that the State had concurrent jurisdiction to regulate subsistence hunting on public lands, so long as its regulation was not inconsistent with federal regulations. Totemoff v. State, 905 P.2d 954 (Alaska 1995).

In addition to the provisions discussed above, ANILCA requires federal agency heads to evaluate the effect of land use decisions on subsistence uses, and to provide notice and hearing if an action would substantially restrict subsistence uses. § 3120. If an action would significantly restrict subsistence uses, the agency head must determine that it is "neces-

sary, consistent with sound management principles" and would involve the minimal amount of
public lands necessary to accomplish "its purpose."
§ 3120(a). "Necessary" in this context is given a
construction of reasonableness; it does not mean
that the action is compelled. Hoonah Indian Ass'n
v. Morrison, 170 F.3d 1223 (9th Cir.1999). The Act
includes many other provisions of general and specific application that are too numerous to describe
here.

Alaska's own hunting and fishing laws continue
to provide a preference for subsistence uses. When
the stocks of fish and game are insufficient for
subsistence and competing uses, competing uses
must yield. There is also a system for determining
preference among subsistence users, although residence may not be used in such a determination.
State v. Kenaitze Indian Tribe, 894 P.2d 632 (Alaska 1995); see Alaska Stat. § 16.05.258. The State
may declare areas where the subsistence preference
does not apply. Kenaitze, 894 P.2d at 639–42. The
Supreme Court of Alaska has disapproved intervention by a lower court to secure a preference for a
particular subsistence hunt; the effects of such a
move on competing subsistence users and the entire
game population must be taken into account. State
v. Kluti Kaah Native Village, 831 P.2d 1270 (Alaska
1992). An intermediate court has held that Alaska's
hunting laws are not merely regulatory, but are
"criminal/prohibitory" for purposes of Public Law
280, see Chapter VIII, Section D, supra, and therefore may be applied on an Indian allotment even if

it is Indian country. Jones v. State, 936 P.2d 1263 (Alaska App.1997).

Several federal statutes of general applicability contain exceptions for Alaska Native subsistence hunting and fishing. The Endangered Species Act provides that endangered or threatened species may be taken for subsistence purposes by "any Indian, Aleut, or Eskimo who is an Alaskan Native who resides in Alaska" or by "any non-native permanent resident of an Alaskan Native village." 16 U.S.C.A. § 1539(e). The exemption has been upheld against an equal protection attack by Native Hawaiians; the classification is rationally based "upon food supply and culture." United States v. Nuesca, 945 F.2d 254, 257 (9th Cir.1991). The Marine Mammal Protection Act imposes a moratorium on the taking of marine mammals, but contains an exception for "any Indian, Aleut, or Eskimo who resides in Alaska and who dwells on the coast of the North Pacific Ocean or the Arctic Ocean." 16 U.S.C.A. § 1371(b). The taking must be for purposes of subsistence or creation of Native artifacts, and must not be conducted "in a wasteful manner." Id. Several treaties regarding migratory birds include protections for Native subsistence, and the Secretary of the Interior is authorized by statute to issue regulations "to assure that the taking of migratory birds and the collection of their eggs, by the indigenous inhabitants of the State of Alaska, shall be permitted for their own nutritional and other essential needs * * *." 16 U.S.C.A. § 712(a). Finally, more distant from the subject of wild game, the Reindeer

Act and its administration have secured a virtual monopoly of the reindeer business for Alaska Natives. See 25 U.S.C.A. § 500 et seq. In order to avoid serious constitutional questions, however, the Act has been interpreted not to prohibit non-Natives from entering the business. See Williams v. Babbitt, 115 F.3d 657 (9th Cir.1997). The number and substance of these various statutory provisions reflect the undeniable importance of hunting and fishing to the Alaska Native culture and economy.

CHAPTER XIV

INDIAN WATER RIGHTS

A. THE APPROPRIATIVE SYSTEM OF WATER RIGHTS

Disputes over Indian water rights are necessarily concentrated in the water-scarce states of the West. To understand these disputes and the evolving legal principles applicable to them, it is necessary to examine briefly the two major systems of water rights in the United States—the "riparian" system of the water-abundant states of the East and the "appropriative" system of the arid West.

Under the riparian system, the owner of land that borders a lake or stream has the right to the reasonable use of the water. That right runs with the land and cannot be separated from it. It continues to exist whether or not it is exercised. The reasonableness of any use of any given amount of water depends entirely on the circumstances of that use, with the primary limitation being that it must not interfere unduly with any other riparian owner's reasonable use of the water. All riparian owners are entitled to a continuation of the flow. If the source of the water is affected by drought, then the right of each riparian owner is diminished proportionally.

The appropriative system operates on entirely different premises. It evolved at a time when nearly all of the land in the West was federally owned, and the primary demands for water were for mining. Mines were often located at considerable distance from the source of the water, and substantial investment was required to construct systems for transporting it. In later years, agriculture became a primary use, and it also required substantial investment in irrigation systems. Miners and farmers both needed assurances of continued supplies of water before they undertook these investments.

The result of these circumstances was the growth of the appropriative system. Under that regime, water rights are not appurtenant to the land. The right to water belongs to the first user who appropriates it and puts it to beneficial use. That appropriator is guaranteed the right to continue to take the same amount of water from the source without interference by any later appropriator. The appropriator retains that right only so long as he or she continues to put the water to beneficial use. "Use it or lose it" is consequently one of the slogans describing the appropriative system.

In case of drought, the entire share of the latest appropriator is lost before the share of the next latest begins to diminish. Appropriation dates are therefore of immense importance, and the older the better. When a stream is almost fully appropriated, new appropriators are at great risk of losing future supplies in short years, but the older appropriators enjoy a high degree of security.

Although the appropriative system evolved on federal land, it is a creature of local custom rather than federal law. Congress by various statutes recognized these customs, and in the Desert Land Entries Act of 1877, 43 U.S.C.A. §§ 321–25, declared all non-navigable water available to appropriation in the present states of California, Oregon, Washington, Idaho, Montana, Wyoming, Utah, Colorado, Nevada, Arizona, New Mexico, and North and South Dakota. These appropriations are governed by state law. California Oregon Power Co. v. Beaver Portland Cement Co., 295 U.S. 142 (1935). State law varies greatly from the relatively pure appropriative system of Colorado to the mixture of appropriative and riparian systems in California and Oregon. Details of state law also differ in regard to requirements for registration of appropriations, the period of non-use that causes forfeiture, priorities of use, and method of resolving disputes. The organizing principles of appropriation remain the same, however: water may be appropriated separately from land; the first appropriator in time is first in right; and water not put to beneficial use is lost to the appropriator.

B. INDIAN WATER RIGHTS: THE *WINTERS* DOCTRINE

Indian water rights do not fall entirely into either the appropriative or the riparian category. Their foundation lies in the Supreme Court decision of Winters v. United States, 207 U.S. 564 (1908). That case involved the Fort Belknap Reservation in Montana, which had been created by an 1888 agreement out of a much larger area previously set aside for the concerned tribes. The agreement described one boundary of the reservation as being the middle of the Milk River, but it made no mention of rights to the use of water. Thereafter, non-Indian settlers off the reservation built dams that diverted the flow of the river and interfered with agricultural uses by the Indians. The settlers claimed that they had appropriated the water after the reservation was established but prior to any use of water by the Indians. The Supreme Court found it unnecessary to determine the truth of the settlers' claims of prior use, because it held that when the Fort Belknap lands were reserved by the 1888 agreement, water rights for the Indians were also reserved by necessary implication. The Court thought it unreasonable to assume that Indians would reserve lands for farming and pastoral purposes without also reserving the water to make those uses possible. The Court also held that this implied reservation of water was unaffected by the subsequent admission of Montana into the Union "upon an equal footing with the original States."

Despite the clear ruling of *Winters*, Indian water rights were largely ignored for many decades thereafter. The United States was far more interested in encouraging non-Indian settlement than it was in developing and protecting Indian water resources. Indeed, during those years the United States represented the tribes in several water rights adjudications that severely compromised the tribes' *Winters* rights, and those decrees in several instances still control the tribes' access to water. See, e.g., Nevada v. United States, 463 U.S. 110 (1983); United States v. Gila Valley Irr. Dist., 920 F.Supp. 1444 (D.Ariz. 1996), aff'd, 117 F.3d 425 (9th Cir.1997). The Supreme Court was not called upon further to define Indian water rights until 1963, in the case of Arizona v. California, 373 U.S. 546 (1963). In that major litigation over the lower Colorado River, the Court had to determine the water rights accruing to tribes along the river whose reservations had been established by both statute and executive order. The Court viewed the question as one of the intention of Congress or the President, and held that neither one could have meant to establish reservations without reserving for the use of the Indians the water necessary to make the land habitable and productive. The Court held that the water rights were effectively reserved as of the time of creation of the reservations.

The other major issue presented by Arizona v. California concerned the quantity of water reserved. Competing users contended that the water rights should be limited to amounts likely to be needed by the relatively sparse Indian population in the foreseeable future. The Supreme Court rejected that measure and instead ruled that the tribes were entitled to enough water to irrigate all the *practicably irrigable acreage* on the reservations—a much more generous measure. Once that quantity was established in the litigation, res judicata precluded claims for additional acreage within the reservation that had not been properly claimed as irrigable. Arizona v. California, 460 U.S. 605 (1983). Reopening was permitted, however, for claims relating to a disputed additional 25,000 acres added to the boundaries of the Quechan Tribe's Fort Yuma Indian Reservation; a defense of res judicata to that claim was raised too late. Arizona v. California, 530 U.S. 392 (2000). There seems little doubt, however, that once the major water rights adjudications are concluded, with tribes and other users awarded a specific quantity of water with fixed priority dates, those figures are not likely to change thereafter.

From the *Winters* and *Arizona v. California* cases, it is possible to summarize some of the characteristics of reserved Indian water rights, commonly referred to as "*Winters* rights":

1.   *Winters* rights are creatures of federal law, which defines their extent.

2.   Establishment of a reservation by treaty, statute or executive order includes an implied reservation of water rights in sources within or bordering the reservation.

3.   The water rights are reserved as of the date of creation of the applicable portion of the reservation. Competing users with prior appropriation dates under state law take precedence over the Indian rights, but those with later dates are subordinate.

4.   The quantity of water reserved for Indian use is that amount sufficient to irrigate all the practicably irrigable acreage of the reservation.

At least one later state decision, however, states this proposition differently: the quantity of water reserved is that amount sufficient to accomplish the purposes of the reservation, which may or may not be agricultural.

5. *Winters* rights to water are not lost by non-use.

It may be seen from this summary that Indian water rights have some of the characteristics of appropriative rights, such as a date of appropriation and the total priority of a prior appropriator over a later one in times of short supply. On the other hand, they also have some of the characteristics of riparian rights; they apply most clearly to water bordering, crossing or within (i.e., appurtenant to) the Indian land, and they are not lost by non-use.

While maximum irrigable acreage provides the measure of Indian water rights under *Arizona v. California*, at least one state court has since diverged from that measure. The Arizona Supreme Court determined that the purpose of a reservation was to supply the Indians with a " 'permanent home and abiding place.' " In re General Adjudication of Gila River System, 201 Ariz. 307, 35 P.3d 68 (2001) (quoting *Winters*, 207 U.S. at 565). Accordingly, it was error for a lower court to use the measure of practicably irrigable acreage. Instead, the needs of the reservation should be determined by attention to a tribe's history and culture, its reservation's topography and resources (including groundwater), the tribe's economic base, past water use, and (with a caution that it should never be the only factor) present and projected population. Id. The fact that this formula is likely to lead to a lower award to the tribes is suggested by the fact that they and the United States urged adherence to the standard of practically irrigable acreage.

The "homeland" purpose played a different role in Wyoming. The master there found that the purpose of the Wind River Reservation had been to provide a homeland, which included but was not limited to agriculture. He therefore awarded water not just for practically irrigable acreage, but for such other uses as mineral development (because the mineral wealth underlying the area was well known at the time the reservation was established). The Wyoming Supreme Court, however, determined that the only purpose of the reservation was agricultural, and so the only measure should be practicably irrigable acreage. In re General Adjudication of Big Horn River System, 753 P.2d 76 (Wyo.1988). The State nevertheless deemed this measure too generous and sought certiorari, which was granted only on that issue. The Supreme Court split evenly, affirming the state court's judgment by an equally divided court. 492 U.S. 406.

As the Supreme Court observed in one of the Arizona v. California opinions, a prime benefit of the measure of practically irrigable acreage was its capability of providing "a *fixed* calculation of future water needs." 460 U.S. at 605. The Court also observed that the measure was a "complete victory" for the tribes. Id. Whether deviation from this standard, if permissible, might in some instances provide more water for the tribes cannot be known, but there is good reason for the tribes to be pessimistic.

The use of practicably irrigable acreage as a measure of water does not require a tribe to engage in inefficient or undesired farming. The special master in Arizona v. California stated that this measure did not necessarily mean that the water had to be used for agricultural purposes. S. Rifkind, Report of the Special Master—Arizona v. California 265 (1962), quoted in D. Getches, D. Rosenfelt & C. Wilkinson, Federal Indian Law 598 (1979). If a tribe decides to use its quantified share of agricultural water for industrial or other purposes, it therefore may do so. See Colville Confederated Tribes v. Walton, 647 F.2d 42, 48 (9th Cir.1981); United States v. Anderson, 736 F.2d 1358, 1365 (9th Cir.1984); but see In re Big Horn River System, 835 P.2d 273, 278 (Wyo.1992). Courts have generally been inclined to recognize the need for flexibility in the manner in which reservations meet the needs of their inhabitants. United States v. Finch, 548 F.2d 822, 832 (9th Cir.1976), rev'd on other grounds, 433 U.S. 676 (1977); Conrad Investment Co. v. United States, 161 Fed. 829, 831 (9th Cir.1908).

When a reservation is established with express or implicit purposes beyond agriculture, such as fishing, then water is also reserved in quantities sufficient to sustain that use. United States v. Adair, 723 F.2d 1394, 1408–11 (9th Cir.1983); Colville Confederated Tribes v. Walton, 647 F.2d at 48.

Although the purpose for which the federal government reserves other types of lands may be strictly construed, United States v. New Mexico, 438 U.S. 696 (1978) (national forest), the purposes of Indian reservations are necessarily entitled to broader interpretation if the goal of Indian self-sufficiency is to be attained. United States v. Finch, 548 F.2d at 827–32.

Winters and nearly all subsequent decisions have dealt solely with surface water, but there are sound reasons for concluding that Indian reserved rights also exist in "ground water" (perhaps better termed "underground water") beneath the reservation. Depletion of that water may defeat the purposes of the reservation as thoroughly as the diversion of surface water. In Cappaert v. United States, 426 U.S. 128 (1976), the United States was held to be entitled to protect a pool of water in Death Valley National Monument from damage by groundwater diversion. The Wyoming Supreme Court, however, held that, for lack of precedent, no groundwater was reserved for the Wind River Reservation even though it agreed that "[t]he logic which supports reservation of surface water to fulfill the purpose of the reservation also supports reservation of groundwater." In re General Adjudication of Big Horn River System, 753 P.2d 76, 99–100 (Wyo.1988). The Arizona Supreme Court weighed in very differently on this issue, holding that there is a federally reserved right to groundwater "when groundwater is necessary to accomplish the purpose of a * * * reservation." In re General Adjudication of the Gila

River System, 195 Ariz. 411, 422, 989 P.2d 750 (1999); see also Confederated Salish and Kootenai Tribes v. Stults, 312 Mont. 420, 59 P.3d 1093 (2002). The holder of such a reserved right can prevent depletion by pumping of groundwater, even though state law would not provide such a remedy. *Gila River,* supra.

An expansive interpretation of *Winters* rights would also reserve for Indian use water from off-reservation sources if determined to be necessary to meet reservation needs. One such award appears to have been made without discussion in the Arizona v. California decree, 376 U.S. 340, 344 (1964); see Note, *Indian Reserved Rights: The Winters of Our Discontent,* 88 Yale L.J. 1689, 1697 n. 54 (1979). Extension of *Winters* rights beyond the reservation is sufficiently disruptive of the entire appropriative system, however, that it is likely to occur only in cases of dire need or where congressional intent is express or clear from a pattern of historical usage. The Department of Justice refused to undertake litigation on behalf of a tribe to pursue a claim to off-reservation water rights based on a treaty right to hunt (and implicitly to fish) on ceded lands. Shoshone Bannock Tribes v. Reno, 56 F.3d 1476 (D.C.Cir.1995).

Many Indian tribes are just beginning to assert their unexercised water rights, and each assertion is almost certain to engender bitter controversy. Non–Indians contend that recognition of long-dormant Indian rights defeats the entire purpose of the appropriative system, which was to create certainty that would stimulate beneficial use. They argue that appropriators who saw unused water and spent large sums in creating transportation and irrigation systems ought not to be shut out today by the Indians. The tribes contend, however, that the reason for their non-use of the water was the failure of the United States to fulfill its responsibility as trustee in developing and protecting water resources, and that it would only compound injury to deprive the tribes of their water forever. *Winters* and its progeny have decided this argument in favor of the Indians, but that outcome has by no means ended the controversy.

The greatest uncertainty resulting from Indian water rights arises from the fact that in many cases the rights have not been quantified. Competing users and the Indians themselves know that a reservation is entitled to enough water to irrigate its practicably irrigable acreage, but no one knows exactly how much water that is. One solution to that problem is adjudication, as in Arizona v. California. Adjudications have not come easily, however. The United States historically has not been vigorous in litigating to establish or preserve Indian water rights. The tribes themselves can bring suit, but the cost of such litigation is frequently prohibitive. Mere service of process in a major river adjudication can run into tens of thousands of dollars and surveys to determine irrigability may cost hundreds of thousands. Expenses of trial itself are even greater. For these reasons, suggestions have been made for quantification of Indian water rights by negotia-

tion, administrative action or legislation, and negotiated settlements are increasingly being reached.
An example is the legislative settlement of the
groundwater claims of the Ak–Chin Reservation in
Arizona. Pub. L. 95–328, 92 Stat. 409 (1978).

C. *WINTERS* RIGHTS IN ALLOTTED LAND

When tribal land is converted into allotments, the
Indian allottees succeed to the tribe's *Winters* rights
for that land. United States v. Powers, 305 U.S. 527
(1939). A non-Indian purchaser of the allotment
acquires rights equal to those of the Indian seller.
United States v. Ahtanum Irrigation Dist., 236 F.2d
321, 342 (9th Cir.1956). The same is true for an
Indian or tribal purchaser. In re General Adjudication of Big Horn River System, 48 P.3d 1040, 1056
(Wyo.2002). A non-Indian purchaser's rights have
been elaborated as follows: (1) an Indian allottee is
entitled to that share of the reservation's irrigation
water rights that his allotment's irrigable acreage
bears to the total irrigable acreage of the reservation; (2) when the Indian allottee sells to a non-
Indian, the purchaser acquires the allotment's reserved water rights; (3) the priority date of those
rights remains the date when the reservation was
created; (4) the non-Indian allottee, unlike his Indian predecessor, loses his reserved right if he does
not use it; he is therefore limited to the quantity of
water from his reserved right that he appropriates
with reasonable diligence after the transfer of title.
Colville Confederated Tribes v. Walton, 647 F.2d 42

(9th Cir.1981). This formulation is a compromise. If no reserved rights at all were transferable, the Indian seller of an allotment would be prevented from realizing most of its value upon sale. On the other hand, if the sale price were maximized by permitting transfer of a right that could not be lost by non-use, the non-Indian transferee might assert dormant claims years later, in competition with reserved rights of the tribe or remaining Indian allottees. The *Walton* rule applies only when a non-Indian acquires an allotment from an Indian allottee; it does not apply to once-tribal land that was ceded back to the United States and subsequently homesteaded. The homesteader must acquire water under state rules. In re Big Horn River System, 899 P.2d 848 (Wyo.1995); United States v. Anderson, 736 F.2d 1358, 1363 (9th Cir.1984).

D.   LEASE OR SALE OF *WINTERS* RIGHTS

It is well established that Indian water rights may be leased to non-Indians along with a lease of Indian lands. Skeem v. United States, 273 Fed. 93 (9th Cir.1921). The practice is quite common. It is less clear whether *Winters* rights may be leased separately to non-Indians for use on other land. Because tribes are not confined to any particular use of their agricultural water, see Section B, supra, there would seem to be no reason to prohibit them from leasing it as an alternative means of making the reservation self-sufficient. Use of such water by non-Indian lessees would not be inconsistent with the trust nature of *Winters* rights so long as the tribe retained the reversionary interest.

Outright sale of Indian water rights might be inconsistent with the trust responsibility, because it would quite possibly threaten the continued existence of the tribal land base. The issue is likely to arise rarely in the future because of extreme resistance by the tribes to the permanent alienation of tribal property.

E. *WINTERS* RIGHTS AS PROPERTY

The question has sometimes been raised whether *Winters* rights are property to which tribes hold recognized title, so that any taking of those rights by the federal government would be subject to compensation under the Fifth Amendment. See Chapter XII, Section D, supra. Although the question has not been settled, it seems almost certain that the status of *Winters* rights is the same as that of the land they serve. As a result, *Winters* rights arising by implication from a treaty or statute establishing a reservation are property to which title is recognized, as are the reservation lands themselves.

When Indian lands are set aside solely by executive order, the tribal title remains unrecognized for Fifth Amendment purposes. See Chapter XII, Section D, supra. It follows that *Winters* rights pertaining to those lands would also be unrecognized and subject to taking without compensation by the federal government.

Winters rights arising from the establishment of a reservation take the date of that establishment as their appropriation date. In some cases, however, a tribe may claim aboriginal occupation of the land long prior to that time. The nature and extent of water rights attending such occupation has only recently come under examination. Initially, these rights would be held under original Indian title and would accordingly be subject to taking without compensation by the federal government (but not subject to taking in any manner by others). The rights become recognized, however, when a reservation is established by treaty or statute on the lands in question. United States v. Adair, 723 F.2d 1394, 1412–15 (9th Cir.1983). Thus the Klamath Tribe's aboriginal hunting and fishing became the foundation for a reserved water right for those purposes when their reservation was established. The amount of water reserved was that quantity sufficient to provide the Indians with a moderate livelihood from hunting and fishing, not the amount enjoyed in aboriginal times, or at the time the reservation was established. The priority date, however, was time immemorial. Id.

F. JURISDICTION TO ADJUDICATE WATER RIGHTS

The United States holds the legal title to *Winters* rights as trustee for the tribes. It consequently is an indispensable party to any adjudication of those rights. It may not, however, be sued without its consent. Traditionally, the United States has not consented to be sued in state court. When it has brought suit itself, it has done so in federal court under the jurisdiction conferred by 28 U.S.C.A. § 1345. As a result, federal court was the customary forum for the adjudication of Indian water rights up to the middle of the twentieth century.

In 1952, however, Congress consented to suit in state court by the McCarran Amendment, which includes the following provision:

43 U.S.C.A. § 666

(a) Consent is hereby given to join the United States as a defendant in any suit (1) for the adjudication of rights to the use of water of a river system or other source, or (2) for the administration of such rights, where it appears that the United States is the owner of or is in the process of acquiring water rights by appropriation under State law, by purchase, by exchange, or otherwise, and the United States is a necessary party to such suit. * * *

Although at one time it was uncertain whether this provision applied to suits involving reserved Indian water rights, that point was settled in Colorado River Water Conservation Dist. v. United States, 424 U.S. 800 (1976). In that case the United States had actually initiated a suit in federal court when a subsequent litigation was begun under the state adjudication system. The Supreme Court held that the McCarran Amendment rendered the United States, as trustee for Indian water rights, subject to suit in state court. It also ruled that the federal court should have abstained in favor of the state litigation, even though the federal court had concurrent jurisdiction. The Court relied on the fact that no proceedings had taken place in federal court except for the filing of the complaint.

The Court also made it clear in *Colorado River* that the nature and extent of reserved Indian water rights remain matters of federal law, even though they are subject to adjudication in state court. Federal question review is therefore available in the Supreme Court. Despite these assurances, the prospect of state adjudication of their water rights causes great apprehension on the part of Indian tribes. They believe that the state forum is likely to be unsympathetic to Indian rights, and that the applicability of federal law does not provide great protection against bias. Indeed, one state supreme court has held that state and not federal law governs the question whether a tribe may change the use of its reserved *Winters* water from agriculture to instream fisheries! In re Big Horn River System, 835 P.2d 273 (Wyo.1992). Even when federal law is acknowledged to govern, water rights cases often depend upon detailed fact determinations, such as the extent of practicably irrigable acreage of a reservation, that are very difficult to upset upon review. For this reason, many tribes have hastened to initiate water rights litigation in federal court, and have attempted to undertake sufficient discovery and other proceedings there to forestall abstention in favor of later-initiated state court proceedings. In general, these tactics have failed, and the federal courts have yielded to the states for general watershed adjudications involving Indian rights.

Legal challenges to state court adjudication have also been unsuccessful. In Arizona v. San Carlos Apache Tribe, 463 U.S. 545 (1983), the United States and several tribes argued: (1) that state enabling acts requiring the states to disclaim jurisdiction over Indian lands precluded the states from adjudicating Indian water rights; (2) that federal Indian policy similarly precluded the states from acting; and (3) that abstention by the federal courts was improper when the suit was brought by a tribe itself, and sought only an adjudication of tribal water rights. The Supreme Court rejected all of these arguments and again strongly endorsed abstention, stating that parallel federal and state proceedings were wasteful and inconsistent with the thrust of the McCarran Amendment.

The United States and the Klamath Tribe challenged Oregon's attempt to adjudicate their water rights on the ground that Oregon's procedure was not a ''suit'' within the meaning of the McCarran Amendment's waiver of sovereign immunity. United States v. Oregon, 44 F.3d 758 (9th Cir.1994). Oregon's procedure was administrative, subject to judicial review when parties filed objections to the administrative report. The court of appeals held that this procedure qualified as a ''suit'' for purposes of the McCarran Amendment. Id. at 765–77. The court also held that the failure of Oregon's adjudication to include groundwater did not deprive it of the comprehensiveness deemed necessary to qualify as an adjudication of a "river system" within the meaning of the Amendment. The United States and the Tribe were therefore required to submit to Oregon's procedure.

More extreme legal challenges to state court adjudication have also failed. One tribe attempted, unsuccessfully, to enjoin federal officers from taking necessary steps to submit the tribe's water claim to state court for adjudication. United States v. White Mountain Apache Tribe, 784 F.2d 917 (9th Cir. 1986).

There is no question, therefore, that the focus of Indian water rights litigation has shifted to the state courts. Several general water rights adjudications involving entire watersheds are under way in the states, and will remain so for several years. The federal courts have correspondingly withdrawn from the field. A federal court will not attempt to clarify rulings of a state adjudication or declare federal rights pertaining to it before that general adjudication is completed. United States v. Braren, 338 F.3d 971 (9th Cir.2003).

On occasion, nevertheless, a federal court is called upon to make a ruling concerning the existence or extent of Indian water rights in order to settle a collateral controversy. The existence of a pending general adjudication in state court, expected to last for years, does not prevent the federal court from acting in such cases. Thus federal courts have been permitted or required to adjudicate tribal reserved rights, at least for purposes of decision, when necessary to protect tribal fisheries. E.g., United States v. Adair, 723 F.2d 1394 (9th Cir.1983); see Kittitas Reclamation District v. Sunnyside Valley Irrigation District, 763 F.2d 1032 (9th Cir.1985); Klamath Water Users Protective Ass'n v. Patterson, 204 F.3d 1206 (9th Cir.1999). In a different move to protect tribal rights, a state court enjoined a state agency from issuing water use permits until tribal rights were quantified. Confederated Salish and Kootenai Tribes v. Clinch, 297 Mont. 448, 992 P.2d 244 (1999). This prohibition applied to groundwater as well as surface water permits. Confederated Salish and Kootenai Tribes v. Stults, 312 Mont. 420, 59 P.3d 1093 (2002).

One other area of collateral jurisdictional contention concerns state power to regulate water use by non-Indians on fee lands they own within reservations. In one instance, where the stream lay wholly within the reservation, the state was held to be preempted from regulating allotted water use. Colville Confederated Tribes v. Walton, 647 F.2d 42, 51–53 (9th Cir.1981). In another, where the stream lay largely outside the reservation and formed a boundary of the reservation only for part of its course, the state was allowed to regulate water use by non-Indians on their fee lands within the reservation. United States v. Anderson, 736 F.2d 1358 (9th Cir.1984). Conversely, a tribe has been held without power under Montana v. United States, 450 U.S. 544 (1981), to regulate non-Indian use of "surplus" water (water in excess of that needed to satisfy *Winters* rights) on fee lands within the reservation or off-reservation. Holly v. Confederated Tribes and Bands of Yakima Indian Nation, 655 F.Supp. 557 (E.D.Wash.1985), aff'd, 812 F.2d 714 (9th Cir.1987).

CHAPTER XV

INDIAN HUNTING AND FISHING RIGHTS

A. INTRODUCTION

Some of the most intense controversies in current Indian affairs are those concerning hunting and fishing. The right to take game and fish has always been of immense economic importance to many tribes, and it has equally great cultural significance for most Indians. Attempts to exercise hunting and fishing rights have brought Indians into conflict with non-Indians who have very strong economic and sporting motivations of their own.

Hunting and fishing rights involve all of the problems of conflicting jurisdiction that exist in the general criminal law and regulatory fields, see Chapters VII and IX, supra. Jurisdiction may thus depend on whether the hunting and fishing is done by an Indian or non-Indian, whether it takes place in or out of Indian country, and whether a treaty modifies the usual jurisdictional rules. In addition to these complexities, migratory fish and game present extraordinary problems of regulation and conservation.

The subject is perhaps best attacked by first examining the basic nature of Indian hunting and fishing rights and then considering the complications introduced by strong state conservation interests. Finally, problems of jurisdiction over non-Indian hunting and fishing in Indian country can be addressed. Issues peculiar to Alaska are treated separately in Chapter XIII, Section D.

B. BASIC INDIAN HUNTING AND FISHING RIGHTS

It is well settled that the establishment of a reservation by treaty, statute or agreement includes an implied right of Indians to hunt and fish on that reservation free of regulation by the state. Menominee Tribe v. United States, 391 U.S. 404 (1968). States have rarely contested the right because of their general lack of power to regulate Indians in Indian country. See McClanahan v. Arizona State Tax Com'n, 411 U.S. 164 (1973). The Indians' immunity from state law applies on the reservation even in states that have been granted criminal jurisdiction over Indian country by Public Law 280, for that statute provides that it shall not "deprive any Indian or any Indian tribe, band, or community of any right, privilege, or immunity afforded under Federal treaty, agreement, or statute with respect to hunting, trapping, or fishing or the control, licensing, or regulation thereof." 18 U.S.C.A. § 1162(b). Nor may state law be applied to Indian hunting and fishing in Indian country by way of the Assimilative Crimes Act, 18 U.S.C.A. § 13. Cheyenne–Arapaho Tribes v. Oklahoma, 618 F.2d 665 (10th Cir.1980). The state may also be preempted from prohibiting the possession or sale off-reservation of fish or game by Indians who had taken them on their reservations. People v. McCovey, 36 Cal.3d 517, 205 Cal.Rptr. 643, 685 P.2d 687 (1984); Mattz v. Superior Court, 46 Cal.3d 355, 250 Cal.Rptr. 278, 758 P.2d 606 (1988); contra Bailey v. State, 409 N.W.2d 33 (Minn.App.1987).

Indeed, the implied treaty right to hunt and fish free from state law has been held to survive a congressional termination of the trust relationship between the tribe and the federal government; the hunting and fishing rights are not extinguished in the absence of a clear indication of congressional intent to that effect. Menominee Tribe v. United States, 391 U.S. 404 (1968); United States v. Felter, 752 F.2d 1505 (10th Cir.1985). Such rights have been upheld even for Indians who withdrew from the tribe upon termination of its trust relationship. Kimball v. Callahan, 493 F.2d 564 (9th Cir.1974), and Kimball v. Callahan, 590 F.2d 768 (9th Cir. 1979); but see United States v. Von Murdock, 132 F.3d 534 (10th Cir.1997). Failure of the federal government to recognize a group of Indians as a tribe does not prevent the group from exercising treaty rights if it descended from a treaty signatory and has maintained an organized tribal structure. United States v. Washington, 520 F.2d 676, 692–93 (9th Cir.1975). A group that fails to maintain cohesion with the treaty tribe, however, does not retain the treaty right. United States v. Oregon, 29 F.3d 481, amended, 43 F.3d 1284 (9th Cir.1994).

A tribe may also reserve by treaty the right to hunt or fish off-reservation. Minnesota v. Mille Lacs Band of Chippewa Indians, 526 U.S. 172 (1999); United States v. Winans, 198 U.S. 371 (1905). Where a treaty reserves the right to fish at "all usual and accustomed places," the state may not preclude access to those places, see *Winans*, nor may it require a license fee of Indians to fish there. Tulee v. Washington, 315 U.S. 681 (1942). The treaty right also encompasses the ability to erect structures at those sites, although their permissible nature and degree of permanence are subject to dispute. See Sohappy v. Hodel, 911 F.2d 1312 (9th Cir.1990). The "usual and accustomed places" are those of the tribes that signed the treaty. A non-treaty tribe that later affiliates with one of the treaty tribes may share the treaty tribe's right to fish its accustomed places, but the affiliating tribe acquires no treaty right to fish *its* own accustomed places. Wahkiakum Band of Chinook Indians v. Bateman, 655 F.2d 176 (9th Cir.1981); State v. Goodell, 84 Or.App. 398, 734 P.2d 10 (1987). If two treaty tribes merge, the resulting merged tribe may exercise the treaty rights of both predecessors. See United States v. Suquamish Indian Tribe, 901 F.2d 772 (9th Cir.1990).

A tribal member exercising the treaty right to hunt on "open and unclaimed lands" within his tribe's aboriginal territory but outside of its reservation cannot be subjected to state season limitations. State v. Stasso, 172 Mont. 242, 563 P.2d 562 (1977). Such a right does not extend beyond the tribe's aboriginal territory, and extends to lands that are publicly owned, not obviously occupied, and that are put to a use compatible with hunting. State v. Buchanan, 138 Wash.2d 186, 978 P.2d 1070 (1999). The right to hunt "upon open and unclaimed land" has been held not to extend to a privately-owned forest. State v. Simpson, 137 Idaho 813, 54 P.3d 456 (2002). An agreement ratified by Congress guaranteeing the right to hunt on ceded lands "in common with all other persons" grants immunity from state season laws. Antoine v. Washington, 420 U.S. 194 (1975). A treaty reserving the "right of hunting" on ceded lands also reserves the right to continue fishing commercially in adjacent waters without a state license. People v. LeBlanc, 399 Mich. 31, 248 N.W.2d 199 (1976). In all of these cases, however, the state may enforce regulations essential to conservation; Minnesota v. Mille Lacs Band of Chippewa Indians, 526 U.S. 172, 205 (1999); see Section C, infra.

It is sometimes difficult to tell at what point a treaty right to hunt and fish off-reservation ends and legitimate governmental regulation (apart from conservation necessity) begins. In Grand Traverse Band of Ottawa and Chippewa Indians v. Director, Mich. Dept. of Nat. Resources, 141 F.3d 635 (6th Cir.1998), a treaty right to fish commercially in the Great Lakes was held to include a right to transient mooring of treaty fishing vessels at municipal marinas because without such mooring the Indians could not fish commercially. In United States v. Gotchnik, 222 F.3d 506 (8th Cir.2000), however, the court held that a treaty right to fish did not exempt Indians from the prohibition against use of motor boats in the Boundary Waters Canoe Area Wilderness; the treaty right of fishing was differentiated from the process of transportation to the fishing area. Similarly, a treaty right to hunt does not create an exemption from the federal law prohibiting felons from possessing firearms; a treaty does not create an exception to a federal law of general application unless it does so expressly. United States v. Gallaher, 275 F.3d 784 (9th Cir.2001).

The status of *temporary* rights reserved by treaty has been somewhat more precarious, but the Supreme Court recently protected such a right in Minnesota v. Mille Lacs Band of Chippewa Indians, 526 U.S. 172 (1999). That case dealt with claims of several Chippewa bands to hunt, fish, and gather under an 1837 treaty guaranteeing those rights "during the pleasure of the President of the United States." The Supreme Court held that this right had never been extinguished. It survived an 1850 executive order that decreed removal of the Indians from the ceded lands and revoked their hunting and fishing rights there. The Court held that the President had lacked authority to order removal (the removal was later abandoned) and the revocation of hunting and fishing rights was not severable from the removal order; the entire order was invalid. Id. at 914–18. The 1837 treaty right also survived an 1855 treaty that relinquished all "right, title, and interest, of whatsoever nature the same may be" in the ceded lands; the relinquishment did not mention hunting and fishing and was held not to apply to those usufructuary rights. Finally, the Court narrowed Ward v. Race Horse, 163 U.S. 504 (1896), and held that the admission of a state, Minnesota in this case, on an equal footing with other states was not inconsistent with a continued Indian treaty right to hunt and fish. Admission therefore did not extinguish the right. Id. at 926–29. The Court affirmed the judgment of the court of appeals, which held the treaty right to be exercisable on all public and private land in the ceded territory open to hunting generally, but not to private land open only with permission of the owner.

In an earlier case, the Seventh Circuit had reached a very similar result with regard to the same 1837 treaty. Lac Courte Oreilles Band v. Voigt, 700 F.2d 341 (7th Cir.1983). The Tenth Circuit, however, had held that a treaty ''right to hunt on the unoccupied lands of the United States so long as game may be found thereon'' was understood to be temporary and was abrogated by the admission of Wyoming into the Union ''on an equal footing with the original States.'' Crow Tribe of Indians v. Repsis, 73 F.3d 982 (10th Cir.1995). The Tenth Circuit relied on Ward v. Race Horse, 163 U.S. 504 (1896), which had held that a continued treaty right was inconsistent with state sovereignty. The Supreme Court's decision in *Mille Lacs Band* puts an end to such reliance on *Race Horse*, however, because it squarely rejects that principle underlying *Race Horse*.

Temporary treaty rights can expire by their own terms, however. A treaty right to hunt, fish and gather on ceded land "until it be surveyed and offered for sale by the President" was extinguished when the land was offered for sale, even if not sold. Menominee Tribe v. Thompson, 161 F.3d 449 (7th Cir.1998).

When a tribe cedes title to lands without any indication of intent to retain hunting or fishing rights, the state is free to regulate Indians there. Oregon Dept. of Fish & Wildlife v. Klamath Tribe, 473 U.S. 753 (1985). In the absence of treaty rights, of course, Indians outside of Indian country are subject to the same state laws as anyone else.

Wholly apart from treaty, a tribe may possess aboriginal rights to hunting and fishing. See Commonwealth v. Maxim, 429 Mass. 287, 708 N.E.2d 636 (1999). Like other aboriginal title, however, it can be extinguished by the federal government. Extinguishment of aboriginal land title also extinguishes aboriginal hunting and fishing rights, unless they are reserved in a treaty, statute or executive order. Confederated Tribes of Chehalis Indian Reservation v. Washington, 96 F.3d 334 (9th Cir. 1996). Aboriginal title may be relinquished by acceptance of a reservation for the tribe, Menominee Indian Tribe v. Thompson, 161 F.3d 449 (7th Cir. 1998), but there may be times when the establishment of a reservation is not intended to end other, aboriginal title. Cf. Oneida Indian Nation v. New York, 194 F.Supp.2d 104, 139–41 (N.D.N.Y.2002). Payment of a claim for taking of aboriginal land title forecloses further enjoyment of an aboriginal right to hunt and fish the lands taken. Western Shoshone Nat'l Council v. Molini, 951 F.2d 200 (9th Cir.1991).

The tribe itself has power to regulate Indian hunting and fishing on the reservation, whether or not it chooses to exercise it. United States v. Jackson, 600 F.2d 1283 (9th Cir.1979). That power extends to the regulation of hunting and fishing by Indians on non-Indian fee lands. Lower Brule Sioux Tribe v. South Dakota, 711 F.2d 809, 827 (8th Cir.1983). The tribe also has the power to regulate Indian hunting or fishing conducted off-reservation pursuant to treaty. Settler v. Lameer, 507 F.2d 231 (9th Cir.1974).

The federal government's plenary power over Indian affairs extends to the regulation of Indian hunting and fishing. Indeed, Congress can wholly abrogate a treaty hunting right, as it did in the Eagle Protection Act, 16 U.S.C.A. § 668(a). United States v. Dion, 476 U.S. 734 (1986). The Secretary of Interior has issued regulations governing Indian fishing on a few reservations, see 25 C.F.R. Pts. 241 and 242, and has provided for identification of treaty Indians fishing off-reservation, 25 C.F.R. Pt. 249. The Secretary has been held to be authorized under the trust power to ban commercial fishing by Indians on their reservation, and he need not show the kind of imminent threat to conservation required for state regulation of treaty fishing. United States v. Eberhardt, 789 F.2d 1354 (9th Cir.1986). The Secretary similarly may regulate Indian hunting.

Northern Arapahoe Tribe v. Hodel, 808 F.2d 741 (10th Cir.1987). In general, however, the federal government has been very sparing in the exercise of its power to regulate Indian hunting and fishing. But see Section D, infra. The matter has accordingly been left largely for tribal regulation. In one instance where the tribe failed to act, federal authorities attempted to prosecute a tribal member under a federal trespass statute that forbids unauthorized entry upon Indian lands for the purpose of hunting, trapping or fishing, 18 U.S.C.A. § 1165. The statute was held inapplicable to Indians. United States v. Jackson, 600 F.2d 1283 (9th Cir.1979). In 1981, however, Congress amended the Lacey Act to prohibit transport of or traffic in fish or wildlife taken, possessed or sold in violation of any federal, state or tribal law. 16 U.S.C.A. § 3372(a). That prohibition was held applicable to Indians in United States v. Sohappy, 770 F.2d 816 (9th Cir.1985). If an Indian is charged under the Lacey Act with violating a state law applicable to Indian treaty fishing, the prosecution must prove that the state law was necessary for conservation of the fish. Id. If an Indian claiming a treaty right is charged under the Lacey Act for a violation of state law that would also constitute a violation of tribal law, no such showing is required. United States v. Williams, 898 F.2d 727 (9th Cir.1990); cf. State v. McCormack, 117 Wash.2d 141, 812 P.2d 483 (1991). Of course, federal statutes of general applicability such as the Airborne Hunting Act, 16 U.S.C.A. § 742j–1, apply to Indians in Indian country just as they apply to everyone else everywhere. United States v. Stone, 112 F.3d 971 (8th Cir.1997).

C. INDIAN RIGHTS AND STATE CONSERVATION; THE WASHINGTON FISHING CASES

The most severe conflict between Indian fishing rights and competing non-Indian interests arose over the right to fish for salmon and steelhead trout in the Pacific Northwest. Those fish are anadromous, which means that they hatch in rivers, then journey far out to sea and ultimately return to their original rivers to spawn. They are sought after not only by Indians, but by non-Indian sport and commercial fishermen both in the rivers and at sea. If too many fish from a particular river's run are caught, then fishing in that river is destroyed and may not be restored for decades, if ever. Wholly unrestricted fishing by all parties would probably lead to that result in some rivers. Consequently, Washington and other states attempted to regulate not only non-Indian fishing, but the entire salmon and steelhead fishery. The result was a number of Supreme Court cases wrestling with the conflicting interests and the issues that they presented.

The first major case was Puyallup Tribe v. Department of Game, 391 U.S. 392 (1968) (*Puyallup I*). The tribes involved in that case had entered a treaty in 1854 which contained the following clause:

The right of taking fish, at all usual and accustomed grounds and stations, is further secured to said Indians, in common with all citizens of the Territory * * *.

Treaty with the Nisqually and Other Indians, art. III, 10 Stat. 1132, 1133 (1854). That clause, or one virtually identical to it, appeared in a number of treaties entered by northwestern tribes in the 1850's. It confers off-reservation fishing rights, which the tribes in *Puyallup I* were exercising by the use of set nets in the streams. The Indians were fishing both for their own needs and for commercial purposes. The State of Washington banned the use of nets in the streams and sought to apply this prohibition to the Indians. The Supreme Court assumed that Indians fished with nets and for commercial purposes at the time of the treaty, but noted that the treaty said nothing to guarantee a particular manner of fishing. The Court then held:

The right to fish "at all usual and accustomed" places may, of course, not be qualified by the State, even though all Indians born in the United States are now citizens of the United States. * * * But the manner of fishing, the size of the take, the restriction of commercial fishing, and the like may be regulated by the State in the interests of conservation, provided the regulation meets appropriate standards and does not discriminate against the Indians.

391 U.S. at 398. The Court noted that the Washington courts had made no finding on whether the particular regulation was a "reasonable and necessary" conservation measure, and therefore remand-

ed the case, with the additional enigmatic comment that the state court's findings "must also cover the issue of equal protection implicit in the phrase 'in common with'." Id. at 403.

Puyallup I was an important departure from prior law because it permitted some state regulation of the exercise of Indian treaty rights. To be sure, that regulation had to meet "appropriate standards." The Supreme Court later explained that "[t]he 'appropriate standards' requirement means that the State must demonstrate that its regulation is a reasonable and necessary conservation measure, * * * *and* that its application to the Indians is necessary in the interests of conservation." Antoine v. Washington, 420 U.S. 194, 207 (1975). Even with that subsequently-developed limitation, however, *Puyallup I* still meant that states for the first time could legally exercise control over federal Indian rights.

After the remand in *Puyallup I*, Washington authorities decided to permit Indian net fishing of salmon, but they banned net fishing of steelhead altogether. The matter returned to the Supreme Court, which pointed out that limiting steelhead fishing to hook-and-line had the effect of granting the entire run to non-Indian sports fishermen. The Court held that this result discriminated against the Indians and consequently did not meet the standard set in the previous *Puyallup* decision. Department of Game v. Puyallup Tribe, 414 U.S. 44 (1973) (*Puyallup II*). Some accommodation between non-Indian and Indian rights had to be found, said the Court, but if a total ban was essential to save the steelhead from extinction, that ban could be applied to Indians.

After the second remand, Washington authorities permitted Indians to net steelhead, but limited their take to 45% of the natural run. At about the same time, an unexpected collateral development took place. A federal court of appeals held that the Puyallup Reservation, which many had thought abandoned, still existed. United States v. Washington, 496 F.2d 620 (9th Cir.1974). As a consequence, many of the "accustomed grounds and stations" dealt with in *Puyallup I* and *II* suddenly were found to be on-reservation sites (although the land was no longer Indian-held). In the third appeal, the tribe therefore argued that the state could not regulate its fishing in those locations at all. The Supreme Court rejected that contention, stating that its prior decisions established that the Indians' right to fish at the accustomed places was not exclusive, and that a fair apportionment of fish could not be made between non-Indians and Indians if the Indians could take an unlimited number of fish within the reservation. Puyallup Tribe, Inc. v. Department of Game, 433 U.S. 165 (1977) (*Puyallup III*). The Court also upheld the standards of conservation necessity applied by the state courts.

In the course of the three *Puyallup* cases, then, the law moved from an original (and perhaps not severely tested) position that the state could not regulate treaty fishing rights at all, to a radically different one permitting it to regulate Indian fishing both on and off-reservation when necessary for purposes of conservation. It was not clear, however, to what degree the state's power over on-reservation fishing was a product of the peculiar history of the *Puyallup* litigation, which began as an off-reservation case and ended as an on-reservation one. It seems clear enough that, where the fishery is shared, the state is entitled to limit the total on-reservation catch so that it does not destroy the non-Indian population's share of the runs. Washington v. Washington State Commercial Passenger Fishing Vessel Ass'n, 443 U.S. 658, 681–82 (1979). The state may also be able to limit Indian fishing methods where essential to preserve the run from extinction. Any regulation beyond that point would appear to run counter to the usual exclusion of state regulatory power over Indians in Indian country. The Supreme Court has cited *Puyallup III* to support the proposition that "in exceptional circumstances a State may assert jurisdiction over the on-reservation activities of tribal members," New Mexico v. Mescalero Apache Tribe, 462 U.S. 324, 331–32 & n. 15 (1983), but instances of such regulation have proved to be rare indeed. See Chapter IX, Section F, supra. The unusual history of the *Puyallup* cases is almost certainly the sole explanation for the unique ruling of *Puyallup III* that the tribe's right to on-reservation stations was nonexclusive; the Court reached a contrary conclusion in *Washington State Commercial Passenger Fishing Vessel Association*, 443 U.S. at 683–84.

Meanwhile, during the pendency of the *Puyallup* litigation, the United States had brought suit in United States District Court on behalf of seven tribes asserting rights under similar treaty clauses. The district court found the Indians entitled to 50% of the harvestable run of fish, minus a few percentage points representing fish that were not needed by the tribes. United States v. Washington, 384 F.Supp. 312 (W.D.Wash. 1974), aff'd, 520 F.2d 676 (9th Cir.1975). The decision was bitterly and in some cases violently resisted. Litigation was begun in state court which culminated in decisions by the Washington Supreme Court holding that the state could not comply with the federal ruling, that the treaty conferred upon the Indians no greater right than that enjoyed by other citizens, and that any other interpretation more favorable to the Indians would violate the Equal Protection Clause. Puget Sound Gillnetters Ass'n v. Moos, 88 Wash.2d 677, 565 P.2d 1151 (1977); Washington State Commercial Passenger Fishing Vessel Ass'n v. Tollefson, 89 Wash.2d 276, 571 P.2d 1373 (1977). The federal district court thereupon issued orders enabling it to supervise the state fishery in order to preserve treaty rights. United States v. Washington, 459 F.Supp. 1020 (W.D.Wash.), aff'd, 573 F.2d 1123 (9th Cir.1978).

These state and federal decisions were all reviewed by the U.S. Supreme Court in Washington v. Washington State Commercial Passenger Fishing Vessel Ass'n, 443 U.S. 658 (1979). The Supreme Court rejected the Washington court's holdings entirely. It ruled that the equal protection issue was foreclosed by the *Puyallup* cases. It also disagreed with the state court's treaty interpretation. While "in common with all citizens of the Territory" might normally be read to confer only an equal opportunity to fish on the same terms as others, the Supreme Court believed that the right of "taking fish" would have been understood by the Indians to guarantee the tribes an actual share of the fish. The federal district court's percentage allocation was therefore approved. The Supreme court in the course of its opinion also set forth the following propositions, which undoubtedly set the future pattern for enforcement of treaty rights in migratory fish:

1.   It is logical to establish a 50% share of the harvestable run as the "ceiling" for the Indian fishery. Reductions may then be made for fish not needed, as when a tribe has dwindled to very small numbers.

2.   The state may set the figure of the harvestable run (the total number of fish that may be caught without endangering the future of the run) for each stream.

3.   All fish from those runs caught by treaty Indians count against the Indian share, whether caught on or off reservation.

4.   All fish from those runs caught by non-Indian citizens of the state count against their share, whether or not caught in state waters.

5. Indians may reserve for their exclusive use all fishing stations within the reservation.

The Court's resolution of this entire controversy probably makes up in pragmatism whatever it lacks in theoretical symmetry. The state continues to be able to regulate treaty fishing rights, but only in the imposition of aggregate catch limits necessary for conservation. Similar limits may be imposed by federal courts adjudicating fishing cases. United States v. Oregon, 657 F.2d 1009, 1016 (9th Cir. 1981). The Indians are guaranteed a substantial portion of the run. The decision is a response to the practical problems attending a shared fishery, and certainly should not be understood as permitting state limitation of Indian rights to take game and fish that never leave the reservation. See United States v. Washington, 694 F.2d 188 (9th Cir.1982).

The Supreme Court's standards have been applied or elaborated upon in continuing litigation of treaty fishing in Washington and Oregon. The Indian share of 50% includes state-produced hatchery fish. United States v. Washington, 759 F.2d 1353 (9th Cir.1985) (en banc). The 50% applies to the whole harvestable run, not simply the total fish actually caught. United States v. Washington, 774 F.2d 1470 (9th Cir.1985). Either party may exceed its share when the other takes less than its share, so long as the total catch does not exceed the harvestable limit. United States v. Washington, 761 F.2d 1404 (9th Cir.1985). Fish caught on-reservation by a tribe that was not a party to any treaty count against the non-treaty share, not the 50%

share of the treaty tribes. United States v. Washington, 235 F.3d 438 (9th Cir.2000). The 50% figure has also been employed in other treaty cases. See, e.g., Lac Courte Oreilles Band of Lake Superior Chippewa Indians v. Wisconsin, 775 F.Supp. 321 (W.D.Wis.1991).

Allocation of anadromous fish among the competing treaty and nontreaty fishing interests has been a continuous process, accomplished largely by agreement of parties under the continuing supervision of the federal courts. See, e.g., United States v. Oregon, 913 F.2d 576 (9th Cir.1990). Controversy continues over the degree of necessity the state must show to support conservation regulations restricting treaty fishing. The state may even close accustomed stations if conservation interests justify. United States v. Oregon, 718 F.2d 299 (9th Cir. 1983); see Shoshone–Bannock Tribes v. Fish and Game Comm'n, 42 F.3d 1278 (9th Cir.1994). The state must show more than mere benefit to the fish run, but it need not show that the fish species is actually endangered. Id. Generally, state regulation of treaty fishing must be the least restrictive alternative consistent with the necessary escapement of fish to preserve future runs; it must treat the treaty rights as co-equal to other uses; and it must accord the tribes a fair opportunity to take, by reasonable means, a fair portion of the fish from each run. United States v. Oregon, 769 F.2d 1410 (9th Cir. 1985). Federal regulation of ocean fishing, by enforcing conservation closures run-by-run, also helps to guarantee that treaty fishermen will have an opportunity to take their share from each separate run. See Washington State Charterboat Ass'n v. Baldrige, 702 F.2d 820 (9th Cir.1983).

A recent application of the Washington treaties concerned shellfish gathering. The treaties providing for a right of the Indians to take fish "at all usual and accustomed grounds and stations" included a proviso: "That they shall not take shell fish from any beds staked or cultivated by citizens." The Ninth Circuit held that the treaty clearly guaranteed a right to take shellfish, and that the proviso excluded treaty Indians only from artificial beds created by private owners; it did not prevent access to natural beds claimed or improved by those owners, nor to artificial beds created by the state. United States v. Washington, 157 F.3d 630 (9th Cir.1998) (amended opinion). In implementing the treaty, the court followed the formula of the salmon cases, awarding the Indians one half of the harvestable shellfish within their accustomed fishing grounds, with an adjustment for harvest from privately-enhanced beds. With regard to natural beds enhanced by private growers, the court awarded the Indians the right to harvest one half of the shellfish that would be produced by such beds without the efforts of the growers to enhance production. Indians had no right to harvest from private beds that would naturally have supported no shellfish population without the owners' improvements. The court also imposed restrictions on exercise of the treaty right arising from the nature of the resource, consisting as it does largely of fixed beds, frequently in privately owned tidelands. Harvest from most beds was confined to five days per year, and owners were given considerable control over the manner of harvest. The Indians were not given a right of crossing private lands to get to the beds unless they showed that there was no other practical means of access. On the other hand, the tribes' rights were not confined to customary shellfish stations, but included all of their accustomed fishing stations for all species. The treaty right was held not to be inconsistent with the admission of Washington into the Union on an equal footing with the original states. The court's implementation of the treaty right represents an understandable compromise. As in the case of anadromous fish, exercise of the treaty right to gather shellfish will require continuous administration, ideally with a high degree of agreement among the competing parties.

The principle of the shellfish decisions was applied to find that the standard treaty provision for taking fish at accustomed stations extended to a tribe's taking of Pacific whiting in the area administered by the National Marine Fisheries Service beyond the three-mile limit. Midwater Trawlers Cooperative v. Dept. of Commerce, 282 F.3d 710 (9th Cir.2002). An allocation by the Service to the Makah Tribe was overturned, however, because it did not purport to be based on scientific evidence regarding the whiting population. Id.

One of the northwest Indian treaties contained a unique clause; it preserved for the Makah Tribe "the right of taking fish and of whaling or sealing

at usual and accustomed grounds and stations."
Treaty of Neah Bay, 12 Stat. 939, 940 (1855). Although the Makah ceased their traditional whaling
in the 1920s, they proposed to resume it and secured federal approval of (and related international
permission apparently allowing) a quota of up to
five gray whales per year. The Ninth Circuit held,
however, that the federal action in moving forward
with the proposal violated the National Environmental Protection Act (NEPA) because an environmental assessment had not been prepared until
after the federal government had committed to help
the Makahs. Metcalf v. Daley, 214 F.3d 1135 (9th
Cir.2000). A new environmental assessment was
then prepared, but the Ninth Circuit held that the
question of substantial environmental effect on local whale populations was sufficiently controversial
and uncertain as to require a full environmental
impact statement under NEPA. Anderson v. Evans,
350 F.3d 815 (9th Cir.2003) (amended opinion).
Even more significantly, the Ninth Circuit held that
the Makah whaling was subject to the permitting
requirements of the Marine Mammal Protection
Act, which applied because the federal government
had geographical jurisdiction, its regulation was
non-discriminatory, and its application to the Makah was necessary to achieve the Act's conservation
purpose. Id. The court noted that the "conservation
necessity" test came from the area of state regulation of treaty rights, but deemed it appropriate for
federal application, although federal powers over
treaty rights were more extensive than state powers

were. The court professed no opinion on whether state regulation would be permitted to the same degree. Id. at *20 n.21. The "fair share" formula of the other Washington fishing cases was held inapplicable when the issue was the taking of marine mammals otherwise wholly protected.

D. THE ALTERNATIVE OF FEDERAL REGULATION; THE GREAT LAKES

Another conflict over Indian off-reservation rights arose in regard to fishing in the Great Lakes. In People v. LeBlanc, 399 Mich. 31, 248 N.W.2d 199 (1976), state authorities charged a Chippewa tribal member with fishing in Lake Superior without a commercial license and with using a prohibited device—a gill net. The Michigan Supreme Court held that the fishing was guaranteed by treaty and that the state could not require a license. It held that the state could, however, impose its gill net regulations, but only if: (1) the prohibition was necessary for the preservation of the fish; (2) the application of the prohibition to the treaty Indians was also necessary for the preservation of the fish; and (3) the regulation did not discriminate against the Chippewas. In so ruling, the court was adhering to the standards set by the Supreme Court in *Puyallup I* and *II* as elaborated by Antoine v. Washington, supra, Section C.

Subsequently, a federal district court held that the state was utterly without power to regulate the manner of exercise of Indian treaty rights to Great Lakes fishing. United States v. Michigan, 471 F.Supp. 192 (W.D.Mich.1979). Shortly thereafter, the Secretary of Interior issued fairly detailed regulations governing Indian treaty fishing in the Great Lakes. The regulations closed certain areas, restricted others, prohibited netting of some species, and regulated the mesh size of gill nets. As a result, the federal court of appeals remanded the preceding district court decision for a determination whether the federal regulations were intended to and did preempt the state law. The preemption issue disappeared, however, when the Secretary permitted the federal regulations to expire; the alternative of federal regulation was accordingly never truly tested. See United States v. Michigan, 653 F.2d 277, 712 F.2d 242 (6th Cir.1981).

There is no question, however, that federal regulations authorized by Congress can supersede conflicting state laws regarding Indian hunting and fishing. Metlakatla Indian Community v. Egan, 369 U.S. 45 (1962). The only questions likely to arise are whether a given regulation is intended to preempt state law and, if so, whether it is authorized by Congress. In People v. McCovey, 36 Cal.3d 517, 205 Cal.Rptr. 643, 685 P.2d 687 (1984), and Mattz v. Superior Court, 46 Cal.3d 355, 250 Cal. Rptr. 278, 758 P.2d 606 (1988), federal regulation of Indian fishing was held to preempt state laws. In Organized Village of Kake v. Egan, 369 U.S. 60 (1962), the Supreme Court held that the general powers conferred upon the executive by 25 U.S.C.A.

§§ 2 and 9 to manage Indian affairs and effectuate any act relating to them were insufficient to support regulation of fish traps in conflict with state law. That case, however, arose under the distinctive historical and legislative conditions of Alaska and no treaty or reservation was involved. It seems likely that the Secretary's powers would be more generously interpreted where a treaty or statute guaranteed the fishing in question.

Valid federal regulation offers a method of meeting conservation goals without permitting state regulation of a federal treaty right. It is most likely to be acceptable where the need is simply for a limitation of the method of fishing, which appears to have been the case in the Great Lakes. Where conservation demands an actual apportionment of the fish, federal regulation could also be the instrument, although it would doubtless meet the same opposition faced by the federal courts, possibly with less success. In any event, apportionment would take the federal executive authorities farther into problems of state fish management than they as yet have been willing to go.

E.   NON–INDIAN HUNTING AND FISHING IN INDIAN COUNTRY

Non–Indian hunting and fishing in Indian country has also given rise to jurisdictional problems. The federal government, the tribe, and the state are all potential regulators.

The federal government unquestionably has power to control hunting and fishing by non-Indians in Indian country, but for the most part it has not chosen to exercise that power. There are two statutory exceptions. One is 18 U.S.C.A. § 1165, which makes it a federal crime to enter Indian lands without permission "for the purpose of hunting, trapping or fishing." The tribes may give permission to enter by means of a licensing system for non-Indians, and hunting or fishing without a tribal permit is then subject to federal prosecution under § 1165. See United States v. Pollmann, 364 F.Supp. 995 (D.Mont.1973).

The other exception is the Lacey Act, which was amended in 1981 to prohibit transport of or traffic in fish, wildlife or plants taken or possessed in violation of federal, state or tribal law. Mere possession of such fish, wildlife or plants in territory within the exclusive jurisdiction of the United States (which includes Indian country, 18 U.S.C.A. § 1152) is also prohibited. 16 U.S.C.A. § 3372(a). Like the trespass statute, the Lacey Act amendments place the force of federal law behind any state or tribal law regulating non-Indian hunting and fishing on reservations. Federal enforcement of both statutes is sufficiently sporadic, however, that they clearly do not substitute for comprehensive regulation of non-Indian hunting and fishing.

The tribe has power to exclude non-Indians from hunting or fishing on Indian lands. Washington v. Washington State Commercial Passenger Fishing Vessel Ass'n, 443 U.S. 658, 683–84 (1979). In Montana v. United States, 450 U.S. 544 (1981), however, the Supreme Court held that a tribe had no power to regulate non-Indian hunting and fishing on fee lands owned by non-Indians within the reservation. The Court pointed out that there were no allegations that the non-Indian activities on fee lands threatened the tribe's welfare, that the state had abdicated its responsibility of conservation, or that its regulations interfered with tribal hunting and fishing rights. Id. at 566 & n. 16. Although this language suggested that tribes in the future might be able to make the necessary showing and regulate non-Indian hunting or fishing on fee lands, such efforts thus far have met with failure. See Lower Brule Sioux Tribe v. South Dakota, 104 F.3d 1017 (8th Cir.1997); South Dakota v. Bourland, 39 F.3d 868 (8th Cir.1994). Tribal success is even less likely after the Supreme Court's decision in Strate v. A–1 Contractors, 520 U.S. 438 (1997), which construed narrowly *Montana*'s exception for threats to tribal welfare.

The federal trespass statute, 18 U.S.C.A. § 1165, does not apply to fee lands within reservations. The Lacey Act Amendments do apply on such lands, 16 U.S.C.A. § 3372(a)(3), but do not enlarge or diminish "the authority of any State or Indian tribe to regulate the activities of persons within Indian reservations." Id. at § 3378(c)(3). The Lacey Act, therefore, can add nothing to the determination of whether the tribe or the state governs the actions of non-Indians on the reservation.

The tribe has power to license hunting and fishing by non-Indians on reservation lands held in trust for the tribe or individual Indians. Montana v. United States, supra; New Mexico v. Mescalero Apache Tribe, 462 U.S. 324 (1983). Tribal regulation of non-Indians has been greatly complicated, however, by Oliphant v. Suquamish Indian Tribe, 435 U.S. 191 (1978), which held that tribes have no criminal jurisdiction over non-Indians. Enforcement of tribal game and fish regulations against non-Indians must therefore be accomplished by the use of civil sanctions. See Montana v. United States, supra. Tribal imposition of a forfeiture of arms or other property of non-Indians has been held an impermissible criminal penalty. Quechan Tribe v. Rowe, 531 F.2d 408 (9th Cir.1976). The remedy of expulsion from Indian lands remains available to the tribe, however, and the aid of federal authorities may be enlisted to prosecute violators of tribal game and fish laws under the trespass provision of 18 U.S.C.A. § 1165 or under the Lacey Act amendments, 16 U.S.C.A. § 3372(a).

In the absence of preemption by federal or tribal authority, the state has the power to regulate hunting and fishing by non-Indians in Indian country. Confederated Tribes of Colville Indian Reservation v. Washington, 591 F.2d 89 (9th Cir.1979); Quechan Tribe v. Rowe, supra. Some tribes cooperate with the state by requiring both tribal and state licenses of non-Indians, or by agreeing to some other division of regulatory jurisdiction. See United States v. Big Eagle, 881 F.2d 539 (8th Cir.1989). The state does not, of course, have the power to authorize non-Indians to enter Indian lands when the tribe chooses to exclude them. United States v. Montana, supra. One state banned all big game hunting by non-tribal-members on all Indian reservations within the state; application of the regulation to a hunter who killed a deer on private land other than her own was held not to violate equal protection or due process. State v. Shook, 313 Mont. 347, 67 P.3d 863 (2002) (opinion and amendment), cert. denied, ___ U.S. ___, 124 S.Ct. 67 (2003).

The greatest jurisdictional problems arise when the tribe purports to enact a comprehensive system of regulation that permits hunting and fishing by non-Indians in a manner prohibited by the state. The tribe's purpose is normally to develop non-Indian hunting and fishing as a source of tribal income, and that purpose is aided if limits or seasons are more generous than the state's. It is positively hindered if non-Indians must pay license fees to both the tribe and the state. The tribes have therefore contended that a comprehensive tribal system preempts state law.

This contention met with mixed results in the lower federal courts, but ultimately succeeded in New Mexico v. Mescalero Apache Tribe, 462 U.S. 324 (1983). In that case the tribe and the federal government had undertaken a joint and extensive program of developing reservation game and fish resources. Resort facilities had been built, in part to attract nonmember hunters and fishermen. The state, on the other hand, did not contribute to reservation game and fish resources, and there was no substantial off-reservation effect of on-reservation hunting and fishing. In light of these facts and the strong federal policy favoring tribal self-development, the Supreme Court held that the state was preempted by federal law from regulating nonmember hunting and fishing on the reservation. Because the Court's preemption analysis involves a fact-specific weighing and balancing of the interests at stake, id. at 334, the possibility exists that other, somewhat less comprehensive tribal programs would be unsuccessful in preventing the state from concurrent regulation of nonmember hunting and fishing. Much of the language of the Supreme Court in *Mescalero* suggests, however, that preemption is to be the rule.

Concurrent jurisdiction would empower New Mexico wholly to supplant tribal regulations. The State would be able to dictate the terms on which nonmembers are permitted to utilize the reservation's resources. The Tribe would thus exercise its authority over the reservation only at the sufferance of the State. The tribal authority to regulate hunting and fishing by nonmembers, which has been repeatedly confirmed by federal treaties and laws * * * would have a rather hollow ring if tribal authority amounted to no more than this.

Id. at 338. The same can surely be said in any other case in which the issue arises. True, the state interest still must be considered, and it would be much stronger in a case where the game or fish

migrated on and off the reservation, and where the
state had contributed to creation and maintenance
of the resources. Absent migration, however, the
result of *Mescalero* will almost certainly follow.
That outcome should surprise no one, in light of the
historical, cultural, economic and proprietary interests of the tribes in their own fish and game.

INDEX

References are to Pages

479

†